COME ALONG

We Are Truth-Bound

Volume One

A Dialogue and Dialectic: Bridging the Great Epistemic Divides

Jacinta Respondowska

Hamilton Books
A member of
The Rowman & Littlefield Publishing Group
Lanham · Boulder · New York · Toronto · Plymouth, UK

Copyright © 2009 by
Hamilton Books
4501 Forbes Boulevard
Suite 200
Lanham, Maryland 20706
Hamilton Books Acquisitions Department (301) 459-3366

Estover Road
Plymouth PL6 7PY
United Kingdom

Library of Congress Control Number: 2008931045
ISBN-13: 978-0-7618-4144-9 (paperback : alk. paper)
ISBN-10: 0-7618-4144-X (paperback : alk. paper)
eISBN-13: 978-0-7618-4279-8
eISBN-10: 0-7618-4279-9

In loving gratitude
to the Triune God for my life such as it has been,
and to my mother, Janina,
for having set my feet on the path of authentic living.

TABLE OF CONTENTS

CHAPTER 1 - DIALOGUE WITH THE READER
"Quest for the Meaning of Life"

CHAPTER 2 - BACK TO THE BASICS
"Quest for the Truth of Reality"

TABLE OF DIAGRAMS AND FIGURES

FOREWORD

Recently, I told a student that I was asked by a friend to write a foreword to her forthcoming book. "What is the book about?," he asked. I sighed, and struggled to come up with an answer that would be both accurate and concise. "Well," I said, "she starts with a single hydrogen atom and works her way up to the Holy Trinity." "Oh," he replied, and we went on walking in silence. Not surprising, really. After all, where would one begin to comment on such a vast enterprise?

I have continued to ask myself that question as I struggled to respond to Sister Jacinta's request that I write the foreword to this volume. Her proposed trilogy is an audaciously ambitious undertaking. Yet at the same time, knowing her as I do, and as is evident from the text, this is also a remarkably humble work. Sister Jacinta is *not* claiming to offer the final word on everything (a criticism often levied by post-modernists against the effort of so-called "system-building"). Instead, she is offering a point of departure, along with a map and supplies for the journey. She is working as a cartographer of the real, knowing full well that the details of the map must be filled in by other explorers with skills and knowledge often different from her own.

In preparing the reader to become an explorer of the real, she provides a set of tools. Her summary and review of the apparatus of logic and dialectic offer the reader a reliable "philosophical toolbox." Readers do not have to begin the venture without resources. Sister Jacinta has made available to them the tried and tested resources of rigorous logic and dialectic. Readers can be sure that they have what they need both to think on their own, as well as engage in vigorous disputation with others as they continue on their philosophical venture.

Preparation for such a philosophical expedition would be incomplete, and its undertaking would be foolhardy, without some acquaintance with the efforts of those who have gone ahead of us in the quest for the real. In order to count ourselves as honest and educated persons, we must be acquainted with the accomplishments and limitations of those who have gone before us. Consequently, Sister Jacinta has provided a remarkably succinct yet highly informative survey of the history of philosophy. She offers a lively account of the advances, missteps, detours and retreats made by the great and near-great in the history of ideas. This part of the book will help the reader to become familiar with the great conversation that has been taking place since at least the time of the ancient Greeks.

A question looms over one who would recommend this book to the reader: Why bother? Given the apparent lack of resolution offered by the history of philosophy, is it not finally time to give up on an account of the whole, and honestly admit that the only progress to be made today is in the advancement of narrow (and most often empirical) specializations?

In reply to this objection, Sister Jacinta makes clear that there is something distinctively human in raising and pursuing "the big questions." This dynamism for wonder in the human spirit is irrepressible. No matter how many advances are made on technological/scientific fronts, the root questions of human nature and identity, good and evil, and human destiny demand answers that the more "practical" disciplines cannot give. We cannot help but philosophize.

Inspired by the writings of Pope John Paul II, Sister Jacinta has answered the call for a "new synthesis," a fresh approach to the great questions, an approach that is at once aware of the accomplishments and errors of the past, and is also open to contributions from the full range of human disciplines and endeavors. She is setting the table for a very long and lively conversation.

She is also acutely aware that she is not setting out merely a new teaching, or a set of facts and concepts to be assented to and memorized. Readers must appropriate for themselves the tools and ideas presented here, or they will not actually make for themselves the journey to the real. What she presents to the readers is not simply information, but an opportunity for transformation. Joining in the venture of the great conversation, which is in fact a communal pilgrimage to the real, readers become more human by fulfilling their natural propensity to philosophize.

In short, Sister Jacinta's project represents an opportunity for human liberation. It offers liberation from the limitations and mistakes of the past. It offers liberation from the despair and exhaustion of those who say that pursuing the great questions is a hopeless task. It offers liberation from the stifling assumption that the real is only what can be measured and manipulated.

I urge readers to move through this book slowly, with a highlighter handy, along with a pen and notebook to record thoughts, comments, objections and questions. I also urge readers to arrange for small and large conversations about this book. Sister Jacinta's project, after all, is not simply a work for individuals—it is a work for all humanity.

Rev. Robert McTeigue, S.J., Ph.D.
Ave Maria University
Ave Maria, FL

PREFACE

Every book traces its inception to some source. This one is no exception. Actually, encouragement for this undertaking traces back to three distinct sources. The first of these came from the deepest recesses of my own being. Ever since the late 1950's when God had far exceeded my loftiest aspirations, I yearned to make Him known and loved. I wanted to become—as I liked to think of it—a herald of the Great King. My personal relationship with God revealed that *He is most worthy of all our love;* I wanted *everyone in the world to experience all I was given;* above all, *I wanted to give God the joy of realizing His fatherly dreams for all of us, each of His children.* I had no idea of how to go about realizing such a goal. Every attempt on my part fell short of the mark. I was at a loss, but the strong desire to do so never left me. On the contrary, it merely intensified with time.

The second source of promptings came from those with whom I occasionally had the opportunity to share the odyssey of my tumultuous life during World War II, which in childhood took me with my mother and a little sister into a labor camp of Siberia and later as a refugee around the globe. Upon hearing some excerpts of my story, their reaction was usually the same: "You must write a book." Some day, perhaps, I'd reply with a smile, when I have nothing else to do. Initially, I had the excuse of a language barrier; subsequently, shortage of time. Teaching, studies, community obligations and eventually also caring for my dear mother during the last phase of her life hardly left room for such a luxury. It was a challenge enough for me to do justice to everything I had to do without sacrificing my life of prayer. Prayer was the one non-negotiable as it was the source of strength I badly needed to carry on. The idea of writing, therefore, was instantly relegated to the background and, until now, rarely given a second thought.

More recently, I heard a calling from the third source. It came from the late Pope John Paul II in an Apostolic Constitution, *Ex Corde Ecclesiae.* In an effort to reverse the trend of ever-greater dissolution of the moral fiber of humanity and fragmentation that plagues individuals and societies alike, the Philosopher-Pope appealed to the educators and scholars at institutions of higher learning to open up fresh lines of research and dialogue. It is his conviction, as is mine, that the lack of adequate understanding, misleading ideologies, and departure from age-old revered truths brought about the confusion of values and the evils of "the culture of death." Contemporary progress in science as well as in technology, he urged, needs to be directed to the service of humanity and to reflect accurately the order and harmony established by God in nature. Human reason is capable of discovering these truths, but the desired goal calls for collaboration among the learned. John Paul II had greatly contributed his part to this end and his words still reverberate.

Although the Pontiff entrusted to theology the task of initiating the needed dialogue, since the question of reality from time immemorial belongs to the discipline of philosophy, and it is philosophy that provides the foundation to all the arts and sciences, I saw philosophy to be cut out for the task. Philosophy, moreover, by its very nature stands a better chance of enticing scholars to join the roundtable discussions. After all, they, too, regardless of the discipline to which they devote themselves, must employ reason to advance human knowledge in their respective areas. In light of this understanding, I felt myself summoned to provide the platform for realizing this worthy goal.

Reflection upon the three promptings to write led me to realize that each of them constitutes a distinct domain and, demanding a different approach calls for a separate book. The thought of executing all three projects seemed daunting. Which of the three books, I wondered, would prove most beneficial to humanity, serve best the ends of human knowledge, and give greatest glory to God? Admittedly, there were considerable gains to be made in each of them. My direction was unclear.

The scale tipped in the direction of my leanings by the request which came from Dr. Laurence W. Mazzeno, at the time President of Alvernia College where I was teaching. He approached me with the proposal of taking up the challenge made by the Supreme Pontiff. I agreed. A single insight subsequently led me to see all three ventures as complementing each other, each an integral part of every human life on its journey to fulfillment. Each of them addressed life on a different level, namely, *natural, intellectual* and *spiritual*—all important. I saw them as important not only because these components of our being co-exist as a part of the integrated whole, but also because each of them completes the other two, sheds light upon them, and ultimately plays a vital role in determining the quality of a person's life.

In light of this understanding, the undertaking is planned as a trilogy. One of the books is planned to depict the *existential journey of human existence*, meaning human life as it is experienced on a *natural level*. The focus here is on human existence in its "subjective" approach to life, which in each case inevitably comes with its own admixture of relativities—well in keeping with the prevailing trends of *existentialism*. From this standpoint, *mutatis mutandis,* it should be easy for any reader to identify with the related story and see the journey of his or her own life in light of it.

Another part of the trilogy, *a philosophical venture,* is an *intellectual ascent to truth*. Its task is to reflect the normal transition from the state of human not-knowing and the initial reporting of one's truths of personal experience, all the way to the objective truths of absolute certainty. To be helpful, this section is both an enactment and an explanation of the *mind's journey to truth*. It takes one up to the knowledge of intellection, disclosing thereby existing avenues to truth. It also exposes the ground of the ontological ascent and one's entrance to it. Conclusions reached at this level are based on deductive arguments that yield indisputable truths. As the dialectic is spiraling upward through the whole gamut of reality delineating various bodies of knowledge, it invites scholars of all disciplines to the roundtable for an enterprising dialogue.

The third part of this undertaking concerns itself with the *ontological* or *spiritual ascent;* it is in fact what St. Bonaventure so accurately called *the soul's journey into God*. Considered here are the specifics that belong to the essential dimension of one's being. By giving direction to one's life these pave the way to the glimpse of the Beatific Vision and, eventually, to union with Him. This knowledge Plato quite aptly named *knowledge of actual beholding*. As planned by God, the human journey of life is meant to terminate in bliss and contentment of mind and heart. It is consoling to learn that the attainment of this end requires of us no more than doing justice to our human nature.

Each of the three areas can be considered as an independent whole; it is in no way contingent upon the knowledge of the other two. However, each area when viewed in isolation lacks the beauty of well-roundedness, vitality, and the compelling force of the coherent whole that human life is meant to reflect. Not unlike the missing pieces in a jigsaw puzzle, one is bound to experience a sense of incompleteness that invites many "ifs" and "buts."

We begin with the philosophical venture proposed by John Paul II for a number of reasons. This order holds the potential of rendering greater service in the overall scheme of things. First of all, a philosophical undertaking takes an *objective approach* to the study of reality, which raises its findings to the trust-worthy, universal status. Secondly, because of its objective nature and universal applicability, there are ramifications of greater import for the academic community, for education, and for knowledge in general—thereby also for the universal church. Finally, it is this part of the trilogy that reveals the underpinnings of the other two approaches and invites everyone to embark with us on the intriguing journey of discovering truth personally. For this reason the book is entitled, *Come Along: We are Truth-Bound (A Dialogue and Dialectic: Bridging the Great Epistemic Divides)*. Peace, order and harmony, the key ingredients of happiness, appear on the horizon here, but they become more enticing in conjunction with the experiences related in the other two books.

Since life is a mystery, the second book of the trilogy to be written will bear the title *Come Along: We are Mystery-Bound (Adventures around the Globe)*. This story is meant to show that the attainment of one's ultimate destiny, as planned by God, does not require ideal conditions to be reached. The reader is bound to find it consoling that there are different ways of arriving at truth and a variety of paths that lead to the attainment of life's goal. Because of it, this goal is accessible to everyone.

Finally, the third book of this sequence, *Come Along: We are Glory-Bound (The Undreamed Dream)*, will manifest the role that spirituality plays in one's life, as also faith's impact upon one's choices and the blessings such life brings. Here we will find likewise firsthand evidence for the conclusions reached in the philosophical dialectic; will see more clearly the basic difference between authentic and inauthentic living.

Needless to say, the philosophical venture, *Come Along: We are Truth-Bound* with which we began, is an outgrowth of a life fully lived on all three levels. Yet, even here, because of the scope of the entire undertaking in this study, discourse limits itself to the basics. This allows the pundits in their respective fields, and the future doctoral candidates in their dissertations, to supply the specifics. It is a project that promises to keep them occupied long into the future. Fortunately, most of the knowledge that is essential, particularly what pertains to authentic living and human happiness, is with us already. It merely needs to be properly inserted into the context of the absolute whole. That is why it requires masters in each field. They already have profound understanding of their respective areas and can, therefore, recognize the connections more readily. It will be, nonetheless, the pure of heart among them who will make the greatest contributions to advancing this knowledge. My intent here, as I have already stated earlier, is merely to prepare the platform for roundtable discussions by providing the foundation and delineating the path sufficiently well to keep the dialogue on track.

Reading, Pennsylvania   Jacinta Respondowska, OSF.
March, 2008

ACKNOWLEDGMENTS

For the initial version of this text, I am deeply indebted to Dr. Laurence W. Mazzeno, President Emeritus of Alvernia College (1997-2005). He not only encouraged me to undertake the project and assisted me along the way, but also made some necessary arrangements toward realizing it. His probing questions led me to develop some concepts more fully. To Dr. Thomas F. Flynn, current President of Alvernia College I am thankful for his continued support. I reserve my greatest gratitude for Sister Madonna Marie Harvath, OSF, General Minister of my Congregation, the Bernardine Franciscan Sisters of the Third Order of Saint Francis of Assisi, who endorsed the plans for this work wholeheartedly, offering enthusiastic support on the part of the Congregation. I am equally grateful to Robert McTeigue, S.J., Ph.D. for writing the Foreword, to Felix Charles Owino, A.J., Ph.D. for his critical reading of the work and to Sue Reese for editing the manuscript and making it more palatable to a non-professional reader.

I take this opportunity to express also profound gratitude to Rabbi Alan Weitzman, a Director of Senior College at Alvernia for his gracious assistance in supplying me with the latest translations of the Hebrew texts and for the information on various topics from the *Encyclopedia Judaica.* This information enabled me to cross-examine writings in both Sacred Scriptures and to provide trustworthy support for my insights in philosophy. Some other persons to whom I wish to express my appreciation include Michael Behe, Ph.D., a biochemist at Lehigh University, and several professors at Alvernia College; namely, John Rochowicz, Ph.D., a professor of mathematics and physics, Stephen Campion, Ph.D., a physical bio-chemist, Professor Elaine Schalck, a chemist and Richard Stichler, Ph.D., a logician. They graciously read the sections pertaining to their discipline and offered their helpful observations. To Florence Kruczek, OSF., Ph.D., my friend and colleague, I owe much gratitude for being my "sounding board." Her input, so willingly rendered was always trustworthy and, therefore, greatly appreciated. I offer special thanks to Michele Spotts and Miroslaw Liwosz, our Multimedia Specialists at Alvernia, for doing an outstanding job on the diagrams, and to Alvernia's competent Librarians for their ever gracious assistance. To Speratus Kamanzi, A.J., Ph.D. I am indebted for help in preparing Bibliography and to Roberta Agnes McKelvie, OSF., Ph.D. for her assistance in preparing the camera-ready copy.

I am no less grateful to my family for being supportive of my project and for being indulgent about my absence at some family gatherings. My sister, Otylia Kornecki, deserves special credit for anticipating my personal needs and for being there for me whenever the need was there. To my brother and sister-in-law, Waldemar and Margaret Respondowski, I extend sincere appreciation for honoring my need of time and patiently awaiting completion of this work.

I would be remiss if I failed to extend a word of appreciation to my students of over thirty years at Alvernia College whose inquisitive minds led me to refine my thinking and who for years have been encouraging me to write and share this knowledge with a wider public. I find myself indebted likewise to the various Publishers for their kind permission to use material from their sources as needed. To these belong Alba House, Cengage Learning, Inc., Penguin Group (USA), Inc., Taylor & Francis Books UK, Yale University Press and the British Province of the Society of Jesus.

Finally, with a prayer for abundant blessings upon them, I extend my warmest thanks to the Editorial Board of University Press of America, Hamilton Division, for giving this work an opportunity to see the light of day. Work's fruitfulness in the lives of readers, its role in education and its service to humanity at large belong to the persons themselves and to God. All that begins *with God* and ends *with God* finds its place *in God*. This truth, in a nutshell, is what this undertaking attempts to exhibit. It took, nonetheless, the cooperation of so many of us—as this acknowledgment shows—to make it accessible to everyone seeking better understanding of reality and of their purpose in life. God created us without us, but He cannot realize His dreams for us without our cooperation. May He be well served, praised and glorified for inspiring this work, guiding its execution and now making it instrumental in bringing His dreams for us to fulfillment!

Jacinta Respondowska, OSF., Ph.D.
Alvernia College
Reading, Pennsylvania
April, 2008

INTRODUCTION

At the click of a mouse, today the whole world opens up to our gaze ready to quench our intellectual thirst on almost any subject. Most of us know this as a fact. The twentieth century ushered in an era of unprecedented progress in information via the Internet. Human genius has unlocked the doors to many secrets that came with an explosion of hitherto undreamt of possibilities in practically every field of human endeavor. New insights contrive to give birth to new solutions, to new theories, even to entire new bodies of knowledge. Growing technology makes us eyewitnesses to scenes almost anywhere around the globe. It is shrinking the whole world to a global village, reducing it to windows on the Internet, while the computer itself is compressed to pocket size and within one's grasp instantly, at any moment.

The most astonishing progress in scientific research appears to be in the realm of human genome. The outcome in many areas, most notably in genetic engineering and medicine, is astounding. Having succeeded in reproducing life by means of *in vitro* fertilization, science now is aiming to reproduce human life by means of cloning, be it for "spare parts" or for combating some diseases, perhaps even to realize some individuals' dream of creating a world of *Übermenschen,* the superior type of human beings.

It is not uncommon at the philosophical conventions to find several sessions devoted to the discussion of artificial intelligence and to a possibility of enhancing human intelligence in due time. Some thinkers vigorously argue that parents, who have a moral responsibility to care for their children's well-being have, on the same ground, a moral obligation to enhance the quality of life of their offspring. This would occur by introducing into their natural genomic structure genes that would not only correct foreseeable defects or remedy beforehand any anticipated shortcomings. It would include genes that would enhance their memory, intelligence, particular talents, as well as height, weight and so forth, enabling them thereby to excel as professionals in their own field of sports, music, business, arts, or any other. Possibilities are endless and contemporary scientists are eager to extend their "know-how" to the limits—supposedly always for justifiable reasons that find a host of supporters.

With increasing progress in technology and information, one would expect to find great strides in reducing the ills of humanity and creating an atmosphere conducive to realizing one's highest aspirations. Alas, the opposite is true. Ambiguity, confusion of values, meaninglessness of life, depression, boredom, and anxiety are the cry of the day. Evils are multiplying. "The culture of death" is claiming the life of the defenseless. Injustice in the use of the world's material goods dominates the scene. Terrorism is prevalent and on the rise. Wars are raging. Nations are geared up for mutually assured destruction. Humanity is on the path of self-annihilation. Clearly, something is awry. Efforts on the part of concerned individuals to reverse these unfortunate trends are meeting with little success.

What is even more disconcerting is that this pandemic has affected not only the business world and social structures; it has permeated many a hall of academia, the very institution to which humanity looks to for guidance and wisdom. In times past professionals at institutions of higher learning had the vision and ability to help us understand the course of history and point out viable alternatives by fostering the ideals that lead to human excellence and harmonious coexistence. Today, hampered by the prevailing worldview, professors, much the same as concerned professionals in other fields, are held back from responding effectively to the needs of their constituents. Seeking to reverse the tide, they are calling for a "fresh start"—a fresh look at reality and human nature, and a "new system of thought" that would enable them to discharge their duties to society more effectively.

The call for a "fresh start" is echoed from different parts of the world and from different disciplines. Alex Mauron, a nuclear biologist and associate professor of Bioethics at the University of Geneva Medical School, in the American scientific journal, *Science,* made the following appeal: "More than ever, we need a richer account of the human condition. To be a human person means more than having a human genome, it means having a narrative of one's own. . . . On the question of human nature, we need a fresh start that cannot be provided by genome alone."[1]

The same plea for a "fresh start" in philosophy comes from John Kantwell Kiley, philosopher and psychiatrist, currently a retired professor of philosophy who taught at Princeton University for twenty-five years. This physician, metaphysician, and author of several books agrees with Alex Mauron regarding his embryological findings, as well as on the grounds of his own experience in his two fields. He writes, "Certainly a fresh start is in order, indeed, it is long overdue."[2] He is urging a new epistemology on "purely metaphysical grounds," as opposed to "genomic metaphysics," for only such metaphysics, he contends, is able to provide a reliable account of reality and human nature (128-33).

David R. Loy, a professor in the Faculty of International Studies, Bunkyo University, Chigasaki, Japan in his article "The Religion of the Market," calls for "a world-view, with ontology and ethics, in competition with other understandings of what the world is and how we should live in it."[3] He argues that formerly religions of the world provided us with the understanding of what the world is and what our role in it is. "Today the most powerful alternative explanation of the world is science, and the most attractive value system has become consumerism. Their academic offspring is economics, the most influential of the 'social sciences.' . . . The discipline of economics," he contends, "is less a science than the theology of that religion, and its god, the Market," he adds, "has become a vicious circle of ever-increasing production and consumption by pretending to offer us a secular salvation" (1).

Loy sees this mentality as a gross misinterpretation of reality and of the purpose of human existence. It is out of this context that he is calling for a new system of thought. "What is most needed," he writes, is "a meaningful challenge to the aggressive proselytizing of market capitalism, which has already become the most successful religion of all time, winning more converts more quickly than any previous belief system or value-system in human history" (1). He argues, "This is not a matter of turning from secular to sacred values, but the need to discover how our secular obsessions have become symptomatic of a spiritual need that they cannot meet." His concern extends to the "environmental catastrophe that has already begun and to the social deterioration we are already suffering" (9). Until the false religion of our age changes, he sees no hope for a better tomorrow.

Theodore Roszak, a professor at the History Department, California State University, much the same as Loy, is calling for a new well-integrated view of reality that takes into account our planet Earth. Not only is he calling for it, he is personally engaged in working toward this end. By means of the Internet, he is extending an invitation to peers from the related disciplines to join him in this venture. In his latest book *The Voice of the Earth*, he envisions reality as a "synergistic interplay between planetary and personal well-being."[4] His explanation of this concept is straightforward. "The term 'synergy'," he states, "is chosen deliberately for its traditional theological connotation linked in the quest for salvation." Restating it somewhat, he says "The contemporary ecological translation of the term might be: the needs of the planet are the needs of the person, the rights of the person are the rights of the planet" (4).

With this goal in mind, he is clamoring for a new science, which he calls "ecopsychology". This science needs to be a synthesis of psychology, cosmology, and ecology. "We need a new discipline," he argues, a discipline "that sees the needs of the planet and the person as a continuum and that can help us reconnect with the truth that lies in our communion with the rest of creation" (1). In his earlier book *Where the Wasteland Ends*, he contends "Until we find our way once more to the *experience of transcendence* [italics his], until we feel the life within us and the nature about us as sacred, there will seem to us no 'realistic' future other than more of the same: single vision and the artificial environment forever and ever, amen."[5] It is his contention that to do justice to the whole person, the new system of thought must arise from *transcendent knowledge*. For the past two hundred years, he notes, it has been "the half person prescribing the whole person's needs" (458). Given the prevailing worldview that is being advanced by the current educational system he places little hope in academia. Seeking a reliable source as the springboard for the new vision, he says "it is the *experience* that must reopen those issues, not academic discourse. If there is to be a next politics, it will be a religious politics." It will be a "vision born of transcendent knowledge" (458).

Among some other leading thinkers of the twentieth century who call for "a new system of thought" we find late Pope John Paul II, a philosopher of no small renown. He makes his appeal to the scholars and educators at the institutions of higher learning, for it is at this level that research is carried on and dissemination of knowledge takes place. His earnest plea is for the disinterested, free search for the whole truth in order to come to humanity's rescue in a world that is besieged by countless problems. "The present age," he writes, "is in urgent need of this kind of disinterested service, namely of *proclaiming the meaning of truth,* that fundamental value without which freedom, justice and human dignity are extinguished."[6]

This "impartial search" for truth, according to him, calls for a dialogue relative to the "relationship between faith and reason" (ECE, 5) and a "fertile dialogue with people of every culture" (ECE, 6). It calls also for a dialogue relative to the "scientific and technological discoveries" and *"search for meaning"*—all of these "in order to guarantee that the new discoveries be used for authentic good of individuals and of human society as a whole. . . . What is at stake here is the *very meaning of scientific and technological research, of social life and of culture,* but, on an even more profound level, what is at stake is the meaning of the human person" (ECE, 7).

Seeing that the task is beyond the grasp of any one discipline because of its legitimate boundaries, John Paul II encourages a joint venture. He proposes an *interdisciplinary approach.* By means of roundtable discussions among scholars of various disciplines, he envisions a synthesis of knowledge on a higher level and, thereby, "an organic vision of reality" (ECE, 20).

These few examples are sufficient to highlight the nature of the contemporary predicament as well as what is needed to meet the challenge we are facing. The calls that are coming from around the globe are dove-tailing. Roszak's "synergistic view of the world" coincides with John Paul's II "organic vision of reality" and with Loy's "world-view with ontology and ethics" that encompasses the environment and social structures. Indeed, only such a view of reality holds the potential of yielding insights into the dilemma confronting us today. Complying with these requests, effort is made to emerge with a system of thought that prepares the platform for the roundtable discussions and delineates the path sufficiently well for the synthesis on a higher level to begin.

Human knowledge is self-corrective provided one's insights are cross-examined against the findings of the related bodies of knowledge. To be visionary and well focused, an interdisciplinary undertaking requires a long-ranged plan that provides a solid foundation and a framework, showing how the various components of reality interlock with each other and, therefore, how the various branches of knowledge supplement each other forming an integrated whole. For it to occur, the right concepts, like the right pieces of a jigsaw puzzle, must first be found, then, properly inserted into their rightful place. It is not sufficient that they fit together; they must complement each other, making the image of reality intelligible. Since the task of explaining reality belongs to the discipline of philosophy, our undertaking is an attempt to do just that—by means of analysis, to find those concepts and to insert them into the context of the whole.

The cries from around the globe reaching us indicate that there is no apathy, lethargy, or indifference to the world's problems on the part of the learned. More books are rolling off the press these days than ever before, yet not many of them are capturing the attention of the general public. There is also much research carried on at the institutions of higher learning and conferences are held regularly by professionals in every field to disseminate new findings. Unfortunately, most of it is self-serving. With the exception of science—and here, too, only selectively—the new insights are not filtering down to the ranks to help make a difference in human lives. Yet, truth is of essence not just for the elite. It is not enough that it be a possession of the select few, the professionals alone. Each person must make his and her own life's decisions and these choices are made in light of one's understanding of who we are and what is good for us. It is obvious that the truth of reality and human existence is not a luxury but a necessity of *every human being.* Therefore, it must be made accessible in some way to *every person.* All people want to be happy; all want to lead a rewarding life.

Challenge: a new approach. While it is true that communication is the primary mode of learning and the ordinary means of disseminating information, because there are levels to reality and degrees to human knowing, surface understanding is not sufficient for making life's weighty choices. Knowledge communicated by others, no matter how profound and clear it is to the communicator, lacks the clarity and conviction issuing from personal discovery and experience. Analogously it can be said, just as no one can see with someone else's eyes, so neither can any one understand with someone else's mind, or choose with someone else's will. Even when one acts upon the advice of another, ultimately, the choice is one's own. The basis of acting upon the advice of another is either the trustworthiness of the source one deems to be good and true or, at least to some extent, one also perceives it to be so. Part of *really* understanding the truth is the process of arriving at it. To facilitate reaching this goal, this book attempts to take you on a journey of your own quest. Because this undertaking comes as an invitation, we entitle the book *Come Along: We are Truth-bound.* And because we are attempting to achieve our goal in *dialogue with each other* by means of a sustained philosophical quest known as *dialectic*, the process by which we will be bridging some "great divides" in knowledge, our sub-title reads: *A Dialogue and Dialectic: Bridging the Great Epistemic Divides.* Effort is made by using diagrams to make the abstract thought intelligible and a rewarding experience.

Put differently, this book is a conversation about the enduring questions of human existence—questions that have challenged the human mind from time immemorial. They are, in fact, the basic questions of philosophy. We encounter them here at the *introductory level*, hoping thereby to prepare you for reading some of the outstanding works of the seminal thinkers who deal with them at greater depth. In its intent and execution, our undertaking resembles current developments in the world of academia. *Active-interactive* approach to learning is but one of the welcome features at the institution of higher learning that is emerging as "The New American College".[7] The revamping of the teaching-learning process takes into account the institution's responsibility to society, directly or indirectly in all its ramifications. The "scholarship of engagement" which is a vital part of it, is seen not as "an esoteric appendage; it is at the heart of what the profession is all about," states David N. Cox.[8] Its aim is to serve the good of all. It is called the "scholarship of engagement" because it involves "active and interactive connection with people and places outside of the university." Direction and goals of scholarship are worked out together with the common good in mind (1).

The new model incorporates the following four components: discovery, integration, application and teaching. "*Discovery* involves adding to the stock of human knowledge. *Integration* involves making connections across disciplines that lead to new understandings. *Application* involves the work of the academy toward more humane ends. . . . *Teaching* . . . can take many forms" (2) [Italics added]. Our *Come Along: We are Truth-Bound*, does on an individual level what "The New American College" undertakes to achieve on a large scale. In keeping with its thrust, this book reaches out to the general public and invites people to engage in a *personal quest*. Its dialogical style evokes the *active-interactive* approach. By engaging you, the reader in the process of intellectual inquiry, it leads you to *personal discovery* and *firsthand understanding* of reality. In so doing, it complies with the first requisite of the new model.

Integration of concepts, its second step, in our study is aided by the use of diagrams that are created along the way by introducing the newly understood ideas into the context of the absolute whole. The process of gradual inclusion of new information into the scheme of things terminates in "a system of thought" that encompasses all of reality. "An Epistemological Atlas" with which the inquiry ends is an integration not only of the categories of reality, but also of the major modes of human knowing that conduce to the understanding of it. Seen vis-à-vis the disciplines, and these also in their relation to each other, you get an image of "what" belongs to which discipline and of the "kind of truth" each discipline contributes to knowledge in general. Put succinctly, our system of thought forms a kind of "scaffold" upon which the human mind makes its ascent to the ultimate Truth. In the process, the reader not only speaks about the ascent; he or she makes the ascent, emerging with the firsthand knowledge of the "truth of intellection."

Application to life, the next step in the new model, was to follow immediately. Given the scope of the undertaking and the variety of topics that fall under its purview, for practical reasons it became necessary to divide this study into more easily manageable parts. As it is, *Come Along: We are Truth-Bound* is being articulated in three parts. Volume I consists of two chapters: the first of these, *A Dialogue with the Reader* introduces a newcomer into the discipline of philosophy and prepares him or her for the philosophical quest; chapter two, *Quest for the Truth of Reality* engages the reader in the dialogue, allowing him or her to arrive at this knowledge personally. The dialectic in this chapter slowly mounts its way to the actual beginning of all that is, the First Principles, which render everything intelligible. Discourse in this chapter terminates in a system of thought that reflects reality as a harmoniously integrated whole.

Volume II, *Quest for Confirmation* enters into a dialogue with a representative thinker from the related disciplines with the view of cross-examining the conclusions reached in the preceding part. Having ascertained the validity of its findings, this volume terminates in what we have called "An Epistemological Atlas." The latter enables one to glean reality in terms of the bodies of knowledge that account for its various aspects. Here also surfaces the answer to the existing antinomies and a resolution to the discrepancies on the spiritual level.

Volume III, *The Saga of Self-Transcendence,* relying on the knowledge thus retrieved, recaptures the story of self-transcendence—first on the Divine, then on the human level—and in light of this understanding addresses matters relative to the journey of human life.

Each of the three parts is a book by itself. Discourse in Volume I begins where we are, on Earth, and by means of the dialectic moves *upward* to the First Principles which prove to be indispensable to the understanding of all that is. Discourse in Volume II, being a dialogue with the representative thinkers from the related bodies of knowledge, moves on a *horizontal level.* And discourse in Volume III, begins from the new vantage point, the First Principles and moves *downward* to us, shedding light on the evolutionary process of creation. This movement yields insight into our human nature and provides a clue to both the path that leads us back to the Source of our being and to the harmonious existence needed to create a milieu conducive to the attainment of life's goals, including that of happiness.

Because of the magnitude and intricacy of reality, the system of thought emerges merely as a "skeleton" of reality, exposing its infrastructure in terms of the basic categories. Converted into the existing bodies of knowledge to which the specific components of reality belong, this framework of "bare bones" is deemed, nonetheless, to be sufficient for inaugurating a meaningful discourse among the scholars. It allows experts in their fields, out of the rich reservoir of their latest findings to supply the sinew, the flesh and the spirit proper to things that fall into their domain. In the wake of this venture there lies the promise of restoring all things back to the life, goodness and beauty that is their birthright.

While we are cognizant that references to the human person(s) require of us neutral terminology of inclusive language, for the sake of authenticity and smooth transition in the use of references we comply with the language of the period.

One final consideration before we begin. Most people tend to shy away from reading philosophy, judging it too abstract and esoteric for them. To overcome their fear and difficulties inherent in dealing with abstract content, the book is articulated in a dialogue form with three characters that reflect three possible approaches to a study: *empirical, intuitive* and *rational.* These characters are created to help you, the reader, to join us on the journey of personal quest by identifying with the approach that best corresponds to your own orientation. Once you become an active participant in the dialogue seeking answers to your own questions, these difficulties will imperceptibly vanish much to your own surprise.

The quest begins in chapter two with an analysis of what-is, the absolute whole, and for the sake of thoroughness moves very slowly—for those with some background in the field, no doubt, too slowly—to give the newcomers into philosophy ample time to assimilate the concepts. This part of the quest is deemed very important because it sets up the foundation upon which eventually the entire system of thought must rest. It is comparable to digging in a rocky terrain for a foundation upon which a huge, elaborate edifice is to be erected. Once the foundation is laid, our pace steadily gains momentum and becomes more intriguing. One of the readers compared the study to Beethoven's Fifth Symphony which likewise begins slowly, but gradually gains momentum and ends with the richness of unique symphonic beauty. Besides, nothing is presupposed; we begin from scratch and diagrams accompany the process of analysis to help us visualize how things fit together. Diagrams are developed along the way as new concepts are discussed and their intelligibility is ascertained.

At the same time, although it is only an *initiation into the field of philosophy,* this book cannot be read like a novel. It is a study that demands an attitude of rumination. The degree of clarity in the understanding that each reader attains, will depend on the personal effort he or she exerts in wrestling with the concepts presented. Since insights surface one at a time and build on the preceding ones, it is imperative that the book be read from cover-to-cover and in dialogue with those concepts. As it can be expected, things become increasingly more intelligible along the way. At the end one discovers not only the path that human "conceptualizing process" takes; one comes to know how the light of truth gradually dispels the darkness of the human intellect upon one's approaching it. At that point one comes to know it not just theoretically, but as a fact, from *personal experience.* What is needed, then, are patience, perseverance and determination to surmount every challenge.

NOTES

1. Alex Mauron, "Is the Genome the Secular Equivalent of the Soul?" *Science,* 2 February 2001, p. 832.

2. John Kantwell Kiley, *Why It's Okay to Get Your Hopes Up,* p. 128, Unpublished Manuscript. Subsequent reference just pages in the body of the paragraph. The author is highly critical of the Darwinian and Marxist theories and finds them to be the root of current incongruities in the world. His major field of interest and research is human consciousness. Among his other books are: *Einstein and Aquinas: A Study in Scientific Method* (1969), *Self Rescue* (1976), *Equilibrium* (1980) and *Brain Sell* (1993).

3. David R. Loy, "The Religion of the Market," *Journal of American Academy of Religion* 65/2 (1997): 275-290. References are cited from the article on the Internet (http://www.bpf.org/market.html), p. 1. Henceforth, just a page number within the paragraph.

4. Theodore Roszak, "Awaking the Ecological Unconscious" *In Context,* A Quarterly of Humane Sustainable Culture, pp.1-5. http://www.context.org/ICLIB/IC34/Roszak.htm.

5. Theodore Roszak, *Where the Wasteland Ends* (Garden City, New York: Doubleday and Company, Inc., 1972), p. 458.

6. John Paul II, *On Catholic Universities, Ex Corde Ecclesiae* (Vatican City, 1990) in (Washington, D.C.: Office for Publishing and Promotion Services, Publication No. 399-X), p. 6. Henceforth: ECE with paragraph number of the document.

7. The concept of "The New American College" was spearheaded by Ernest Boyer in 1990. Although not universally endorsed, the idea is catching on. Much research is being done along this line and there are currently over twenty institutions of higher learning in the United States that subscribe to it. ANAC (Associated New American Colleges Bulletin), Spring, 2006, lists the member institutions. http://www.anac.org/.

8. TP Msg. #726 "The scholarship of Engagement: What Is It? Sponsored by The Stanford University Center for Teaching and Learning, pp.1-3. http://ctl.stanford.edu.

CHAPTER ONE

DIALOGUE WITH THE READER

"Quest for the Meaning of Life"

The search for truth begins with a dialogue between Jason and Diotima who are intent on finding answers to the questions Jason has about the purpose and meaning of human life. By means of this dialogue, Diotima hopes at the same time to oblige the academic community with respect to their call for a new system of thought. Jason is a young man who in this dialogue reflects the spirit of Jason in Greek mythology, the young hero who sailed in search of the Golden Fleece, except that this Jason is seeking wisdom as his treasure. Diotima, who is leading Jason to his treasure, is, in Greek mythology, a priestess of Apollo who has firsthand knowledge of things divine. In Plato's dialogue Symposium *(the theme of which is love), Socrates relates how Diotima introduced him to the Great Mysteries and explained to him how the lover of wisdom "is led" and "must approach" the "sanctuary of Love." The journey here (as in both other scenes that of the mythical Jason and Socrates) is long because "the lover of wisdom" advances by means of "scanning beauty's wide horizon," but when he "draws near the final revelation . . . there bursts upon him that wondrous vision which is the very soul of the beauty he has toiled so long for" (Symp. 210e-211a).*

Toward the end of the chapter, two other characters enter the scene to represent two other approaches to the study of reality. This is done to help you, the reader, to identify with one of those characters so that you could join us on the journey of personal quest from the standpoint with which you feel most comfortable.

Since philosophy is "love of wisdom" and its function is to lead one to the treasure that Jason and the concerned thinkers are seeking, the dialogue begins with the intent of meeting this challenge but inevitably lapses into the discussion about philosophy.

I. PREPARATION FOR THE JOURNEY

Diotima: Greetings, Jason! Come in! I'm so delighted you've decided to come. We have a big challenge ahead of us.

Jason: What do you mean?

Diotima: Calls are coming from concerned educators around the globe for a "new system of thought" in philosophy. They want it to be articulated in light of contemporary knowledge and do justice to God, to the universe and to human nature. Isn't this wonderful? We are long overdue for such a system of thought.

Jason: You must be kidding! My purpose for coming here is to get my own questions answered. I'm in no position to address any of these concepts, much less to design a system of thought!

Diotima: Actually, the answer to your questions, Jason, is found *within* a system of thought. In an effort to oblige those who are calling for it, you will find answers to your own questions. They are proposing a "fresh start."[1] This means that a system of thought needs to start at the very beginning and gets devised as one's quest moves along, answers surfacing one at a time. Nothing is presupposed, Jason, that you must know beforehand.

Jason: The prospect is certainly intriguing. I'm not sure, though, that another system of thought is needed, or that I could place much faith in it. By now, there is probably in existence every imaginable philosophy to meet the fancy of every ideology. Isn't it so?

Diotima: You're right. One has only to look into the volumes of the History of Philosophy to see all there is at everyone's disposal already. Scholarly journals, moreover, are regularly rolling off the press detailing the latest insights on the minutest aspects of reality—each being a product of painstaking inquiry and each attempting to meet world's current needs.

Jason: Good as that information may be, I think relatively few draw upon it.

Diotima: Why? Do literary productions have to be warm off the press to capture interest of contemporary minds? Doesn't anyone other than scholars read philosophy anymore?

Jason: Most of the people don't even know that this information exists, even though a great deal of it is easily accessible on the Internet. More important than this, philosophy has lost its appeal, so of what good is it?

Diotima: Why do you think that, Jason?

Jason: Let's face it: Who can understand it? Philosophy seems to be written for the elite, not for an average person like me, with or without a college degree. Philosophy is abstract to begin with, which makes it difficult to understand. Its cumbersome style and sophisticated terminology are enough to discourage even the most inquisitive of minds. Besides, I am not interested in all the intricacies of philosophical systems. I just want to make better sense of life. I am looking for answers to the big questions of human existence.

Diotima: Quite a formidable charge you level here against philosophy, my friend. Yet, your criticism is not without some merit. If I understand you correctly, your charges are as follows: 1) that philosophy is just for the intellectuals; 2) that philosophy's cumbersome style and sophisticated terminology make it inaccessible to the general public; 3) that philosophy is abstract and difficult to understand; and 4) that the intricacies of philosophical systems are beyond the pale and interest of the general public. Is this a fair summary of your criticisms?

Jason: Yes, that's exactly what I am trying to say.

Diotima: Alright, Jason. Let us address these charges one by one. We do so not just to provide some justification for what cannot be changed, but also to see how we might be able to overcome the barriers you mention. Let us begin with your first point.

Right at the outset let me assure you that philosophy is not just for the elite. It is meant to be of service to everyone. Before we begin to wrestle with the difficulties inherent in reading and doing philosophy, however, let us first determine whether or not you consider it worth the effort you will need to exert to find the answers you are seeking. Philosophy is about life, about the meaning and purpose of one's existence—about living one's life well so as to be genuinely happy. It is about the world we live in, and about a host of other things that bear directly upon the quality of one's life. Is this knowledge important to you? Is it, in your opinion, important to others?

Jason: Of course, it is. This is exactly what I have been looking for. Perhaps my difficulty stems from the fact that I don't expect to become a philosopher.

Diotima: That is what most people say, mistakenly so. The truth is we are born philosophers. Prior to whatever else we become, be it scientists, mathematicians, psychologists, educators, technicians, that is, whatever our trade, profession, or vocation in life eventually turns out to be—we are philosophers.

Jason: Really? How am I to understand this?

Diotima: Philosophy begins with *wonder* and it is sustained by *wonder* about what-is. When we come into this world, we are full of wonder about everything. Endless questions of children, which at times drive parents to their wit's end are an undeniable proof of it. Unfortunately, this wonder all too often is stifled, sometimes totally extinguished, by society and by the very system of education that should be capitalizing on it and cultivating it to the fullest extent. There can be too much emphasis placed on memorizing facts. In learning, some memorizing is inevitable, but memory should work hand in hand with reasoning: the process of critical thinking and discovering answers personally. Many students who come to philosophy classes, if they are not majoring in the field, want only answers so that they could regurgitate them on the test and pass the course. *This is not philosophy.* Memorized answers, moreover, are quickly forgotten. Memory has been found to be our weakest faculty. When such students are asked: Would you like to take a test on a course you have just completed last semester? Their answer inevitably is, "No! No!" This is true of most of us, not just of students. The answers about life we have merely memorized will be back to haunt us, often with a vengeance. As you will see it for yourself, moreover, the answers you are getting now will satisfy you only temporarily; the *wonder* of what lies ahead will be spurring you on to ever new and more profound questions. That's the nature of philosophy. Plato says: "This sense of wonder is the mark of the philosopher. Philosophy indeed has no other origin."[2] Only truth succeeds in satisfying the human mind, which is why we have undertaken this study.

Jason: Is there any knowledge we can acquire with clarity and conviction, apart from what one gains through personal experience, more often than not through a painful experience?

Diotima: Yes, indeed. That's what education is all about. The whole objective of education through the study of various disciplines, especially through a study of arts and sciences, is meant to help us arrive at just such knowledge and thereby to reduce those "trying lessons of life" to a minimum. The arriving, however, is the work of one's own effort. The instructor is meant to be only a knowledgeable guide. What we attain personally we know best, for part of *really understanding* the answer is the process of arriving at it. In going through the process, one gains insight into things. These insights, being bits of knowledge, enlighten one's mind and transform one into a more enlightened individual. Whatever we learn this way, therefore, becomes a part of us, thus "our new vision." As John Powell, S.J. says, it becomes our new "frame of reference, a basic perception of reality through which we integrate, evaluate, and interpret new persons, events, and ideas."[3] We are speaking here of the *intrinsic value* of knowledge to which we have alluded in the introduction. A good course in philosophy, or in any art or science for that matter, can do just that. A book that challenges us to think critically can achieve a comparable purpose. These engage one in the process of discovering truth personally, rather than thoughtlessly accepting answers on the authority of another. Philosophical discourse, in addition to helping one gain personal understanding of reality, can assist one in assessing the views of others. As a result, both parties in a dialogue arrive at truth on a higher level. They come to understand it more accurately—to use your terminology—"with greater clarity and conviction." Would you consider such knowledge to be important to everyone's life?

Jason: Positively.

Diotima: Philosophy, then, *cannot* be "just for the elite." Can it?

Jason: I suppose you are right. What about the people who do not go to college or perhaps have never heard the word "philosophy"? Likewise, the folks who lack education entirely—the illiterate, how do they arrive at truth?

Diotima: Some never arrive at it and that is a part of their misfortune. There is no guarantee either that those who complete college, even those who hold terminal degrees in their respective fields, will possess the truth that is the object of philosophy. There are, nonetheless, other reliable avenues of acquiring this truth. We will eventually come to discover what they are. A good conversation, however, the kind of dialogue we are having right now, can ignite within anyone the true spirit of philosophy and lead them to some valuable insights. At least most people, if not all, have an opportunity to know the truth that is at the heart of philosophy. Whether they accept it or not, that is their choice. If this provisional answer to your first objection satisfies you temporarily, we can move on the next point.

Jason: Let's go on. I'm especially eager to hear what excuses you'll have to offer in defense of the dull, belabored language in philosophical literature.

Diotima: These may sound like lame excuses to you, Jason, but the fact remains that writing is an art difficult to master for most of us. Some words are laden with meanings, and it is challenging to write something without having it be subject to misinterpretation. Even when one tries to communicate simple ideas of common-day occurrences, what people perceive is often a far cry from what one was trying to relate.

Did you ever hand in a paper to your instructor feeling you did top quality work, then having it returned with all kinds of markings? Some of those markings, apart from grammar and punctuation, were perhaps questioning what you meant by a statement, because "the meaning was unclear"? Some other remarks may have been challenging the truth or accuracy of your statement. Perhaps upon the subsequent discussion with your professor, you realized your articulation lent itself to an interpretation you never intended?

Jason: Oh, absolutely! I've had a number of such experiences. At times, I've argued with my professor only to be shown that my understanding was correct, but it was not what my written words communicated to the reader.

Diotima: Or a letter to a friend may be totally misunderstood and cause much pain unnecessarily because one's message did not come through clearly. Awareness of this problem is the primary reason for the cumbersome style of philosophical writing. Mindful of the fact that most people are not on the same wavelength, the concerned thinker tries to communicate concepts with utmost accuracy. This in itself sometimes accounts for a long-winded explanation. Given that philosophical statements have far-reaching implications and the same words carry many meanings that open the door to unwanted interpretations, the thinker who can foresee possible pitfalls, tries to forestall them. His or her desire to help the reader to understand the concepts accurately is what makes for the belabored style in philosophical literature. Immanuel Kant's writings are a classical case in point. He was a brilliant philosopher of the Modern Period, highly respected by everyone, who is a good example of it. Can we fault any philosopher for that? Furthermore, since human language is adapted to the physical world of reality with which everyone is familiar, the philosopher must apply the same language to the metaphysical domain. A philosopher's challenge, as you can see, is enormous. In the process of our current undertaking, you will have ample opportunities to face the same dilemma. Your experience with this dilemma is likely to make you more sympathetic toward, than critical of, the philosopher attempting to communicate truth. The experience of "wresting truth from its concealment," to use Heidegger's expression, is the primary task of every thinker. Difficult as it may be, the outcome of this effort is invaluable to one's own understanding of reality and to the understanding of other thinkers' systems of thought.

As to the "sophisticated terminology" in philosophy, to use your phrase, there is hardly a remedy for that. Virtually every field of academic or business endeavor has its special terminology. Terms like "market share," "net profit," "marginal difference," and the like have special meaning in the business world and we just have to learn them if we are interested in this field. Some terms just go with the territory; the content of each discipline determines that. No harm is done in learning new terms. We just have to be careful to explain those terms sufficiently well in order to make them intelligible. Coining new terms is an alternative, but it does complicate matters even more. Relatively few individuals appreciate such creativity; fewer yet capture the real meaning of the newly coined words. Still others puzzled and estranged by this device, walk away empty-handed and the world is only impoverished thereby. Heidegger tried to do just that and it was anything but appreciated.[4]

Jason: If a professional, an author of a book, has this to say about creating new words, I am convinced that even if the words were easier but unfamiliar, they would hardly do us any good.

Diotima: Wonderful, Jason! I am glad you get the point.

Thus far, we have clarified, hopefully to your satisfaction, the first two points. We may only add that the problem with a written language is not new at all. You may find it interesting to learn what Plato had to say about it two and a half thousand years ago. He writes, "Writing, Phaedrus, has this strange quality, and is very much like painting; for the creatures of painting stand like living beings, but if one asks them a question, they preserve a solemn silence. And so it is with the written words; you may think they spoke as if they had intelligence, but if you question them, wishing to know about their meanings, they always say only one and the same thing. And every word, once it is written, is bandied about, alike, among those who understand and those who have no interest in it, and it knows not to whom to speak or not to speak; when ill-treated or unjustly reviled, it always needs its father to help it; for it has no power to protect or help itself" (Phaedrus, 275d-e).

This we can expect will be our difficulty as well, despite our resolve to communicate living thought with utmost care. Consequently, while there is much more that can be said regarding the nature of difficulties connected with language, let our brief discussion of it suffice for now, for what is looming upon the horizon is a much weightier matter.

Your underlying and perhaps biggest concern addresses the content of philosophy, which we have listed as your third point. You say, "Philosophy is abstract . . . difficult to understand." This is true, because the content of philosophy consists of ideas and ideas are abstract by nature. There is hardly a remedy for that. Abstract though they are, they are very important. The whole world is built on ideas. Ideas rule the world, nations, principalities; they also govern our lives. Their significance can hardly be overestimated. Unfortunately, not all ideas human beings propose are good, which is why they need to be examined. Good ideas reflect order and harmony in nature; they bring peace, order and joy into our lives. Apparently, these ideas are true, for truth is symphonic by nature; moreover, it brings enlightenment and happiness. Bad ideas, on the other hand, produce conflicts, discord and chaos. They lead to all kinds of aberrations and loss of happiness. We are led to conclude that what produces such results is neither good nor true, for the good and the true always seem to appear in concert. Since the quality of one's life is determined by the ideas one chooses to live by, and the contemporary scene is full of destructive elements and unhappiness, it is certain that some choices people make are hardly good. Consequently, discourse about ideas is inevitable. The goal of philosophy is to help us arrive at the wise choices. What is beyond our power to change, we must accept. Understanding the reason for it can make our grappling with the abstract content that much easier.

Jason: But doesn't every person want what is truly good?

Diotima: Yes, everyone wants what is good, but what appears to be good is not always truly good. The ideas human beings advocate and choose to live by are contingent on the quality of their thinking. Superficial thinking leads to ambiguous ideas, poor judgments and artificial living. Profound thinking leads to sublime ideas, wise judgments and meaningful living. Philosophy seeks to dispel ignorance in the realm of the sublime, for primarily it is ignorance that is at the bottom of poor judgments, distorted values, unwise choices and misuse of freedom. These, in turn, result in confusion as well as in loss of inner peace and happiness. The unhappiness in the world today may very well be due to lack of knowledge of what is truly good. That is why we are attempting to re-examine the origin and the quality of ideas that rule our world. To all evidence, the thinkers who are calling for a new system of thought have serious misgivings about some of these ideas. A "fresh start" with an objective look at reality in its totality holds the potential of revealing an oversight in the system of thought that currently rules the world. This oversight may be at the bottom of the contemporary problems and unhappiness. Our challenge at the present time lies in finding a better starting point for our study. Everything in the universe seems to be entwined and interrelated. Already Plato noted this fact, for he writes: "All nature is akin" (*Meno*, 81d). There is also much wisdom in the observation of Nietzsche, who said something to the effect that *to gain insight into a single thing is to shed light on everything, and to misinterpret a single thing is to obscure everything.*

Given that reality is so vast and diverse and ideas abstract, a sustained discourse on the metaphysical level does present no small challenge to the thinker and to the reader alike. Knowing, however, that ingenious thinkers have surmounted this difficulty in the past, gives us reason to believe that we can surmount it as well. In communicating their insights philosophers occasionally appeal to analogies, myths, metaphors, models, charts, and the like to help clarify abstract concepts. Plato's divided line and his cave allegory are excellent examples of it. Appeals to objects from nature are particularly effective because everyone has familiarity with these things. Through such examples, *mutatis mutandis,* that is, with all due adjustments or modifications having been made, abstract thought becomes more easily intelligible to human mind. All such helps, Ian T. Ramsey points out, are "rooted in disclosure and born of insight."[5] Even the most rigorous thinkers such as Max Black, Stephen C. Pepper and Richard Whately, despite their rigor, share the view that aids such as the ones we've mentioned above are not expendable in the cognitive domain. Black writes: "A memorable metaphor has the power to bring two separate domains into cognitive and emotional relation by using language directly appropriate to the one as a lens for seeing the other; the implications, suggestions, and supporting values entwined with the literal use of metaphorical expression enable us to see a new subject matter in a new way."[6]

In our study of what-is, in addition to the aforementioned devices, we shall also employ diagrams. We will draw a map, as it were, of all that is and like the geographers do, so shall we insert into its contour all that we find belongs to it. Using this visible device should do much to help us see all things in relation to each other, and to find more clearly our place in the overall scheme of things. At the same time, it should also reduce ambiguities and facilitate discussion amid mounting abstract concepts. A visual image, we are told, is worth a thousand words. We shall have the opportunity to test the adage.

Jason: That should prove to be an immense help, especially to individuals like me who are visual learners. Since what we are seeking is of such great importance, we shall appreciate any help so long as it leads us to truth.

Diotima: Only a lover of wisdom could have given such a response, Jason. You reveal a truly philosophical spirit. Our journey promises to be most interesting. I cannot wait to embark upon it. Alas, there is one more area that calls for a comment—your fourth point. You remarked that neither you nor the general public is interested in the "intricacies" of philosophical systems, that you "want answers to the big questions of life." Isn't that correct?

Jason: Yes, I did say that and I still hold to it. I am confident that once I understand the big picture of reality, I'll be able to figure out the rest myself.

Diotima: I am sure you will. Since the great thinkers have already worked out most of the details, there is really no need for us to go into those intricacies. Besides, those minute components are parts of some larger wholes. Consequently, by inserting the big concepts into their proper place for our benefit, we will have taken care of the details as well. If the new insights truly contribute accurately to the knowledge of something, they will fit right in. A clash with surrounding bodies of knowledge will reveal an inadequacy and call for a careful re-evaluation on both sides. It is like fitting pieces into a jigsaw puzzle. Although that is a prerequisite, it is not enough that the piece fits in perfectly into a particular place; it must also complete the image the jigsaw puzzle portrays by blending in with every other piece content-and-color-wise. It is only then that the representation reveals its beauty and becomes fully intelligible. Would you be able to recognize the piece that fits into a particular place but fails to comply in other respects?

Jason: Upon careful examination, I am sure I would recognize it.

Diotima: This is exactly what we ourselves must be attentive to in our discussion of reality, when we are inserting new concepts into the context of the whole. In saying this, it looks as if we have accidentally stumbled upon a criterion for the work ahead of us.

As to the answers you are eager to obtain, we shall have to discover them first. Philosophy is not a catalog of answers, but an activity of the thinkers who search for them. When philosophers find them, they share them with us through the system of thought they devise. As you already know, these answers never turn out to be simple or readily understood—all because of the magnitude and richness of all that is.

Jason: I'll try to understand.

Diotima: At this point of our dialogue, we have a fairly good idea of our goal. It is not quite as obvious yet, I am afraid, as to how our study should be conducted and where we should begin. Since our work is in philosophy, we need to conduct the study in accordance with the discipline and methods proper to philosophy. Consequently, instead of relying on any of the philosophers, let us look to philosophy itself for the direction. By saying this, I am proposing that we look at the word "philosophy" to see what the name itself reveals and get direction from what we learn. The Greeks, you must know, had the uncanny knack for conferring appropriate names on things. So their names disclose something about the object named. For instance, the Greek word for "thought", *dianoia*, comes from two words: *dia*, which means "through" and *nous*, which means "mind," defining thought as "that which comes through the mind." Another interesting example of it is the word "theory," the Greek *theoria*. This term likewise comes from two words: *théā*, "a view, a thing seen, sight or spectacle" and *oraio*, "to see, to look at, to behold or perceive." A theory, therefore, is an account of that which disclosed itself, that came into view or appeared to one's sight. This means further that theoretical seeing is an intellectual seeing or understanding of something that showed itself in one's sense experience. The word "philosophy" is no exception. It, too, comes from two Greek words: *philia*, which means "love" and also "friendship," and *sophia*, which means "wisdom." The nominal definition of philosophy, therefore, is "love of wisdom" or "friendship with wisdom."

In addition to the nominal definition, that is, what *nomos*, the "name" itself means, philosophy is an activity of the mind that inquires into the nature of things. Since there are many different areas into which one may inquire, there are many descriptive definitions. These differ in accordance with the subject matter of their specific concerns. Thus, the definition of Ethics, Logic, Cosmology, Epistemology, Ontology, Metaphysics, and so on, will differ in accordance with the content of its inquiry. Each of these names reveals what the discipline is all about. Since these branches of philosophy incorporate all that is, it is obvious that we need to look to the *basic definition* of it to point us in the right direction.

II. CLOSER LOOK AT PHILOSOPHY

The nominal definition of philosophy being "love of wisdom," we immediately see that the *goal* of philosophy is *wisdom*. Upon reflection, we note that wisdom applies only to human beings and that wisdom has to do with life and choice. In ordinary parlance, we hear people make statements such as: "In choosing to pursue college education, she made a wise decision." "Giving two years of his life to Peace Corps at this time, was a wise choice on his part." Both of the statements indicate that what the two individuals decided to do was good for them; it would profit them as human beings, if not immediately, then in the long run.

Statements of this nature, in turn, imply the perennial questions of philosophy, namely: Who am I? Whence do I come? Where am I going? and What am I doing in this world? Otherwise, on what basis could one judge that something is good for a person, unless it is in keeping with human nature? That is to say, in some respect it is compatible with who one is. The choice is wise precisely because it takes one in the direction one ought to be moving. The answer to Who am I? in turn, depends on the answer to the question Whence do I come?, the source of one's true identity. To use an analogy: I can judge adequately the identity of the liquid in the glass I am holding, only if I know from where it comes. Is it from the running spring? A rusty faucet? From some muddy river? A contaminated lake? Or, perhaps, from the brewery or a vine press? When I know from where the liquid I am holding came, its source, I will know what it is and what I *ought to* do with it. So, too, is the case with the question of human identity. Once I know from whence I come, I know who I am. Knowing my true nature, I will know what I *ought to* do with my life. It is because I am an intelligent and by nature an inwardly propelled being, that I can know "toward what" I am being impelled. Once this awareness dawns, I will know what I *ought to* be doing in this world, that is, what direction my life *ought to* be taking. Everything depends on the proper understanding of the *true source* of our identity. As we can see, on this knowledge depend the answers to the remaining perennial questions of philosophy. These questions in unison reveal our true nature. Wisdom has to do with living in accordance with our nature. Consequently, choices that lead us to the attainment of our highest good and enable us to reach our highest destiny are said to be wise. They are wise precisely because they are in keeping with our nature. By living in accordance with our nature, we attain the end for which we were born: the realization of our potential, excellence of our being, a sense of fulfillment and genuine happiness—all those things the human heart relentlessly craves.

Unfortunately, not all the thinkers agree on what the source is and, therefore, on what is human nature. Conflicting opinions are rampant, confusion prevails, and there appears to be little hope of seeing them resolved in light of the knowledge that is being propounded today. This is the big question of metaphysics, the branch of philosophy that inquires into the nature of reality itself. Kant called it "a battlefield of endless controversies." His tedious, painstaking effort was aimed at resolving the problem. Alas, his thorough explanation—much the same as that of many other thinkers'—is hardly intelligible to most readers. How, then, can one appreciate the wisdom it conveys? Their findings, moreover, stand in sharp opposition to the prevailing contemporary schools of thought. So the battle rages on. Necessarily so. For the human mind will not rest until Truth dawns in all its splendor and beauty.

Jason: Truth in all its splendor and beauty? What a tantalizing thought! The very idea of it does something for my heart. Tell me, how can I know who are those thinkers who would lead me to this Truth?

Diotima: I am afraid you cannot know it, unless you conduct the study personally and discover it yourself. Only then, not before, will you be in the position to know *what-is as it really is*, and be able to assess other systems of thought objectively. My giving you the answer would rob you of the joy of discovering it yourself. Besides, you would be accepting it from me on faith or on my authority, without a personal conviction on your part. When confronted by some shrewd rhetorician, how would you be ready? Would you have to capitulate to him? Only if you had retrieved the truth on your own, would you be able to defend it.

Jason: How then do I go about retrieving it personally?

Diotima: Ah, this brings us to the discussion of *what philosophy is*. From our earlier discussion, we already know that philosophy *begins* with *wonder*. We also know that the *goal* of philosophy is *wisdom* and we know why we need it. Now, since we have to philosophize, to carry on the process of doing philosophy, we need to understand what it is that we need to be doing.

Philosophy is an *activity* of a philosopher and this activity is called *dialectic*. The word's origin and evolvement have a long history to it. But in essence, it means a sustained argumentative discourse. The word "dialectic" comes again from two Greek words: *dia*, "through" and *legeine*, "to speak, to argue, to converse"; thus a "dialectician," *dialecticos*, is one who is "skilled in discourse or argument." We can say then that dialectic is an argumentative discourse among thinkers in which conflicting views are brought to collide. Through such a discourse of clarification of arguments and successive revisions, agreement is finally reached.

Such a philosophical argumentation is often explained in terms of the thesis and the antithesis, or the confrontation of opposing views. Through clarification of each, a synthesis is reached. This synthesis then becomes one's new thesis until it meets its antithesis. Again through a dialogue of disagreement and successive revisions discourse terminates in a new synthesis, now on a higher level. The process of this dialectic carries one aloft until the light of truth dawns.

Jason: So, the dialectic is an argument through dialogue, disagreement, and successive revisions out of which comes agreement and understanding?

Diotima: Excellent, Jason! Well put, my friend. Listen further. See if you can also agree with the reasoning put forth in the next statement.

Since philosophy is dialectic, an activity of the thinker we call a philosopher, it follows that there is no philosophy apart from the philosopher. Because it is this activity that yields insight along the way and results in understanding, it is equally apparent that part of knowing the answer is the process of arriving at it. A correct answer is very important, even if it is memorized. It is certainly extremely important for children to be pointed unto the right path of life at a time when they are just beginning to form their own vision. But a memorized answer lacks much needed understanding. So when such an answer or belief is attacked by its antithesis, one is at a loss to defend it.

Jason: I can understand now why you are reluctant to give me your answers.

Diotima: Insights, one by one, enlighten the minds of the dialecticians by dispelling the darkness of their ignorance and lead them to the light of truth. Through this process we can see that the *effect* of philosophy is *excellence of one's being.* For by this means one is transformed into an enlightened individual. The effect, which a sound philosophy has on one's life, is in fact the fourth characteristic of philosophy.

The above characteristic rounds out our understanding of what philosophy is. Since good pedagogical practice calls for a summary statement of the topic at the end of the discussion, let us conclude our discourse on philosophy by defining it now in terms of its four characteristics. Put succinctly, we can say: philosophy is a *dialectic* which begins with *wonder* that leads to the search of *wisdom* in order to attain *excellence of one's being.*

Jason: Now that I understand it, this definition of philosophy makes more sense to me, but I do not see as clearly the relationship between truth and wisdom. Does it mean that philosopher's work is completed when the dialectic reaches its end and truth dawns upon the horizon of one's mind? Didn't we say that philosophy's goal is wisdom?

Diotima: Yes, indeed. That is exactly what we have said and that still holds. In reaching the truth, philosophy has discharged its primary role, for wisdom presupposes truth. Wisdom demands the second step, the application of truth to life. Only the one who lives in accordance with truth can be said to live wisely, for wisdom essentially is truth in action, truth applied to life. Thus, not everyone who knows the truth is necessarily a "lover of wisdom," but only the person who strives to live in accordance with it. It is this second step that is the distinguishing mark of the true "philosopher." None of the others deserve the name. Here also we see the relation and difference between knowledge and wisdom. The two, as we have intimated earlier, are not the same, but neither are they antithetical.

Jason: So the first of the "*great divides*" has been bridged. I cannot help but wonder, however, who among us mortals can claim to be wise? Most of us humans depart from truth at one point or another in our life—sometimes not even through ill will, but through weakness or plain ignorance.

Diotima: How true! This is why Plato has Socrates say, "real wisdom is a property of God" (Apology, 23a-b). Likewise, "Only gods are wise, and those who become friends of God" (Timaeus, 54 d-e). Can you see now why communication with God is so important and truly needed, if we want to live wisely? Real philosophers do not see themselves as "wise," only as "lovers of wisdom." They know that they do not know, so they rely on the wisdom of God rather than on their own opinions. Sophists, as their very name indicates, were the ones who enjoyed the pretentious title of being "wise men." They were the itinerant teachers in the Greek city-states of their day. According to Socrates, though, they were often merely loquacious jugglers of words. We can talk about them at some other time, or you can read about them yourself. At this point, I am just interested in knowing, given what you have learned, what you would reply to a sincere inquirer, who approached you with the question: What is the relevance and function of philosophy?

Jason: Relevance of *sound* philosophy, I can see could hardly be over-estimated primarily because of what it does for us. I would, therefore, have no difficulty singing its praises. But if I were asked about its function, I would be at a loss to provide a fitting reply.

Diotima: I like Plato's explanation, Jason. He presumably came up with the analogy for the function of philosophy by observing his master teacher, Socrates, who to this day is acclaimed as the greatest philosopher of all times.[7] In the Dialogue *Theaetetus* Socrates compares philosophy to "midwifery." A midwife, as we know, is a person who assists at birth—in those days always a woman—who helped to deliver a baby. Please note, she was not the one giving birth, but the one who helped to deliver the new life safely. So, too, is the function of philosophy. Philosophy does not give birth to ideas; it merely assists us in delivering ideas that are good, beautiful and just—ideas that have "instinct with life and truth" in them (Theaetetus, 150 b-c).[8] These are the ideas that are worth living and dying for, as Socrates proved it by his own life.

Jason: I like this analogy. I hope we can achieve this enviable end ourselves. I wonder, however, how does one go about giving birth to such ideas? We certainly don't want to emerge with just another system of thought that is only going to complicate matters still further. Do we?

Diotima: Your question, Jason, brings us to the discussion of the method proper to the discipline of philosophy, namely, logic. Logic, strictly speaking, is not philosophy. As Aristotle pointed out, logic is a prerequisite for doing philosophy. It is, if you will, a tool of philosophy. There is nothing more objective and more reliable than logic in helping one to think soundly. It is precisely because logic is objective and knows no favorites that it is able to keep one's dialectic on track and help one arrive at reliable conclusions in spite of the preferences of the logician. For this reason, it is a fair arbitrator and can resolve conflicts in favor of truth.

Jason: You seem to hold it in great esteem. I wish I knew more about it. All I heard about it is that it is difficult and boring.

Diotima: Considering that I am going to hold you responsible for the soundness of the arguments we formulate, I must make sure you understand what is essential to our dialectic—by no means shall we attempt to cover all there is to know about it! Logic, you must know, is a science in its own right. Books in logic appear under titles such as: *Introduction to Logic, Formal Logic, Informal Logic, Symbolic Logic, Practical Logic, Understanding Arguments, Applied Logic, Critical Thinking* and so on. Each of such books is anywhere between 250 and 400 pages long. Even if we moved at a rapid pace, it would require much more time to cover everything than can be allotted here. Basic knowledge of it, however, is indispensable, if we are to rely on logic in conducting our dialectic.

Jason: I'd like you to go over at least the essentials of it, please. I assume this will be a sort of crash course in logic.

Diotima: Not even that much, Jason. However, to appreciate the conclusions we will eventually reach, it is important that we have an understanding of the structure of the logical arguments and know the difference not only between an opinion and a fact, but also between the deductive and the inductive arguments. Otherwise, they will not mean much to you and you will be no better off at the end than you are now at the beginning. Even with this understanding it will take much vigilance on the part of both of us to reach our goal, for there are many "slippery slopes" in reasoning.

Jason: I will try my best.

III. UNDERSTANDING SOME LOGIC

Diotima: Since you are a visual learner, Jason, let us enclose a diagram to get a big picture of the science of logic (Diagram 1). Sometimes a cursory look at the content as a whole can be advantageous. Seeing first particular concepts in their relation to each other with a logical structure and sequence to them can facilitate understanding of the specifics in a given subject matter.

Jason: I'm sure this will be very helpful particularly in logic where the subject matter is abstract and for most of us hardly captivating.

Diotima: You may be amazed, but there are some thinkers who are greatly intrigued by logic. Fascinated and challenged by its subtleties and aware of its potential service to human knowledge, they devote their entire life to the study and teaching of it. These are the logicians to whom we are indebted for the understanding of the internal structure of logic and for all there is to know about its application to matters of human concern.

Looking at Diagram 1, we can see that logic consists of two branches: *formal* and *informal*. The formal branch provides rules and forms for the construction and/or examination of logical arguments; the informal logic, applying these guidelines to specific content concerns itself with arguments that argue "for" or "against" some position. Arguments, in turn, can be *deductive* and *inductive* and both of them can be sound or unsound, valid or invalid, true or false. These arguments, furthermore, can be *categorical, conditional,* and *disjunctive.* Before we attempt to understand what all of this means, notice please the similarity between the deductive and the inductive arguments as well as what is required of them.

Jason: All of it looks simple, at least in its layout. Once I understand what it all means, I shouldn't have any difficulty with the arguments, should I?

Diotima: We'll see. Let's begin with the definition of logic. Were you surprised when I introduced logic as a "science of correct reasoning"?

Jason: Yes, somewhat. When I hear the word science, I tend to think immediately of the physical and natural sciences. Since the method of inquiry proper to them is one of observation, experimentation, measuring, testing and the like, or, as is the case in any social science, observation, polling, and testing, I wondered how such a method could be applicable to logic.

Diotima: You're right, Jason, in assuming that none of these practices apply to logic. Logic must be understood as a science in a broader sense. It is a science in that it is an intellectual enterprise, which, like all other fields of academic and scholarly pursuits, is a systematic inquiry into its subject matter with the view of

BASIC STRUCTURE OF LOGIC

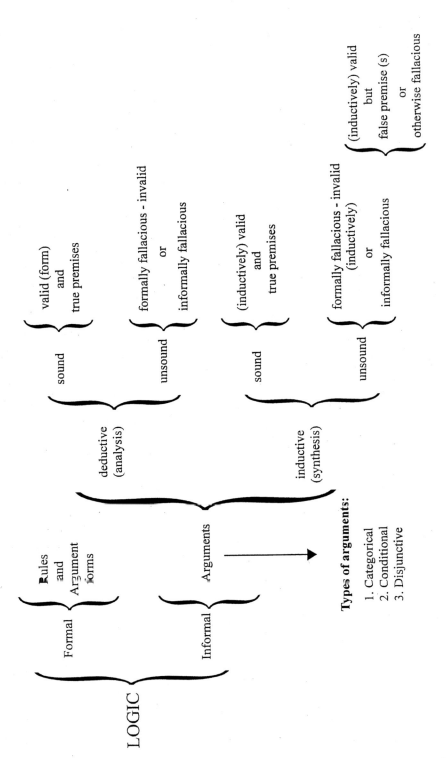

Diagram 1

arriving at reliable conclusions. Unlike the other sciences, which inquire into some particular, concrete aspect of reality proper to their respective discipline, logic inquires into the way we think. All those sciences are said to be *descriptive* because they describe what they find in the process of their investigations. Logic, like Normative Ethics, on the other hand, is *prescriptive* in character, because it prescribes ways we need to think to arrive at reliable conclusions.

Our thinking is often erratic. Ideas do not come to us in an organized way. Consequently, when we communicate them before we had a chance to organize them, what we express, whether orally or in writing, often lacks clarity and logical coherence. That often leads to misunderstanding and unintended implications. Logic helps us to remedy this weakness so that when we are dealing at least with matters of great importance, we may know how to order our thinking so as not to be misled, or have to regret later the judgments or decisions we have made due to fallacious thinking. Understanding this to be the purpose of logic, let us next turn our attention to its branches.

Jason: I thought that the purpose of logic was to convince others about the things we believe.

Diotima: There are times when we ourselves are seeking an answer to something, as for instance to what is true, how to judge matters, or what to believe. At other times, we may want to defend our claim or, as you have noted, we may want to persuade others of a conviction we hold worthy of belief. Logic makes a provision for all such cases. We just need to know how to formulate an argument to attain the desired end. This general, introductory statement about logic as a discipline brings us to its first major subdivision.

Jason: The diagram shows that logic consists of two branches: formal and informal, but how do they differ?

Diotima: Formal logic, as its name suggests, is concerned with the *form* of correct reasoning, that is, with the "internal structure" of arguments. It can be said that formal logic is a kind of "logic of logic." It provides the *rules* and *argument forms* that are dictated by logic itself. This is to say, these rules and argument forms are based on logical necessity, rather than on any whimsical preferences or consensus on the part of the logicians. Because these rules and argument forms are merely

directives for constructing arguments, formal logic is *abstract*. It is abstract because it lacks concrete content. The following examples illustrate this fact.

(a) All A's are B's.		(b) All A's are B's.		(c) No P's are Q's.
All B's are C's.	or,	C is an A.	or	Some S's are P's.
Therefore All A's are C's.		Therefore, C is a B.		Therefore, some S's are not Q's.

These are valid *argument forms*. One does not argue here "for" or "against" anything in particular; there is no specific content to them. However, because each such form is a neutral model of a *valid* argument, it can be applied to any content with equal cogency. Thus, when one of these forms is applied to the content in accordance with the rules for constructing arguments, and the premises of the argument are true, the conclusion of the argument will be necessarily sound. The arguments based on the above argument forms are called *syllogisms*. Traditionally they have been known to consist of two premises and a conclusion.

Informal logic is in fact "applied logic," for it applies the rules and models of formal logic to arguments. It converts *argument forms* into *arguments*. Thus, if in the first instance we let A stand for "human beings," B for "mammals," and C for "air-breathers," the argument form (a) becomes the argument that reads:

All human beings are mammals.
All mammals are air-breathers.
Therefore, all human beings are air-breathers.

From this example we can see how the directives of *formal logic* become the backbone of *informal logic* and why informal logic is known as "applied logic." We can also see that the content of applied logic consists of arguments that address matters of a *concrete nature* and lead to sound conclusions. Having understood the relationship and the difference between formal and informal logic, let us now turn the spotlight on the arguments themselves.

Understanding Logical Arguments

In light of what we've just said, it is obvious that a *logical argument* is not a disagreement among individuals over something. It is rather *an attempt to justify the claim of truth for a given assertion or, to arrive at an answer to some question by reference to the truth of other assertions that support it or, are evidence of it.* In short, an *ar-*

gument is a justification for the claim one makes, or it is a search for a solution to a given question or problem. If the argument begins with a *claim*, one must provide supporting evidence for it. If one has a *question*, one must appeal to what is already known about the particular matter and draw the conclusion from it. By means of what is known, it is possible to arrive at the answer one is seeking. Let us take a closer at each of these approaches.

If an argument is a *claim* and the claim is: "Bound paper burns slowly," then the supporting evidence for it would be: *because* "bound paper has little air" and "whatever has little air burns slowly." Another way to state it would be: *Since* bound paper has little air and whatever has little air burns slowly, bound paper burns slowly. Set up as a syllogism, the argument would be:

> Bound paper has little air.
> Whatever has little air burns slowly.
> Therefore, bound paper burns slowly.

Since truth is understood to be a correspondence with facts, if in fact "whatever has little air burns slowly," then my claim is justified. If not, then my claim is untenable. In this case we know that the supporting evidence is true, therefore, the conclusion is sound.

But not all arguments begin with a claim. They may begin with a *question*. If the question is: "Why does bound paper burn slowly?" the answer requires a *reasoning process* that moves from the "known" to the "unknown." This process can be demonstrated as follows:

Question: *Why does bound paper burn slowly?*	Unknown
I know that *bound paper has little air.*	Known
I also know that *whatever has little air burns slowly.*	Known
Therefore, I now know why *bound paper burns slowly.*	Unknown solved

Whether the starting point is a *claim* or a *question*, the argument remains the same.

In a syllogistic argument if the general principle is known, one may begin with it. In such a case the argument would be expressed as follows:

> Whatever has little air burns slowly.
> Bound paper has little air.
> Therefore, bound paper burns slowly.

This example illustrates the *reasoning process* by means of which a great deal of human knowledge is attained. Though not exclusively, this method is employed primarily by the disciplines whose subject matter is metaphysical and as such eludes observation and analysis proper to empirical disciplines. It is a *forte* of the philosophical discourse.

What is often very challenging is that not all arguments appear in this succinct form. Some of them are expressed in a paragraph; others that are more complex may require several paragraphs to arrive systematically at a conclusion.

Jason: If that's the case, how does one recognize an argument?

Diotima: Good question, Jason. Even when something is expressed in three statements that are in some sense related, does not necessarily make them an argument. To be specific:

> The sun is shining brightly.
> Birds are chirping.
> It is a beautiful spring day.

Do you see any cohesion in the content of these statements?

Jason: Yes, positively! They express common experiences in spring and summer.

Diotima: Would you say that these statements constitute a logical argument?

Jason: Since they do not argue "for" or "against" anything, my answer would have to be "no."

Diotima: And you're right, Jason. In an argument there has to be a movement to thought that reflects a *cause-effect* relationship. The latter can be readily recognized by its "clue words." Words such as: *because, since, for,* because they reflect the reason of such a connection are seen as "reason markers" and words such as *therefore, then, thus, hence, accordingly, so,* because they lead to the conclusion, as "conclusion markers." All of these words are clues to recognizing arguments.

The reasoning process of going from "the known to the unknown" and possesses the above mentioned "clue words"—whether it is concise as these examples exhibit it, or it is extensive, consisting of several paragraphs—is an ordinary way of recognizing arguments. It is also a legitimate way of obtaining much of human knowledge. You can expect to encounter this process of reasoning in reading about matters in life that are of great significance to us humans, for such things by their nature escape direct observation.

Jason: Do you mean things in life such as soul, death, immortality, God, freedom and the like?

Diotima: Precisely, Jason. Given the importance of such matters, let us take a brief look at the next point of importance in logic.

Structure of Syllogistic Arguments

Having seen that in an argument, whether it begins with a claim or with a question, the *reasoning process* always moves from "the known" to "the unknown," we now note that the solution to it is gained by means of the *intermediate information*. The intermediate information is called a "middle term." Without it, solution would be unattainable. For the sake of expediency, let's gain this understanding by means of the example we've just employed.

Bound paper   because it has little air   burns slowly.

(*subject* of the quest)   *middle term*   (*predicate* of the quest)

S   M   P

(Letters S, M, P, stand for the italicized word above)

As this example illustrates, the justification or the answer is obtained by means of the *middle term*. Converted into an argument, it is as follows:

The question: *Why does bound paper burns slowly?*

Subject defined:	Bound paper (S) has little air. (M)
Known general principle:	<u>Whatever has little air (M) burns slowly. (P)</u>
Conclusion:	Therefore, bound paper (S) burns slowly (P).

Please note that the *middle term* (M) defines the subject (S) and that it is *shared.* That is, it appears in both assertions and is found between the subject and the predicate. It thereby *mediates* the two assertions and *connects* the subject (S) with the predicate (P) in the conclusion. In other words, the solution emerges by means of the *middle term.* This is why the first rule of logic states: *The syllogism must have three terms.* And the second rule: *The middle term must be distributed at least once.*

In a valid syllogism, it is unimportant which assertion is stated first. If the general principle is known, the same argument can begin with it.

Whatever has little air (M)   burns slowly. (P)

<u>Bound paper (S)   has little air. (M)</u>

Therefore, bound paper (S) burns slowly. (P)

In either case, the *middle term* in the syllogism is the same, it is *distributed* and it leads to the same *conclusion.*

Jason: According to Diagram 1, arguments can be *categorical, conditional* and *disjunctive.* Although their names connote their nature, I'm not sure that my understanding is adequate.

Diotima: First, let's take a closer look at the *categorical* arguments, for we already know some things about them and they are more complex.

Components of the Syllogism

Categorical syllogistic arguments, as we already know, consist of "two assertions" and a "conclusion." The assertions are called *premises*. In a syllogistic argument the premises consist of *three terms*; these are: the *major term*, the *minor term* and the *middle term*. Consequently, one of the first rules states: *The syllogism must have three terms.*

Jason: How do we know which of the premises is "major" and which "minor" term, especially if both of the statements have universal premises, as in our example (a)?

Diotima: The answer to your question is found in the conclusion. The *subject* of the "minor term" and the *predicate* of the "major term" always appear in the conclusion. For instance, when studying parallelograms if we have learned that all rectangles are parallelograms and we want to know if squares fall into the category of parallelograms, the argument starting with the known would run as follows:

All rectangles (M) are parallelograms (P).
<u>All squares (S) are rectangles (M).</u>
Therefore, all squares (S) are parallelograms (P).

Which of the premises in this instance is the major term?

Jason: The first premise, because it meets the requirements: both, the subject (S) of minor and the predicate (P) of major terms appear in the conclusion and the middle term (M) appears in both premises, linking the two.

Diotima: Did you notice that the *middle term* always appears once in each premise and *never* in the conclusion?

Jason: I didn't, but I can see it now.

Diotima: Two other rules are closely allied with the one on distribution; one of them is: *The subject term cannot be distributed in the conclusion, if it is not distributed in the premises.*

And the other: *The predicate term may not be distributed in the conclusion if it is not distributed in the premises.*

Jason: These rules seem to complement and complete the one requiring that the middle term be distributed at least once, if I understand them correctly. They just look at the syllogism from the standpoint of the conclusion. My question is: What if I am not sure whether the conclusion is sound?

Diotima: To assess the soundness of the conclusion, one must ask two questions:

1. Is the argument valid?
2. Are the premises true?

Validity, we must remember, is always determined by the *form*, hence by the rules and models of formal logic. When this fact is ascertained, next we need to examine the assertions of both premises to see if they are true. To determine the validity of our last argument we need ask: Is it true that squares are rectangles? The answer, of course, is "yes." Is it true that rectangles are parallelograms? Again, the answer is "yes." However, if I am uncertain about the truth of either assertion, I must first verify the meaning of the things involved to ascertain their truth. It is only when I am certain that the assertions are true that I can determine the status of the conclusion. In this case it would be necessary to have an accurate meaning of parallelogram, rectangle and square. Since a parallelogram is "a plane figure with four sides, having the opposite sides parallel and equal" *(Webster's New World College Dictionary*, Fourth Edition, 1999), and both squares and rectangles fit this definition, both assertions are true. Given that the argument is valid, and both premises are true, the conclusion is necessarily sound.

While assertions in the argument are called *premises,* the error in reasoning is called a *fallacy.* We will look at some of them as soon as we finish our discussion about arguments and the rules that guide them. We're not there yet.

Jason: Do you have in mind the distinction between the *deductive* and *inductive* arguments?

Diotima: That's one of them. We have also to observe that among the syllogistic arguments there are some that *affirm* (or *connect*) and some that *deny* (or *separate*) two things by means of the "third." This leads to *affirmative* and *negative* propositions. Each of these is governed by its own rule. The rule that governs the affirmative propositions states: *Whatever is affirmed of all in any class (or thing) is affirmed of every one in that class (or thing)*. Of the three valid argument forms given at the outset, example (b) reflects the structure of this rule. To be concrete: if *all the members of the Crusader basketball team are excellent players*, then *John, who is one of the members of the Crusader basketball team, must be an excellent player*.

> All the members of the Crusader basketball team (M) are excellent players (P).
> John (S) is one of the members of the Crusader basketball team (M).
> Therefore, John (S) is an excellent player (P).

And conversely: Whatever is denied of all in a class (or thing), is denied of every one in that class (or thing). Example (c) exemplifies this case. The rules that govern the arguments with a negative premise, state: *If one premise is negative, then the conclusion must also be negative*. And, *If the conclusion is negative, then one premise must be negative.*[9] In conjunction with these, some logicians add one other rule: *A valid syllogism must not have two negative premises*. This is because nothing follows from two negative premises. In such arguments there is no connection between the major and minor terms. For this reason this rule is sometimes omitted as unnecessary. The error is spotted by the rule regarding the middle term.

Jason: I can understand why. It would be helpful now to see all the rules listed together and have an example or two of how they are violated.

Diotima: We will do just that as soon as we address your earlier question regarding the kinds of arguments. As you have noted, there are two kinds of arguments: *deductive* and *inductive*. These arguments differ in a number of ways. The first distinction exists in the "reasoning process" itself.

In the *inductive arguments*, the reasoning process moves from the particular instances to universal conclusions, from the parts to the whole, from the specifics to the general, and from the many to the one. The reasoning process here is one of *synthesis*. This reasoning process is employed by all the sciences. From the many particular cases under observation, experimentation, testing, polling, and so on (proper to each discipline) a scientist draws an *inference*. The conclusion called an "inference" is a *generalization* and a generalization is an *educated guess*. It is an educated guess because on the basis of *the known* in the class (or thing), one draws a conclusion about *all* in that class (or thing).

The reasoning process in *deductive arguments* moves in just the opposite direction, hence: from the whole to the parts, from the universal to the particular, from the general to the specific, and from the one to the many. Given that deductive arguments begin with a *totality*—the *all* or the *whole* of something, what is true of the whole is necessarily true of its parts. If you have an apple pie and divide it into pieces, no matter how pieces there are, every one of them will be an apple pie. The reasoning process here is one of *analysis*. Since the conclusion is *deduced* from the premises, it is called a *deduction*.

Jason: I can understand why there could be a big difference in the kinds of conclusions their arguments render.

Diotima: Provided the argument is sound, the conclusion of an inductive argument is *very likely true*, but not necessarily so in every case. It is held to be true because it has been formulated by means of fair amount of evidence accumulated from the factual data secured through a method proper to the respective discipline. The conclusion, nonetheless, is only probable. Since nature comes with all kinds of surprises and it is impossible to study *every case*, that always leaves room for exceptions and deviations from the conclusion, thereby weakening its status. The following example illustrates the point.

> Every Norwegian I have ever met was tall and blond.
> Mary is a Norwegian.
> Therefore, Mary is (necessarily?) tall and blond.

Upon meeting Mary I may find out that she is anything but tall and blond. A trip to Norway may prove that Norwegians are a fair mix of all types of individuals. However, by and large, they may in fact be tall and blond. It is, therefore, wiser to modify the conclusions of the inductive arguments by prefacing them with words such as "most likely" true, or "probably" true, to allow room for the exceptions.

On the other hand, "counter example" is just that, a counter example. As such, it does not nullify the generalization that was made on the basis of ample evidence secured by the legitimate method proper to the discipline. Since most of human knowledge is attained by means of the empirical sciences and consists of generalizations, were we to nullify generalizations on the basis of counter examples, we would have to dismiss most of human knowledge.

Jason: Can you give me an example of it?

Diotima: By all means! Let us look at the medical profession to see how such a scenario is played out in real life. It is commonly accepted that physicians provide competent medical care with compassion and respect for dignity and human rights. Suppose someone's physician fails to uphold the standards of his or her profession, is dishonest, or places personal gain above the well-being of the patient. Does that mean that we must now hold suspect or distrust all physicians and the medical profession as a whole because of one person?

Jason: The answer is obviously "no."

Diotima: Clearly, a counter example is, for the most part, only a counter example and one should not be flustered and thrown into confusion when one is trying to make a valid contribution to knowledge and someone brings up a counter example in an effort to discredit it.

Jason: I must confess that here I, too, am a culprit. I always felt that if I succeeded in finding a counter example then I have refuted my opponent's view and have won the dispute. Not so, I see.

Diotima: I am glad, Jason that you can now recognize the counter examples for what they truly are. Fortunately, conclusions of deductive arguments never face such a dilemma. If the argument is sound, deductive conclusions are always guaranteed and indisputable. They are indisputable because, unlike the generalizations of inductive arguments—*deductions* never claim more in the conclusion than what was already accepted in the premises. Deductions are characterized by "necessity and universality," that is, they are *necessarily true* and *universally so.* These conclusions can be derived *a priori,* that is, independently of human experience, just on the basis of logical coherence. Scientific conclusions, on the other hand, initially, are derived *a posteriori,* that is, from experience, on the basis of their observation, experimentation, or whatever other method is employed. It is only when the scientists succeed in expressing their insights in terms of mathematical formula that they are certain their insights are accurate. Being a neutral and an exact science, mathematics can render objective validity to any content to which it is applied.

Jason: Given this understanding, I find it very surprising that we generally put so much faith in the conclusions of science and pay so little attention to sound logical reasoning.

Diotima: Keep this in mind also that inductive and deductive arguments are meant to complement, rather than compete with each other. When we come into this world, we begin our learning process by means of experience. This knowledge comes primarily through our senses. As we encounter new objects, we learn names for them. Slowly we build a repertoire of vocabulary and are able to communicate our thoughts. This is achieved by means of the synthesis of ideas and words.

The process of synthesis continues as we learn new subjects. Initially, our accumulation of knowledge is inductive. It is only gradually that we become capable of understanding universal concepts such as goodness, beauty and justice, or patriotism, freedom and loyalty and learn to analyze objects, concepts, issues, and the like. We, too, when we have completed our inquiry shall synthesize the analyzed concepts and by means of this method eventually arrive at truth. In due time, we will have much more to say about these procedures. Right now, we need to complete our discussion of logic. For thus far we have dealt only with *categorical syllogisms.* But there are two other kinds of arguments we've mentioned. Do you remember what they are?

Jason: The diagram in front of me makes the answer easy, so let's move on to them.

Conditional and Disjunctive Arguments

The three "argument forms" we have portrayed at the outset, as you now well know, are all examples of the *categorical syllogisms.* You may have noticed that all categorical syllogisms contain "All" or "No" (or an equivalent of these words, like "every" or "none") in the major premise. Sometimes these words do not appear; they are recognized from the context and the clue words. These two argument forms have comparable clue words.

Conditional arguments are the "If . . . then" arguments. The word "If" in the major premise expresses the *condition* of the argument; the conclusion depends upon it. The valid form for it is:

> If A, then B.
> A.
> Therefore B.

This form converted into the argument may be: *If* all human beings are mammals, and you are a human being, *then* you are a mammal. The important thing to remember about this type of argument is that the major premise, which begins with an "if," stipulates the condition for the soundness of the conclusion. Thus, the reverse arrangement form would not hold true. For instance,

> If A, then B.
> <u>B.</u>
> Therefore A.

This is an "invalid argument form," because the conclusion is not based on the condition of the argument, namely, A. Translated into an argument, it would read:

> *If* Anthrax X is a deadly powder, *then* anyone who inhales Anthrax X will die.
> <u>Susan died.</u>
> Therefore, Susan inhaled Anthrax X.

The fact that Susan died is not a guarantee that she inhaled anthrax X. She may have died of a heart attack or from some other cause.

Disjunctive arguments are the "Either / or" arguments.

> Either A or B.
> <u>Not A.</u>
> Therefore B.

> Either Jack or Jill went to the store and did the shopping.
> <u>It was not Jack.</u>
> Therefore, it was Jill.

In "either/or" arguments it does not matter which term appears first, because the case has been narrowed down to just two options. Thus, if not one, then it has to be the other.

Jason: I don't anticipate having any difficulty with these two types of arguments. If what follows is just as simple, I should be in good shape.

Diotima: Having roughly secured basic understanding of the structure of arguments, we are at last ready to honor your request with regard to listing all the rules and seeing how they are violated. If you have further questions, this is the time to raise them.

Rules for Constructing Arguments:

> *1. The syllogism must have three terms and only three terms.*
> *2. The middle term must be distributed at least once.*
> *3. The subject term may not be distributed in the conclusion if it is not distributed in the premises.*
> *4. The predicate term may not be distributed in the conclusion if it is not distributed in the premises.*
> *5. A particular conclusion cannot be derived from two universal premises.*
> *6. If one premise is negative, then the conclusion must also be negative, and if the conclusion is negative, then one premise must also be negative.*
> *7. A valid argument can not have two negative premises. (Nothing follows from two negative premises, because there is no connection between the major and the minor term.)*

Jason: Who decided on these rules? Or, how were these laws derived?

Diotima: These rules were derived by the logicians in logic in the same way that the natural and kinetic laws were derived by the scientists in their field of endeavor. Studies in both areas have revealed that things operate consistently in a certain manner under the *natural to them conditions*. When these conditions are violated, it was found that the same results are unobtainable. This led logicians to postulate these rules or laws in logic and scientists to those in their own realm.

Jason: Thanks. I get the idea.

Diotima: Looking at the first rule: *The syllogism must have three terms, and only three terms,* do you remember what those three terms are and do you have any questions regarding this rule?

Jason: I think that I remember them; they are: a *major term*, a *minor term* and a *concl* . . . No! I should say: a minor term, which is the *subject* (S) of the proposition, a *middle term* (M) that is *distributed*, and a major term, which becomes a *predicate* (P) in the argument. By being distributed in the premises, the *middle term* connects the two premises and links the subject with the predicate *in the conclusion*.

Diotima: Your answer covers the second rule as well.

Jason: But how is rule one violated?

Diotima: Rule one is violated when the *middle term*, though one term, has two meanings. This leads to four terms, which obscures the argument and leads to the *fallacy of equivocation*. For instance,

> Angels are pure created spirits.
> <u>My sister is an angel.</u>
> Therefore, my sister is a pure created spirit.

Jason: I can see the ambiguity in the meaning of the word "angel." The term "angel" is employed here in two different senses. This is the reason for the fallacious conclusion. This fallacy, if you notice, is the first one listed below.

Diotima: Do you want to go through the process of how each of the rules is violated, or would it suffice for now to just name the fallacies that violate those rules?

Jason: Since I am eager to get to the answers of greater urgency to me, at this point let's proceed. As long as you do not deem this understanding to be of essence to our quest, we can get to consider these things in greater depth when we have more time.

Diotima: Good. I am sure that you will find some of the fallacies to be self-explanatory. However, if, or when we encounter some other fallacy along the way that calls for better understanding, we'll deal with it then.

The Corresponding Fallacy for Each of the Rules when it is violated:

1. *The Fallacy of Equivocation.*
2. *The Fallacy of the Undistributed Middle.*
3. *The Fallacy of the Illicitly Distributed Subject.*
4. *The Fallacy of Illicitly Distributed Predicate.*
5. *The Fallacy of Deriving a Particular Conclusion from Universal Premises.*
6. *The Fallacy of Deriving a Negative Conclusion from two Affirmative Premises or the Fallacy of Deriving an Affirmative Conclusion with a Negative Premise.*
7. *The Fallacy of two Negative Premises.*

Validity, Truth and Soundness

As you can see, all arguments can be valid or invalid, true or false, sound or unsound. *Validity* is determined by "form," *truth* by "premises" and *soundness* by the combination of both of these. We have already seen that *validity* is established by the rules of logic that provide valid argument models to safeguard against error in reasoning. *Truth* is found in "premises": in "inductive arguments" it is determined by the *correspondence with empirical facts*; in "deductive arguments" it is derived by *logical coherence in the reasoning process*. Premises are either true or false, but never both.

We also know what those *argument forms* and *rules* are and what *fallacies* accrue when these rules are violated; we know likewise how the *truth of the premises* is ascertained. With these points in mind, we direct our gaze to the possible combinations of truth and falsehood. Looking at a few examples you will have an opportunity, Jason to test your knowledge of what you've learned thus far.

There are four possible combinations of truth and falsehood in the premises and conclusions:

1. Premises and conclusion can both be true.
2. Premises may be true but conclusion false.
3. Premises may be false and the conclusion true.
4. Both premises and conclusion may be false.

An example of the first combination would be:

> All human beings are mortal. T
> Jane is a human being. T
> Therefore, Jane is mortal. T

Jason: It is plane that conclusion is sound because here we have a valid form and true premises.

Diotima: Is this an inductive, or a deductive syllogism?

Jason: Since we know this not by the reasoning process but from experience, like scientists empirically, I'd judge it to be an *inference* of inductive knowledge.

Diotima: What about the following combination of truth and falsehood?

> All men are mortal. T
> All women are mortal. T
> Therefore, all men are women. F

Diotima: Can you name the reason for the false conclusion?

Jason: Since both premises are true, the fallacy is due to the invalid form. This becomes readily apparent when I convert the argument into the argument form.

> All A's are B's.
> All C's are B's.
> Therefore, all A's are C's.

I see the second rule violated. The argument exhibits *the fallacy of the undistributed middle*. There is no middle term connecting the two premises. Consequently, the conclusion is false.

Diotima: Good, Jason. We must keep this in mind when we are formulating our arguments. Strict adherence to the dictates of formal logic is absolutely necessary, if our conclusions are to be sound. Can you do as well with the next argument?

> All squares are circles. F
> All circles are parallelograms. F
> Therefore, all squares are parallelograms. T

Jason: This case is just the opposite of the former one. Now we have a valid argument form but false premises. It is the false premises that make this argument unsound.

Diotima: What about the fourth combination?

> All triangles are circles. F
> All circles are parallelograms. F
> Therefore, all triangles are parallelograms. F

Jason: This is another instance of a valid form but an unsound argument because of the false premises.

Diotima: These examples demonstrate that both, the inductive and the deductive arguments can be sound or unsound. The rules are the same for both. There is, however, one difference between them we must note regarding *unsoundness*.

As Diagram 1 shows, both deductive and inductive arguments can be *unsound* in two ways: *formally* and *informally*. They are *formally fallacious* when they are invalid, even when the premises are true. They are *informally fallacious* when they are valid but have false premise(s). But inductive arguments can be *fallacious other-*

wise as well. This can occur in a number of ways, but all have to do with *fallacious reasoning*. These arguments are known as: begging the question, ad hominem arguments, *post hoc, ergo poster hoc* arguments, red herring arguments, arguments by counter-example, mere assertion, vicious circle, and many others. Since we will be very careful in observing the rules of correct reasoning so as to avoid these mistakes, we shall look only at a few of these that you may see the difference between these fallacies and the ones we have studied.

Jason: Among these there is one I already know. I know the argument by counter example from personal experience. Most likely I am guilty of some others as well, but don't know it.

Diotima: Let's look at the most common ones. In the event you need further explanation, please don't hesitate to ask.

Begging the question is a fallacious argument because it accepts as a premise something that is supposed to be proven or demonstrated. It uses a statement as both a conclusion and a part of it as a premise for that conclusion. Example: Terrorism is immoral because it is wrong. If asked: Why is it immoral? The answer is: "because it is wrong." Since immoral means morally wrong, the argument uses part of its conclusion as a premise, which itself needs to be demonstrated. Thus, the conclusion begs the question. The main problem with this kind of argument is that it lacks sufficient evidence to support the claim.

Jason: This argument seems to lack the major premise providing the middle term.

Diotima: The *ad hominem* argument is fallacious because, as its name in Latin reveals, it attacks the person (in Latin, *homo*), rather than speaks to the issue. Fallacies of this sort are not infrequent during political campaigns. For example, we may hear one of the contenders for governmental office, attack his opponent, rather than defend his or her own position. Ordinarily this occurs when the person feels he or she is losing ground on the platform. Unable to refute the issues advanced by the opponent, one tries to defeat him or her by attacking person's character.

The *post hoc, ergo propter hoc* argument, literally means "after this, therefore because of this." It is fallacious in that it jumps to the conclusion without sufficient evidence. It asserts that just because something occurred after some event took place that it was caused by it, when in fact there is no evidence connecting the two occurrences. Let's say the forest is on fire. Just because the boy scouts had their meeting there earlier, is no evidence that they are responsible for having set the forest on fire.

The *red herring* argument is one that deliberately introduces an irrelevant issue into the discussion for purposes of deception. Such a fallacy is readily recognized.

Jason: I've encountered such arguments, but I did not know that they are called by this name.

Diotima: Mere assertion is not event an argument because it consists merely of stating one's view without providing supporting reasons for it, yet expecting others to accept it as a logical argument.

Jason: It sounds as if such a person is claiming to speak with authority, which apparently it lacks.

Diotima: There is an argument that logicians call a *fallacy of appealing to authority.* The weakness of this argument lies in that it cites authority instead of giving reasons to support what one claims. While there is nothing wrong with appealing to the authority of experts for support of what one says—we often appeal to lawyers, economists, doctors and other qualified individuals in the area of their expertise—this evidence should come as a confirmation for the reasons one offers, rather than in place of them.

The *vicious circle* argument is something like begging the question argument; it lacks sufficient evidence to support one's view. Both assume what needs to be demonstrated. The vicious circle argument consists in using two or three propositions or arguments to support one another without any other support. For example: "All people should love one another." Why? Your reason is, "because the Bible says so." The question is: Why does the Bible say so? If you say, "Because God said it," you have not added any new evidence to support your claim, because the Bible is understood to be the word of God. For you this may be reason enough, but not for one who does not believe in God. If he rejects God, he automatically rejects the Bible. The fallacy consists in assuming what needs to be demonstrated. Using these assertions to support each other is called a *vicious circle*. More evidence is needed to demonstrate the point you want to make.

There is, nonetheless, what some logicians call a "virtuous circle" as well. One might attempt, for example, to provide an answer to a complex issue or to articulate a whole system of thought. To do so, one might need to make use of a series of sound arguments to arrive at the final conclusion. Each argument in the series serves as a stepping stone, as it were, that eventually brings one full circle and yields an intelligible conclusion. This kind of reasoning reflects a *virtuous circle.*

Jason: I suspect this is something we will be striving to achieve.

Diotima: Good premonition, Jason. Needless to say, there are many more fallacious arguments than these and there is much more to be said in behalf of logic as a science. Unfortunately, we have here neither space nor time to go into them. For our purposes, this much will suffice.

Jason: Even this much is a big help to me. It certainly will make me a more careful thinker and less eager to jump to conclusions without adequate evidence.

Diotima: By way of summary, we can say that the function of logic is three-fold. Logic tells us how to 1) formulate sound arguments to arrive at reliable conclusions; 2) reason to persuade others to accept our views; and 3) examine the arguments of others for their soundness. The same rules and models serve as the criterion for all three, which is what makes logic the most objective science of all.

There is one more point I must make. The examples we've employed in explaining arguments have been, for the most part so obvious that they did not need to be set up as arguments for one to be convinced of their conclusions. This was done deliberately, to make the principle at work fully intelligible. Ordinarily this is not how the argumentative discourse occurs. Sometimes relevant information is insufficient, conflicting, or difficult to choose and assess. In most cases, arguments are long-winded and complex. They can, nonetheless, be reduced to the basic premises and examined in light of the criteria provided by formal logic. Fortunately, we do not need to be concerned in this study with examining other people's arguments. We just have to make sure that our arguments are correctly formulated, and for this we have adequate understanding, or do we, Jason?

Jason: I think we do. Time will tell. At least I understand the basics of it.

Diotima: What is of essence here is that we know we have the right tool and an approval of scholars for conducting our study as proposed. For Black writes: "There will always be competent technicians who . . . can be trusted to build the highways 'over which the streamlined vehicles of a highly mechanized logic, fast and efficient, can reach every important point on fixed tracks'."[10] We can be certain, therefore, that as long as we do not deviate from the principles of logic, our procedure, as well our appeal to analogies, diagrams, metaphors or models is legitimate and can help us reach the goal we have set for ourselves.

Jason: If the masters in the field speak of logic in such glowing terms and approve of those additional aids whenever the need is there, I have every reason to believe that we have chosen the right means for achieving our goal. There is, notwithstanding, a lingering question in my mind: What will make our study relevant and appealing to the contemporary person? After all, we don't want to be selfish and keep the truth to ourselves when we find it, do we?

Diotima: By no means, Jason! I doubt that anyone who caught a glimpse of truth could keep it to oneself. If we humans have a great need of sharing our joys with others whenever some great fortune comes our way, you can be sure that when it comes to the ultimate Truth, we would not even be able to contain the joy of it within ourselves. With the light of truth, you will recall, come all the blessings that the human heart craves. Finding it is like finding a treasure—a joy not easily concealed.

As to finding an appealing style, one that reflects contemporary trends in communication, we need to take a brief look at the History of Philosophy in terms of the major periods. To be honest, Jason, I for one never understand anything adequately independently of its context. Neither can I do justice to anything in explaining it apart from its context. Such an attempt inescapably invites all kinds of "why" and "how." Seeing things in their proper setting and arriving at the understanding in a systematic way, strikes me as a wholesome way to acquire and to disseminate knowledge. You may find it beneficial as well.

Jason: This, I still must learn. Eventually I will let you know if I found an historical approach helpful.

IV. QUICK GLANCE AT THE HISTORY OF PHILOSOPHY

Diotima: From our earlier discussion of philosophy, we already know that philosophy in its quest for the "being" of beings is concerned with all that is. Also, that at the heart of it, there are the perennial questions. Do you remember what these questions are?

Jason: I believe I do, because these questions are of special interest to me. Tell me if I have them right: Who am I? From where do I come? Where am I going? And, what is the best way to get there?

Diotima: I like the way you have rephrased the last question. Actually, the question: "What am I doing in this world?" implies and leads to your question: "What is the best way to get there?" I agree. It does seem to follow naturally upon the third question: "Where am I going?" While it is true that the answers to all four perennial questions are essential to the meaning of human life, wisdom, if you remember, applies most directly to the fourth question. It points out the best way of getting there, wherever the "there" turns out to be. On the other hand, the answer to this question, you may recall, hinges primarily on the first question "Who am I?" It is this question that reveals the true nature of our identity. Consequently, to discover the answer to these questions we need to start with . . .

Jason: Excuse me. I'm sorry for interrupting, but I am puzzled. What is the need of bringing up these philosophical questions again? You said earlier that these questions are perennial, that is, that human beings of every century from time immemorial have been asking them. So why do we need to raise these questions anew? Are you implying that no one up to this point has found reliable answers to these questions?

Diotima: No, I am not implying that at all.

Jason: If these answers are already available, then why sweat looking for them? Isn't it like trying to reinvent the wheel? Can't we just go to the thinkers who found the answers and learn from them?

Diotima: If no one in the past had succeeded in arriving at them, we would be in an even greater predicament, lover of wisdom. For then we would have to wonder what chances are there of our finding them? Don't you agree?

Jason: I guess you are right. But what's wrong with relying on the answers of others? Don't we do plenty of that in everyday life? Human life is based 99% on the trust we place in what others tell us. What we are speaking of here is not for the average person. Given the depth and the nature of the perennial questions, those who have emerged with reliable answers must have been profound and trustworthy individuals. Shouldn't their answers be accorded, at least, as much credibility as the answers of others?

Diotima: The problem is that the answers bequeathed to us by them do not coincide. Thinkers do not agree on the question of human identity. Without first arriving at our own answer, we are at a loss to know which answer reflects the truth. The perplexing thing about those views is that there appears to be some truth in all of them. Yet they have different implications. As a result, there is a great disparity in the final conclusions that thinkers reach. This is why I was about to suggest that we take a quick look at the History of Philosophy. We can get there an idea of what our predecessors had to say on this topic, and then understand better the reason for the controversy and the implications thereof. Along the way we hope to discover an appropriate style for our study, one that is likely to resonate with the contemporary mind. If you recall, this was our initial intent.

Jason: Well, go ahead as you have planned. I forgot about that. I'm just impatient and can't imagine that we can reduce several volumes of the History of Philosophy to a few pages, and make it intelligible.

Diotima: Oh, no! This will be barely a glance at history, Jason. We will dive in only for the answers we are seeking. What we want is just a gist of a given philosophy to know how the thinker derived his view of human identity. We need this information to understand where our challenge lies. For the sake of brevity, we will limit ourselves also to the historical perspective in the Western World only. Rest assured it will be the shortest treatment of history you have ever seen.

Jason: I am amused by the prospect, so let's go!

Diotima: As you most likely know, Greece is the cradle of the Western World. It is also the birthplace of western philosophy. While the history of this civilization takes us back to the Bronze Age (c. 3000 B.C.), even beyond to the Neolithic Era (c. 7000-3000 B.C.),[11] the question of human identity had surfaced only about 500 B.C. It was approximately at this time, amid great achievements in all other arts and sciences, that literature and drama reached the status of superior eminence. Formal systems of education did not exist as yet, but poetry— initially the epics of Homer and Hesiod, later also lyrics of other poets— served to teach children the alphabet and reading, as also the values of culture and the ideals of patriotism. Drama, on the other hand, became the main vehicle of moral and religious education of the adult populace. Festivals of this nature were held throughout Greece and were well attended. Because they provided entertainment and education, they were held in high esteem. To make them easily accessible to everyone, performances took place in the outdoor theatres that were very large and free of charge. In those days, the government was responsible for enhancing the life of its citizens. It is estimated that the beautiful theatre at Epidauros accommodated approximately 18,000 spectators (Goff, 63). The most famous theatre is said to have been in Athens, the city viewed as the center of Greek culture. Please note, education and entertainment served the same end: to ennoble the person and to enable one to reach the excellence of one's being, morally and otherwise.

Jason: Interesting! Things have really changed!

Diotima: It is the playwrights of that period who give us the first hint about the nature of human identity, even though they do it indirectly.

Jason: What do you mean?

Diotima: They did not give us the answer directly. The answer is inferred from the plot of the story and the conduct of the characters in the cast.

Jason: Do they agree in their views on human nature?

Diotima: Unfortunately not, but they do reveal an interesting pattern of answers that has been recurring throughout the centuries. Let us consider briefly each of the playwrights to see what each of them sought to communicate.

Jason: How many were there? Do we know who they are?

Diotima: Apparently, there were many contestants, but we know of the most famous three, namely, Aeschylus, Sophocles, and Euripides—all of them tragedians. Several of their plays have survived the ravages of time and continue to be studied with much interest even today.

A.   Presocratic Playwrights

Aeschylus (c. 525-456 B.C.) was the earliest of the three. Put succinctly, he envisioned man as *a spiritual, moral being—a God-like being.* "Aeschylean tragedy," state Goff and his contributors, "is concerned with major moral and theological issues" (Goff, 63). In fact, Aeschylus sometimes has been "accused of being much more a preacher than a dramatist, for all of his plays carry a clearly stated message" of moral nature, write Cross and his collaborators.[12] Aeschylus stressed that "evil would breed evil unless vengeance was tempered by wise deliberation" (Goff, 63). The most detestable of evils was human arrogance or pride which the Greeks called *hubris.* Because this evil led to all kinds of vices and crimes, in Greek mythology *hubris* was punishable by the goddess of retributive justice, *Nemesis.* Aeschylus advocated moderation in all things. All his plays seek to develop a personal sense of responsibility and a strong sense of justice in light of human freedom. They also disclose the delicate nature of human freedom (Goff, 63).

Sophocles (c. 496-406 B.C.), a student of Aeschylus, seems to have outshone his master. Judging by how many plays he produced and the number of times he was awarded the first prize, he seems more famous. Sophocles portrays man as a *rational being.* It is because man by nature is a rational being, he contended, that he can become a moral, God-like being. In the absence of moderation, however, man could become just the opposite. Sophocles maintained "fate was irresistible and placed human beings within certain limitations; to try to exceed them, especially, by challenging the gods, was *hubris* and invited destruction" (Goff, 63-64).

His plays carried the message that "life was full of suffering, even for the innocent," but suffering had the power to build one's character. It is the "inborn character traits, whether despicable or admirable," that were responsible for the decisions one makes. He counseled an attitude "of resignation before the superior wisdom of inscrutable deities," and like his master, he encouraged moderation in all things (Goff, 64).

Jason: Now I can see more clearly how philosophy is embodied in literature and why at college we had to take some courses in fine arts, regardless of what our major was.

Euripides (c. 485-406 B.C.), a contemporary of Sophocles, was the third of the tragedians of the same period. Strongly influenced by the sophistic mentality, Euripides gives us an image of man as merely a *natural being.* Reading his plays one is tempted to see man not just as being merely human, but to use Nietzsche's phrase, "all-too-human." His colorful characters depict psychological abnormalities, explosive emotions, a supercharged sexual appetite and a vengeful spirit. In his plays, especially *Hippolitus, Bacchant Women,* and *Medea,* even the gods display these flaws of character. "Euripides equated the traditional anthropomorphic gods with irrepressible compulsions within the human psyche" (Goff, 65). In his drama, Euripides questioned traditional social and moral values in the critical spirit of sophistic skepticism.

Jason: We said at some point that we all need to develop a critical attitude toward what we read and hear. Why, then, was the critical attitude of the sophists not seen in this light?

Diotima: Some of their questioning was indeed constructive, but some of it led to the demise of the Greek culture. Experimenting with their newly found personal freedom that came with the birth of Greek democracy, some sophists carried it to an extreme. That led people down the alley of relativism. Protagoras, viewed by history as the leading figure of the movement at the time, enthroned "man as the measure of all things," meaning man is the highest authority; each man has the right to decide for himself. Along the line of this reasoning, the later soph-ists moved toward the positions that the "laws were merely a set of men's opinions." Consequently, if any indi-vidual held a different opinion, his opinion was "as valid for him" as were the laws (Cross, 65). This thinking un-dermined the laws of the nation, whose purpose was to provide order, unity and a fair system of justice to its citizens. Aeschylus and Sophocles sought to hold back the rushing tide of moral decadence bound to result from such relativistic mentality. However, the Protagorean view of unbridled freedom was too appealing to human na-ture to be restrained. It caught on quickly and took hold of the society at large. Once relativism took over, moral-ity fell victim to lawlessness and gradual decadence ensued. The rich culture's disintegration became merely a matter of time.

The result was inevitable. The conflicting views having obscured people's understanding of human nature, the movement terminated in confusion, fragmentation and dissatisfaction with life. There was therefore the need to turn to *reason*.

At approximately the same time, philosophy of the Western World was being born. The thinkers of this pe-riod are called Presocratics.

Jason: Didn't the Presocratic thinkers begin with wonder?

Diotima: Yes, they did. Their wonder, however, was not about the perennial questions of philosophy. These thinkers were of a scientific bent. Fascinated by the beauty, order and harmony of the cosmos, they directed their energies toward discovering how all things came to be and to what they are ultimately reducible. In the language of philosophy, theirs was the search for the "first principles."

Jason: What precisely is the difference between the Presocratic playwrights and these philosophers?

Diotima: The Presocratic playwrights relied on *intuition* and addressed themselves primarily to the issues of *life,* whereas the Presocratic philosophers, though likewise deeply intuitive, made a shift toward *reason* and to *nature.* As they observed nature and intuitively apprehended the splendor and beauty of the world of phenomena, they began to question the *whence* of it all. In other words, they were the first to look *rationally* for the first prin-ciples of reality.

With regard to their contributions to knowledge, it is commonly accepted that their merit in philosophy lies more in the profoundness of the questions they asked than in the answers they provided. Yet—judging by the ex-tant fragments—it is there that we find the first insights into the three basic interpretations of reality, which coin-cide with the three theories of human nature. At that time also there surfaced all the epistemological and human problems that challenge philosophy to this very day. A closer look at these thinkers, you may find, will reveal depth much greater than what is ordinarily credited to them.

B.   Presocratic Thinkers

Taking their name from the place of their birth, or from the predominant concept of the theory they advanced, Presocratics fall into five groups: Ionians, Eleatics, Pluralists, Atomists, and the Sophists whom we have encoun-tered earlier. While all of them offer some valuable insights, Aristotle and that school of thought consider De-mocritus to be the greatest among them. Yet, many scholars of that period maintain, like Plato that the most pro-found and subtle among them were the Eleatics, notably Parmenides, Pythagoras, Xenophanes, and Zeno. Their knowledge borders on the mystical, if it does not find its origin there. From among the Presocratics, Parmenides, Anaxagoras and Democritus can be selected as the *trio* that best corresponds to the three interpretations of human nature we have discussed already. It must be noted, however, that their understanding of human nature is not a mere endorsement of the views of their predecessors. Far from it! It derives from their understanding of the cos-mos.

Jason: I'm really eager to see how they were able to arrive at the same views from so distant a route.

Parmenides (c. 530-444 B.C.) is identified as the first Greek thinker who was a metaphysician or ontologist in the full sense of the word. He was the first to articulate the philosophical doctrine of idealism, and the first to argue for "the real" or "what-is" as "the one" or "being" (*to eon*). This being, he states, is a "pure form" which is ungenerated, unchangeable, indivisible, continuous and unique.[13] According to Albert E. Avey, he is likewise the first to argue for what subsequently became known as the three laws, or principles of thought: the Principle of Contradiction, the Principle of Identity and the Principle of the Excluded Middle. These laws have been acknowledged ever since to be the beginning and the bedrock principles of all philosophical discourse; they are what makes logical discourse possible.[14]

Jason: What are these principles all about? Why are they so important?

Diotima: We shall have to become acquainted with them when we are ready to undertake our own search for the truth of reality. Discussion of them at this point would get us off the track of our current goal.

Jason: I understand. In that case, let's get back to Parmenides.

Diotima: The being of Parmenides is apparently an intelligent being, a thinking being. "For it is the same thing to think and to be," he says, or "For thinking and being are identical" (Frs. 2-3).[15]

From the synopsis on Parmenides in *The Cambridge Dictionary of Philosophy* we learn that some sources indicate he was a physician by profession. Extant ancient fragments from the second part of his allegorical poem *Opinions,* dealing with the embryological themes seem to confirm it. In the same section of the poem are also recorded "four scientific break-throughs" some of which doubtlessly, it is maintained, "were Parmenides' own discoveries: that the earth is a sphere; that the two tropics and the Arctic and Antarctic circles divide the earth into five zones; that the moon gets its light from the sun; and that the morning star and the evening star are the same planet."[16]

According to the same source, many philosophical groups of thinkers and movements from about the middle fifth century on, directly or indirectly, have been influenced by Parmenides' thinking. Among them are mentioned Empedocles, Anaxagoras and Democritus. We find his thinking in Plato's writings, particularly in conjunction with his theory of Forms, and recognize it in the basic features of the Aristotelian corpus, especially in "the priority of actuality over potentiality, the unmoved mover, and the man-begets-man principle" (CDP, 647). Clearly, Parmenides stands high above the others.

As to the "Truth" about what is, the true reality, he tells us he received it from the goddess who thus instructed him. She explained that there are two paths: "the path of Truth," and "the path of Opinion." Only the path of Truth leads one to the knowledge of this being and to the correct understanding of the world. The realm, to which he was borne aloft to receive this knowledge, is far beyond "the paths of the mortals" who follow the path of Opinion. Opinion cannot bring one to this knowledge. Parmenides couches his experience in the allegory with which he begins his Poem; through it also he communicates his philosophy. It is by means of this "privileged experience" that this knowledge came to him, he tells us. The unmitigated conviction of utter certainty with which he communicates it, however, makes it questionable that what he says is merely an allegory, a philosophical device, or even a deduction of reason. None of the rational thinkers—philosophers or not!—thereafter, actually no one else apart from the mystics, ever exhibited comparable conviction. Scholars ascribe the obscurity inherent in his writing to the fact that he communicates in verse rather than in prose. This undeniable difficulty comes, however, in addition to his already subtle thought.

Jason: Is Parmenides suggesting that a certain kind of knowledge can be had only by means of a divine revelation?

Diotima: This is what he is implying—a divine revelation given *in experience.* Being the first philosopher to speak of this being and speaking of it with such confidence, suggests that what he describes in his Poem was *his personal experience* of it. It is this firsthand knowledge, we judge, that constitutes the basis of his contention.

Anaxagoras (c. 534-462 B.C.)[17] was one of the pluralists. He was singled out by Socrates as having provided the most sensible answer to account for the origin of the cosmos. He postulated *nous* (mind) as the first principle of reality. Fragments 11 and 12 seem to indicate just that. He states, "In everything there is a share of everything except mind; but in some things there is also mind" (Fr. 11). "All other things partake of a share of everything, but mind is unlimited and self-ruling and is mixed with no thing, (*chrema*), but is alone itself by itself. . . . It possesses all understanding of everything and is endowed with the greatest power" (Fr. 12).

The cosmos, as in Parmenides, is a mixture; it partakes of *nous.* The many substances that make up the cosmos are composed of particles called "seeds." The seeds are mingled together and are dispersed throughout the cosmos, but mind sets up the movements of the heavens into the order in which they are. Albert E. Avey suggests this "regulating mind" of the cosmos looks like "an early argument from the design to prove the existence of God" (Avey, 16). Too few fragments have survived to know exactly what his theory was; for which reason, writes Owens, "The various modern interpretations of Anaxagoras' basic doctrine differ widely and radically" (Owens, 114). Since the scholarly analyses of the existing fragments have no bearing on our study, we shall forego discussing them.

There are nonetheless a few other bits of information from the writings of his contemporaries that shed interesting light on his views. For instance, according to Theophrastus, Owens states, "Anaxagoras taught that 'the earth is flat in shape, and remains suspended aloft on account of its size and because there is no void, and because the air being very strong carries the earth upon it'" (Owens, 121). Some other ideas attributed to Anaxagoras are that "the sun was larger than Peloponnesus, that eclipses of the moon are caused by the interposition of the earth between the sun and moon, and that there are many inhabited worlds like ours. Also he believed in biological evolution and *panpsychism* or the omnipresence of consciousness in the universe" (Avey, 16). Whatever his theory of the cosmos was, it must have had some inconsistencies. The main reason Socrates gives for abandoning it is that instead of explaining how the *nous* is operative in nature, Anaxagoras turned to the natural causes to explain the objects of nature. Besides, for Socrates, understanding man's ethical life was more important than understanding the universe. That is why he devotedly espoused the concerns of ethical life.

Democritus (c. 460—c. 370 B.C.) was an atomist, the first philosopher to give a developed, purely materialistic account of nature. His account of reality is in terms of the "atoms," whence the designation "atomist." Democritus taught that all substance consists of indivisible, tiny, invisible particles, called atoms that come in great variety of forms and move in an empty space. The space or void is real. The void is infinite and an infinite number of atoms collide with one another in it. The various combinations of these atoms account for the diversity in nature. According to him, even Parmenides' "being" is composed of them. All atoms share the same characteristics; they are ungenerated, indestructible, eternal and indivisible. "Under the right conditions a concentration of atoms can begin a vortex motion that draws in other atoms and forms a spherical heaven enclosing a world" (CDP, 217). Our earth is flat. It is surrounded by the "heavenly bodies carried by a vortex motion." Besides ours, there are other worlds that may be different from ours. It is not necessary that they have living beings in them. The cosmos is guided by rigid natural laws.

As to the living things, "living things, including humans, originally emerged out of slime. Life is caused by fine, spherical soul atoms, and living things die when these atoms are lost. Human culture gradually evolved through chance discoveries and imitations of nature."[18]

Democritus was a brilliant man. The wide range of interests that absorbed his mind testifies to it. His studies included astronomy, meteorology, agriculture, medicine, mathematics, music, poetry, painting and diction, but his moral concerns prevailed over all the rest. Owens writes that fragments 35-115 are "Maxims of Democritus" but in addition to these, there are many more fragments devoted to moral wisdom. Michael Nill is even more encompassing in scope on this point. He writes: "Although he [Democritus] is best known for his atomic theory of matter, virtually all 298 fragments ascribed to him consist of one-or two-sentence gnomic statements about ethical matters."[19] Here Democritus draws upon conventional wisdom of Greek life. He recommends an ethics of moderation and advises a disposition of cheerfulness in life for which he offers excellent advice.

Cheerfulness (*euthymia*) Democritus stresses does not result from maximizing any particular pleasure. It results from a "balance of pleasures." Cheerfulness is a sign of being a good moral individual. It is a consequence of acts that are just and lawful. "So strongly does he believe in the compatibility of morality and the pursuit of self-interest or *euthymia* that he adopts (or anticipates) the Socratic claim that committing an injustice does more harm to one's soul than suffering an injustice" (EE, 390, Frag. 45).

Democritus bases his view on compatibility of cheerfulness with morality on two claims: "(a) laws are imposed to prevent strife which has its origin in jealousy (frag. 245); and (b) jealousy and ENVY are incompatible with *euthymia* because they create disturbances in the soul, cause dissatisfaction, and make one an enemy of oneself" (EE, 390). The latter finds its endorsement in Karl Marx's theory of historical materialism, albeit adapted to his own system. We will discuss Marx's theory later. Actually, much of what Democritus advises for a happy life, we could apply with great profit to our own lives in this troubled, fast-paced, ambitious world of ours.

As to knowledge, because atoms are invisible, "we cannot have direct knowledge of anything." All that senses can provide is "bastard" knowledge. There is, however, "legitimate" knowledge. "It is based on reason which takes over where senses leave off" (CDP, 217).

Democritus had no immediate followers. Although Aristotle mentions him in his writings, his views were overshadowed for at least a century. We suspect there were at least two reasons for it. First, philosophers changed focus from nature to the pressing moral and political matters to which Socrates drew everyone's attention. Second, Plato's Dialogues and Aristotle's writings held public interest captive at that time. It is Epicurus who brought forth Democritus' ideas to light. And it was the Epicurean school of thought, subsequently, that transmitted Democritus' atomic theory to the Modern Period.

Jason: Amazing! What a brilliant man! We tend to think of ourselves as being so wise, as "the-know-it-all." And we consider the people of ages past as "know-nothings." Yet I wonder how many persons today can equal the depth and range of knowledge that we find in these men.

Diotima: This is why studying history is so important. We learn from it that "we are standing on the shoulders of giants."[20] We also discover that our achievements today, be it in science, art or technology, are possible because someone else laid the foundation for them. As you will soon see, the concepts of the past form the climate of today.

Unfortunately, Sophistic thinking was gaining an upper hand. It is the charismatic archenemy of sophistry, Socrates, who averted the tide that threatened to send humanity, certainly that of the Western World, down the path of decadence and destruction. His critical approach and the high-minded ideals of moral excellence by which he lived and for which he died were instrumental in reversing the trend. His death evinced an enormous influence on his followers. Owing much to his students, primarily to Plato, and subsequently to Aristotle, Greek culture and with it Western Civilization was borne aloft to its heights. That excellence had never been known before, and one wonders if it was ever surpassed thereafter. This was indeed the Golden Age of Greece, which is now known in history as the Classical Period.

Jason: What was the thrust in thought during this period that led to such an extraordinary achievement? Did these philosophers find a conclusive answer to human nature?

Diotima: In their pursuit of truth, the philosophers of the Classical Period relied on *reason*, but they looked to *nature* for discovering it.

Jason: Could we say, then, that there is a kind of merging of the interests at this time pursued by the Presocratic playwrights and those of the Presocratic thinkers?

Diotima: Good observation, Jason, except that this occurred spontaneously. Nature and we belong together; we are its product and its crowing glory. Since without nature we do not exist and independently of it we cannot understand ourselves, it was only reasonable to look to nature for the answers. As to your question regarding our identity, the answer is "no." Despite the profoundness of their thought, the same divergence in views surfaced once again. Let us take a look at the three major thinkers of the Classical Period who are viewed by the history of philosophy as the main shapers of that civilization. They also happen to be the proponents of the same three views on human nature.

C. Classical Period

Plato (427-347 B.C.) Known as an ideal philosopher, Plato identified human nature with that of Aeschylus. Human beings are *God-like, moral beings* in virtue of their *spiritual soul* that traces to the *cosmic soul* (*Tim.,* 30a-d). Because of its link with the cosmic soul, the human soul is immortal. "The soul," he says, "is most like that which is divine, immortal, intelligible, uniform, indissoluble, and ever self-consistent and invariable, whereas body is most like that which is human, mortal, multiform, unintelligible, dissoluble, and never self-consistent" (*Phaedo*, 80b). But human beings must be well educated and developed to attain that status. They need to understand themselves correctly and lead a virtuous life. It is the practice of virtues, especially those of self-control, moderation or temperance, courage, and prudence that is of great importance (*Phaedo*, 68a-69d). Prudence is a kind of wisdom that in concert with the other virtues enables the soul to attain excellence of its being and makes it possible for it at death to go to the "Islands of the Blessed" (*Rep.* VII, 519c-520b; *Symp.* 179e), "a place that is like itself, glorious, pure, and invisible—the true Hades or unseen world—into the presence of the good and wise God" (*Phaedo*, 79c-d). His system of thought traces all of creation to the divine as "the first principles" of reality. The created world, in turn, is a copy of the eternal model because the artificer (*demiourgos*) while fashioning it wanted to make it as good as possible.

In light of their perfections, Plato has many appropriate sets of names for the first principles, the most basic of which are the Good, the Beautiful, and the Just. On the basis of these principles he erects his system of thought and traces the path of human life to the attainment of its glorious destiny. Because we begin our life in this world, the "World of Becoming," and lack knowledge of both the origin and the goal of our existence, in the *Republic* (the Dialogue central to his system of thought) Plato allegorically depicts the journey of human life as an ascent out of a cave into a region of Light. The former represents the World of Becoming, the latter, the World of Being. Plato's Theory of Forms is fundamental to the truth of reality and to the thrust of human existence. His is the first complete system of thought in the history of philosophy. This system of thought, however, must be assembled, for the parts of it are developed in the various Dialogues. Most likely, Plato's notes of his lectures at the Academy, the school he founded, contained a systematic exposition of his philosophy. Unfortunately, those writings were lost during the Peloponnesian War. What we have is a collection of Dialogues that he wrote for the general public. Those writings, Dialogues and Letters, that survived the ravages of war and time, have been collected and now appear in the volume under the title, *Plato: Collected Dialogues.*

Elaborate system of thought as it is, Plato succeeds in portraying reality by means of his ingenious *divided line.* The divided line aligns all that is in its diversity, yet presents it as a single, well-integrated whole. It also traces the path of human ascent from the darkness of ignorance to the light of truth. As such, it denotes the degrees of the enlightenment of the soul. While one's mind is led to the knowledge of the Being that is the cause of all that is, it is Love, a "powerful Spirit" that leads one to the "actual beholding" of the Good, the Beautiful and the Just. Only upon reaching this moment does one *really* come to know whence one comes, where human life is headed, and what one's *real identity* truly is.

Aristotle (384-322 B.C), Plato's student of twenty years, identified with the view of Sophocles. Man is a *rational animal.* One's soul (*psyche*) is the form or principle of the body with the potentiality for life. This principle of life and motion consists of many faculties, powers or capacities through which man functions and achieves his goals. Although Aristotle states that the human soul has no boundaries and opens out upon the infinite, he rejects Plato's Theory of Forms and with it the spiritual world. There is only one world, the world of the phenomena given to our senses. This world is eternal. The highest form of activity that the soul is capable of is that of contemplation, but not in a spiritual sense. It is an intellectual activity, the kind of activity in which a philosopher engages.

The son of a physician, Aristotle from the earliest years of his life was exposed to the interests of the human body and the physical reality. Making this reality intelligible became his life-long commitment. Aristotle is a scientist, analytical thinker and keen observer of "the given" in the empirical sense, as opposed to Plato who is an artist, a poet, a rational, speculative thinker, and a mystic besides. Aristotle's system of thought, as it can be expected, begins with the perceptible phenomena of nature. According to him, reality is analyzable into four principles or causes. These are: material, formal, efficient and final. The *material cause* he defines as "the primary substratum of each thing, from which it comes to be without qualification, and which persists in the result" (*Phys.*I, 9.30). This cause, as its name suggests, is matter. The *formal cause* is the "principle of life"; it has to do with the *function* or *nature* of each thing, and "*nature is a source or cause of being moved and of being at rest in that to which it belongs primarily,* in virtue of itself" (*Phys.* II, 1.20). In case of the inanimate substances it is energy which comes with attributes; in the animate entities it is life with its powers; and in human beings it is a rational soul with its powers. The *efficient cause* is "the primary source or cause of change or coming to rest; e.g. the man who gave advice is a cause, the father is a cause of the child, and generally what makes of what is made and what causes change of what is changed" (*Phys.* II, 3.29-30). And the *final cause* is "that for the sake of which something is done, e.g. health is the cause of walking about" (*Phys.* II, 3.32-33). In man's case, the efficient, formal and final causes coincide. The *soul* is the *formal cause* of one's being, it is likewise an *efficient cause* in that it functions "in accordance with its own nature," and it is its *final cause* because it acts with a purpose of achieving its own *final end,* the completeness of its own being. Matter is equated with potency, act with a form, and cognition with life that has a form, but is immaterial.

As to the world at large, "since its movement must be eternal, there must be an eternal mover and one whose essence is actuality." If its essence is potency, "the movement will not be *eternal* movement, since that which is potentially may possibly not be" (*Metaphysics* XII, 6, 1071b17-20). The eternal mover or the "prime mover" originates motion; but being actual, it cannot be moved, which is why it is said to an "unmoved mover." The unmoved mover is God. He is one, eternal, the highest form, the perfect form. Since the highest activity is that of thinking or contemplation and "contemplation is what is most pleasant and best . . . God is always in that good state in which we sometimes are. . . . And life also belongs to God; for the actuality of thought is life, and God is that actuality; and God's self-dependent actuality is life most good and eternal. We say, therefore," he adds, "that God is a living being, eternal, most good, so that life and duration continuous and eternal belong to God; for this *is* God" (XII, 7, 1072b1-29). Unlike Plato's God who cares for humans and to whom we pray (*Tim.* 27c), Aristotle's God is a separate entity that contemplates itself (XII, 9, 1074b 9-19, 25-26, 33-34).

A HISTORICAL PERSPECTIVE

Presocratic Playwrights

Intuition

Aeschylus - a spiritual, moral, divine-like being
(525-456 B.C.)

Sophocles - a rational being
(c.495-406 B.C.)

Euripedes - a natural being
(c. 484-407 B.C.)

Result: confusion, sophistry and dissatisfaction with life, therefore a need to appeal to **reason.**

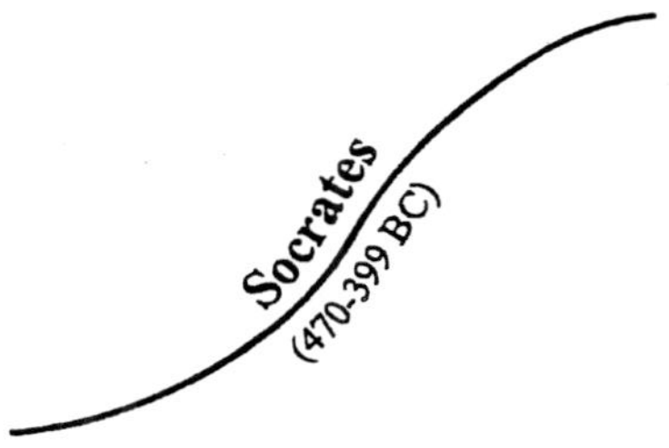

Socrates
(470-399 BC)

Classical Period

Reason → Nature

Plato
(427-347 B.C.)

Aristotle
(384-322 B.C.)

Epicurus
(242-270 B.C.)

Result: Shallowness of life, decadence and distrust of reason, therefore turning to **Faith.**

Presocratic Thinkers { Parmenides (c. 485-399 B.C.)
Anaxagoras (c. 500-428 B.C.)
Democritus (c. 460- 360 B.C.)

Diagram 2.1

In agreement with his theory of reality and the understanding of man, where each natural object "by nature" seeks its own good, Aristotle's ethical theory is based on virtue, an action that is in keeping with human nature. Virtue is an "excellence" in fulfilling a particular function. Because man is a *rational animal*, there are two kinds of virtues, moral and intellectual. Moral virtue consists in "the golden rule," the "median" or the intermediate state between "too much" (excess) and "too little" (deficiency). For instance, the virtue of *generosity* is a mean between the excess of wastefulness and deficiency of stinginess. Moral virtues (virtues of character) such as *honesty* and *justice* and intellectual virtues (virtues of thought and intelligence) such as *deliberation* and *right reasoning* lead one to the excellence of one's being and to happiness—man's final end. Although the two thinkers differ on what constitutes the final end of man, like Plato, Aristotle maintains that habitation (naturally conducive environment), careful training and good upbringing are indispensable to the development of moral excellence in a person. The latter is important because it forms one's character.

Jason: A very positive view, I gather. Nonetheless, if I understand it correctly, his view of the human person as a *rational animal* is already a step down from Plato's spiritual stance. His explanation of the human soul seems to lack the spiritual component that links us to the divine. Does it not?

Diotima: According to Aristotle, the soul's rational activity likens it to the divine. You are right, though, in observing disparity in the two views. Neither are his explanations of God and the soul's relationship to God, nor the soul's final end on par with Plato's. Apparently Parmenides was right in stating that certain knowledge is not attainable from the natural standpoint.

Jason: It will be very interesting to see how this scenario plays out.

Diotima: Diagram 2.1 helps us to see what we have come to understand thus far. It incorporates the third thinker of the Classical Period, Epicurus, whose worldview had partly contributed to the period's demise.

Epicurus (341-270 B.C.) is another Greek thinker who founded a School in Athens. His school gave rise to a new movement in Hellenistic philosophy. The movement is named after him. It is called *Epicureanism*. In his view of man, Epicurus aligns himself with the third position, hence with that of Euripedes, though with a different slant to it. Man is a *natural being*; consequently, Epicurus contends, the best life is a pleasant life. He saw pleasant life as a natural state of man to which man was directed "by nature." Everything therefore, virtues and values, are subordinate to it. The only evil is pain and this evil, he contends, can be reduced by living simply. By "simple life" he means one that is free from political and social involvements and not bent on amassing great wealth. Because Epicurus based life on a *pleasure principle,* his ethical theory in time became synonymous with *hedonism*. While it is true that his theory of the universe and of man is atomistic, like that of Democritus, and he led the kind of life that he advocated, his life was not what hedonism came to mean, a life of excessive pleasures.

Epicurus distinguished two kinds of pleasures: the lower pleasures, those of the body, and the higher pleasures, those of the mind. He saw the higher pleasures as more compatible with pleasant life. Fear of the gods and death are irrational, he maintained, because natural phenomena are not threatening and at death one's body being nothing more than a "composite of atoms" simply yields to disintegration. At that point one returns to a state prior to one's coming into existence.

In his assessment of this view Matthias Steup writes, "Epicureanism enjoyed widespread popularity, but unlike its great rival Stoicism never entered the intellectual bloodstream of the ancient world. Its stances were dismissed by many as philistine, especially its rejection of all cultural activities not geared to the Epicurean good life" (CDP. 269-271). His school of thought, however, continued to flourish and his theory slowly carried to excess hastened the death of the period that was already for some time on its downward course.

Jason: I am puzzled. All three thinkers derive their views of human nature by means of *reason* and all three look to *nature* to explain their stance. Yet, each of them emerges with a different interpretation? How can this be?

Diotima: Before we address this question, Jason, one other point is worth noting. A look in retrospect, with the help of Diagram 2.2 helps us to capture the big picture of history. With one bold, sweeping generalization we can say: the Medieval Period was a return to the Aschylean – Platonic view of human nature; the Modern Period, to the Sophoclean – Aristotelian view, and the Postmodern Period (in which we presently find ourselves), gives evidence of exalting the natural view. Can you see the pattern?

Jason: I most certainly can. Looking at this image, however, my mind is assailed by many questions. First of all, does each successive period presuppose a death of the preceding one?

Diotima: That is what history tells us had happened.

Jason: Could it be that each of the periods exhibits the same three-fold pattern regarding human nature that we have encountered thus far?

Diotima: I see you are catching on.

Jason: How did people know that a new philosophical system was replacing the ideas of the former one?

Diotima: They didn't know it at the time, for such things do not take place instantaneously. Change on a large scale occurs gradually, over many generations. It takes time for some ideas to fade away; it takes even longer for the new, life-giving ideas to catch on, and it takes sometimes centuries for them to permeate the culture. What is unfortunate in the scenario of the downward trends is that from one generation to another, there is a steady, gradual, barely observable change that occurs before the stark reality dawns. And when it does dawn, those who perceive it find themselves powerless to do anything about it. For when they speak out, they find themselves at odds with the masses that blindly revel in their shallow existence. In societies where democracy rules and the majority view prevails the chances of altering people's vision and values are even slimmer.

Jason: How does humanity succeed to rebound from such an unfortunate state? How, for example, did humanity of the Medieval Period manage to rise to its own heights from the death of the Classical Period?

Diotima: It usually takes centuries, Jason. It took over a thousand years for the Medieval Period to rebound and reach its heights. With the death of a period, inevitably always the experience of darkness, confusion and a loss of direction accompanied by a sense of helplessness prevail first. Humanity finds itself disoriented, frightened and at a loss to do anything about it. There is, however, a positive side to it, too. Death of a period usually gives birth to a whole new wave of concerned thinkers who through soul-searching, profound thinking and authentic living emerge with fresh insights that creatively respond to the crisis of the time. Born of the anguished spirit and tested in the crucible of suffering, their insights give impetus to a new orientation in life, making it richer and inwardly rewarding. It is these insights, then, through some charismatic individual, whose vision is clear swings the pendulum in the opposite direction, giving new focus to the upcoming generations of thinkers. As the new ideas catch on, gradually, with a sustained effort on the part of many, humanity emerges out of the crisis. The new way of life leads to a birth of a new period which, then, over the centuries slowly rises to its greatness. In other words, Jason, between each of the major periods there is always an *intermediate period* during which spadework is done for the birth of the new major period.

Jason: This is remarkable. It looks as if we should never lose hope, even in the worst of times.

Diotima: Crises challenges us. When things are moving smoothly and all is well, we tend to become complacent and lead superficial life. Not so when darkness descends upon one's world and one's life is threatened. At such times the indomitable human spirit rises to its potential. On the one hand, when man begins to think deeply he becomes creative and resourceful; on the other hand, history in its unfolding provides new avenues for humanity to rebound.

Jason: When did the Classical Period die and in what way did history help humanity to recover from the death of the Classical Period?

Diotima: Historians tell us that the lights of this great period had fallen dim already around 323-322 B.C.[21] with the passing away of three important figures of that world: Alexander the Great (323 B.C.), the conqueror of Greece who sought to capture the whole world known at that time; Aristotle (322 B.C.), the great philosopher and teacher of Alexander; and Demosthenes (322 B.C.), the famed orator of Greece who fiercely resisted Alexander's invasion. Epicurean philosophy, which took over as the new way of life, brought it to its final demise. You may be surprised to learn that in due time, the same orientation in life was instrumental in bringing about the dissolution of the Roman Empire as well. The latter, you may remember from your history classes, fell prey to the enemy from the outside only because it was weakened by its enemy from within, the love of ease, pleasure and moral corruption.

To answer the second part of your question—the role of history in rebounding—a look in retrospect reveals that while the Classical Period died, the ideas and ideals of that period, primarily those of Socrates, Plato and Aristotle in reality never died. In conjunction with those of Epicurus, they gave rise to three *New Schools of Thought* known as: *the Neo-platonic School* with *Plotinus* (205-270)[22] as its most prominent philosopher; *the Stoic School* which embodied Aristotle's views with *Epictetus* (c. 60-c. 137) as its foremost proponent; and *the Epicurean School* with *Lucretius* (c. 96-c. 55 B.C.) and *Horace* (c.65-8 B.C.) as its ardent advocates. These three schools of thought form the *intermediate period* between the Classical and the Medieval Period.

A HISTORICAL PERSPECTIVE

Presocratic Playwrights

Intuition

Aeschylus – a spiritual, moral, divine-like being
(525-456 B.C.)

Sophocles – a rational being
(c.495-406 B.C.)

Euripedes – a natural being
(c. 484-407 B.C.)

Result: confusion, sophistry and dissatisfaction with life, therefore a need to appeal to reason.

Socrates
(470-399 BC)

Presocratic Thinkers {
Parmenides (c. 485-399 B.C.)
Anaxagoras (c. 500-428 B.C.)
Democritus (c. 460- 360 B.C.)
}

Classical Period

Reason → Nature

Plato
(427-347 B.C.)

Aristotle
(384-322 B.C.)

Epicurus
(242-270 B.C.)

Result: Shallowness of life, decadence and distrust of reason, therefore turning to **Faith**.

Medieval Period: Return to the spiritual/moral

Modern Period: Return to reason (Age of Science)

Postmodern Period: return to the natural with the admixture of everything else.

Diagram 2.2

D. Transitions to the Current Worldview

1. Three New Schools of Thought

It is important to emphasize that the thinkers who preserved for us the rich heritage of the Classical Period did not do so without some modifications. Being persons of their own time, on the one hand they imperceptibly assimilated the prevailing spirit and values of their time, and on the other hand they were instrumental in shaping the worldview for future generations. How one shapes it, for better or for worse, is always determined by how one lives. Each person speaks from the abundance of his or her own heart. One speaks what one knows, and one knows what one lives. We can see this readily in the thinkers of this intermediate period.

Plotinus (205-270 A.D.), himself a mystic, reflects closely, though in a limited way, the vision of Plato. He adds to it, however, insights from the wealth of his own spiritual experiences of the Divine. Thanks to his students who have collected and edited them, we have his thoughts recorded in six *Enneads*. According to Plotinus reality consists of emanations from the One who is an eternal Being and the source of all that is. Man is a composite of *body and spirit*. As such, he belongs to the world of the spirit and to the world of matter. To attain climatic experience of one's life, which is union with the One, one must turn away from the inferior things of this world and turn toward "the inner reality" of his soul. As in Plato, the human soul is a part of the World-Soul. Through this link, the human soul is endowed with immortality. Arab, Jewish and Christian philosophers have been influenced by his thought. Karl Jaspers, a twentieth century German philosopher held him in great esteem. He considered him to be one of the greatest philosophers of all time.

Epictetus (c. 60-c. 137 A.D.) was a Greek born in Phrygia, Asia Minor who lived around the middle of the first century. Sources do not agree on the date of his birth or of his death. Likewise, little is known of his early life until he was in Rome at the height of the Greco-Roman Period. While a slave to Epaphroditus, a freedman of Nero, Epictetus—despite the cruel treatment by his master that left him lame—had an opportunity to attend lectures in Stoic philosophy. Sometime before the year 89 he was granted freedom and became a teacher in Rome. Since Stoic philosophy viewed *reason* as the dominant faculty of man and Stoicism was born shortly after Aristotle's death (322 B.C.) with Zeno the Stoic (c. 335-263 B.C.), this philosophy was seen as an extension of Aristotelian thought: man was viewed primarily as a *rational being*. There were, however, some differences between the two schools of thought.

As we have seen in the previous instances, so, too, Stoic philosophy was not a pure endorsement of Aristotle's thought; it was a notable departure from it in a number of ways. For instance, Aristotle distinguished between reason and emotions, but saw both of these components in man play an important role in developing one's life of virtue, character and the good life. Stoics saw reason and emotions as warring factors that lead one in opposite directions. **F**eelings and emotions are *irrational* by nature, hence opposed to the judgments of reason. Seeing the sad consequences in the world due to Epicurean school of thought that catered to them, Stoics steered clear of emotions. Instead, they advocated a life of discipline and high moral standards. Their life was tough, but it had many staunched followers from every social class. Marcus Aurelius (121-180), an emperor of Rome, was one of them.

Unlike Aristotle and more like Plato, Stoics saw human reason as a "spark of the divine" *in us* and held on to the judgments of reason. Since nature is a product of divine reason, to live in conformity with nature is to live in conformity with divine reason. This was, therefore, the way of life they advocated. Reason was given to us to help us distinguish between the petty human concerns and those that really matter. Stoic philosophy demanded self-discipline; it was "designed to cope with the tragedies and injustices" of life. It placed emphasis on "detaching oneself from the "absurdities of life" through reason. "Stoicism was an extreme philosophy," write Robert C. Solomon & Kathleen M. Higgins, "but one that would serve many souls well in difficult and troubled times. It became an immensely popular philosophy in Rome and throughout the Roman Empire."[23] According to historians, this philosophy was "the single most successful and longest-lasting movement in Greco-Roman philosophy" (71).

While Stoic philosophy had a system of thought that encompassed all of reality, Epictetus is said to have focused only on the moral and religious aspect of it. He was a "moral activist" who insisted on "rigorous, continuing moral instruction and effort" and a "daily self-examination." He wanted every person to see that each man alone is responsible for his actions and, therefore, must learn to judge his deeds well and to deal with them firmly. It is because man is gifted with the power of freedom that he must take full responsibility for what he does. "The faculty of choice and refusal . . . was the power even Zeus himself could not interfere with," he says in the *Discourses*.[24] Like the thinkers of the Greek world, he understood man to be a citizen of the universe, rather than a product of local convention. Epictetus is known for having lived and preached simple life; he modeled what he taught. In spite of the harsh treatment that was his lot in life, he was an image of personal gentleness and moral integrity.

Epictetus left no writings. What we know of his thought comes from his students, primarily "his disciple, the Greek philosopher and historian Arrian, who complied from his master's lectures and conversations the 'Discourses and Encheiridion' [Manual]."[25]

Jason: I'd like to learn more about him and his thought. He is an inspiring personage and offers a challenging philosophy, to say the least.

Diotima: You can be sure that the time you devote to it will be well worth it.

Lucretius (c. 96-55 B.C.) and **Horace (c. 65-8 B.C.)** are Roman thinkers who were devoted followers of Epicurean philosophy. There is no need of going into their thinking. They reflect the third position; namely, man is merely a *natural being*. We already have a fairly good idea of what this means.

Jason: Horace brings us almost to the doorstep of the new millennium, closer to our times, doesn't he?

Diotima: Yes, indeed, and this occurs with a momentous event at that! With the year 8 B.C., which marks the death of Horace, we find ourselves on the threshold of the extraordinary event in the history of humanity. This event marks the beginning of a new epoch, an event without which St. Augustine and the entire Medieval Period would be completely unrealizable. That event is obviously the birth of Jesus of Nazareth. His coming was announced two millennia earlier and had been prophesied for centuries thereafter. This singular event was so important that it gave the world a new reckoning to time. It marked the beginning of the new calendar in the history of the Western World: all that took place prior to it was marked B.C. for "Before Christ" and all that occurred after it, A.D., from the Latin *Anno Domini*, "the year of Our Lord."[26] Apart from some older cultures, like the Chinese for instance which retained its own calendar, this designation has been in use for twenty centuries in the Western World. In the latter part of the twentieth century a "B.C.E." (Before Common Era) was introduced to replace the B.C. In either case, though, it is still the same epochal event of Christ's birth that marks the crossroads of time in the history of the world.

Jesus Christ was born when the glory of Greece had faded away and Roman Empire basked in the glory of its own grandeurs. The newly erected magnificent structures bespoke of Rome's splendor. Roads were built throughout the empire to make travel easier. Yet, relatively few people could read and communication was mostly through word of mouth. In the absence of cars, trains and airplanes, much the same as of printing press, radio, television and computer—inventions that would make their debut gradually centuries later—the mission of Jesus was confined to Palestine, the region of His native place. His disciples were commissioned to carry his *good news* "to the whole world." Jesus not only told them exactly who He is, whence He came, why He came and where He was going, but also gave ample evidence of it by His own life and works. It is because His disciples took their commission seriously that the *Good News* slowly but surely, spread far and wide, first to the neighboring countries around Palestine and then, against all odds, to all the continents of the world.

Among those who received the good news of Jesus Christ was Augustine of Hippo, now better known as St. Augustine. His restless life wondrously transformed by Christ's teaching, he spared no effort or time in sharing it with others. Because his copious writings did much to propagate Christ's teachings in the then-known-world he is, like Socrates earlier, *the transitional thinker* who paved the way to the greatness of the Medieval Period (Diagram 2.3). It took several centuries and many generations, however, for this period to reach its "Golden Age."

Jason: How do you justify bringing Jesus into philosophy? Is he considered one of the philosophers?

Diotima: A valid question, Jason. No, ordinarily Jesus is not included in philosophy. Jesus is not a "lover of wisdom," He is "the bearer of divine wisdom." The reason we need to incorporate Him here is that the wisdom He brought gave a new direction to philosophy. As we have just stated, without Jesus, St. Augustine's philosophy and at least the next thousand years after him would have been inconceivable. Humanity at that time considered truth to be more important than the source from which it came. What was at stake here, moreover, was not some theory about the universe or the nature of things in general; it had to do with human life, with living it well now in order to attain contentment of heart for all eternity.

A HISTORICAL PERSPECTIVE

Presocratic Playwrights

Intuition

Aeschylus - a spiritual, moral, divine-like being
(525-456 B.C.)

Sophocles - a rational being
(c. 495-406 B.C.)

Euripedes - a natural being
(c. 484-407 B.C.)

Result: confusion, sophistry and dissatisfaction with life, therefore a need to appeal to **reason.**

Socrates
(470-399 BC)

Classical Period

Reason → Nature

Plato
(427-347 B.C.)

Aristotle
(384-322 B.C.)

Epicurus
(242-270 B.C.)

Result: Shallowness of life, decadence and distrust of reason, therefore turning to **Faith.**

St. Augustine
(374-430)

Medieval Period: Return to the spiritual/moral

Modern Period: Return to reason (Age of Science)

Postmodern Period: return to the natural with the admixture of everything else.

Presocratic Thinkers { Parmenides (c. 485-399 B.C.)
Anaxagoras (c. 500-428 B.C.)
Democritus (c. 460- 360 B.C.)

New Schools of Thought { Neoplatonic: Plotinus (205-270)
Stoic: Epictetus (60-117)
Epicurean: Lucretius (96-55 B.C.)
Horace (65-8 B.C.)

Diagram 2.3

Jason: The importance of leading a good life was neither new, nor was it held only by Christian thinkers. Isn't that right?

Diotima: Just listen to what the pagan philosopher, Plato had to say four centuries B.C. on the subject of life, death and preparation for the life beyond. I have briefly alluded to it earlier, but here you can see it in the context of the advice he offers to his friends. He states, ". . . although it is very difficult if not impossible in this life to achieve certainty about these questions, at the same time it is utterly feeble not to use every effort in testing the available theories, or to leave off before we have considered them in every way, and come to the end of our resources. It is our duty to do one of two things, either to ascertain the facts, whether by seeking instruction or by personal discovery, or, if this is impossible, to select the best and most dependable theory which human intelligence can supply, and use it as a raft to ride the seas of life—that is, assuming that we cannot make our journey with greater confidence and security by the surer means of a divine revelation" (*Phaedo*, 85c-d). Neither Socrates and Plato, nor Aristotle and Epicurus had the luxury of a divine revelation, but humanity after Christ's coming did. Since the Classical Period proved *reason* by itself to be inadequate, philosophers of the Medieval Period turned to *faith* as the more reliable way to face the turbulent waters of the sea of life.

Turning to *faith*, however, did not mean turning away from *reason*. In fact, scholastics, as the medieval thinkers were called, sought to wed the two. Faith provided the truth Christ revealed, and reason served to explain it. Research and teaching at the universities, which sprang from the heart of the Church at least partially for this purpose, became the chief means of securing and disseminating that knowledge to an ever larger number of those who had the means to profit from it. The Church herself sought to enlighten the people at large.

In Christ's message, the people of God found strength and consolation; they also found meaning and a sure direction for life. Having accepted His teaching with utter confidence, they believed God created the world, ruled it and sustained it in existence. They understood He created the world for man and man for Himself. Eternal life with God was man's destiny, and this life was a preparation for it, or better, a journey to it. It is this knowledge, which they received on faith, that enabled them to endure the harsh conditions of the medieval life and reap abundant blessings spiritually. Music, art and architecture, particularly the cathedrals of that period, are the proud monuments to the lofty vision, spirit and ideals of the Medieval Period at its height. And what the cathedrals were in stone, so the writings of the scholastics, particularly those of Albert the Great, St. Thomas, St. Bonaventure, Duns Scotus and others were in thought. Man was created for heaven. Becoming a saint was considered the finest goal of human life on earth, and the universal church, well endowed by Christ, was properly equipped to provide the means to its attainment. It was all so simple, so clear, and so intelligible for a thousand years! That is, of course, where it was embraced lovingly and lived authentically. Of this period Cross writes: "Within this time was built a body of knowledge and a keenness of pure intellectuality which has seldom been equaled" (Cross, 241). It paved the way for the renaissance of the human spirit and led to the period of the Enlightenment.

Jason: How would you sum up the accomplishments of the Medieval Period?

Diotima: Put succinctly, we can say that this period reached new intellectual heights, produced many saints, and achieved synthesis between *faith* with *reason*. Unfortunately, despite scholastics' agreement on the essential identity of human nature as a *spiritual being* and on the importance of both, faith and reason, the period ended with a split between the two.

Jason: Who or what caused this rift to occur?

Diotima: The third position in every *trio* is always a departure from the prevailing movement of thought at the time. William of Ockham's "razor" is said to have inaugurated the breakdown of scholastic philosophy. Ockham, however, did not reduce human nature to just a natural level, nor did he ever depart from his Catholic Faith. True to the rigorous spirit of philosophy, his "razor-sharp" mind merely challenged and thereby undermined some of the tenets of his contemporaries. It is primarily the disputes about faith and reason that weakened the bonds of unity. With his thinking emerged the conflict between *nominalism* and *realism*, about which we will speak later.

In addition to these concerns, there developed some intellectual combats among the scholastics. At the center of the controversy was the disagreement regarding the extent and limits of human reason: what can and what cannot be known by reason alone, an issue Kant would subsequently try to resolve. This controversy raised the question of proper methodology in doing philosophy. In conjunction with the disparity in these views, there surfaced likewise the squabble about the preeminence of intellect and reason, with St. Thomas Aquinas as its most eminent supporter, versus charity or love and free will with St. Bonaventure as its outstanding contender. These discrepancies, in combination with the new developments in science that began to explain the world independently of God eventually led to the death of the Medieval Period.

Jason: Are we going to discuss the rest of the periods?

Diotima: Interesting as it may be, for the sake of reaching our destination sooner we may need to settle for just a short conversation about them. I think you have the idea of the pattern. What may be more profitable to mention at this point is that although our sweeping generalization about the major periods is predominantly true, when we look with sharper lenses we discover that each of those periods had—and will always have—advocates of all three views of human nature. This is inevitable.

Jason: Why?

Diotima: New generations keep coming into existence and we humans begin our life with the darkness of the intellect. Progress in knowledge on the personal level takes time, on the cultural level understandably much longer. Because there will always be people at different levels of maturity, there will always be persons on different levels of enlightenment and consequently, always some who will align themselves with each of these three views. While there are many external factors that affect—contribute or impede—one's progress in enlightenment, one's culture plays a crucial role. For culture creates a milieu for human growth and development; what it promotes influences the direction that most people take and this, in turn, determines the quality of life most people lead.

Jason: How is this so? Can you explain it?

Diotima: This occurs through the values the culture promotes and the ideals it fosters by means of its educational, economic, and political systems. Since the views projected by the intellectuals of the prevailing branch of knowledge are not only taught in school but are also embodied in the visual arts, music, literature, architecture, society and so on—the world of one's everyday lived experience, these create the climate of the time, determining the style of life one leads and, thereby, the level at which the majority of people in a particular culture by and large live their life.

Fortunately, because there are always proponents of all three views even in times of crises, there are always, albeit few persons whose vision is clear and spirit of the dawning age vibrantly alive—persons of the time, who become protagonists in pointing humanity in a new direction. Advancing an idea whose time has come, one of them usually succeeds in making himself heard and becomes a *transitional figure*. With the help from above, through reason, authentic living and the ideals by which the person lives, such an individual paves the way for the new age.

Jason: Isn't this just what Socrates and St. Augustine did? Each of them in keeping with the needs of his time, as we have seen, steered humanity in a better direction, to a path that led individuals personally to the fulfillment on a deeper level and humanity at large, eventually, to a "Golden Age."

Diotima: Yes, you're right, Jason. The philosophers who devote all their energies to steering humanity in the right direction are either rational thinkers, or they are mystics. Despite the difference in their methodology, because of their life of faith and careful reasoning there is a striking similarity in their conclusions. It can be said, therefore, that both philosophical approaches, the mystical and the rational, serve well the interests of philosophy and the good of humanity at large, provided one is living authentically.

Jason: What is the relationship between mysticism and philosophy? I thought these were two different realms of knowledge.

Diotima: Yes, indeed, so much knowledge has been garnered in each of these areas that they do constitute two distinct bodies of knowledge, but they are not antithetical. In fact, it is in their reciprocity that there lies man's greatest advantage. The rational approach is predominantly theoretical, the mystical, preeminently practical. The theoretical is for the sake of the practical. And the practical advances the theoretical. Wisdom is for the sake of living one's life wisely. Philosophy being "love of wisdom" is for the sake of life. With philosophy shedding light upon life and thus paving the way, the "lover of wisdom" advances forward until eventually he or she arrives at the ultimate Truth with absolute certainty. The journey of life that is accompanied by "firsthand glimpses" of what-is is called *mysticism*. While the firsthand glimpses into the mystery of reality are the phenomena of mysticism, the knowledge thus secured is called *knowledge of intellection*, or of *actual beholding*. Thinkers such as Parmenides, Socrates, Plato, Plotinus, St. Augustine and St. Bonaventure are examples of the mystical philosophers. Because such thinkers had those firsthand experiences, they speak with great confidence and are not likely ever to change their stance; if at all, it is only to clarify further some point.

Jason: So that is the secret behind the disparity in philosophical systems of thought!

Diotima: You may recall we have said earlier that there is no philosophy apart from the philosopher. Systems of thought—in addition to different branches of philosophy and the particular philosopher's specific area of inquiry—differ in their approach because of the thinker's innate predisposition. Philosophers are, basically, *empirical*, *rational* and *intuitive* thinkers. These, in turn, differ in the quality of life they lead and the degree of enlightenment to which each personally attains. Because they, like every other human being, are in the process of becoming enlightened and knowledge comes in degrees, when they advance in knowledge and approximate the Truth, they often modify their explanation of reality. For this reason, not infrequently do we find philosophers changing their stance on things. It is only when the light of Truth dawns upon one and one finally comes to see what-is *as it truly is*, that one attains understanding with incredible clarity and can, with conviction, articulate a system of thought with Truth as one's starting point. The whole system of thought then is an attempt to reflect one's understanding and, thereby, to help others with the acquisition of the same knowledge. Such is the case with the mystical philosophers. Reason alone falls short of the mark. Later on when we shall personally undertake the process of discovering what-is, what I have just said here should become amply intelligible to you. Remember, part of *really* understanding the answer is the process of arriving at it.

Jason: Even this brief explanation leads me to see that the philosophical systems of the mystical thinkers are not some perverted attempts to accommodate revealed truths, but that they are in fact genuine attempts to help reason lead one at least to the threshold of the ultimate Truth. I can also see now why Socrates and St. Augustine were so effective in pointing humanity in the direction that led their period to the Golden Age.

Diotima: Notwithstanding, Jason, lest you are left with a mistaken view about the "golden periods" in history, I must adduce that while the periods at such times exhibit great achievements in thought, art, music, drama, sculpture, architecture and the like, they often do so amidst very difficult conditions. Certainly, life for most of the people is far from ideal. Cross and Lindau write, "Whenever one considers the city of Athens at the time of Pericles (the peak of the Golden Age) one is tempted to exaggerate the good qualities of the city. One is tempted to forget that the entire culture was based on slave labor, that women were completely disregarded in the life of the city, that rival political factions warred within the town, that it was the enlightened Athenians who put Socrates to death, and that the final decline of Athenian culture came about because of the traitors within the city more than from the work of external enemies. One sees the magnificent buildings of the Acropolis, and forgets that the Athenian home was only a rude shelter. All of these accusations are true and must not be forgotten."[27] The values and the ideals that the thinkers promoted at the time were meant to create a milieu conducive to growth in excellence for all, but not all lived by them and not all profited from them.

Something comparable can be said of the medieval world, even at its height. Life based on feudal system was extremely difficult—a real struggle for survival. According to the historians it was a period of great contrasts: of abject poverty and relative wealth, of plundering and yet some sense of security, of deep religious faith and destructive warfare, of humble dwellings and majestic cathedrals, and of illiteracy and great learning. In spite of the harshness of life, poverty, starvation, widespread rebellion, wars and the Bubonic plague known as "Black Death" that claimed a third of Europe's population, thinking and the arts were advancing, reaching new heights, and renaissance was in the making. It is the humble, unobtrusive works of this period, the seeds it planted, that eventually gave birth to the Renaissance Period and led to the Enlightenment.[28]

Jason: This certainly is a sobering thought. It puts these periods for me in a new light.

Diotima: It also leads us to conclude that no matter how great the achievements of humanity may be in any area of human endeavor at a given time, there will always be the need of working toward creating a world of lived experience with equitable conditions for all. History reveals that while in each successive period this awareness surfaces with ever greater urgency, the challenge remains. Sadly, sometimes instead of moving forward the world finds itself submerged in even greater disrepair.

2. Transition to the Modern Period

Jason: Who was instrumental in swinging the pendulum in the opposite direction after the death of the Medieval Period? How did it happen?

Diotima: We place René Déscartes (1596-1650), a French philosopher as the *transitional figure*, for he is regarded by history as the "father of modern philosophy." His *cogito ergo sum*, "I think, therefore I am," points to *consciousness* as the focus for the new age. It was his method of doing philosophy that led him to his insight, but he was not the only one to point thinking in this direction. Much had transpired before Descartes' arrival on the scene and the Modern Period's dawn from the time the first signs of medieval dissolution began to be noted. While history repeats itself and every ensuing period comes with an admixture of everything that preceded it in time, it never manifests itself in the same way, nor does the change occur suddenly. The Modern Period was no exception. We may trace the change primarily to two developments.

Jason: One of them, I surmise, had to do with the split between faith and reason that was mentioned earlier. And the other ?

Diotima: The other traces back to great discoveries in astronomy, mathematics and physics, in short to science.

Toward the end of the Middle Ages, and certainly during the Renaissance Period, man's vision of the world had changed. With the insight of Nicolaus Copernicus (1473-1543) that the Earth revolves around the sun, rather than the other way around, man's confidence in the power of reason has been greatly bolstered. This is not to say that there were no individuals prior to this time who had the same awareness. Most certainly, there were; we have met some of them. They displayed the power of reason brilliantly, beyond a shadow of a doubt. Now, however, humanity at large became conscious of it. The *homo faber*, man the worker, of the agrarian society on the continent of Europe began to understand himself as *homo sapiens,*[29] man the thinker, the seeker of wisdom, to whom the whole new world opened up. Life became exciting. It took on a new meaning.

With the dawn of reason, there came also a sense of greater freedom, which manifested itself in an outburst of intellectual creativity both in the area of science and in the humanities. The Renaissance was seen as a birth of a new era in the history of humanity. In science, astronomers Kepler and Galileo had refined the theory of Copernicus about the universe and carried forward this understanding of it in terms of mathematics. In humanities, it is sufficient to name men such as Leonardo da Vinci, Raphael, Michelangelo, Rembrandt, Shakespeare, Machiavelli, Thomas More, along with Descartes to get a sense of the period. It would be mistaken to think, though, that ideas advanced in just one direction. "New discoveries and new ideas flooded the world in such profusion that the whole of the Renaissance became a vast chaos. Born during this time was the scientific spirit, which was eventually to triumph over all other aspects of life and furnish the foundation of the epoch which succeeded the Renaissance."[30] That new epoch became known as the Age of Enlightenment, which in turn gave birth to the Age of Reason, the Modern Period.

What began with the profound insight of the Copernican heliocentric world, through Galileo, Kepler, Descartes and Bacon, led to the understanding of the universe as a vast machine operating in accordance with natural laws. Since these laws could be understood by science independently of God, in light of this perception God became superfluous. His existence itself became suspect (Cross, V2, 106). Francis Bacon (1561-1626), in fact, counseled to shift our sights from inquiries into the nature of man and concerns with God to concentrate on the world. The purpose of human life, according to him, was to master the world in which we live. In his work *Novum Organum* (1620) he laid out the plan for realizing this goal. Bacon called for clearing the ground of all medieval thinking, mysticism and the concepts inherited from the past. Science had the authoritative answers to human life. Protagorean dictum: "Man is the measure of all things" now became the position of science.

As man's vision of the world changed, so changed his understanding of himself. With life becoming less austere and offering better opportunities for improving man's lot here and now, a more relaxed attitude toward religion became manifest. The religious, otherworldly attitude toward life became replaced by values of this world. Life was worth living for its own sake. The Epicurean trend to seek the pleasant life became attractive once again. "A love of the rich, the ornate, the sumptuous . . . spurred men to strive for earthly power beyond all things" to the extent that living for the sake of "eternal rewards" became of secondary importance. This spirit was strongly reinforced by the pagan writings of the Greek, Roman, Jewish and Arabic thinkers, whose manuscripts were now being read, translated, copied and quoted. (Cross, V2, 4). Human life began to reflect the secular spirit advanced by science. It gave rise to a new form of humanism, which with the passing of time became strongly entrenched in the human psyche.

Jason: What about philosophy?

Diotima: Scientific strides and the evolving culture found ready supporters in the field of philosophy, which addresses human life from a different perspective. Among them were Thomas Hobbes, John Locke and Jean Jacques Rousseau, the *social theory philosophers* who were interested in the areas of morality and political philosophy.

Jason: Which interpretation of human nature did these thinkers support?

Diotima: Hobbes, in agreement with his friend Bacon produced a theory of man consonant with the scientific view, hence man as merely a *natural being.* According to this view, the world was a machine and man himself was nothing more than a mechanism; both were matter in motion. As to Locke and Rousseau, though they saw things differently and neither of them dispensed with God or man's obligation to obey God's laws, both of them articulated a theory that placed on the shoulders of government the responsibility for life in society and for man's right to happiness. Since people personally determine their own goals and have the right to their own brand of happiness in light of their inherent freedom, Locke maintained in contrast to Rousseau, that the "individual's personal good" supersedes the common good of society. For this reason Locke's theory is known as *individualism*.

Jason: So this is where we find the roots of the contemporary individualism. These can also be considered the underpinnings of the American form of government.

Diotima: Not all the thinkers of that period agreed with these views. During the seventeenth century there were also those like Blaise Pascal, George Berkeley, Benedict Spinoza, Joseph Butler and Gottfried W. Leibniz, to name a few, who made significant contributions to human knowledge in a number of areas. Their contributions align themselves with the other two interpretations of human nature, but it is the ideas of the social theory thinkers that carried over to the Modern Period. Thus it is that in philosophy at this time the orientation turned out to be *reason* looking to *social consciousness*, and in science, *reason* looking strictly to *empirical facts* retrieved from *nature*. These two trends made the Modern Period the Age of Reason.

The goal of the Modern Period was: objective, logical, systematic, universal knowledge of reality, devised in the spirit of the time, hence by means of reason alone. Immanuel Kant (1724-1804), Georg W. Hegel (1770-1831) and Karl Marx (1818-1883) can be named as the outstanding *trio* best representing this period. Each of them designed an elaborate system of thought, his understanding of reality providing the basis for the interpretation of man. By and large—though as always with some differences—their systems of thought correspond to the three views of human nature with which we are already familiar.

Jason: When did the Modern Period end and what are its merits?

Diotima: For quite some time it was held that the Modern Period ended in the nineteenth century with Marx and that at the turn of the twentieth century with the *reaction to modernism* the Postmodern Period began. Contemporary thinkers, however, as we shall soon see, have second thoughts about it. As to its merits, the Modern Period indeed made progress in science and gave a systematic view of reality, but in failing to do justice to human nature, it obscured man's understanding of himself. There was therefore a need for the shift of focus to human existence. The philosophy that espoused this concern came to be known as *Existentialism*. The latter, because its basic orientation remained secular, the Postmodern Period became known as that of *Secular Humanism*.

Jason: Why didn't the death of the Modern Period result, as in the past, in turning away from what caused its downfall?

Diotima: There was some turning away, but on the superficial level only, thereby, plunging humanity even deeper into turmoil. It was a turning away from the tenets that guided the Modern Period, for the approach in the Postmodern Period turned out to be *subjective, relative, unsystematic* and *personal*, just the opposite of what the Modern Period sought. The awareness at the deeper level, of what *really went wrong* has not yet dawned upon the horizon of *the world's consciousness*. This is a sure sign that we are still in the time of crisis; consequently, that *modernism*, as this orientation is sometimes called, did not die yet. All progress in science continued to move in the direction of the *purely natural* understanding of the world. What's more, the new evidence coming from the different branches of science appeared to converge, leading humanity to believe that scientific vision reflects objective truth.

Jason: What evidence are we speaking of now?

Diotima: In 1830, Charles Lyell published *Principles of Geology*. His research showed that "the contours of the landscape were shaped by geological forces, not by the hand of God, and that the earth was much older than Bible stories claimed."[31]

Jason: I never heard about Charles Lyell and his research.

Diotima: This is presumably because new scientific findings surfaced in rapid succession and the other proclamations overshadowed Lyell's. In those days, without the current media of instant communication, it took a long time for scientific discoveries to filter down to the general public. And it was only eighteen years later, in 1848, that Marx published his *Communist Manifesto*. His theory, as we already know, received wide acclaim rather quickly. Then, only eleven years later, in 1859, Darwin published *The Origin of Species*. His theory shocked the world. It was, as the saying goes, "the last straw that broke the camel's back," because the people who already entertained serious doubts about God's existence, this theory had extinguished the last spark of faith they had. Undeniably, the arrival of the theory was met with suspicion, if not with disbelief, at first. At our point in history, however, this theory is enjoying scientific status, precluding even the possibility of creation.

Darwin's theory was confirming and refining the Democritean assumption that all forms of life, including man, evolved from the basic stuff of the world, namely, *matter*. Building on that theory, Darwin in his publication was speaking of life in its later stages of evolution. According to him, this evolution occurred by means of biological adaptation over the stretch of millions years, rather than instantly at the word of God, as the Bible says.

Then, Nietzsche (1844-1900) announced that "God is dead." The news was received by the people without a blink of an eye, which proved that the "madman making the announcement" was right, in one sense—God was dead in their lives. Finally, Freud (1856-1939) concluded that God is merely an "illusion" or a "vague abstraction" of an insecure human mind, which is only creating "inhibitions" and causing all kinds of psychological and mental problems in people's lives, hence in need of being abandoned. This thinking projecting into the twentieth century found further support in the *Pragmatism* of John Dewey (1859-1952), *Logical Positivism* of Alfred J. Ayer (1910—89), *literature* (novels and essays) of Albert Camus (1913-1960) and *Existentialism* of Jean-Paul Sartre (1905-80) that carried it to the ultimate. Of course, not everyone subscribed to their views either.

As of late, because of the observed disparity in thought among the leading philosophers of the twentieth century, Peter A. Lawler rightfully interprets the Postmodern Period as having diverged into two distinct camps, as it were: the "Ultra Modern" and the Postmodern Period rightly understood, a "Return to Realism."[32] Since the Modern Period, having distanced itself from faith and become an ally of science pursued strictly secular orientation with the schools of thought mentioned above pushing it to the extreme, the thinkers pursuing this trend of thought are seen today as belonging to the first, the "Ultra Modern" camp. Edmund Husserl (1859-1938), Karl Jaspers (1883-1969), Gabrielle Marcel (1889-1973) and Martin Heidegger (1905-76) are examples of the twentieth century thinkers comprising the second camp. These philosophers explicitly had distanced themselves from their contemporaries in the first camp. Each of them gives ample evidence of "returning to realism" with the *sapiential dimension* of the pre-modern era that we saw alive and well during the Medieval Period. This direction is currently being advanced with much vigor by many philosophers in America who want to restore the correspondence between faith and reason. It is because *modernism* is leading the world to self-annihilation that the truly *postmodern thinkers* from around the globe are calling for a "synergistic view of reality," a "return to realism," hence a system of thought where God, the universe and we humans are reflected as a part of a single integrated whole.

One day, Jason, history will consign the twentieth century to the intermediate position, with the Philosopher-Pope John Paul II most likely as the *transitional personage* who will be seen—in concert with the truly postmodern thinkers—as having shown humanity the path out of the crisis and to a new age that probably will be called the Contemporary Period. By his pointing out the direction to "the organic vision of the whole" and the need of "synthesis of knowledge on a higher level," an army of new thinkers working out those details will lead humanity to the greatest "Golden Age" ever! Of course, such will be the outcome only if we embrace the truth of reality for what it is and make it the guiding light of our life.

Jason: Your vision offers much hope.

Diotima: In saying this, however, we are far ahead of history. Let us return to where we left off.

Anticipating the need of understanding better divergence of thought reflected by the two "camps," with an eye on the twentieth century we have lingered a bit on the Medieval Period to clarify the meaning of *realism.* Now, to understand better the concept of *modernism,* we need to go to Marx, for that is where we find the underpinnings of the current worldview. Subsequently we will look at the two outstanding thinkers of the current period who depict these two movements: the philosophy of Sartre where we find the ultimate expression of *modernism* that swept the world over, and the philosophy of Heidegger, Sartre's contemporary, where we discover the path "from there," that reflects a *return to realism.* In conjunction with this understanding we are apt to comprehend more readily the two choices available to us at this point in history, better to judge which path holds the potential of leading us to the verdant pastures of our dreams.

Karl Marx (1818-1883), the third major figure of the Modern Period, was a German thinker. He is well known in our century as a social philosopher, economic theorist and a revolutionary. Since he saw man as merely a *natural being,* he focused on improving man's life on earth. Dismissing God as a non-entity and religion as "the opium of the masses," he provided a system of thought that can be best understood in two parts: one, *Dialectical Materialism,* the other, *Historical Materialism.* In formulating this philosophy, he drew upon the concepts of the past.

We have noted earlier that Epicurus in his day revived the evolutionary, purely materialistic theory of Democritus. Now, Marx, having carefully studied them, revived both of those theories. These two theories form the underpinnings and the ideal of his system of thought. Marx's *dialectical materialism,* in the spirit of Democritus, explained the world and everything in it in terms of matter in motion. This explanation coincided with, and was strongly reinforced by the scientific understanding of the world at that time. Since—as it was then held—matter can neither be created nor destroyed, the world is indestructible and eternal. It operates in accordance with natural laws independently of any Creator. "Nature is its own cause. . . . That materialist formula signifies that nature is in no need of a creator standing above it, that nature itself possesses the attributes of infinity and eternity which the theologians falsely ascribe to God."[33] To understand the basic laws of material change is to gain insight into the evolution of the world. In short, *dialectical materialism* was an attempt to explain the laws of dialectic operative in the world at large.

Historical materialism, in turn, attempted to explain how the dialectical laws of material change work to produce different kinds of beings, and eventually, a thinking being, man. With the appearance of man, the history of the human race began. Thus, history, man and everything else in the world, which is not primary matter, is a product of it.

Marx's philosophy attempted to resolve the *alienation* caused by capitalism and ownership of property. Both lead to social injustice. "Marx understood alienation as a state of radical disharmony (1) among individuals, (2) between them and their own life activity, or labor, and (3) between individuals and their system of production" (CDP, 538). Consequently, these concepts became the building blocks of his system of thought.

The elaborate system consisted of two major components: the economic relations and the socio-ideological relations. The former was the *basis,* that is, the economic structure of society incorporating all relations of production. The latter, the *superstructure,* incorporated the sum-total of socio-ideological relations. Among them were ideology, social psychology, organizations and institutions such as the state, church, courts, etc.—what shaped the life of society.[34] Changes in the *basis* would produce changes in the *superstructure.* These changes, by means of the dialectical laws upon which the system was erected, would eventually lead a given society to the state of perfect *communism.* The latter would bring about "the fulfillment of all the potentialities and desires of man for a genuinely good and truly human life" (Varga, 72-3).

The system as envisioned by Marx and Engels, later also by Lenin, aimed to do away with capitalism, for it created an unfair class strata and led to all kinds of inequalities. The goal being equality in a classless society, the first phase of communism was that of *socialism.* Private ownership of all the means of production was to be abolished. Scientific socialism provided the rational structure for the production of goods to satisfy all human needs. In the early stage, the motto was: "From each according to his ability, to each according to his work." But once the system was up and running for a while, it would be: "From each according to his ability, to each according to his needs." In other words, initially the amount of one's production or contribution to the common good would determine how much each person would receive; later on, even though each person as before would be expected to contribute according to his or her ability, one would be given what one needs, regardless of how much one has contributed.

The final result of Marx's system would be the elimination of money. Because of the abundance of goods, all the needs of material and cultural nature would be satisfied without payment. Moreover, since all kinds of vices and evils in society are due to scarcity, human disposition would improve with the abundance of goods to satisfy everyone's needs. Peace, order and harmony would replace the evil. Everyone would be *comrad* and *tovarishch,* a comrade and a friend to everyone else. In such an atmosphere, there would be no need of a legal system; eventually, no need even of a government.

Jason: The ideology seems to have promised an ideal co-existence, almost *utopia.* It is no wonder *communism* spread like fire around the globe.

Diotima: It lasted in the place of its birth for seventy-five years and it is still alive in some parts of the world. Alas, the system anticipated much more than what it could deliver. The golden era of communism, to which historical dialectic was to lead the world, was never realized. Communism in the Soviet Union, the place of its birth, crumbled as soon as the satellite countries, overtaken during World War II, succeeded to free themselves of the communist yoke of oppression. The supply of goods having halted, turmoil erupted and the Soviet Union itself splintered into individual States of the Republic, all claiming their own independence. Owing to contemporary television media, many of us were eyewitnesses of its dramatic demise under Mikhail Gorbachev in 1991, when his own life was in peril.

Jason: Why didn't the system work as it was envisioned?

Diotima: The fact that so many states in the world embraced the Marxist ideology does prove that the promised peace, order and harmony, as well as the ideas of friendship and comradery are seen by humanity as noteworthy goals to strive for and to live by. Regrettably, the system was not without its faults.

Unquestionably, much good was intended. It is the uncritical attitude of society unable to separate the good from the bad that must at least in part accept the blame for its failure. By embracing Marx's thinking in its entirety, the communist world plunged humanity into a crisis worse than any other before. Leaving God and religion out of the equation soon gave way to a full-fledged materialism, socialism and militant atheism. That led, in one sense, to the death of the Modern Period itself. We can say, then, that the Modern Period made progress in science and gave us a systematic view of reality, but in neglecting to do justice to human nature, it obscured man's understanding of himself. Therefore, there surfaced the need for a shift of focus on *human existence,* which resulted in a philosophy known as *Existentialism.* The latter took the form of *secular humanism.*

Jason: How can it be said that man was neglected? Weren't all the systems we have mentioned sought for the greater good of humankind?

Diotima: Looking back to the social theory thinkers we began to discuss, the answer to your question is "yes, they were," but they had to do with improving life in society, with the external circumstances, as it were. Creating better government and a social climate conducive to human growth and development is important; however, it is not enough. Human beings have an inner life as well, hence also inner needs. It is these needs that were being overlooked. Some philosophers in another European country tried to address themselves to one of these needs.

Jason: Who are they?

Diotima: Approximately at the same time when Hegel's philosophy dominated the intellectual atmosphere on the Continent and Marx was working on his theory in Germany, Jeremy Bentham and John Stuart Mill endeavored to formulate a theory of human happiness in England. Well in keeping with the spirit of the time, they, too, focused on *social consciousness.* Owing to their genius, we have a theory known as *utilitarianism* deeply entrenched in our society. Derived from Epicurean *hedene* or pleasure, this theory is based on the pleasure/pain principle. Where there are choices, the wise choice is one that will bring greatest pleasure. Bentham calls the property of an act that produces pleasure "utility," whence the name *utilitarianism.*

Jason: So by happiness Bentham means "pleasure and absence of pain."

Diotima: Agreeing with Bentham that happiness is the goal of human life and that happiness is pleasure, Mill writes: "The creed which as the foundation of morals 'utility' or the 'greatest happiness principle' holds that actions are right in proportion as they tend to promote happiness; wrong as they tend to produce the reverse of happiness. By happiness is intended pleasure and the absence of pain; by unhappiness, pain and the privation of pleasure."[35]

Unlike Epicurean theory, utilitarianism is founded on the *Greatest Happiness Principle*; it aims at *personal happiness* as well as that of the *community.* It comes with *qualitative* and *quantitative* qualities. Yet, it holds, as Epicurus did, that pleasures of the intellect are higher than those of sensation. Mill writes, "It is better to be a human being dissatisfied than a pig satisfied; better to be Socrates dissatisfied than a fool satisfied. And if the fool, or the pig, are (sic) of a different opinion, it is because they only know their own side of the question. The other party to the comparison knows both sides" (10).

Jason: I can see that *utilitarianism* complements Marx' natural theory of man. Even though it incorporates the intellectual component of our being, it does not take into account the spiritual dimension of our human nature.

Diotima: If now you recall what we have said earlier about thinkers who followed them; namely, Lyell, Darwin, Nietzsche and Freud, only to be followed by Dewey's *Pragmatism,* Ayer's *Logical Positivism* and scientific dominance that continued to hold sway, you can see that the climate of our time is a product of several centuries and that Sartre's *Existentialism* is merely a natural consequence of it. Let him tell us himself *why* and *how* he became an atheist as also what his thoughts were toward the end of his life. His autobiography is a masterpiece from the psychological point of view. It tells us in unambiguous terms where *modernism* terminates.

Jason: While I look forward to hearing what Sartre had to say to see *modernism* in its ultimate form, I am glad to learn that we cannot take the full blame for the existing state of affairs in the world. I realize, however, that neither can we plead excuse and do nothing about it. Now I can see why you've said to me when I came, that great challenge is ahead of us.

3. Divergence of Thought in the Postmodern Period

a. Effects of "Ultra Modern" School of Thought: Sartre's Existentialism

Jean-Paul Sartre (1905-1980) was a French philosopher who is perhaps the best known of the twentieth century existentialists. Like Marcel and Camus, his contemporaries, Sartre was orphaned at a very early age. His father, Jean-Baptiste, "a marine engineer, died from a fever contracted in Indo-China, shortly after Jean Paul's birth"[36] After his father's untimely death he and his mother, Anne Marie, moved into the home of her parents, the Schweitzers, where he was raised.

In his autobiography, *The Words*, Jean Paul Sartre recalls having been treated by his grandparents with much affection and tenderness.[37] Yet, he attributes his attitude of "dis-belief" to the lack of an example of authentic living and the absence of a spiritual atmosphere at that home. He writes: "I was led to dis-believe not by a conflict of dogmas, but by my grandparents' indifference. Nevertheless, I believed. In my nightshirt, kneeling on the bed, with my hands together, I said my prayers everyday, but I thought of God less and less often. . . . My grandfather had done such a thorough job that I regarded priests as odd animals. . . . It was my grandfather who hated them through me" (100-101). Unlike Jaspers and Marcel who also grew up in a Godless atmosphere but eventually altered their lifestyle, Sartre lived the life he learned in childhood. Since he was given the title "father of existentialism," atheism became the hallmark of existentialism. It is because of the atheistic slant on existentialism that a number of thinkers, including Jaspers, Marcel and Heidegger—even though they shared the concern for human existence—refused to be identified with it.

Jason: Why was this title conferred on Sartre, rather than on some other thinker who shared the same concerns and had preceded him in time? Could it be that people popularized his philosophy? And people popularized it because, by and large, they identified more closely with his thinking in that their experiences of life resonated more closely with Sartre's writings rather than with any of the other thinker's? Or was it perhaps that the novels and plays by means of which Sartre chose to communicate his thought, were easier to understand and having been read widely overshadowed the writings of others?

Diotima: There is some truth to everything at what you are hinting here. More importantly, Sartre himself made an exclusive claim to it by stating that his form of existentialism best reflects the reality of human existence. Speaking of it, he writes: "this theory alone is compatible with the dignity of man, it is the only one which does not make man into an object."[38] He claimed, moreover, that his theory was based on an "absolute truth"—a strange claim indeed coming from one who did away with all absolutes and argued exclusively for the subjective/relative orientation to life.

Jason: What, then, did Sartre mean by *existentialism?* Whence his preeminence?

Diotima: In the lecture entitled "Existentialism is a Humanism" where he tries to defend the position he developed in *Being and Nothingness (L'être et le néant),* Sartre explains: "existentialism, in our sense of the word, is a doctrine that does render human life possible; a doctrine, also, which affirms that every truth and every action imply both an environment and a human subjectivity" (288). If that were all to it, this broad definition would have been phenomenological, which automatically means that it is *subjective* and that it is bound up with *consciousness.* It is the further elucidation that reveals his brand. He writes: "Atheistic existentialism, of which I am a representative, declares with greater consistency that if God does not exist there is at least one being whose existence comes before its essence, a being which exists before it can be defined by any conception of it. That being is man or, as Heidegger has it, the human reality" (290).

This amplified explanation of existentialism, please observe, points out two major differences: first, that his brand of existentialism is atheistic; and second, that in the case of man, "existence precedes essence." The first point needs no clarification; the second point, however, is a puzzle. It is also a crux to understanding Sartre's thought. One cannot help but ask: How can existence precede essence when existence is always an existence of "something"? Existence presupposes some form of "being"—"that which exists." Philosophers in the past referred to that "something" of which existence can be posited as "essence"; hence they called it an "essent" or a "being." In the absence of an "essent" or "being," there is "nothing." Nothing is the opposite of being. If "nothing" is, nothing "exists" and so nothing can be said about it. The two terms are inseparable; their fate is sealed together. To say, therefore, that "existence precedes essence" is tantamount to saying that to begin with a "nothing" exists. And to say this of man, is to say, that to begin with "man is nothing" and, therefore, that man first exists as "nothing." But that is exactly what Sartre says: "man to begin with is nothing" (290). We ask him: How can that be? What do you mean? "We mean," he replies," "that man first of all exists, encounters himself, surges up in the world—and defines himself afterwards. If man as the existentialist sees him is not definable, it is because to begin with he is nothing. He will not be anything until later, and then he will be what he makes of himself. Thus, there is no human nature, because there is no God to have a conception of it. Man simply is" (290-91).

Jason: What about the world? If there is no God, how did the world come to be?

Diotima: No one was there to see it, is his reply. The world already is and we are in it. This is our starting point. And what is, the world, according to Sartre, admits of two modes of being: being "for-itself" *(l'être pour soi)* and being "in-itself" *(l'être en-soi).* These two modes of being by their nature are very different and are mutually exclusive. The being "in-itself" consists of inanimate objects, the *things* of this world that lack consciousness. They make up the world in which we live. The being "for-itself" is man alone, and man must be understood in conjunction with "consciousness" and both, man and consciousness, as "nothingness."

Being "for-itself" is, first of all, "consciousness" and consciousness is always a consciousness of "something." Agreeing with Husserl, Sartre maintains that consciousness automatically posits an object, which necessarily transcends it and is different from it. In *Being and Nothingness* Sartre explains the fundamental relation between the two. "All consciousness, as Husserl has shown, is consciousness of something. This means that there is no consciousness which is not a positing of a transcendent object, or if you prefer, that consciousness has no 'content.' . . . All consciousness is positional in that it transcends itself in order to reach an object, and it exhausts itself in this positing."[39] Consciousness is nothing in itself; it is an activity of a being that is conscious of something in the world. Lescoe explains, "All consciousness is consciousness of something . . . this means that consciousness in its inmost nature is a relation to a transcendent being . . . it means that transcendence is the constitutive structure of consciousness, that is, that consciousness is born, supported by a being which is not itself. . . . To say that consciousness is consciousness of something is to say that it must produce itself as a revealed-revelation of a being which is not it and which gives itself as already existing when consciousness reveals it" (E, 280). Consequently, consciousness and the self do not have an independent existence; the self is the object of consciousness, which defines it.

In light of the above, since the existence of an object is an absolute necessity for the existence of consciousness, there is no need to justify the existence of the object. Being the condition of possibility of consciousness, the object needs only to be acknowledged. In other words, as long as consciousness is, the object necessarily is.

Jason: How, then, can consciousness be understood?

Diotima: One can understand it by analogy, the analog being a mirror. "A mirror has content only when objects are reflected in it. Of itself, it is empty. In like manner, consciousness has no content except the objects which it reflects. These objects are always other than consciousness itself" (E, 280-81).

Apparently Sartre was one of the philosophers who thought he understood Heidegger, for he compares his "for-itself" to Heidegger's *Dasein.* He says we could apply to consciousness the definition which Heidegger reserves for *Dasein,* "a being such that in its being, its being is in question." Lescoe notes, however, "it would be necessary to complete the definition and formulate it more like this: consciousness is a being such that in its being, its being is in question insofar as this being implies a being other than itself" (E, 281). Although Sartre's concept *pour soi* and Heidegger's *Dasein* the two thinkers hold out do not share the same meaning, there are some similarities between them. Just as Heidegger's *Dasein,* that is always a "not-yet" being, so Sartre's "for-itself" is a never finished being. And just as Heidegger's *Dasein* is "futural," always "projecting itself out" and realizing its being, so, too, Sartre's "for-itself" is always "something which propels itself towards a future." Both of them are always in the process of being constructed, fashioned, or created by the actions each performs.

Elaborating on his understanding of man, Sartre says man is what he wills to be, that is, "what he wills, and as he conceives himself after existing—as he wills to be after that leap towards existence. Man is nothing else but that which he makes of himself. That is the first principle of existentialism" (EH, 291). This, he tells us, is what he understands "subjectivity" to be: man himself determining his own identity. And it is this subjectivity that places man above other things in the world like a stone or a table. It is this subjectivity that gives man his dignity. "Man is, indeed, a project which possesses a subjective life, instead of being a kind of moss, or a fungus or a cauliflower. Before that projection of the self nothing exists; not even in the heaven of intelligence: man will only attain existence when he is what he purposes to be. Not, however, what he may wish to be" (291). It is what he "wills" to be. Willing is a conscious act, it is a decision which is possible only "after we have made ourselves what we are." The "nothing" of man, therefore, is not an absolute nothing, for something "surges up" or, as some other translations have it, something simply "turns up." But what "turns up" is nothing predetermined by nature, for which reason it cannot be defined and is, therefore, called by Sartre "nothing." It is only in the process of existing, by acting, through the choices one makes that one creates his or her own identity and becomes what he or she wills to be. It finally becomes clear that what "surges up" is really the "self" or better, the "nothing" that eventually emerges as the "self." And consciousness is "nothing" because it is not a thing or being, but an "activity" of the self.

Jason: If existence precedes essence and man becomes what he chooses to make of himself, then isn't man responsible for what he turns out to be?

Diotima: That is exactly what Sartre contends. He says "the first effect of existentialism is that it puts the entire responsibility for his existence squarely upon his own shoulders" (291). There is no God to tell him how to live. If God as the creator existed, he could rightfully be conceived as "a supernal artisan." In creating he would know exactly what he created and why. He would have these concepts in His mind each imaging something definitive. Making use of an analogy he explains, "the conception of man in the mind of God is comparable to that of the paper-knife in the mind of the artisan: God makes man according to a procedure and a conception, exactly as the artisan manufactures a paper-knife, following a definition and a formula. Thus each individual man is the realization of a certain conception which dwells in the divine understanding" (290). But God does not exist and the existentialist "finds it extremely embarrassing that God does not exist, for there disappears with Him all possibility of finding values in an intelligible heaven. There can no longer be any good *a priori*, since there is no infinite and perfect consciousness to think it. . . . Dostoevsky once wrote 'If God did not exist, everything would be permitted'; and that, for existentialism, is the starting point" (294-95). As a result, man is forlorn, he has no one but himself to count on and he is without excuse about what he makes of himself. "For if indeed existence precedes essence, one will never be able to explain one's action by reference to a given and specific nature . . . man is free, man *is* freedom. . . . Nor . . . if God does not exist, are we provided with any values or commands that could legitimize our behavior. Thus we have neither behind us or before us in a luminous realm of values, any means of justification or excuse. We are left alone, without excuse. That is what I mean when I say that man is condemned to be free" (295). On the other hand, for that very reason "there is a future to be fashioned, a virgin future that awaits him" (295).

Jason: Isn't he thereby advocating an individualistic view of morality?

Diotima: No. Man is responsible not just for his own individuality. He is responsible for all men, Sartre asserts.

Jason: How can this be if every man can choose according to his own will?

Diotima: Sartre finds an answer to it in the two-fold meaning he ascribes to subjectivity. He contends: "Subjectivism means, on the one hand, the freedom of the individual subject and, on the other, that man cannot pass beyond human subjectivity. It is the latter which is the deeper meaning of existentialism. When we say that man chooses himself, we do mean that every one of us must choose himself; but by that we also mean that in choosing for himself he chooses for all men; . . . we are unable ever to choose the worse. What we choose is always the better; and nothing can be better for us unless it is better for all. . . . Our responsibility is thus much greater than we had supposed, for it concerns mankind as a whole" (291-92).

Anguish, abandonment and despair are experiences bound up with freedom, for man can blame no one but himself for the choices he makes. He makes himself by "the choice of his morality, and he cannot but choose a morality, such is the pressure of circumstances" (306). Man is condemned to be free. Freedom is his greatest prerogative and the greatest burden. On the other hand, "once a man has seen that values depend upon himself, in that state of forsakenness he can will only one thing, and that is freedom as the foundation of values. . . . We will freedom for freedom's sake, in and through particular circumstances. And in thus willing freedom, we discover that it depends entirely upon the freedom of others and that the freedom of others depends upon our freedom" (306-07).

Jason: Given this understanding of freedom, what is Sartre's view on other people? How do they affect our life?

Diotima: Yes, others do enter into the picture. Just as Heidegger devoted much space in *Being and Time* speaking of *Dasein* "in-the-world" as being a "being-with-others," so does Sartre devote about two hundred pages in his *Being and Nothingness* to the section entitled "Being-For-Others." The two thinkers, however, do not see the "other" in the same light. For Heidegger, although *Dasein* can lose itself in the world of the "they-self," *Dasein* needs the "other" to become an authentic self. Being-with-others is constitutive of *Dasein's* existence in the world. For Sartre, the "Other" is a threat to me. The Other inhibits me, disrupts my world, robs me of my freedom. The presence of the Other evokes at times fear in me; at other times it makes me feel shame. My whole existence is disrupted and in danger. Roger Mehl captures the image quite well when he writes: "The existence of the Other is my negation. It endangers me. By the attention which it places on me and which reaches me right in my heart, the Other attempts to fix and freeze my destiny for all time. Under the attention of the Other, I am reduced to being only a thing, to being only a means or an obstacle for the realization of the projects of the Other. It would be necessary for me to escape the attention of the Other, but this is impossible" (E, 302). Sartre claims that this feeling and reaction is mutual. Paraphrasing Sartre Lescoe writes, "Everything which may be said of me in relation with the Other applies to him as well. While I attempt to free myself from the hold of the Other, the Other is trying to free himself from mine; while I seek to enslave the Other, the Other seeks to enslave me. . . . *Conflict is the original meaning of being-for-others*" (E, 303).

Conflict with the Other, furthermore, is a source of all kinds of problems. It manifests itself not only in fear and in shame. It manifests itself also in masochism and sadism, in hate and even in love. According to Sartre, love is in fact the most striking example of mutual conflict between two individuals. For here each of the parties strives to appropriate what is most vital to a person, the freedom of the other. Under ideal circumstances love should be "a fusion of consciousness." By preserving one's own otherness one would be in a good position to build up the other, but such is not the case. Each of them instead seeks to enslave the other through love. In *No Exit,* a play with only three characters where the central theme is love, Sartre through one of the characters concludes, "Hell is other people."

Toward the end of *Being and Nothingness* Sartre says that man's desire is to be in-and-for-itself, to become the proof and foundation of his self; he wishes to free himself from contingency, that is, to become God. But that, of course is impossible, and so man turns out to be "a useless passion" *(une passion inutile).*

Jason: How does Sartre arrive at this conclusion?

Diotima: It is impossible for man to become God, he reasons, because the concept "God" demands a being "for-itself-and-in-itself," and given his understanding of "for-itself" and of "in-itself" that is impossible. Self-identity excludes consciousness. That is precisely the reason why he concluded God does not exist. "For consciousness means presence to oneself as distant from oneself, whereas being-in-itself means the absence of that fissure or rift which is essential to consciousness. It is thus impossible for *pour-soi* and *en-soi* to be united in one self-identical being. . . . It is not simply that God does not exist as a matter of fact: there can be no God. For to affirm the existence of God is to enunciate a self-contradictory proposition. There can be no God. And man's striving after divinity is doomed to frustration" (CP, 188). Because man wants to be God and cannot, he is a "useless passion" and so "life is absurd."

Jason: What does Sartre mean by "existentialism is a humanism"?

Diotima: Sartre explains: "In reality, the word humanism has two different meanings. One may understand by humanism a theory which upholds man as the end-in-itself and as the supreme value. . . . But there is another sense of the word: Man is all the time outside of himself: it is in projecting and losing himself beyond himself that he makes man to exist; and on the other hand, it is by pursuing transcendent aims that he himself is able to exist. Since man is thus self-surpassing, and can grasp objects only in relation to his surpassing, he is himself the heart and center of his transcendence. There is no other universe except the human universe, the universe of human subjectivity. This relation of transcendence as constitutive of man (not in the sense that God is transcendent, but in the sense of self-surpassing) with subjectivity (in such a sense that man is not shut up in himself but forever present in a human universe)—it is this that we call existential humanism. This is humanism because we remind man that there is no legislator but himself; that he himself, thus abandoned, must decide for himself; also because we show that it is not by turning back upon himself, but always by seeking, beyond himself, an aim which is one of liberation or of some practical realization, that man can realize himself as truly human. . . . Existentialism is nothing else but an attempt to draw the full conclusions from a consistently atheistic position. . . . Existentialism is not atheist in the sense that it would exhaust itself in demonstrations of the non-existence of God. It declares, rather, that even if God existed that would make no difference from its point of view" (EH, 310-11).

Jason: Given Sartre's understanding of existentialism, what kind of an effect did this orientation have on his life? Seeing himself as the only "legislator" of his life with "a virgin future awaiting him," and an "absolute, unqualified" freedom "to create himself" according to his own will, how did he fare in the end? Do we have any inkling of it?

Diotima: Yes, we have. The answer comes in two different ways, directly and indirectly. Directly, it comes from his autobiography, *The Words,* where at the end of it he writes: "I was a prisoner of that obvious contradiction, but I did not see it, I saw the world through it. Fake to the marrow of my bones and hoodwinked, I joyfully wrote about our unhappy state. Dogmatic though I was, I doubted everything except that I was the elect of doubt. I built with one hand what I destroyed with the other, and I regarded anxiety as the guarantee of my security; I was happy.

"I have changed. . . . The retrospective illusion has been smashed to bits; martyrdom, salvation, and immortality are falling to pieces; the edifice is going to rack and ruin; I collared the Holy Ghost in the cellar and threw him out; atheism is a cruel and long-range affair; I think I've carried it through. I see clearly, I've lost my illusions. . . . For the last ten years or so I've been a man who's been waking up, cured of a long, bitter-sweet madness, and who can't get over the fact, a man who can't think of his old ways without laughing and who doesn't know what to do with himself. I've again become the traveler without a ticket that I was at the age of seven. . . . I've given up the office but not the frock; I still write. What else can I do?" (*Words,* 252-53.)

Indirectly, the answer comes from three sources, each confirming the one above. The first of these is his novel *Nausea*, which commentators see as his other biography, a fact Sartre himself had confirmed. In his autobiography he admitted that he himself was Antoine Roquentin. "I was Roquentin; I used him to show, without complacency, the texture of my life" *(Words,* 251).

We get another idea of it from what Sartre has to say about love between two individuals drawing upon his subjective experience of personal relationship with Simone de Beauvoir, his life's companion of forty years. It turned out to be a partnership of "contingent loves,"[40] the partnership that according to her writings was tainted by incidents of infidelity and proved disappointing to both of them.[41] Finally, we get it from the disheartening assessment of her life, which again casts a shadow on both lives. She who redefined the socialized role of woman and created her own future according to "her own choice," toward the end of her life had this to say: "If it (my life) had at least enriched the earth. If it had given birth to . . . what? A hill? A rocket? The promises have all been kept. And yet, turning an incredulous gaze toward that young and credulous girl, I realize how much I have been gypped."[42] Lescoe adds, "And so the world-famous author of *The Second Sex,* the classic which expounded woman's discontented state in modern society, now finds herself empty, useless and unfulfilled" (E, 273). So the re-defined role of woman turns out to be a big disappointment in the end. Jean-Paul and Simone had no children. Toward the end of his life, Sartre adopted a daughter, a twenty-eight years old Algerian-born girl, Arlette Elkaim, who was to be his legal heir.

In light of what we have learned, it is obvious that Sartre, being true to the spirit of our time lived and advocated *subjective/relative* approach to everything in life.[43]

Jason: It is a powerful testimony that Sartre offered about his life and vision. Did people know what he had to say about himself and his philosophy in the end?

Diotima: Undeniably, it was a humble, honest confession about the outcome of the philosophy by which he lived and which he promulgated by his writings. As to whether or not people knew about the effects of it on his life, most probably the answer is no. There are at least two good reasons for it. Sartre began to publish in 1936 and his autobiography appeared in print only in 1964. By then his views were widely endorsed around the globe. Secondly, since he was so popular, the negative consequences of his views did not receive equal attention in the media. The majority of people, most likely, do not know about them even today. A good number of people identify with his views currently, even if they did not receive them directly from him. The younger generation may have received them at home as children, or they may have imbibed them from the cultural atmosphere in which we live, for our social milieu is permeated with that thought. Be that as it may, this is one of the options that will always be available to us as human beings. Our freedom allows us to determine our personal course of life. Once we make the choice, we must live with the consequences of it, even as did Sartre. Hopefully, before he died he recovered the faith into which he was born.

Jason: It's unfortunate that people do not know it. I believe that if people who are committed to following his philosophy knew where it ends, they would have second thought about it. After all, everyone wants to be happy.

Diotima: This, in any event, is where "ultra modern thinking" leads. Let us now move on to Heidegger to see what he had to say. He is said to be an *ontologist,* rather than an *existentialist* because he looks at human existence from the fundamental standpoint of human existence by raising the question of the Being of our being—the question that for centuries had been forgotten and is now in dire need of being resurrected. It is his contention that in this answer resides the hope of reversing the thinking that is leading humanity down the path of devastation. By returning philosophy to its roots, he is returning it to *realism.*

b. Return to Realism: Heidegger's Vision

Martin Heidegger (1889-1976) was another German philosopher, who initially aspired to become a Jesuit. Soon in his life, however, he switched his orientation first to mathematics and subsequently to philosophy (CDP, 370). He is regarded as one of the most influential thinkers of our time. His work in philosophy being in the area of ontology provides the foundation for existentialism and raises *subjectivity* to a new status.

Heidegger's approach is phenomenological. He took over this method from Husserl with whom he collaborated for some time. Much to Husserl's disappointment, Heidegger modified it. He did so to overcome the duality construed by Husserl's *epoché,* that is, bracketing the external aspect of a phenomenon given in human experience, the very component studied by empirical science.[44]

The central point of philosophy, and indeed, of human existence, Heidegger maintains, is the question of Being. He begins the Introduction to his famous *Being and Time (Sein und Zeit)* with the section on "The Necessity for Explicitly Restating the Question of Being." There he writes: "This question has today been forgotten. . . . It is one which provided a stimulus for the researches of Plato and Aristotle, only to subside from then on *as a theme for actual investigation.* . . . And what they wrested with the utmost intellectual effort from the phenomena, fragmentary and incipient as it was, has long since become trivialized."[45] Heidegger, therefore, sees the need for resurrecting this question, which he then proceeds to develop with utmost care.

Jason: How does he go about retrieving the concept of Being?

Diotima: Being as such, he states, cannot be studied directly. Heidegger finds access to it by analyzing the being of man. For although Being is expressed in many ways, for example, mountains, flowers, water, animals, and so on, man is that expression of Being where being becomes conscious of itself. Heidegger calls man *Da-sein,* the "there-being," the name man holds in common with Being. In his book *Kant and the Problem of Metaphysics,* he writes, "Man is man only on the basis of the *Dasein* in him."[46] In his essay "The Way Back into the Ground of Metaphysics" where he attempts to clarify this concept misunderstood in *Being and Time (B&T),* Heidegger writes: "To characterize with a single term both the involvement of Being in human nature and the essential relation of man to the openness ('there') of Being as such, the name of 'being there' [*Dasein*] was chosen for that sphere of being in which man stands as man."[47] Since man is intimately concerned with being, he is the key to the understanding of Being.

"*Dasein* always understands itself in terms of its existence" (*B&T,* 33). But the word "existence" is not a synonym for *Dasein,* "being-there."

Jason: What, then, does he mean by "existence"?

Diotima: Heidegger explains: "In *B.&T.* the term 'existence' is used exclusively for the being of man. . . . The being that exists is man. Man alone exists. Rocks are, but they do not exist. Trees are, but they do not exist. Horses are, but they do not exist. Angels are, but they do not exist. God is, but he does not exist. The proposition 'man alone exists' does not mean by any means that man alone is a real being while all other beings are unreal and mere appearances or human ideas. The proposition 'man exists' means: man is that being whose Being is distinguished by the open-standing standing-in in the unconcealedness of Being, from Being, in Being.[48] The existential nature of man is the reason why man can represent beings as such, and why he can be conscious of them. All consciousness presupposes ecstatically understood existence as *the essentia* of man—*essentia* meaning that as which man is present insofar as he is man" (WBGM, 213-214). In other words, man is the only being whose being is distinguished from all other entities by "existence," that is, by concernfully maintaining himself in a state of openness to discovering who he really is as he stands in relation to the Being who is present to him and is revealing itself as *the Being of man's being.* The "unconcealedness" (Greek *alethea* for truth) is therefore a disclosure "of Being," as it comes "from Being" and is "in Being," that is, in the nature of who man ontologically is. Put in a still simpler form, the truth of who man is ontologically comes in the process of man's existence through the openness of his being to the Being who discloses it.

Jason: How does this occur?

Diotima: Human existence is always ecstatic *(ekstasis).* It has to do with Dasein's "projecting" itself out in *care* "toward the truth of Being. . . . We must think at the same time, however, of standing in the openness of Being, of enduring and out-standing this standing-in (care), and of out-braving the utmost (Being toward death); for it is only together that they constitute the full essence of existence" (WBGM, 214).

Jason: What is man's stance toward the world according to Heidegger?

Diotima: Man does not stand in opposition to the world. He is the most refined part of the world. Nor is man just another object in the world, like a bird or a tree. He is *subjectivity.* He is not just objectively there, he is there as feeling happy or sad, fearful or joyful, and so on. Man gives meaning to everything in the world and he himself is the reason for the world's existence. Man, moreover, not only gives meaning to the world, he also transforms the world for his own use, because man's basic orientation in life is that of *care (Sorge).*

Jason: Does man accomplish this on his own, or with the help of others? What role, if any, does Heidegger ascribe to others?

Diotima: He sees them in a positive light. They are in fact indispensable to one's growth in authenticity. Man is Being-in-the-world being. This involves him with others. Man is Being-with-others being (*Mitsein*). He is also Being-one's-Self (*Selbstsein*). This being-with others is part of man's very constitution. Human existence is a shared existence. The social interdependence of our every day existence is primary and constitutive. My full self-consciousness and my full self-affirmation come from my being conscious of others. I do not begin with myself and go to others. I begin as a being-with-others-being (*B&T*, 149 ff).

Being-with-others helps man to become authentic. Inauthentic man does not live in the world of others, nor does he make his own choices. He reduces others to the "they" (*das Man*) existence, and conforms his life to what "they-say." Man must have *genuine concern (Sorge) for authentic being*. This concern leads him to freedom and selfhood. Coming to terms with himself means coming to terms with Being in its greatness.

Concern brings man also to *angst*, almost dread, at the nearness of non-being in death. Man *is*, but it is possible that he will not be. This depends upon the way he chooses to use his freedom. In *angst*, man is no longer concerned with the superficial everyday world, he begins to experience human existence itself, and the thrilling reality of true freedom. Authentic man is fully conscious of himself, and of his "I" who is freely creating his future. He understands that his future is in his own hands. Man's meaning lies in his freedom to work out his major project of life—the self. Concern and *angst*, conscience and guilt, deepen man and open him to his true self, to his fellow human beings and to Being. They call his attention to his "lostness" in the "they-self" of the inauthentic living. And they call him to take charge of his own life with "resoluteness," to be true to self and to Being.

Dasein in the world is always a "not-yet" being. It is always "*ec-static*", "projecting" itself into the future. It is always in the process of becoming and attaining its own authentic fulfillment and identity. This occurs through the choices it makes and the acts it performs, for *Dasein* is a "being of possibilities." It does so, because *Dasein* is "futural," it has a destiny. But *Dasein* is likewise "temporal," a "being-toward death (*zum Tode*)." Death brings to a halt all further possibilities (*B&T*, 264, 266, 279ff). There is only so much time that *Dasein* has for making Presence present to itself before returning to the Being of his being precisely because *Dasein* is temporal. *Dasein*, moreover, is a steward of its being. At death, upon "homecoming," *Dasein* must give an account of stewardship of its being to Being.

This whole drama is enacted in the world. Man never loses the world. He is never alone. He is in communion with Being, with the world, with his fellow creatures. But man can be lost, he can betray himself and turn traitor before Being. This is the effect of inauthentic living, of being lost in the "they-being."

Jason: Is Heidegger's Being God?

Diotima: No. God is, but he is given to man in a religious experience, not in philosophical analysis. Man's concern in the world is with Being. Man can come into contact with the "ground" of his being only through Being. Because of the forgetfulness of Being contemporary man cannot find God. God in our world is known only by his absence.

Jason: How, then, would you characterize Heidegger's philosophy?

Diotima: Ontological in his undertaking, Heidegger's approach is *subjective/objective*. It is the subject, he rightly contends, who raises human understanding to the objective level. In other words, *objectivity is grounded in subjectivity* unless, of course, we accept on faith revealed knowledge, which is objective in nature. Yet, even in this case, correct understanding still depends on the subject's accurate interpretation of it.

Jason: There is something in Heidegger's thought that I find very relevant. However, if the language in all his writings is like the passages that were quoted, I would not have the courage to read his works. Isn't there anything that could help one to understand in clearer terms what precisely he means by Being?

Diotima: It is possible that the clue you are seeking, Jason, can be located in one of his earlier works that appears under the title *What Is Philosophy?* In it Heidegger bewails the plight of the current state of philosophy. He says that by departing from the concept of Being—so central to Socrates, Plato and Aristotle, even already to Heraclitus and Parmenides before them—philosophy lost its focus and thereby direction. Forgetfulness of Being has become a problem for philosophy and for *Dasein*. Heidegger sees the contemporary crisis as a direct result of it. Since overcoming the crisis—which at this point threatens the very existence of *Dasein* and of the world—hinges upon reinstating Being to its rightful status, and this task belongs to philosophy, Heidegger's philosophy is an effort to achieve just that. The two major reasons why philosophy is so important, according to him, are: first, because it "concerns us personally, affects us and, indeed, touches us in our very nature," and second, because philosophy "is not only something rational but is the actual guardian of reason."[49]

Jason: What's the clue, how does he get at it?

Diotima: To understand the clue to Heidegger's meaning of Being requires of us to see it in the context of his discussion of philosophy. It is interesting how he himself comes to this understanding. Considering that Heidegger's answer is in harmony with our own findings, it is worth giving it the time it will take to surface. Don't you agree?

Jason: By all means!

Diotmia: In view of the fact that Greeks, "and only Greeks," as Heidegger puts it, had the uncanny knack for conferring names on things whereby the name revealed the very being of "what was named," and the name "philosophy" traces to Heraclitean *philosophos*, Heidegger begins by recovering the meaning Heraclitus intended to communicate by this word. Concluding that *philosophia*, that is, philosophy, at that point did not yet exist, he takes a penetrating look at the word *philosophos* and carries out his inquiry as only a scholar adept in Greek language could do.

Speaking of Heraclitean *philosophos*, Heidegger writes, "An *aner philosophos* is *hos philei to sophon*, he who loves the *sophon; philein,* to love, signifies here, in the Heraclitean sense, *homolegein,* to speak in the way in which the *Logos* speaks, in correspondence with the *Logos*" (47). Correspondence, Heidegger argues, implies the "inner dialectic" between the parties engaged in speaking. "Speaking—to be speaking—requires correspondence," we are told in the footnote. In other words, speaking requires receptivity on both sides, for speaking is a dialogue, not a monologue. "This correspondence," Heidegger goes on to explain, "is in accord with the *sophon*. Accordance is *harmonia.* That *one being* [italics in this case ours] reciprocally unites itself with another, that both are originally united to each other because they are at each other's disposal—this *harmonia* is the distinctive feature of *philein,* of 'loving' in the Heraclitean sense"(47).

Philosophos is "one who loves *sophon,*" but what does *sophon* mean? "What this word means for Heraclitus is hard to translate," Heidegger says. "But we can explain it according to Heraclitus' own interpretation. According to this the *sophon* means, *Hen Panta,* 'One (is) all.' 'All' means here, all things that exist, the whole, the totality of being. *Hen,* one, means, the one, the unique, the all-uniting. But all being is united in Being. The *sophon* says—all being *is* Being. In this instance 'is' speaks transitively and means approximately 'gathered together,' 'collected.' Being gathers being together in so far as it is being. Being is the gathering together—*Logos*" (48-49).

Having said that, Heidegger comments that to most people the fact that "all being is in Being" may sound trivial, irrelevant; it may even be offensive to the contemporary person. "And yet, just this fact that being is gathered together in Being, that in the appearance of Being being appears, that astonished the Greeks and first astonished them and them alone. Being [small "b"] in Being—that became the most astonishing thing for the Greeks" (49).

Now, do you know, Jason, what Heidegger means by the concept "Being"?

Jason: He seems to have connected the beings of this world to the concept of Being and the concept "Being" to *Logos,* but I am not sure what all of this means. Besides, I still do not understand what Heidegger means by philosophy, and when was philosophy born if it still did not exist at the time of Heraclitus and Parmenides.

Diotima: Heidegger insightfully points out that Heraclitus and Parmenides belong to the "greater" thinkers in that they were in touch with the Being of beings.

Jason: In what sense were they greater?

Diotima: Heidegger writes, "Heraclitus and Parmenides were 'greater' in the sense that they were still in harmony with the *Logos,* that is, with the 'One (is) all'" (53). This harmony was disrupted and the relationship with the *Logos* severed by the Sophists. Socrates and Plato gave birth to *philosophia,* philosophy, because they were the first to re-establish the harmony with the "One (is) all." They and Aristotle "became those who *strove* for the *sophon* and who through their own striving awakened and kept alive among others the yearning for the *sophon.* The loving the *sophon,* that already mentioned harmony with the *sophon,* the *harmonia,* thus became an *orexis* [yearning], a *striving* for the *sophon*" (51). Ever since then the effort to re-establish harmony with the *sophon* continues.

Jason: Why?

Diotima: Heidegger says: "Because the loving is no longer an original harmony with the *sophon* but is a particular striving *towards* the *sophon,* the loving of the *sophon* becomes '*philosophia.*' This striving is determined by Eros" (51). Given the departure of *Dasein* from its being in Being caused by the forgetfulness of Being, the central question of philosophy becomes the question of Being. "What is being, in so far as it is?" This leads Heidegger to conclude, "Only now does thinking become '*philosophy*'" (53).

Jason: How did Socrates, Plato and Aristotle succeed in re-establishing that harmony? Perhaps therein lies the clue for our achieving the same end?

Diotima: They did this through philosophical *logos,* a *discourse,* that is a dialogue and dialectic. This discourse, Heidegger explains, is a *dialogue* because it is a "conversation" among the thinkers who, then and subsequently throughout history, are seeking to recover the original harmony between the Being and beings by uncovering the *correspondence* between "the first principles and causes that constitute the Being of being" (57). And because this *discourse* is a kind of "tuning" which through gradual "attunement" to Being leads to the initial harmony, it is *dialectic*. Since this is what philosophy does, *philosophy is a dialogue and dialectic* that eventually leads to the *unconcealment* of Being—unconcealment, *aletheia,* being the Greek word for truth. This is what Socrates, Plato and Aristotle did, each in his own way, to re-establish harmony with the *sophon,* and this is exactly what we are getting ready to undertake.

Lest it elude our notice, it is important to underscore what Heidegger just pointed out, namely, that philosophy is a two-fold discourse: one with other thinkers, the other, with the Being of being. Heidegger explicitly states philosophy "consists in our corresponding to [answering to] that towards which philosophy is on the way. And that is—the Being of being" (71). This requires of us to be "in conversation with that to which the tradition of philosophy delivers us, that is, liberates us . . . the Being of being" (71). It is through one's *conversation with the Being* that the "unfolding" of Being occurs. For this reason, we must first make an effort to establish this correspondence. "For . . . although we do remain always and everywhere in correspondence to the Being of being, we, nevertheless, rarely pay attention to the appeal of Being. The correspondence to the Being of being does, to be sure, always remain our abode. But only at times does it become an unfolding attitude specifically adopted by us" (75). In light of this understanding Heidegger sums up his view of philosophy as follows: "Philosophy is the correspondence to the Being of being, but not until, and only when, the correspondence to the Being of being is actually fulfilled and thereby unfolds itself and expands this unfoldment" (75). It is equally significant that the correspondence and subsequent unfolding can occur in different ways. It depends on "how the appeal of Being speaks," whether "it is heard or not heard," and whether "what is heard is said or *is* kept silent" (75). Given the possible responses on our part, Heidegger contends, "*Philosophia* is the expressly accomplished correspondence which speaks in so far as it considers the appeal of the Being of being. The correspondence listens to the voice of the appeal. What appeals to us as the voice of Being evokes correspondence. 'Correspondence' then means: being de-termined, *être disposé* by that which comes from the Being of being" (75-76). This is to say, our being is de-termined or shaped by what the *sophon* reveals, by responding in agreement with the *logos,* or the *speaking* of Being.

Jason: Is there any evidence of such a discourse, particularly of "listening to the voice of Logos" and of "corresponding to it" in the writings of Socrates and Plato?

Diotima: Yes, there is ample evidence of it in the both senses Heidegger adduces. However, as you may already know, Socrates left no writings. What we know of him, we know through the writings of his contemporaries, most notably through Plato's Dialogues. And since Plato made Socrates the major speaker in nearly all of his Dialogues, we have reason to believe that the views Socrates propounds are equally those of Plato. Otherwise, we would have nothing of Plato. Insofar as the various Dialogues are a "conversation" among thinkers seeking to arrive at a correspondence, a harmonious view on the topic under discussion, they give evidence of philosophy as a *dialogue and dialectic* in the first sense. The evidence in the second sense we find in Plato's *Symposium* where Socrates seeks correspondence in a discourse with the Being of his being. Before making his appearance at the house of Agathon where the philosophers were gathering to give speeches in praise of Love, Plato tells us that Socrates on the way to the party with his companions, lags behind only to withdraw to a neighbor's portico, as he was often want to do, where he gets lost in contemplation. At such times he did not want to be disturbed. "You'd much better leave him to himself. It's quite a habit of his, you know; off he goes and there he stands, no matter where it is" (*Symp.* 174b 175 o). In those moments, we are told, he was communing with the voice within and imbibing divine wisdom, for "there is a divinity in human propagation, an immortal something in the midst of man's mortality which is incompatible with any kind of discord" (206c). We have reason to believe that it is "this something within us," the Being of our being, that calls us to correspondence and, when we heed its voice, there is established the *harmonia* between us and the first principles.

It is worth noting that already Plato makes the point of the "forgetfulness of Being" so central to Heidegger's thought. For Agathon, the tragedian (the fifth speaker at the gathering), begins his speech by drawing everyone's attention to the fact that speakers up to this point in their eulogies on love "have forgotten to extol the god himself, and have thrown no light at all upon the nature of our divine benefactor. Yet surely, if we are to praise anyone, no matter whom, no matter how, there is only one way to go about it, and that is to indicate the nature of him whose praises we are to sing, and of the blessings he is the author of " (194e-195a). As you can see, Jason, in Plato's *Symposium* we find not only a demonstration of both forms of philosophical discourse of which Heidegger speaks, but also an explicit reference to the first principles. This lends further validity to Heidegger's elucidation of the nature of philosophy.

Manifestly, for Heidegger human existence is inextricably bound with the Being of our being and receives its meaning from it. In view of the fact that one who lives authentically becomes conscious of the presence of Being

(*Sein*) within oneself and hears its appeal, Heidegger states that the name *Dasein*, "there-being" applies to both, the Being and the human person. As we have seen earlier, "Man is man only on the basis of *Dasein* in him" (*KPM*, 237). In *Being and Time* Heidegger undertakes to uncover the ground of our being, to recover the nature of an authentic relationship between *Dasein* and *Logos* and, by exposing the roots of inauthentic living, he reveals the nature of the contemporary crisis with the hope of averting the trend.

Jason: I wish I were able to see all this in more concrete terms.

Diotima: You will, Jason, when we undertake the study of reality on our own. At that time we shall make use of diagrams to help us see things as on a map. Some of what Heidegger says should become intelligible in conjunction with our study of reality, and some of it in the course of our discussion of the perennial questions of philosophy. When we arrive at our understanding, we will be in a better position to figure out what Heidegger must have meant by what he said. At that point also, I have reason to believe, you will muster enough courage to read Heidegger's books on your own. This is why I have been telling you that a personal quest is indispensable to *real* understanding of the answer.

At the next session, my partner, we shall sharpen our focus on the specifics of the journey, otherwise we might lose time meandering.

Jason: That's great! We have covered so much that at this point I am not completely clear about the direction we're to take. Since you've put me in charge of staying on track, sharpening our focus will be very helpful.

Diotima: Yes, we'll do that, Jason, for your sake and mine. A guide, too, must have a clear vision of where he or she is leading and must figure out the best way to get to the staked out destination.

Jason: There is one more question I have. Actually, it's a request.

Diotima: Speak freely, my friend.

Jason: The things I have been learning here I've been discussing with my friends. Some have shown a great deal of interest in these matters. One in particular has asked if you would have any objections to her joining us. Is it alright if she comes along to our next session?

Diotima: Oh, by all means! Feel free to invite others as well, if they are truly interested. They will only enhance the journey of our quest. Apparently you have done an outstanding job in sharing your information with them to have evoked such a response on their part. Just refresh with them our discussion on logic.

Jason. I will. Thanks.

* * * * * * * * * * * * *

Diotima at the next session: Welcome to all of you! What a pleasant surprise! We have two guests instead of one. And who are they, Jason?

Jason: This is my friend, Sophie, who was eager to join us. And this is Thomas, my buddy, who usually gives me a hard time, especially when we're discussing ideas that are beyond the scope of science. Since I often find myself ill prepared to counter his arguments, I encouraged him to join us.

Sophie: I don't think Tom is trying to be difficult. I believe he's just looking at things from a different standpoint, but this is enough to confuse us.

Diotima: A warm welcome to both of you. What a fine addition to our discussions! No doubt, Sophie, as your name suggests, you bring wisdom. And you, Thomas, with your salient mind bring challenge, an invaluable component of philosophical dialectic.

Thomas: I'm not so sure that I have a salient mind, but I do tend to see everything from the scientific point of view. For this reason I'm skeptical about things that fall outside the pale of science. I am serious, nonetheless, about truth, especially about the truth regarding the perennial questions of philosophy. Like Jason and Sophie, and the rest of humanity, I, too, want to live a good life and be happy.

Diotima: You are truly a gift to us, Thomas. I trust you will always feel free not only to raise questions, to voice your objections, or to register your reservations, but also to offer your insights. You play a crucial role in our quest for truth. This holds true for you as well, Sophie and Jason. We all must feel at ease with each other, to speak honestly and to challenge each other's opinions, if we are to arrive at truth. To this end, there are two points we must keep in mind. First of all, we must approach the study with an open mind that the light of truth may enter in, and once truth dawns, we must be willing to relinquish our opinion, even if it is contrary to our liking. Sometimes we have to wrestle with it for a while, because it is not enough that the mind apprehend the truth—that's only the first step to it—the will must embrace it. Often, that's the rub, for we are proud creatures and prefer to hold on to our own views. The second point is, we must be open to the challenges of others and not take another's objections personally. It is not the person but the opinion that will be challenged. And our opinion will be challenged for the sake of being examined in order that truth may surface in all its splendor and beauty.

Thomas: Are you saying that we are free to challenge your views, too?

Diotima: Absolutely! This is indispensable to your arriving at clarity and convictions.

Jason: It is obvious to me that in the absence of these attitudes, there would be no point in undertaking our dialectic.

Diotima: Very well then. Are we ready now to map the course for our journey? I am certainly glad you two have joined us in time to be at the drawing board. A good, crisp start and a clear vision of what one is about are always very helpful, especially when one sets out on a trip like ours proposes to be.

V. SHARPENING THE FOCUS

Diotima: First of all we have to be clear about our *goal*, that is, the destination of our dialectic.

Jason: By now you all know that my goal is *truth with respect to the perennial questions of philosophy.*

Sophie: I am looking for *wisdom* and a better understanding of *why* it is important that *everyone should strive for it.*

Thomas: Lest I disappoint you, my goal is only *to understand reality* from the standpoint of philosophy in order to complement my empirical understanding of it.

Diotima: All genuine goals of philosophy! While your goals differ, they are in fact closely bound up with each other. The answers to the perennial questions presuppose an understanding of reality, for we are a part of it. So Tom's goal must necessarily be addressed first. It is this understanding that will disclose the answers to the perennial questions and meet your goal, Jason. And once we know who we are, whence we came, and where we are destined to go by our nature, we will know what we ought to be doing in this world. Since choices that are in keeping with our human nature are said to be wise, Sophie's goal will come to the foreground. And because it belongs to the domain of wisdom to pave our way throughout life and to carry us aloft to truth, when that wondrous vision bursts forth upon us, if we act wisely, we shall attain not only the light of truth regarding excellence of our being, our destiny and genuine happiness, but will also know why everyone should strive for it.

Does each of you see your own goal fully incorporated into the fabric of the whole, as also the order we need to follow?

Sophie: Yes, I see that our goals do fit together and that this order is preferable.

Thomas: It does make sense to me, too. I am glad also that I don't have to wait long to have my goal met.

Jason: I see the rationale for the order in pursuing our goals likewise so let's get started on the journey of our quest.

Diotima: What approach do you think will serve us best?

Sophie: Subjective, I suppose, since we are the subjects who are going to engage in this quest.

Thomas: Perhaps we should call it subjective/relative since at this point we seem to feel strongly about our own opinions which do not coincide.

Jason: Yes. I think Tom is right. I hope, however, that through logic we can raise our understanding of subjective perceptions and personal experiences to the level of objective knowledge.

Diotima: That is the function of logic. And if I read you correctly, you are prepared to draw upon every source of knowledge that is accessible to us human beings.

Sophie: Given that there are different sources of knowledge and each yields something different, wouldn't we be depriving ourselves of something if we eliminate any given source? That, I suspect, could prove to be an obstacle to gaining access to the whole truth. Don't you think?

Thomas: I'm willing to accept only what can be demonstrated, or proven true in a rational way.

Jason: I take it, Tom you would accept logical or mathematical demonstration, as also a possible human experience to be an adequate proof. Am I right?

Thomas: Yes. I see these as belonging to the scope of reliable human knowledge.

Diotima: Since human knowledge has its origin in sense perception and feelings of personal experience, which we all possess, and we will try to follow the normal track of human development, it looks as if we have a starting point that is acceptable to everyone. It is important that we all agree on the starting point. Otherwise our dialectic would have to end right here. Incidentally, did you brush up on logic?

Sophie: We did, but I must confess that logic is not my forte. I seem to hear things better when I listen with the heart.

Diotima: You must be an intuitive person, Sophie. Most women are. Philosophers would call you an *intuitionist*. Thomas, do you know how you would be identified?

Thomas: Yes, as an *empiricist*.

Diotima: And you, Jason?

Jason: Since I seek to be guided by reason, I suppose I would be regarded as a *rationalist*.

Diotima: What an ideal combination!

Sophie: I'm not sure if I fully understand what all of these terms mean, but if my understanding is close, this combination sounds complementary and very interesting!

Diotima: We will clarify these terms in conjunction with our analysis of reality. And now that we know what our *goal* is and how we will *approach* it, we need to determine our *starting point* and to plan the *direction* our study needs to take.

In an attempt to give a fresh start to philosophy in his day, Edmund Husserl, "the father of phenomenology" began his quest with the cry: "Back to the things themselves." We begin with the cry: "Back to the Basics." To be specific about our undertaking in this area let us keep in mind that this is going to be our "Quest for the Truth of Reality." As we proceed to explore the geography of what-is, we will be drafting a map of it to help us see more clearly where we are, whence we come and, thereby, who we are; also, where we are impelled by our nature to go, and what is the best way to get there. Reaching the ultimate Truth regarding these questions will have us traverse the world of knowledge and make use of different methods available for the attainment of knowledge. Before addressing your question, Jason, and Sophie's, we shall conclude this discourse with the *summary* of insights we gain along the way, and a *synthesis* of the specifics pertinent to the process of attainting knowledge. The first part of our quest, then, being an ascent to Truth, will terminate in a "System of Thought" and "An Epistemological Atlas," as we shall call our succinct synthesis of knowledge. This knowledge, in turn, will serve as the basis for the remaining areas of our quest.

With this explanation, my friends, comes a question: Seeing that this is only the beginning and that it will take several other rounds of discourse to get to the answers you are seeking, do you still have the courage to pursue your goals?

Jason: The undertaking does seem daunting, but my restless spirit will know no peace until I've found the answers to those perennial questions of philosophy. I am resolved to move on. Are you with us, Sophie and Tom?

Sophie: By all means! I have only one life to live. I don't want to waste it, or to find out at death that I have missed the purpose for which I was born. I want to make my life truly worth living. Since the attainment of this goal presupposes truth, I am determined to find it.

Thomas: Life itself challenges us to reach out for something. It seems to beckon us to ever-new horizons. I see our search as a part of human adventure and I'm ready for it.

Diotima: Marvelous! We shall launch out into the deep at our next session.

NOTES

1. Reference here is made to the thinkers introduced in the Introduction: Alex Mauron, a nuclear biologist, John Kantwell Kiley, a psychiatrist and philosopher, David R. Loy, a philosopher and theologian, Theodore Roszak, a historian and John Paul II, the Philosopher-Pope. All these thinkers issue the same clarion call for a "fresh start."

2. *The Collected Dialogues of Plato,* ed. Edith Hamilton and Huntington Cairns, (New York: Pantheon Books, 1966), *Theaetetus*, 155d, Translated by F.M. Cornford. Future references to this volume: name of the Dialogue and number.

3. John Powell, S.J., *Fully Human Fully Alive* (Allen, Texas: Tabor Publishing, 1976), p. 4.

4. Arland Ussher writes, "In the whole production of Heidegger you will rarely find an image, a homely phrase, a concrete term; and the abstract terms are limited to a few dozen (almost all interchangeable and often bewilderingly interchanged), recurring within sickening monotony like wooden horses in a merry-go-round. If the Absolute could speak, one feels, this might well be its language. Over the entire glacial surface of Heidegger's work, there is no relief for the eye, no handrail, no foothold; this might be the philosophical equivalent of Scott's Last Post in the Antarctic. Only a collusc—or a professor—could project himself through these wastes, or nourish on such aliment . . . actual flavor of Nothingness!" Arland Ussher, *Journey Through Dread* (New York: Bilbo, Tannen Booksellers and Publishers, 1955), pp. 64-65.

5. Ian Ramsey, *Models and Mystery* (London: Oxford University Press, 1964), p. 50.

6. Max Black, *Models and Metaphors: Studies in Language and Philosophy* (Ithaca, New York: Cornell University Press, 1962), pp. 236-7.

7. Since Socrates never wrote a word and Plato, to show his indebtedness to him, made Socrates in his Dialogues the spokesperson for his own ideas, we have no way of knowing whether the ideas Plato puts on the lips of Socrates are his own or those of his master. Regardless, knowing the truth is far more important than knowing who said what. To this we can expect everyone will agree.

8. Socrates provides here the full explanation of the art he is practicing. He says: "My art of midwifery is in general like theirs; the only difference is that my patients are men, not women, and my concern is not with the body but with the soul that is in travail of birth. And the highest point of my art is the power to prove by every test whether the offspring of a young man's thought is a false phantom or instinct with life and truth.... The many admirable truths they bring to birth have been discovered by themselves from within. But the delivery is heaven's work and mine" (*Theaetetus*, 150 b-d).

9. This rule in the modern interpretation is seen as not needed, because the syllogism that violates this rule violates also the rule of distribution. For us who are just being introduced to logic, it may be helpful to incorporate it.

10. Max Black, op. cit., p. 242. The quote within Black's quote is taken from Kurt Lewin's *Field Theory in Science* (New York, 1951), p. 3.

11. Richard D. Goff, George H. Cassar, Anthony Esler, James P. Holoka and James C. Walts, *A Survey of Western Civilization*, Volume One (St. Paul, MN: West Publishing Company, 1987), p. 24. Henceforth: Goff and page.

12. Neal M. Cross, Robert C. Lamm, and Rudy H. Turk, *The Search for Personal Freedom*, Volume I, Fourth Edition (Dubuque, Iowa: Wm. C. Brown Company Publishers, 1972), p. 59. Henceforth: Cross and page.

13. Joseph Owens, C.Ss.R., *A History of Ancient Western Philosophy* (New York: Appleton, Century, Crofts, Inc., 1959) pp. 112-127. Henceforth: Owens and page.

14. Albert E. Avey, *Handbook in the History of Philosophy*, Second Edition (Barnes and Noble, Inc., 1961) p. 14. Henceforth: Avey and page.

15. Owens, p. 61, footnote 9.

16. *The Cambridge Dictionary of Philosophy*, Second Edition, Robert Audi, General Editor (Cambridge University Press, 1999), pp. 646-47. Henceforth: CDP and page.

17. Sources disagree on the dates, but the studies of Owens provide circumstantial evidence in support of the dates furnished here.

18. CDP, p. 217. Here we note a link between Marx's *historical materialism* and the views of Democritus on the emergence of culture.

19. *Encyclopedia of Ethics*, Second Edition, Volume I, Lawrence C. Becker & Charlotte B. Becker, Editors (New York: Routledge Publishers, 2201), p. 389. Henceforth: EE and page.

20. Isaac Newton's full statement reads: "If I see farther than other men, it is because I stand on the shoulders of giants." And Bernard of Chartres put it as follows, "We are dwarfs but standing on the shoulders of giants."

21. Will Durant, *The Story of Philosophy* (New York: Washington Square Press, Inc., 1962), pp. 94-95.

22. Plotinus is a mystic who developed his own system of thought that places him in the category of Parmenides and Plato.

23. Robert C. Solomon and Kathleen M. Higgins, *A Short History of Philosophy* (New York: Oxford University Press, 1996), pp. 71-73.

24. *The Encyclopedia of Philosophy*, Vol. 3 (Crowell Collier and MacMillan, Inc. 1967), p. 1.

25. The Harvard Classics Edited by Charles W. Eliot, LL.D., "The Golden Sayings of Epictetus" Trans. Hastings Crossley (New York: P.F. Collier & Son Corporation, 1968), p. 116. "The Golden Sayings of Epictetus," 115-185, "Fragments,"183-185.

26. The A.D. was seldom used. When the B.C. did not appear with the date, it was understood that the event under discussion took place in the A.D. period of history.

27. Neal M. Cross and Leslie Dae Lindau, *The Search for Personal Freedom*, Vol. I, Second Edition (Dubuque, Iowa: Wm. C. Brown Company Publishers, 1961), p. 94.

28. *The Middle Ages*. Just the Facts Learning Series. (Thousand Oaks, California: Full Circle Entertainments, Inc., 2001).

29. The word *sapiens* comes from Latin *sapientia,* which translates as "wisdom, good sense, discernment, prudence," especially "proficiency in philosophy, in science, or in any department of knowledge." *Cassell's Latin Dictionary* by D. P. Simpson, M.A. (New York: Macmillan Publishing Company, 1968), p. 534.

30. Neal M. Cross., Robert C. Lamm, and Rudy H. Turk, *The Search for Personal Freedom,* Volume 2, Fourth Edition (Wm. C. Brown Publishers, 1974), p. 4. Henceforth: Cross, V2 and page.

31. Andrew Newberg, M.D., Eugene D'Aquili, M.D., Ph.D., and Vince Rause, *Why God Won't Go Away* (New York: The Ballantine Publishing Group, 2001), p. 169.

32. This observation is offered by Peter Augustine Lawler in his book *Postmodernism Rightly Understood* with the subtitle *Return to Realism in American Thought.* (Rowman & Littlefield Publishers, Inc., 1999).

33. Gustav A. Wetter, *Dialectical Materialism* (New York: Praeger1958); *Soviet Ideology Today* (London: Heinemann, 1966). Cf. Andrew C. Varga, *On Being Human: Principles of Ethics* (New York: Paulist Press, 1978), p. 71. Future reference: Varga and page.

34. F.V. Konstantinov et al., *The Fundamentals of Marxist-Leninist Philosophy* (Moscow: Progress Publishers, 1974), p. 336. Cf. Andrew C. Varga, *On Being Human: Principles of Ethics,* op. cit., p. 72.

35. John Stuart Mill, *Utilitarianism.* Edited with an Introduction, George Sher (Indianapolis: Hackett Publishing Company, 1979), p. 7.

36. Jean-Paul Sartre, *The Words.* Translated from French by Bernard Frechtman (New York: George Braziller, Inc. 1964. First Vintage Books Edition, 1981), p. 23. Henceforth: Words.

37. Speaking of his grandfather when he was little, Sartre recalls: "My mere presence would fill him to overflowing. He was the God of Love with the beard of the Father and the Sacred Heart of the Son. There was a laying on of hands, and I could feel the warmth of his palm on my skull. He would call me his 'tiny little one' in a voice quavering with tenderness. His cold eyes would dim with tears. . . . He worshipped me, that was manifest" (p. 23).

38. Jean Paul Sartre, "Existentialism is a Humanism" (pp. 287-311) in *Existentialism from Dostoevsky to Sartre.* Edited, with an introduction and prefaces, and new translations by Walter Kaufmann. Meridian Books (New York: The World Publishing Company, 1956), p. 302. Henceforth: EH. Further references to this essay will be given only page numbers, unless they follow some other cited source. In that case, EH and page.

39. Jean Paul Sartre, *Being and Nothingness: An Essay of Phenomenological Ontology.* (1943) Translated by Hazel Barnes (New York: Citadel Press, 1964), pp. 11ff. Henceforth: B&N.

40. Whether to spurn the "bourgeois values and conventions" of society, or to prove their philosophy of "absolute, unqualified freedom," they never went through the ceremony of marriage. And when that "marriageless marriage" turned out to be only a "contingent love" relationship, neither did they seek a divorce. Lescoe, p. 272.

41. Under the guise of fiction, Simone de Beauvoir describes some of those affairs in *She Came to Stay* (1943), *The Mandarines* (1954), and *Force of Circumstances* (1963).

42. Simone de Beauvoir, *Force of Circumstance,* trans. Richard Howard (New York: G. Putnam's Sons, 1965), p. 658.

43. Vincent Miceli offers both, an excellent summary and a penetrating assessment of Sartre's philosophy when he writes, "Sartre has rendered mankind some useful service. He analyzed sin with deep penetration. It is the bitter estrangement from God and from our fellow man. It is the great divine-human schism. He has exploded the secularized myths that guarantee man happiness in and through temporal achievements. No present, no future earthly condition of man will ever make life worth living. He has stressed, once again, in a stark manner, man's personal responsibility for making his own being and world. He has focused the mind and heart of man on his great power of freedom with all its dangerous possibilities. He has ruthlessly unmasked the poses men take to escape hard decisions. He has re-created the confrontation between freedom and grace. He has forced the collectivized atheism of positivism and Marxism to come out from behind their protective wall of science and politics in order to prove to the individual that absurd existence is not worth living. He has put their panaceas to a severe test.

But in the last analysis, Sartre's philosophy leads logically and directly to despair and suicide. His doctrine of salvation leads man to the abyss of social atomism. His first and final word on life, liberty and love is that they just happen and are always absurd, contradictory and doomed to frustration. His world of atheism is a kingdom of nothingness plunged into intellectual darkness, convulsed with spiritual hate and peopled by inhabitants who curse God and destroy each other in their vain attempt to seize His vacant throne." Vincent Miceli, S.J. *The Gods of Atheism,* (New Rochelle: Arlington House1971), pp. 245-46.

44. The *epoché* was a two-step intellectual act. The first act consisted of bracketing the phenomenon, the external dimension of an object along with what one had learned of it through any discipline. The second act focused on the *essence* of an object (the Greek *eidos*), that is, the very "being" of an object as it is intuitively given to consciousness. Here, just as in mathematics, for instance, we have the intuitive awareness of the "number concept" and the "symbolic intention" of it.

45. Martin Heidegger, *Being and Time.* Translated by John Macquarrie & Edward Robinson (New York: Harper & Row, Publishers, 1962), p. 2. Henceforth: B&T.

46. Martin Heidegger, *Kant and the Problem of Metaphysics.* Translated by James S. Churchill (Bloomington: Indiana University Press, 1968), p. 237. Henceforth: KPM.

47. Martin Heidegger, "The Way Back into the Ground of Metaphysics." *Existentialism from Dostoevsky to Sartre* Edited with an introduction, prefaces, and new translations by Walter Kaufmann. Meridian Books (New York: The World Publishing Company, 1956), p. 213. Henceforth: WBGM.

48. Since this statement of Heidegger is already his attempt to explain what he said in *Being and Time*, it is not difficult to imagine what that language is like. Both parties complain: Heidegger complains that he is being misunderstood, and scholars complain about the meaning of his newly coined terms because they don't know what he means. Some translators say that to do justice to Heidegger's thought, his German has to be translated first into standard German and only then translated into other languages.

49. Martin Heidegger *What Is Philosophy?* Translated with an Introduction by William Klubach and Jean T. Wilde (New Haven, CT: College and University Press, 1956), p. 23. Henceforth: WIP.

CHAPTER TWO

BACK TO THE BASICS

"Quest for the Truth of Reality"

I. PRELUDE TO THE DIALECTIC

Diotima: Some preliminary remarks are in order here to get us off to a good start. First of all, thus far we have said nothing about how a philosophical system of thought should begin. Neither did we mention the three basic principles of thought, the rock bottom principles of all philosophical discourse upon which we will need to rely along the way. These are indispensable to keep us on track. Let us begin, however, by first defining the word "principle" to make sure we understand precisely what philosophers have in mind when they discuss principles.

A. Meaning of "Principle" in Philosophy

According to the *Webster's New World College Dictionary* (1999) there are six definitions of the word "principle." Some of these definitions come with several nuances, because the word "principle" has many meanings. It has a different meaning, moreover, in the field of medicine, in science, in morality, in business, and so on. Every lexicon proper to a different discipline carries its own shades of meanings. Since our study is in the area of philosophy, it seems only logical that we consult the dictionary of philosophy.

The Dictionary of Philosophy tells us that the word *principle* comes from Latin *principle,* from *principium,* which means a "beginning." Given this meaning, a principle is a "fundamental cause or universal truth; that which is inherent in anything. According to Aristotle, the primary source of all being, actuality and knowledge."[1] In other words, a principle is "that upon which" a system of thought is built, and "that which" renders reality intelligible.

Sophie: If the primary principle is both "the fundamental cause" of all that is and "the universal truth," then when we reach the end of the dialectic, namely truth, we should find ourselves at the beginning and understand everything.

Thomas: You mean our discourse will make a full circle? That's clever!

Diotima: Yes, that is the plan. Notice, moreover, that according to this definition, the *first principle* as "the fundamental cause and universal truth" is "inherent" in all things. It is the *primary source* of their being. This implies that what we are looking for is with us already, but it is somehow concealed from our sight.

Jason: So the purpose of the dialectic is to let it come to light?

Diotima: Exactly. Just remember: Reality is what it is. It has a being and identity of its own. Reality does not change. This is why we can have knowledge of it. If reality kept on changing, neither language nor truth would be possible—this Plato noted already four centuries B.C.—for nothing would be retaining its identity from one day to another. The change, therefore, has to occur within us.

Thomas: How?

Diotima: By sharpening our minds and seeing it more accurately. The more profoundly we think, the more accurately we shall come to understand *what-is* as *it is*.

Jason: Does it also mean that the first principle by disclosing the truth of reality will provide answers to the perennial questions of philosophy?

Diotima: That is what the definition of the word "principle" designates, but whether such is the case, depends upon the principles that form its foundation, the starting principles. This brings us to the discussion of the first point we have set out to clarify, namely, a good beginning for a system of thought in philosophy.

B. First Principles of Philosophy

Diotima: There are two preferred beginnings. Philosophers call these beginnings "first principles" precisely because they are used as the starting point of a system of thought. By definition, the first principles are those *axioms* or *assumptions* from which a philosophy begins. These principles must be solid and indisputable, but they do not have to be the principles one first believed.

Please note, we have said *axioms* or *assumptions*. That means that there are two ways a philosophy can begin. A philosophy that begins with an *axiom* is one that begins with a self-evident proposition. And by *self-evident* proposition is meant a statement that is obvious, so fully intelligible that it requires no proof or argument to support it. Every normal rational adult would understand and agree with it. The purpose of the system of thought in this case consists of rendering all of reality equally intelligible in terms of this principle, or principles, as the case may be.

A philosophy that begins with an *assumption* begins with an hypothesis or a *supposition* that something is true. The whole system of thought then consists of proving or demonstrating the truth of that hypothesis and in the process of explaining reality itself.

Thomas: This is also the procedure employed by science. When one's hypothesis is shown to be tenable, it is accepted as a theory.

Jason: But isn't it true that some scientific theories that were once accepted as true representations of reality had to be later modified? Besides, scientific theories are usually of concrete things and when we are looking for wisdom or answers to the perennial questions of philosophy, we're looking for more than just knowledge of the empirical reality. Taking into account that our quest is for the truth of all that is, this approach would be inadequate for us. Am I not right?

Thomas: What do you mean? Can you give me an example of it, Jason?

Jason: Years back scientists, notably, geophysicists, astrophysicists and cosmogonists, believed that the beginning of the universe occurred about five billion years ago. All the findings of these disciplines, supposedly derived independently of each other, seemed to confirm that conclusion. Now we are told that in light of some new insights, the origin of the universe has to be set at about fifteen billion years. And this, too, is only an inference, an educated guess. Is it not?

Thomas: That's true, but look at the span of time involved in such a theory. Besides, when we look at the origin of the universe, we are speaking of time before anything existed. Doesn't it stagger your mind when you think of it! Theories of the specific phenomena, such as light, heat, or sound are more accurate because they are with us to be studied. What occurred so long ago is naturally more difficult to determine.

Sophie: That's true, Tom, but going back to philosophy, what if one did not agree with the assumption someone is proposing?

Diotima: Then that would be the end of the dialogue. You see, one has to have a starting point that is acceptable to the parties involved, or at least one must be willing to give one's partner in dialogue the benefit of the doubt. In such a case, one would have to examine carefully the evidence being advanced in support of the assumption. The demonstrations and/or arguments would have to be scrutinized to make sure that they are valid and that the conclusions are sound.

Thomas: Your discourse on the first principles began by saying that there are two "preferred" beginnings. Can a philosophy begin in any other way?

Diotima: Yes, it can begin with a question about anything, but the truth in all its clarity will not dawn until discourse makes a full circle. Starting anywhere in the middle will make it that much more difficult to make a full circle and return to the starting point. This is because at each step of the way, every new answer evokes a number of new questions in one's mind. These questions can take one in different directions and get one off the track in pursuing the answer to the original question. This is inevitable because as you will eventually come to see everything is entwined, nothing exists in isolation. Beginning at the beginning, therefore, makes one's inquiry easier.

In any event, by the exchange of your ideas I am led to conclude that you see the self-evident principles as the more reliable approach.

Jason: By far!

Thomas: Yes, I see the point you're making.

Diotima: Given our consensus, let me then propose the four self-evident principles upon which we shall build our system of thought. I will list them first, and then we shall examine each of them carefully to see if these principles are fully intelligible to all of us.

The self-evident principles are:
1. Nothing comes from nothing.
2. No one can give what one does not have.
3. An intellectual activity presupposes an intelligent being.
4. The intelligence of a being is always at least on par with its activities.

Jason: Does the first principle mean that nothing can come from absolute nothingness?

Thomas: Yes. I believe this principle in science is comparable to: There are no causeless phenomena. Everything that exists presupposes a cause.

Diotima: What about you, Sophie? Is this principle self-evident to you?

Sophie: Yes, without any reservations.

Diotima: How about the second principle? "No one can give what one does not have."

Thomas: Can you give us an example?

Diotima: Suppose I say to you: Thomas, give me a hundred dollar bill. Can you give it to me?

Thomas: No. I don't have it, at least not with me.

Diotima: Can you give us a brief explanation of Einstein's General Theory of Relativity, Sophie?

Sophie: Sorry, I can't. I have never studied it or read about it.

Thomas: I can give it to you.

Diotima: Thank you, Thomas. Please keep this experience in mind for future reference. As to your knowledge of this theory, you will have a chance to share it with us later. And now let me make my final request. Describe to us the experience of Buddhist state of nirvana, Jason.

Jason: Can't do it. I know very little about Buddhist spirituality and nothing from experience about the state of nirvana to be able to describe it.

Diotima: How about you Thomas or Sophie?

Thomas and Sophie: I can't. Neither can I.

Diotima: Do you think that a Buddhist guru would be able to provide us with a reliable description of it?

Sophie: Definitely. There are, however, books written about it so we can learn something about it from them. That understanding, I suspect, would be somewhat obscure. For it would be like any theory we study, a second-hand knowledge to us. It would lack the clarity of firsthand experience that a guru has.

Diotima: Well said, Sophie. So you have accepted, I see, our second principle as self-evident. Please note that the principle holds true on three different levels. On the *physical level* of $100 bill, as in the case of Thomas, on the *intellectual level* of Einstein's General Theory of Relativity, as Sophie's example demonstrated it, and on the *spiritual level* regarding Jason's experience of nirvana.

In this discussion, you brought out two other points worth noting: one, that none of us knows everything, but that we can learn things from others, from those who know; and two, that there is a difference in the quality of knowledge we attain directly, through personal experience, and the knowledge we acquire from other sources, whether through others' theories or descriptions, be they oral and written.

Jason: It is likewise true that we can get initial understanding of things by learning them first from others, and subsequently we can deepen that knowledge by pursuing the matter on our own until it becomes fully intelligible to us.

Thomas: Isn't this how human knowledge begins in every person's life? None of us comes into this world with a ready supply of it. Someone has said that human mind to begin with is a *tabula rasa,* a clear slate as it were, upon which we inscribe the things we learn.

Sophie: It was John Locke, I believe, who gave us this analogy.

Diotima: Now that we have no doubt about the intelligibility of the second principle (One cannot give what one does not have), what about the third one on our list? "An intellectual activity presupposes an intelligent being."

Jason: The third and the fourth principles seem to be related to intelligence and both can be readily affirmed. Let me explain how I understand them by means of an example. Suppose one afternoon after a windy morning I walk out the door and find on the ground a paper with a blueprint of some building. I instantly know it was produced by an intelligent human being, and not by a dog, a deer, or an ape. That's my example of the third principle. Furthermore, I also know that the blueprint was not produced by a first-grader, but by an accomplished architect. The production reveals the intelligence of the producer. The first-grader, even though s/he might be very intelligent and some day produce works of even greater sophistication, would hardly be able to produce a blueprint of a building at that early age. The same would apply to any work of art, a composition in music, a system of thought in philosophy, a scientific theory, or anything else for that matter. The production always reveals something about the intelligence of the producer. So the fourth principle: "The intelligence of a being is always at least on par with its activities" is also self-evident and it complements the third principle. Does anyone of you have any misgivings about my explanation or about the principles themselves?

Sophie: None! That's good, Jason. I take it though this does not mean that the master, whatever the area of his or her creativity, could not produce some other works that are superior to his or her previous achievements. Does it?

Thomas: Right, Sophie. That is why the principle incorporates the words "at least." However, a particular piece of work is usually judged to be somebody's masterpiece only at the end of the person's career, when all the productions are taken into consideration. . . . So yes, all four principles are truly self-evident.

Diotima: As long as there is an honest agreement among us on the validity of all four principles as self-evident, these will form the foundation upon which our system of thought will be erected. And now, setting this matter temporarily aside, let us move on to our second point.

C. Three Principles of Thought

Diotima: In conjunction with studying the fundamentals of logic, we have looked at several principles against which we have to guard. They told us what *not to do.* What we have missed but need to incorporate, are the three laws of thought that tell us what *we must do* to arrive at sound conclusions. Traditionally, already since the time of Parmenides in the sixth century B.C., albeit in a simpler form, these principles have been perceived as indispensable to all thought. They are what makes logical discourse possible. These principles are the laws that guard against inconsistencies in thinking and guide the reasoning process to sound conclusions. As before, we shall list them first, and then clarify them, if need be.

1. *The Principle of Non-contradiction:* Nothing can, both be and not be, at the same time, place and in the same   respect.
2. *The Principle of the Excluded Middle:* Something either is, or it is not.
3. *The Principle of Identity:* Something is what it is.

Diotima: Do you have any difficulties in understanding these principles?

Sophie: An example of each principle would be helpful, just to make sure we understand them correctly.

Diotima: Fine. Let us take Thomas as an example. According to the first principle, it is impossible for Thomas "to be" *and* "not to be" *present here*, "in the same place and at the same time." Suppose Thomas retorts: "Only my body is here. I am with my girlfriend." Is it possible that this could be the case?

Thomas: Yes, of course.

Jason: But you would have violated the first principle by making that statement?

Thomas: Prove it.

Jason: You would have violated the third condition of it, which requires that the terms be employed "in the same respect." By changing the meaning of the word *present,* there automatically ensued ambiguity, a sure sign of some inconsistency or a contradiction. The last part of the principle catches up with such errors in reasoning.

Sophie: Jason is right. By making that statement, Tom, I got confused. I knew instantly what you said was wrong, but at first I did not know how to explain why it was wrong.

Diotima: Good thinking and a good defense of the principle. For the principle stipulates not only that something cannot both "be" <u>and</u> "not be" "at the same time and in the same place," but also that it must be "in the same respect." As long as there is any inconsistency in terms, confusion sets in; and even if only a part of the principle is violated, that contradiction makes the conclusion unsound. Because a contradiction is an error in reasoning, and the principle seeks to guard against contradictions, it is aptly called the *Principle of Non-Contradiction.* You may encounter it in some books as the *Principle of Contradiction,* for that is how it was called originally. But the meaning of it was the same.

Admittedly, this example was quite simple, purposely so, for it was meant to help us understand the principle *in principle.* In philosophical discourse, however, such is not always the case, especially when discourse is about issues of a more subtle nature. This is why all of us must be alert and very sensitive to any discrepancies in thought. One contradiction is sufficient to derail the train of thought and hamper one's attainment of truth. Consequently, if you have any reservations about the meaning of a word, or anything else for that matter, please do not hesitate to ask for the clarification at once. This will prevent backtracking and save time in the long run.

Thomas: What about the second law of thought?

Diotima: Sometimes, when people feel strongly about their divergent views, but do not want to part as enemies, they opt for the middle ground, which is really a compromise. This often happens when the controversy is about God, freedom, love, and some such thing. If neither party succeeds in convincing the other of its view, let us say about God's existence, the solution comes in these or comparable words: "I believe in God, therefore, for me God exists. You do not believe in God, therefore, for you God does not exist." Such a solution is inadmissible because it violates the second principle. The truth is either that *God exists,* or that *God does not exist.* Logically, there is nothing in between. The question of what and why I, or you, believe or do not believe in God is a different matter. Because the principle excludes the middle position as logically untenable, it is appropriately called the *Principle of the Excluded Middle.*

Sophie: The third principle strikes me as a completion of the second principle.

Jason: How?

Sophie: The third principle elaborates on the second principle in that once you establish that something is or exists, the next step is to determine *what that something is,* this is to say, what its *true identity* is.

Diotima: Good reasoning, Sophie. Entities have being and identity that are unique to them. The identity of a particular entity is revealed primarily by its form and its nature, namely by the shape of the body and by what it does. A *name* assigned to it denotes who, or what, it is, hence its *identity.* For instance, there is an entity called a "fish." A fish has a being and identity of its own. The identity of a fish is revealed by its elongated bodily form with gills and fins and its unique nature. The nature of a fish is to swim and to live in water. Thus, when we hear or see the word "fish," we automatically have an image in our mind of an entity that swims and lives in water. While fish admit of classes and of different species and come in a wide variety of shapes and sizes, they all have a body that is adapted to their nature and habitat. Since fishes are grouped into classes, they have their class names such as jawless, cartilaginous and bony fishes. And because they come in different species, they also have names such as perch, salmon, monk, swordfish that are proper to their species. But the name "fish" denotes their *essential identity,* which is common to them all.

Something comparable can be said of a bird, except that the main features of a bird are its light body, feathers, wings, two legs and a bill or beak. Its nature is to fly.[2] Its form and powers are adapted to its form of life. Yet birds divide into land birds, water birds, tropical birds, birds of prey, perching birds, game birds and flightless birds. These again sub-divide even further so much so that there are about 9,000 species of birds and 30,000 subspecies.[3] In spite of these differences among them, when we hear the word "bird" we instantly have a winged creature in mind. The case in the kingdom of flora is no different. The complete classification of a single species includes in plants includes division, subdivision, class, subclass, order, family, genus, species, and variety of sub-species.[4] We can say then that just as the zoologists try to identify the distinctive features proper to each species of animals and in light of their identity seek to bestow upon them an appropriate name, so the botanists do the same with the plant life. The anthropologists (from Greek *anthropos,* man), in turn, study human nature with the same goal in mind. However, because the human race is very complex, there are several bodies of knowledge that seek to account for human identity. We will, in due time, inquire into them to learn what these disciplines have discovered about our identity. Our purpose in that venture will be to cross-examine our own findings. As for now, what we have said should be sufficient for us to understand what the *Principle of Identity* denotes when it states *something is what it is.*

Thomas: It's clear to me. I have, nonetheless, a different question. If the physicists are trying to uncover the identity of the physical fields, forces, and phenomena, the chemists of solids, liquids and gases, and the biologists of the living things that subdivide into plants, animals and human beings, what are the philosophers looking for? Into what do they inquire?

Jason: Tom, was your question meant to be a joke, or are you serious about it?

Thomas: A little of both, but what is your answer on the serious side?

Jason: Did we not say earlier that philosophers inquire first of all into *reality* in general? They want to know how all the things we have named came to be in the first place. It is in light of this understanding, then, that they inquire into *human identity.*

Sophie: They also inquire into *wisdom!* Philosophy by its very definition is *love of wisdom,* so we cannot leave *wisdom* out of the picture.

Jason: Tom, remember our personal goals? Those goals are also the goals of philosophy.

Diotima: Oh, there is more to philosophy than that. Soon you will discover that nothing falls beyond the am-bit of philosophy, but do concentrate on your personal goals. The rest will come as a bonus. . . . And now, what do you say: Are we ready to launch out into the deep?

All: Ready and eager to proceed according to the plan we have mapped out.

Diotima: Just remember that to move forward safely, as in driving, presupposes an occasional glance at what's behind and on the sides. So don't be surprised if occasionally I draw your attention to something in either direction.

II. REFLECTIONS ON REALITY

A. Personal Views of Reality

Diotima: As of now you are philosophers at work, so let us begin with your own understanding of reality. What is reality? How do you define it?

Thomas: Reality is all that I can see, feel, smell, hear and touch. It is the world in which we live, the whole cosmos. In short, it is everything that is reducible to matter or energy.

Sophie: My concept of reality includes the physical world, but it incorporates also things like love and friendships, family and relatives, freedom and virtues such as honesty and justice, also religion and morality, knowledge and values, God, angels, eternity—everything!

Jason: You may find my definition a bit abstract, but for me in a nutshell, reality is everything that exists, both visible and invisible.

Diotima: Keep these definitions in mind to see how your personal views of reality compare with the existing interpretations that find their advocates in every century.

B. Existing Interpretations of Reality

Diotima: There are three basic interpretations of reality: pluralism, dualism, and monism. *The Philosophical Dictionary* defines these as follows:

1. *Pluralism* is "the doctrine that there is not one (Monism), not two (Dualism) but many ultimate substances" (PD, 240). In other words, pluralism is the view that reality is comprised of many independent substances, none of which is reducible to any other. This view is based on a simple observation of what we see in nature. It is sufficient to look at the world around us to find confirmation for it. A star, a blade of grass, a grain of sand and a rock, a fish, a bird, a lion and a human being are all so unlike each other that there seems to be no way of reducing them to a common denominator, as it were. Sense perceptions give ample evidence of this view, which upholds the stance of empiricism. Empirical knowledge is said to be *a posteriori,* that is, based on human experience that cannot be denied. With such a vast diversity and plurality of existing things, *pluralism,* many people contend, is the most accurate reflection of what is.

2. *Dualism* (from Latin *duo,* two) is a "theory which admits in any given domain, two independent and mutually irreducible substances" (84). The provided examples of the two domains include Plato's dualism of the visible and intelligible worlds, Descartes' categories of mind and matter, Leibnizian actual and possible worlds, Kantian worlds of noumena and phenomena and Hegel's sensible and supersensible worlds. In simple terms, dualism is a theory that acknowledges the existence of two kinds of reality: the physical and the metaphysical. It sees them as different in their nature, therefore irreducible to each other. According to this view, all the examples provided by pluralism fall into the category of the physical realm; they are the things that can be known by our senses. Whereas mind and things of the mind, such as ideas, knowledge, wisdom, and soul—whatever can be understood, but not perceived through the senses, constitutes the metaphysical realm. Since the nature of these two categories is distinct, they are irreducible to each other. This view does not exclude the empirical world; it simply acknowledges another category of reality that is even more permanent than the passing things of this world. This knowledge is established *a priori,* through reason, independently of human experience.

3. *Monism* (from Greek *mones,* single) is "the view that there is but one fundamental reality" (201). This view does not deny the diversity of existing things, but it maintains that reality is ultimately one in that there is something that binds it together into a single whole. While there are many monists at heart, they all do not agree what that one "silver thread" is that is responsible for the unity of all that is. There are in fact three kinds of monism: materialism, neutralism and idealism.

a. *Materialism* is the philosophical theory which holds "that matter is the primordial or fundamental constituent of the universe . . . and everything is explainable in terms of matter in motion, or matter and energy" (189). This is it. There is no other reality, materialists argue. Science has a handle on it.

b. *Neutralism* is "a type of monism, which holds that reality is neither mind nor matter, but a single kind of substance of which mind and matter are but appearances or aspects" (209). Thinkers do not agree, however, about what that neutral substance is.

c. *Idealism* is "any system or doctrine whose interpretative principle is ideal. Broadly, any theoretical or practical view emphasizing mind (soul, spirit, life). . . . The term Idealism shares the unavoidable expansion of such words as Idea, Mind, Spirit, or even Person" (136). Like the former views, Idealism is also subject to various interpretations.

To complicate matters more, there is also a voice of the *intuitionist* who bases his knowledge on "the logic of the heart" rather than on the knowledge of the senses or of reason. Here, one's claim is to the direct and immediate apprehension of reality. This knowledge, the intuitionist challenges, is superior to all other forms of knowing. It is innate, primordial and most reliable of all, especially in philosophy. Reason can err and misinterpret, senses can deceive and mislead, but what we intuit with the heart, is directly given and as such it is free of such pitfalls (149-150).

Thomas: It seems to me that materialism refutes pluralism.

Sophie: And dualism rejects materialism as the only reality.

Jason: At the same time, neutralism refutes dualism.

Diotima: And idealism negates neutralism? Does that mean that idealism wins the contest and that intuition is the way to it? To put it differently, we can say that empiricism rejects intuitionism, that rationalism undermines empiricism, and that intuitionism underrates rationalism—yet all speak of the same reality! And all make their claims in the name of truth! Who is right? Where is the truth? Are all these interpretations contradictory? Are they all just as good? Could it be that it is all simply a matter of choice?

Jason: Truth can never be a matter of choice. I just do not see how one arrives at it.

Diotima: As you can see, there are a number of divides that we will have to bridge along the way to get to the truth in order to be able to do justice to it all. Give it some thought. This will be our challenge at the next session.

III. EXPLORATIONS OF WHAT-IS

A. Concept of One and the Whole

Diotima: I assume that all of you feel you know the meaning of what the simple concepts "one" and a "whole" mean. But your definitions and our exposure to the existing interpretations of reality bring their meaning into question. When we are speaking of reality, are we speaking of the same whole? Moreover, in what sense is reality one? In what sense is it a whole? Just look at your own definitions. You all are defining the same concept *reality* as a whole. Do your definitions intend the same whole?

Jason: No, they do not. Tom's definition limits reality to the cosmos. My definition implies two kinds of reality. And Sophie's definition suggests that a plurality of things makes up reality. It certainly looks like our own views of reality are a fair representation of monism, dualism and pluralism.

Thomas: As I look at Sophie's definition of "the physical world that incorporates things like love and friendship, family and relatives, freedom and virtues, religion and morality, knowledge and values, God, angels and eternity," it seems to me that each of the things she names could be considered as one and a whole all by itself.

Diotima: On the basis of your own observations we can establish several points that will prove helpful as we move along. First of all, the concepts "one" and "whole" are *convertible. Any object we name* can be thought of as *one* and a *whole* by itself. For instance, the pen I am holding, the chair you are sitting on, the book you are reading, the car you are driving, a tree, a bird, a house, each of these is one by itself; it is also a whole by itself. Since these concepts can be used interchangeably, it is said that they are *convertible.*

There are, however, different *kinds* of ones or wholes. They can be small or large, simple or complex, composite or aggregate. What would you consider to be the smallest whole?

Thomas: An atom.

Diotima: And a large whole?

Thomas: A mountain.

Diotima: What would be a good example of a simple whole?

Sophie: A piece of chalk.

Diotima: Judged from the standpoint of sense perception, yes. And a complex whole?

Sophie: A computer.

Jason: A human being! I don't think there is anything more complex than a human being.

Diotima: You may be right, Jason. I assume you are making this judgment on the basis of your experience. Maybe this is so because we are so richly endowed. Leaving this question temporarily aside, let us have an example of a composite.

Thomas: Water. It is a composite of hydrogen and oxygen (H_2O).

Diotima: Good, but here we are relying already on scientific knowledge. This fact is not apparent to the naked human eye. Neither is it given in any of our experiences of water. We accept it as a fact on the basis of scientific analysis, trusting experts in the field. And now, can anyone of you give an example of an aggregate?

Jason: Since an aggregate is a total number of things considered as a whole, a college campus, a city, a government, even our planet earth would be an example of an aggregate. The name of each of these entities comes in a singular form, which indicates that they are one as a whole, but this whole is a composite of many smaller wholes each of which is one by itself.

Diotima: And what is the largest aggregate you can think of? Anyone?

Thomas: The universe or the cosmos.

Sophie: The universe is, indeed, the largest physical whole. But it does not incorporate everything I have named in my definition of reality.

Diotima: That means that we need to find a name for the whole that would encompass absolutely all that is— all that you, Sophie, have named, and all that Jason sought to encompass in his definition, "all that is visible and invisible." Does anyone of you have an appropriate name for this largest whole that is going to be an aggregate of all the aggregates?

Jason: If you say this whole has to encompass absolutely all that is, why not call it an absolute whole?

Sophie: That's a great name for it! Don't you agree, Tom?

Thomas: It certainly names what it intends to encompass. Yes, I'm certainly comfortable with this name.

Diotima: Excellent! I doubt that I could come up with a better name for it myself. Can you also come up with an appropriate symbol for the absolute whole?

Thomas: I suggest a circle, for a circle can symbolically encompass absolutely all that is. But why do we need a symbol?

Diotima: The philosophical quest, unlike that of science, proceeds by means of pure concepts, ideas and forms. These are abstract. It is difficult to maintain discourse on an abstract level for a long time without getting confused, or worse yet, lost.

Sophie: That's true. Ideas are abstract and my mind is concrete. It is difficult for me even to envision all that we have named as a single whole. How will I be able to hold on to this image when we start introducing other concepts? I think a symbol can be a great help.

Diotima: I would not say, Sophie, your mind is *concrete*, but there is truth to what you have said. Our minds are more adept at dealing with concrete, tangible objects than with abstract thought. Some of us, moreover, are visual learners, so having an appropriate visual representation can be of help. Use it, if you find it helpful. Otherwise just ignore it.

Sophie: I am one of those people who appreciate visual aids. Tom, your symbol, by the way, is exceptionally good. Thanks.

Jason: Because the large circle representing the absolute whole will be one and a whole by itself, yet it will be encompassing all the other ones each of which is an independent whole, we will have the largest aggregate possible—the whole of all the wholes. That certainly should leave nothing out from our purview.

Diotima: Good, and since the smaller wholes will be representing different aspects or components of reality along with their respective bodies of knowledge, that should enable us not only to secure "the organic vision of the whole," but also to see how the individual aspects of reality are entwined with each other, how they constitute a single whole and how the respective bodies of knowledge can help us arrive at the understanding of it.

Jason: Do you remember the analogy of the jigsaw puzzle? I believe it is very appropriate in this case as well.

Diotima: Finally, just to be sure we know what exactly comprises the absolute whole let us name once again all that we think belongs in it. Please pay close attention as I name the items so that if I leave anything out, you can remind me of it. Because we are building up to the absolute whole we need to begin with the smallest thing we've named. With this statement, however, comes one more directive: as I name something, you will be incorporating into your vision all the particulars that fall under that name. You remember our discussion about the meaning of the word "fish" and "bird", don't you? That's what I mean. Otherwise, we will be stuck here forever! Incidentally, if it helps you to close your eyes to envision the image you are creating, please do not hesitate to do so. Are we ready?

All: Yes.

Diotima: Hydrogen atom (hence also all the atoms), a speck of dust, a pencil, a chair, this room, this building, our city, our state. . . . Are you already on the map?

All: Yes.

Diotima: Is your whole getting progressively bigger?

All: Yes.

Diotima: Moving on, let us extend this whole to our country (hence all the countries in the world), the planet earth, the solar system, local star system, Milky Way, outermost galaxies—everything in space! . . . Do we have everything?

Sophie: We did not include people, plants and animals.

Jason: When we included the planet earth, Sophie, we have included everything upon earth so all these things are included. However, what about knowledge?

Sophie: How about heaven, God, angels, religion and morality, virtue and vice—all those other things I named earlier? They all are very important.

Diotima: These have not been included yet. Since heaven is understood to be the place where God, angels, and all holy beings reside, let us incorporate them along with the concept of heaven. And since God is said to possess all perfections and knowledge is one of these perfections, knowledge necessarily belongs there, too. Finely, given your list, let us add also religion and morality along with virtue and vice and all such things. Anything else?

WHAT-IS:
THE TRUE REALITY

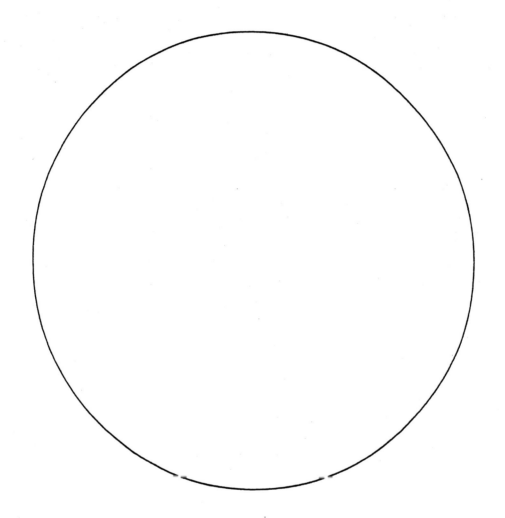

The Actual Object of Knowledge

Diagram 3.1

Thomas: If heaven, then also hell. If there is heaven because that is the place where God is and where good people go, then there has to be also hell, because not everyone is good even by human standards. Consequently, hell too must be a part of reality.

Diotima: Absolutely! Hell, too, and whoever might be in hell as well. If names name aspects of reality, then what they name must be somehow a part of the total scene.

Thomas: What if there are any other planets, galaxies or worlds that scientists have not discovered yet?

Jason: Then it will be up to those who discover them to insert them where they belong.

Sophie: When we've said "everything in space," also "everything in heaven and in hell," Tom, we have covered all the areas where anything else could possibly be. Don't you think so?

Diotima: In saying this we seem to be ahead of ourselves both in space and in time. We shall do well enough if we succeed in understanding what-is. For the time being, therefore, let us concentrate on what you have named. Of course, there is no guarantee we might not stumble upon something new along the way. That, I am sure you will agree is different from looking for something we do not know exists.

Before we move on to our next undertaking, let me draw your attention to the fact that in securing our understanding of the absolute whole, we have been faithful in observing the process proper to human nature. We have started with one item at a time, moved to include the many objects of our sense experience and eventually transcending them, we have advanced to encompass absolutely all that is. We have secured the image of the absolute whole by means of the process of *synthesis,* that is, by adding on new objects and subsequently moving "from the many to the one," the many wholes to the single whole.

Now that we have reached the absolute whole, we find ourselves at the new beginning ready to undertake the arduous task of *analysis* of what-is—the reasoning process "from the one to the many."

B. Analysis of the Absolute Whole

Diotima: As of now, we have the big circle (Diagram 3.1), our symbol for *the absolute whole*. By the absolute whole we mean "what-is" or "all-that-is." We hyphenate these words to indicate oneness or unity of this whole. And we understand this whole to be *the actual object of human knowledge*.

Currently the circle is empty. Like the geographers in preparing a map of a specific locale start with a blank page, so, too, we start with an empty circle. And just as they carefully study the surroundings before they start charting the territory, so will we in charting ours. This should enable us to see more clearly the relationship of each thing to everything and in its position to reality as a whole. We know what belongs in it, but we are not going to include into it anything until, through a dialogue, we discover on the basis of logical necessity how and why it belongs there. The first and possibly the greatest challenge lies in discovering *the basic categories* of what-is. We initiate the quest by asking: What are we really looking for?

Thomas: Knowledge.

Jason: Truth.

Sophie: Understanding.

Diotima: To have knowledge of something is to have the truth of it, and to have the truth is to have an understanding of it. So, all your answers are good. Let us stay with the first reply. We are seeking *knowledge,* but knowledge about what?

Sophie: We all had a different goal.

Diotima: True, but how did we see these goals in relation to each other? Do you remember the logical order that would lead us to these answers?

Thomas: We said we had to discover first what reality is.

Diotima: Good, Thomas, *reality*. So we have now two categories: *knowledge* and *reality*. Our next question is: How does human knowledge ordinarily come?

Thomas: It comes through communication.

Diotima: There are different forms of communication. Can you be more specific?

Sophie: The most common form is speaking. That's how we begin to learn.

Diotima: Yes, but communication through speaking presupposes knowledge of something.

Jason: Language.

Diotima: Excellent! Actually all your answers are good. The Greek word *logos* denotes all those meanings, and much more, besides. It means also a word, an account, a study and reason. You do not need to be concerned with all these meanings just yet. In any event, we now have *knowledge, reality* and *language.* Which of these is the most important?

Jason: I suppose reality.

Diotima: You're right. Unless there is reality, there could be no knowledge, for knowledge is about reality. In fact, if there were no reality, there would be nothing at all. There would be no one to ask any questions and nothing to ask about. Since you and I are, and we are a part of this magnificent reality, we are able to ask questions and to seek knowledge about it. So, yes, reality is necessarily first. And by *reality* we understand *something that is,* that *has a being and identity of its own* independently of our minds. Its existence is not contingent on our knowing it.

Jason: Fortunately so, for that would shrink reality beyond recognition.

Diotima: As to language, since language communicates knowledge, language presupposes knowledge; therefore *knowledge* has to be second and *language* third.

Notice, however, that knowledge is not only about reality. Knowledge is also about language and knowledge is about knowledge as well. If you were to study *epistemology,* the Greek word for knowledge, you would be learning things about knowledge itself. You would be seeking answers to questions such as: how is knowledge possible, what kinds of knowledge are there, what are the degrees of certainty, what forms of reasoning lead to it, what are the types of judgment, what truths, what principles, etc. And, of course, you would be using language to search for those answers.

Something comparable is true of language. Language communicates knowledge about reality, about knowledge and about itself. When you were studying English, or any language for that matter, you have employed language to learn things about that language, things like grammatical syntax, punctuation, documentation, etc. We can say then that *language is the medium through which human knowledge ordinarily comes.*

Sophie: Why did you say "ordinarily"? This word implies that there are other ways knowledge can come.

Diotima: There is a sign language and a body language. When you are driving, traffic lights, a stop sign, speed limit signs are all communicating something to you without any words. Likewise, a particular nod of the head communicates "yes" or "no," a stern look of a person communicates disapproval, a raised hand of the police officer means "stop," etc. But knowledge can also come directly. Much can be communicated by a meaningful exchange of looks. Looking directly into the eyes of another, one can see deep into the person's soul. Love has a language of its own; so does hate. A smile, an embrace, a kind gesture, a facial expression are all examples of human communication. The non-verbal language sometimes can communicate more eloquently and more honestly than words often do. Yet language remains the ordinary means of human communication. All the arts and sciences rely upon it; so does formal education and our dialectic as well.

Sophie: I never thought of those other forms of communication as "non-verbal language." I see it now.

Diotima: We now understand the order of these categories to be *reality, knowledge* and *language.* Next, since we are looking for *the basic categories of what-is* and want to be certain all three are truly basic, before we insert them into their context, let us cross-examine them. Perhaps they could be reduced further.

We've already seen that reality is the non-negotiable part of what-is. The question is: Can we dispense with knowledge?

Thomas: Knowledge is indispensable to us human beings. In the absence of knowledge we would be reduced to . . . ?

Jason: Exactly, Tom. Without knowledge we would be reduced to the highest species of animals. None of the animals are concerned with knowledge. They know what they need and go about providing for their needs. I don't see them show any concern for knowledge.

Diotima: Animals are "intra-worldly" beings. They belong to this world. Their desires are for what is found in the environment. And the environment has everything they need to satisfy their desires. Knowledge, truth, wisdom—these are uniquely human needs.

Thomas: But animals have intelligence.

Diotima: Animals have practical intelligence and powers appropriate to their nature. These abilities vary from species to species and, like the members within the species, come in different degrees. The most gifted species exhibit admirable abilities but abstract knowledge and reasoning, studies have shown are not within their grasp. We will elaborate on that point at the proper time. Suffice it to say, knowledge of reality and the answers you are seeking are beyond their interest and need.

Sophie: Definitely, however, humans cannot dispense with knowledge. It is currently our greatest need. This is why we are here and engaged in this search.

Diotima: Alright then, what about language?

Jason: If there were no language, how would knowledge be possible? Language is the very first thing we learn when we come into this world. Learning everything else depends upon our knowledge of the language—well, practically everything else.

Thomas: I agree. The fact that we begin our life with learning the language is evidence enough that language is one of the basics.

Diotima: Are we ready then to insert *the three basic categories of what-is* into the absolute whole?

Sophie: Wait, I'm still not clear why language is not a part of knowledge. We have to learn it as we do all other knowledge.

Diotima: Language presupposes knowledge, but language communicates knowledge and opinion, truth and falsehood, certainty and doubt, conviction and skepticism, clarity and ambiguity, whereas knowledge denotes only the first term in these sets. *Knowledge is the light of the mind about what-is.* To have knowledge about something is to be enlightened on it. That, in turn, means to understand it *as* it is. The second term in each of these pairs is in fact an indication of a lack of adequate understanding, whence ambiguity, doubt and skepticism result. Not infrequently language itself, because of an inaccurate expression of thought, is responsible for ambiguity. It is for this reason that language cannot be equated with knowledge.

Sophie: This explanation makes much sense now. Thank you. I finally understand the difference between the two and am ready to see *reality, knowledge* and *language* entered into the absolute whole as *the three basic categories of what-is.*

C. Focus on Reality: Question of Origin

Diotima: With the three basic categories in place (Diagram 3.2), we now turn our gaze on reality itself to see what it can reveal to us about itself. I am glad you have a pencil and paper handy for we shall begin with a written exercise. Looking around the room, can you write a list of things that had no beginning?

Diotima: What seems to be the matter? You cannot find anything here? Expand your horizon. Look out the window to see if you can find anything in nature that had no beginning. Don't hesitate to make use of your scientific knowledge as well.

Diotima: Still nothing? We are now facing the fundamental question of philosophy: How did it all come to be? How is it that there is something rather than nothing?

Thomas: The Big Bang Theory answers this question for me.

Sophie: I say: God created it.

Jason: These are the two popular views that have been in conflict for ages now. Is there any way to resolve them?

Diotima: This is the challenge that faces us, friends. We'll see where the dialectic takes us and with what conclusion each of you personally will emerge.

Since the answer to this question is not apparent, let us reason further. This time, it will be a mental exercise requiring you to make use of imagination. Do you remember all the things you have named as making up the absolute whole? Imagine them all being now inside the circle. I will name those things again one by one, as before. Now, however, using the same procedure as before, you will *take them out* of the absolute whole and think them away from existence. For example, when I say "the planet Earth," you will think away from existence the Earth and everything upon it. Are you all clear about what you are to do?

All: Yes.

Diotima: Let's begin: a hydrogen atom (hence all atoms), a speck of dust, a pencil, a chair, this room, this building, our city, our state. …

Please note that when we are thinking away these things, we are simply going back to the time when they did not exist yet. For there was a time when each of the items we have named did not exist. You may want to look up the records to see when your state, city, and this building came into being. That date will indicate the time, prior

WHAT-IS:
THE TRUE REALITY

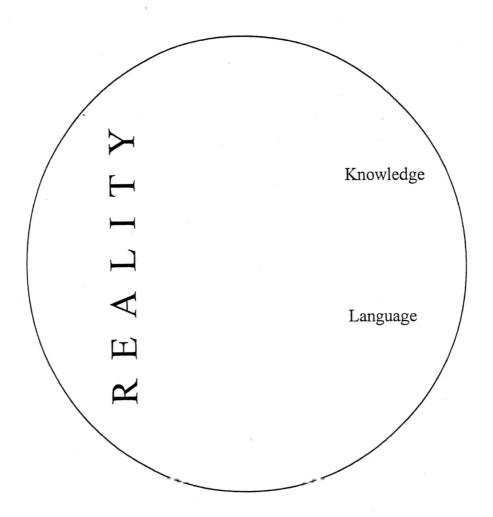

The Three Basic Catagories of What-Is

Diagram 3.2

to which they did not exist. Keeping this fact in mind, as I continue to name things you will be moving back to the time when those other things did not exist yet. The exercise, as you can see, has its basis in reality.

Since the last thing we have mentioned was the state, let us now think away the existence of our country, the planet earth, the solar system, the local star system, Milky Way, the outermost galaxies, everything in space, hence matter or energy—the whole universe! Finally, we include in this list knowledge, God, angels, holy souls, heaven and hell, and all those who may be there. Is there anything left in your mind?

Jason: Nothing.

Diotima: Sophie, you had your eyes closed. What did you see when you have removed absolutely everything?

Sophie: Nothing but darkness.

Diotima: Jason and Thomas, would you also like to close your eyes temporarily to conclude personally if you could see anything other than darkness?

Jason: I see just darkness.

Thomas: Same here.

Diotima: Please keep your eyes closed and dwell in this darkness for a while as I pose to you my next question. The question is: Can anything come into being out of this absolute nothingness?

Jason: No way!

Diotima: What if we wait for it a little longer?

Thomas: Nothing comes from nothing.

Sophie: That's our first self-evident principle!

Diotima: I am glad you have recognized it. Now you also understand the full significance of this principle in philosophy. The question facing us now is: How did all-that-is come into being?

Thomas: My understanding is that it all started with the big bang and then by means of evolution it developed into what it is.

Jason: What caused that big bang if there was nothing there to begin with?

Thomas: According to this theory there was matter. All matter in the universe was drawn together by gravity into the center and formed one huge, hot ball called a "primordial atom." With an increased pressure, this ball condensed. Pressure and temperature reached enormous levels. When the outer layers rushed inward and all matter was drawn into the center, a critical point was reached, the massive cosmic ball exploded. This explosion is called the "big bang."

At this point the matter was flung in all directions. Slowly it began to coagulate and form into clusters of stars. As these began to drift away, they formed into galaxies. And as matter began to cool off, planets began to form. In due time different forms of life began to appear. This, of course, took billions of years before the universe evolved into what it is today.

My description here is a highly condensed account of the theory that has been advanced by Philip Morrison as the Big Bang Theory. While attempts have been made by other physicists to give a different explanation, and there are other theories like the Steady-state Theory by Sir Fred Hoyle and the Pulsating-universe Theory by Allen Sandage, evidence seems to mount in favor of the Big Bang Theory. The major distinction between the Big-Bang theory and the other two is that this theory insists on there being just one big bang, whereas the other two theories find a one-time explosion as too accidental for the workings of nature. Events in nature occur in a cyclic manner. Scientists develop their theories by means of observation of those recurring events. This one-time event doesn't seem to be right, yet evidence coming from little understood "quasars" lends strong evidence in support of it. Since that single explosion the universe, we are told, is "running down" as it moves to its final dissolution.

Jason: So the Big Bang Theory does not begin with nothing. It presupposes the existence of something.

Thomas: It presupposes the existence of matter.

Sophie: How could matter give us intelligence when it doesn't have it? Didn't we see earlier that no one can give what one does not have?

Diotima: Whether God or matter, we must admit something has to be *eternal* and it is this "eternal something" that must be responsible for the origin of what-is. Keep in mind that all the possibilities thought of for centuries have been narrowed down to these two sources, God or matter. As in the past, so it is now: the theists believe God is the origin of all things; the non-theists cast their lot with matter. Whichever one it turns out to be, one thing is certain; "that something" must be *eternal*, and by eternal we mean, "always was, is and will always be." At this point in our dialectic it is not clear which of the two, God or matter is to be credited for the origin of the universe. Sophie's observation, however, cannot be dismissed lightly.

Jason: It seems to me that we ourselves are divided on this score.

Diotima: Until light dawns, let us leave this dilemma temporarily aside. Instead, let me help you, by way of analogy, to gain some insight into reality, as we know it.

D. Analysis of Reality

Diotima: At the center of our roundtable is a beautiful vase of flowers, against the wall there stands a book-shelf, in the corner of the room we see a coat rack. Any one of these objects would make a good analogy, but let us take as an example the most common thing there is, a wooden chair, one of the six around this table. Look at it. How do you think this chair came to be?

Thomas: It was obviously made by someone.

Diotima: Is it possible that these pieces of wood fell into this position by chance?

Thomas: That's absurd.

Diotima: Why is it absurd?

Thomas: It's obvious that the chair was designed to take this particular form. The individual pieces were care-fully crafted and accurately measured in order to fit together. Besides, the whole thing had to be properly assem-bled. The chair might even be patented. There are six identical chairs around this table, an unmistakable proof that they were made according to a design that can now be multiplied by any number.

Diotima: Did designing of this chair presuppose knowledge?

Thomas: Most certainly. The chair had to be designed in such a way as to be able to hold up the weight of the person. It's not enough that the pieces fit together. The designer had to have more knowledge than it may seem to the unskilled eye.

Diotima: Is it possible that a chimpanzee designed this chair?

Thomas: This, too, is a ridiculous question. Chimpanzees are very intelligent creatures, but they lack knowl-edge of such things. Perhaps with some help from man they could.

Diotima: Do you know of anything we are using that chimpanzees have produced with human help?

Thomas: No. Neither do they have any need of such things like chairs.

Diotima: Yes, their intelligence and abilities are appropriate to their style of life in the wild. As to the chair, do you know who designed it?

Thomas: I don't, but if I look it over I will probably find some kind of a trademark that will tell me either the name of the company that produced it, or the store that sold it. It may even have the patent number. This evidence, in turn, can lead me eventually to the designer of it.

Diotima: You can take that up as your future project, Thomas. In the meantime, I have another question for you. Can you tell us what logically had to come first, the chair or the design of the chair?

Thomas: The design.

Diotima: And what does the design presuppose?

Thomas: A designer.

Diotima: Jason and Sophie, do you agree with Thomas?

Sophie: Yes, of course.

Jason: Positively.

Diotima: If yes, then look around to see if you can notice something comparable in nature? Clearly, nature is more creative and science has those answers ready for us. Yet, even apart from scientific knowledge, if you look attentively you will notice there is a design to flowers, bushes and trees, just as there is a design to animal species. There is, for instance, an orchid tree that comes in 15,000 species, yet all their flowers retain the basic structure of an orchid.[5] An apple tree, which also comes in a rich variety, contains and retains from year to year the same basic features of an apple tree and inevitably produces the fruit known as an apple. Pear trees and cherry trees have their own identity by which they are recognized. And they too are faithful to their nature. Stars, in turn, the first of the cosmic bodies to come into being have been so designed as to gradually produce new elements of matter capable of forming new substances out of which, in turn, would come new forms of existence. In spite of the changes that occur in individual entities as they go through the process of becoming, there is stability and order to nature as a whole. Greeks called the universe *cosmos,* which means, "an ordering" because they saw all things in it harmoni-ously ordered. The ordered things in the universe, too, presuppose ordering and an orderer, much the same as the designed entities presuppose designing and a designer.

Thomas: Why can't it be granted that things came by chance?

Diotima: What happens by chance never happens the same way producing the same results. Take a deck of cards and release it from your hand several times without changing the circumstances while you are carrying out the experiment. The answer to your question will become exceedingly clear. Even three pebbles, or pennies, can make the same point if you carry out the experiment several times in the same way. Yet in nature, seasons follow in the same order and though they manifest themselves differently, we know beforehand what changes we can expect to occur in each.

Thomas: But I can argue that the seasons don't happen in the same way either. Temperature and rainfall vary from year to year, there were ice ages once before that do not exist now, and so on. Why can't we say that seasons never happen in the same way either?

Diotima: Seasons, Thomas, are something like human beings and the other species in nature. They are all different, yet all the same. They all have their own *specific features*—philosophers like to call them "accidental qualities"—but *in essence* they are all the same. Notice, winter is always followed by spring, summer and autumn, each with a character, beauty and giftedness of its own. Because their essential nature is basically the same, things like a school year, sports activities and social events are scheduled accordingly well in advance. This is true of nature in other respects as well.

Sophie: That's true. Each season produces different results. We know, for instance, when to expect certain flowers, different fruits, grain, berries, and produce in general. These are determined not only by climate and kind of soil, but also by season. So there is enough stability to seasons to know what each will bring and the order in which it will occur. Not so with the deck of cards and things which happen by chance.

Thomas: Granting these things, I can see that the application of those names to reality is a possibility, but I will have to see that design in it first to be convinced.

Jason: If knowledge is a true image of reality and there is a design to it, that design should emerge. I, for one, have no difficulty in seeing a pattern to seasons, to days and nights, and to various developmental processes in nature. This is how we gradually accumulate knowledge about things and that's what makes progress in knowledge possible. It is because by now we know what constitutes their normal development, when something hinders their normal growth, experts in their respective fields can identify the problem and subsequently, in light of their findings, search for the remedy.

Sophie: Judging by what came to light we can say that reality can be analyzed into three categories: designer, designing and the designed.

Diotima: Not to confuse this set of distinctions with the previous one, since we have called the former set the *three basic categories of what-is,* let us name this set of distinctions the *three classes of reality,* unless, of course, you prefer *realms* or some other name.

Jason: Let's keep it simple. *Classes* sounds fine. We can, however, refer to them at times as realms without any difficulty. We know what we mean by them.

1. Classes of Reality

Diotima: With the help of Tom's analogy of the chair, we have reasoned to there being three classes of reality. Temporarily we shall call them simply: Class I, Class II and Class III. Any suggestions on how these classes should be entered into the context of the absolute whole?

Jason: Since the objects that make up the cosmos presuppose the designing and the designer, cosmos should constitute Class III. The mental activities such as thinking, designing, ordering, etc. should be Class II and above it, should be Class I, the realm of the intelligent living being, the designer.

Diotima: Do we know if there is one or more of those intelligent living beings?

Jason: No. So let us add in parenthesis letter "s" to being, just in case there is more than one.

Diotima: For Class I, then, we have a general name "Intelligent Living Being(s)" that Jason is suggesting. For Class III, Thomas fittingly gave us "Cosmos." What would be a good designation for Class II?

Jason: The realm of the thinking mind.

Thomas: The realm of thought.

Diotima: Remember the Greek word for thought, *dianoia* and its meaning, "that which comes through the mind"? As you can see, your answers complement each other. Both are good. May I suggest, however, that we name Class II the realm of "pure thought"? We need to distinguish this thought from the thought that is embodied in some form as, for example, in the sound of music, in language, in some work of art, and so on. By "pure" we simply mean thought in its pristine form, unmixed with anything, just as it is in the mind of the thinker before it is externalized in some way.

And now, to make sure we see clearly the relationship of the concepts to which we have reasoned earlier as applicable to the three classes, let us look at them again. This time let us look with a critical eye to see if there be any discrepancies between those sets of names and the names: The Intelligent Living Being(s), Pure Thought, and Cosmos. Perhaps you can come up with some additional names.

2. Appropriate Names for the Classes

Sophie: In keeping with the order of our discussion, the first set was: *the designer, designing* and *the designed.*

Thomas: *Orderer, ordering* and *the ordered.*

Jason: *Knower, knowing* and *the known.*

Sophie: *Creator, creating* and *the created.*

Thomas: This set of names, Sophie, is a little premature. It is only your assumption. We have not established this fact yet. We can, however, add *thinker, thinking* and *the objects thought.*

Jason: It seems to me that *eternal* would apply to the first class, but I do not know what would be the corresponding names for the other two classes. So let's just drop this name.

Thomas: *Composer, composing* and *the composed.*

Diotima: Sufficient for now. The repertoire of names will grow as our image of reality becomes clearer. Can you detect any discrepancies among these sets of names? As you know, at every step along the way we have to be mindful of the Principle of Non-Contradiction. Cross-examining one's concepts is what helps one to steer clear of contradictions.

Incidentally, did you notice that what holds true on this large scale, is true also of us human beings on a smaller scale? We, too, after all are intelligent beings, thinkers, designers, composers, artists and planners, and so forth. To avoid confusion in the future as to which thinkers we have in mind, let's agree always to capitalize the names that refer to the first class.

Sophie: Fine, that should make the distinction clear. I also like your analogy of the human thinker to gain insight into the Eternal Thinker. Keeping this analogy in mind can help us to understand better some of the concepts about reality in general, especially those that are imperceptible to the human eye with which we are unfamiliar.

Diotima: Those aspects of what-is that are intelligible but imperceptible to the human eye, that is, our three upper categories of the absolute whole, are referred to in philosophy as *metaphysical,* meaning, not physical. The Greek word *meta* means also "after" and/or "beyond." Since these categories come after the physical realm and are beyond it, here you have another reason for calling that realm "metaphysical." Aristotle's Metaphysics, known also as the First Philosophy, traces to this meaning.

Sophie: Thanks. This is helpful. I can also see why Metaphysics would be called the First Philosophy.

Diotima: With this clarification, let's see what else we might be able to observe by taking a closer look at what we already know.

3. Total Number and Order of the Categories

Diotima: Incidentally, where do you think human beings belong?

Thomas: Since we're on Earth and the planet Earth is a part of the cosmic realm, we must be somewhere within the cosmic realm, hence in class three.

Diotima: Good reasoning, Thomas. As we look at Diagram 3.3, we notice that knowledge is a link between the Designer and designing, for designing presupposes knowledge and the Knower. Language, in turn, is a link between pure thought and the cosmos, because language in communicating knowledge communicates thought by means of cosmic sound. This means then that everything is connected and that there are five categories in all. How do you think these categories should be reckoned? Where do we start?

Thomas: We start with the cosmos, for that is where we are.

Jason: To start at the beginning is to start with class one.

WHAT-IS:
THE TRUE REALITY

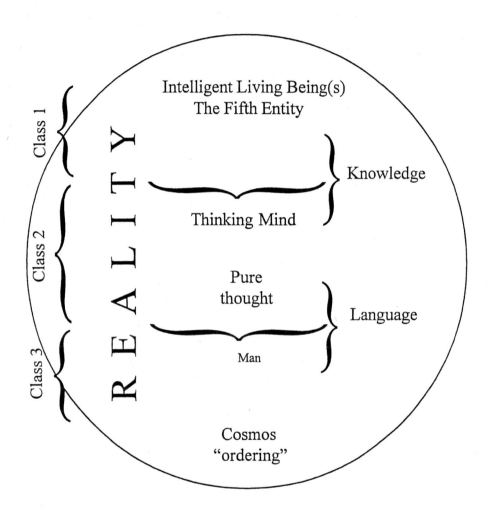

Five Categories of What-Is

Diagram 3.3

Diotima: Both answers can be justified. There are, indeed, two ways of looking at what-is. Jason is right in that he is pointing out to *the actual order,* beginning at the real beginning, with the Eternal Entity. We then move down to knowledge, pure thought, language and the cosmos. Thomas is also right in that this is the *order from the human standpoint,* the way we humans come to know all-that-is. When we are born into this world, we first see things in this world, we learn the language next, through language we become acquainted with ideas, and through ideas we acquire knowledge. Knowledge, in turn, leads us to the Knower. Consequently, from the human standpoint, cosmos is first, language is second, pure thought is third, knowledge is fourth, and fifth is the Intelligent Living Being(s) or the Fifth Entity, so mark them in this order.

Sophie: Given this ordering, knowledge of the Fifth Entity naturally comes last. It's no wonder people have so many misgivings about its existence.

Jason: It's true that no one has any doubt about the existence of the natural entities in this world, even if they haven't seen them or don't understand them. This is presumably because these are objects of possible experience. On the basis of what they know, they can with the help of imagination extend this knowledge to encompass what they still don't know.

Given the opportunity, they can subsequently come to know it personally. But if the Fifth Entity is reached last, it is obvious that knowledge of it would not be accessible to everyone.

Sophie: Yes, because we're all at a different level of understanding and people make progress in knowledge at a different pace—this, already in addition to the differences in age and person's maturity.

Jason: When I think of it, it is really not so surprising that initially we think this world is all there is. When we come into this world, all we see are things of this world. Since the world is so large and we find there is always so much more to learn about it, it is only natural to think that this world is all there is. And when this world is the only reality we know, to talk about any other world strikes us as a fiction, it appears to be incredible, even amusing, at first.

What brought me to suspect that there is more to reality than just this world is the sudden death of my friend who was killed in a tragic car accident. His death made me question the purpose of life, the meaning of death and the possibility of there being an afterlife. It also brought into my mind the question of values. I cannot believe that he no longer exists. This is why, as you may have noticed, I relentlessly seek answers to the perennial questions of philosophy. Since I could not find these answers in the world of perception, I began to look beneath what meets the eye. You know now what brought me to philosophy; you know the real reason for my quest.

Diotima: The answers to these questions are indeed of paramount importance to human life. When these questions surge up from within, it is a sure sign that a person is ready to take a leap ahead in life's journey. We have only to reflect

momentarily on the earliest days of our existence to gain insight into the mystery of our life. The infant's world is at first extremely small. It begins with the mother's womb. When we're born, our world is limited to the mother and the crib. As we begin to develop our eyesight and mental powers through the loved ones speaking to us, our world gradually extends to the father, siblings, household, and subsequently to one's neighborhood, church, school, and so on. With the acquisition of language we become acquainted with ideas that go beyond the tangible objects of everyday life, and by means of education we begin to acquire knowledge of the world at large. By the time we ask questions about knowledge, we are already half way into it. The process takes place so naturally and inconspicuously that we're not even aware of it. But learning about the particular aspects of reality and attaining knowledge of professional fields gradually leads to questions about knowledge of reality in general. That is where we are right now. Our knowledge continues to expand by encompassing more and more of what-is until we gain the vision of reality as a whole. Since philosophy is concerned with all-that-is, progress in our undertaking should lead us eventually to the knowledge about the Fifth Entity and to the organic vision of the absolute whole.

Sophie: Is it the knowledge of the Fifth Entity that renders everything intelligible?

Diotima: Do you remember what we've said about the first principles of philosophy? To reach the Fifth Entity is to reach the beginning, hence to reach "the first principles" in light of which everything becomes intelligible. I agree; the name "first principles" sounds a little strange for the Intelligent Being(s). In our common everyday language we don't associate the word "principles" with living beings. We consign it to science, mathematics, logic, and so forth. Later on, however, we will understand why this association makes sense in philosophy.

Sophie: I am actually getting excited about the direction we're taking. This is getting very interesting!

Jason: I can see also the reason for doubt, suspicion, dis-belief, even for the rejection of the Fifth Entity as also of the entire metaphysical reality when one's horizon is too limited, or when one's learning stops prematurely. Until one's vision encompasses absolutely all-that-is, I suspect that questioning will never cease.

Thomas: No one doubts the existence of what is given in one's own experience, even if only in a possible human experience. Experience provides firsthand knowledge and with firsthand knowledge comes unshakable conviction. One never surrenders these convictions, even if the rest of the world wouldn't believe what one holds as truth.

Diotima: You're right, Thomas. Keep this poignant observation of yours for future reference. You may need to remind us of it on occasion, and we, in turn, may need to remind you of it. It will prove helpful along the way.

Sophie: Could it be that the convictions about God's existence come from the people who have come to experience Him? And this is the reason why they are holding on to their beliefs even if half of the world doesn't believe in God?

Thomas: But is the experience of God a possible experience for everyone?

Diotima: This question can be answered best in light of our understanding of human nature. Since the understanding of human nature depends upon our understanding of reality, perhaps we should first move on with our quest and complete our analysis of the absolute whole. Before we do so, however, allow me to draw your attention to one point with regard to the five categories in general. Please note that the upper three categories, namely, pure thought, knowledge and the Eternal Knower, are *purely metaphysical* and, as such, are supersensible, whereas the lower two categories, cosmos and language, are sensible, hence perceptible by our senses. This means that the upper three categories can only be understood, while the lower ones can be known through sense perceptions. We begin our knowledge with concrete objects of our world, but the higher we move, the more subtle and abstract things become.

Thomas: Indeed, there is already some difference between the tangible objects of nature and language, even though spoken language makes use of the cosmic sound and written language makes use of the visible characters. We don't see the words with the same concreteness as we do the physical objects of the world that these words name.

Diotima: Yes, the visible characters of language are symbols of spoken words, and spoken words are symbols or images of both, pure thought and sense perceptible objects.

One other point is worth noting with regard to what-is; namely, that these five categories form a "chain of wholes."

Thomas: How can we envision this without obscuring the image of what we've just established?

Diotima: We can draw one oval around the cosmos and language, another one around language and pure thought, the third one around pure thought and knowledge, and the fourth one around knowledge and the Knower (Diagram 3.4).

Thomas: I see. Each of the categories can still be considered as a whole by itself, but in reality they do not exist independently of each other. We always find them in relation to something else.

Diotima: This is why Plato concluded that all nature is akin, and by "nature" he meant everything that is. We, too, shall soon see how it is so. Do you have any further questions or comments? It looks as if we have a consensus, so we can move on to the next step.

E. Analysis of Each of the Five Categories

Sophie: I'm glad that we're going to look at each of the categories because I want to know the difference between a thought, a concept, an idea and a form.

Diotima: This isn't a bad category to begin with, Sophie, for as you see thought is at the center of all-that-is.

1. Pure Thought

Diotima: A pure thought is a concept, an idea or a form. A *concept* is an abstract notion, or a universal idea that does not present or evoke any image in one's mind when it is encountered. For example, goodness, beauty, truth, justice, freedom, number, sound, love, these are all concepts. They can be understood but not imaged, which is why they are more difficult to understand. By seeing many beautiful things we get an understanding of the concept "beauty." By learning different numbers, we come to understand the concept "number," and so forth.

An *idea* is a thought that is always of something definitive, like a tree, a bird, a blade of grass, a star, and so forth. When you look at a tree, you get an idea of a tree. When you look at a rock, you get an idea of a rock, and so on. Later on when you hear the word "tree" or a "rock" you immediately have an image of it in your mind. Ideas are of particular objects, persons and things. Because ideas take a form and usually have a corresponding object/entity given in experience, they present and evoke an image of that form in one's mind. For this reason ideas are easier to understand than concepts.

Pure forms are geometrical figures such as a circle, a line, an oval, a sphere, a triangle, and the like. In nature we find them combined with ideas. A ball, a moon and a planet are ideas that took the form of a "sphere." Spruce trees are a combination of a triangle and lines; other trees reflect more a circle or an oval and lines. In studying art, for instance, when you take a basic course in drawing you discover that all the objects in nature have some geometrical form as their base, including a person and a human face. The more intricate the object, the more diversified is the combinations of those forms. Objects made by human beings follow the same pattern. A house, for instance, can be a combination of a variety of these forms. The more elaborate it is, the more forms it will incorporate. It is the filling out, or the aesthetic finishing touch to things that covers over and conceals those basic forms.

Viewed from our standpoint, concepts, ideas and forms are first *in the mind of the thinker,* human or otherwise, but they seldom remain there. They get expressed or externalized in some way. In the cosmos they are *externalized in matter,* in language they are *expressed in words,* spoken and written. In *knowledge, they themselves* constitute *its tiny components.* Finally, they are *in the mind of the Original Thinker(s), the Fifth Entity,* for that is where all categories begin.

Thomas: That would follow, unless, of course, matter turns out to be eternal and it is the beginning of our cosmos.

Diotima: In due time, Thomas, we're going to focus directly on matter to consider the possibility of it being eternal and the beginning of all-that-is. That analysis will provide an excellent cross-examination for our current understanding.

Sophie: We've established earlier that knowledge is the light of the mind. Does it mean that each of us can hope to become enlightened by means of the concepts, ideas and forms we are now discussing?

Diotima: That's the purpose of our quest, Sophie. The journey to this light, however, is long and tedious, for concepts, ideas and forms enable us to make progress in knowledge one insight at a time. Reality, as you already know, is incredibly vast while our intellectual abilities are limited. The slow progress in knowledge is to our advantage nonetheless. Were our intellect to receive full knowledge all at once, we would only be blinded by it, much the same as we are blinded by the brilliant summer sunlight in mid-day when we come out from a dark room. Because we begin our life with the darkness of the intellect with only the potential for knowledge, we begin to build our reservoir of it by first getting acquainted with the particular objects, children's toys. These tangible little forms lead gradually to the understanding of the living forms in nature that these toys represent and gradually to an understanding of all kinds of forms, including the forms of the cosmic bodies.

Through the visible forms of objects in nature, furthermore, we come to understand abstract concepts, ideas and forms. Initially, we merely get exposed to them. Subsequently, as questions relative to them surface in our mind, we discuss them independently of their counterparts in nature. At this stage we're not only able to carry on a discourse about them on a purely abstract level, but also to raise questions about knowledge regarding them. Eventually we ask questions about the origin of knowledge as well. It's the questions about the latter that leads us to the Ideal Form(s) of the Fifth Entity, the Knower(s). For knowledge, as we've concluded earlier, presupposes a Knower. Since knowledge is the light of the mind and ideas "bits of light," when we get good ideas about something, our mind is enlightened and we come to understand the object of our inquiry. That's how ordinarily human knowledge is acquired and how it is communicated.

Sophie: I get it! Concepts, ideas and forms are really at the heart of reality. They are truly at the center of every category and at the center of all-that-is.

Thomas: Apparently this is why no matter what we study, whether it is physics, biology, art, or music, mathematics, literature, theology or philosophy, we are always receiving and communicating concepts, ideas and forms. That's quite an eye-opener for me. I have never noticed that before.

WHAT-IS:
THE TRUE REALITY

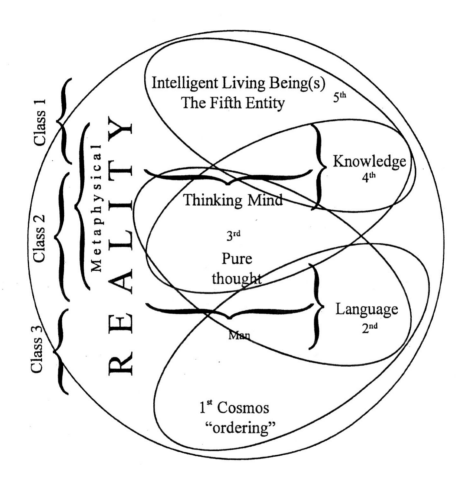

Bonding of What-Is

Diagram 3.4

Diotima: There is much more that can be said about concepts, ideas and forms, but since we will be dealing with them right along, we will have ample opportunity to upgrade our understanding of them. Let's now take a brief look at the rest of the categories.

2. The Cosmos

Diotima: The universe consists of the physical fields, forces and phenomena, as well as of the elements of matter, the natural objects of nature and the various forms of life. But all of the aspects of the cosmic whole are ultimately reducible to the *embodied concepts, ideas* and *forms.*

Sophie: Embodied in what?

Thomas: Did you forget, Sophie? They're *embodied in matter.*

Diotima: If so, then, we have two more names for the third class: *the realm of the embodied, concepts, ideas and forms,* and *the realm of matter.*

Jason: No wonder it's said that the world is built on ideas and that it is governed by ideas. This is literally true!

Thomas: By studying cosmic phenomena, scientists retrieve the concepts, ideas and forms that are embodied in matter. In turn, they embody them in theories by means of language and appropriate formulae—all symbols of thought.

Diotima: Since what is "embodied" in something is *concealed,* when we study anything, whether these be theories in science, humanities, or philosophy, every insight is at once an "in-sight" or "a seeing into the mystery of reality" and a "discovery." And every discovery is, in fact, nothing other than the "un-covery" or a "re-covery" of the concepts, ideas and forms upon which that particular component of reality was built and/or of the powers with which it has been endowed. Since to "recover" this knowledge is to arrive at truth, the Greek word for truth is *a-letheia,* which means *un-concealment.* As we move along, we shall find ample evidence in support of understanding truth as the "unconcealment" of what-is.

3. Language

Sophie: What then are the basic components of language?

Diotima: Agreeing with Plato,[6] we note that language, which we have been using all along as a medium of communication, when analyzed into its simplest components can be said to exist first of all, of a *word* or a *name* naming each and every part of speech. With these words we give a *description* of what we wish to communicate. And what we wish to communicate is some *image.* So the basic components of language are: a *word/name, description* and *image.*

Thomas: What precisely do you mean by an image?

Diotima: It could be an image of anything that is a part of the three classes of reality (cosmos, pure thought, and the Fifth Entity). Or it can be an original image, or a design, of something we have in mind and wish to communicate.

Sophie: Am I to understand that the description could be either of the physical or metaphysical forms?

Diotima: Yes, except that the description of the metaphysical forms will be more difficult to describe and it will be even more difficult to understand if one does not have firsthand knowledge of them.

Sophie: According to this reasoning, wouldn't it follow that we, too, are embodied ideas of the Thinker.

Diotima: Absolutely! We're embodied ideas that are uniquely endowed. This truth will eventually come to light and we will have every reason to be proud of what we are.

Jason: I'm interested in knowing how something comparable can be said about knowledge. Can knowledge be analyzed as well?

Diotima: Yes. Let's move right on to it.

4. Knowledge

Diotima: Until now we've taken knowledge for granted. With the help of Tom's analogy of the chair, we saw the importance of knowledge. By means of it we've also seen that an orderly, intelligible design presupposes an intelligent designer. Mental exercise led us to conclude that the Designer of the cosmos has to be eternal and, since the cosmos reveals an orderly, intelligible design, that the cosmos presupposes knowledge and the Knower. It's therefore safe to say that there is knowledge and that knowledge traces back to the Fifth Entity and, therefore, belongs to it. The picture changes somewhat when we raise the question of *human knowledge*. At this point our opinions are divergent. Since to have knowledge is to have truth and truth is one, if we don't agree on what-is it is a sign that we lack knowledge. It also follows that opinion is not knowledge.

We know firsthand that there is knowledge because we have been making some progress in attaining it. This knowledge comes to us in addition to the knowledge we've acquired earlier at home and in the course of receiving our formal education. Plato contends that particular knowledge, such as we gain by means of various theories is a *true opinion*. This is not a bad name for it.

Sophie: What exactly is the difference between an "opinion" and the "true opinion"?

Diotima: An opinion is a personal view one holds about something for which one lacks objective evidence to prove it. It is something one believes that comes from one's perception or public opinion. The "true opinion" reflects "some truth" about the content in question, but one still lacks full understanding of it. There are other questions one has with regard to it. In other words, what is known is true, but there remains more that needs to come to light to render "that something" really intelligible.

Sophie: So it's a partial truth, as it were?

Diotima: Yes. Upon discovering answers to those puzzling questions, we reach the second level of knowing, namely, *understanding*. We really never fully know anything, however, until we understand it in terms of the first principles. It is only when this level of understanding is reached can we say that we have *knowledge.*

Knowledge implies understanding of the thing itself, an understanding of it in relation to other things, and also in terms of the first principles. When we achieve such an understanding of something and are able to explain it by providing objective evidence in its support without contradicting ourselves, only then can we claim to have knowledge of it. Once this knowledge dawns, we are able to communicate it in a way that is appropriate to its nature. I say "appropriate to its nature," because the content of the three classes of reality differs in nature, so does the knowledge of it. There are, therefore, three *kinds* of knowing, which are, in fact, *three degrees* of human knowing: *true opinion, understanding* and *knowledge* (Diagram 3.5).

Please observe that in our search for knowledge we are slowly but surely approaching the Eternal Knower. And as we are approaching the Eternal Knower, we are approximating knowledge of the Fifth Entity.

Needless to say, much more needs to be clarified for us to be able to claim even an "understanding" of what knowledge is. However, since knowledge is the object of our study, it is only at the end of our quest that we can hope to emerge with a fairly satisfactory understanding of it. At this point, if you can accept *the three kinds and degrees* of human knowing stated above as a "true opinion," then we can move on to the last category on our list.

Jason: There's certainly no contradiction in that designation, as far as I can see that would prevent us from adopting the view.

5. The Fifth Entity

Thomas: I have noticed that thus far everything came in sets of three's. Is that a hint that we should expect there to be three Intelligent Beings?

Diotima: Plato tells us that the whole world is a copy of the Eternal Model.

Sophie: What does he say is the Eternal Model?

Diotima: He has several sets of names, but the basic one is: the Good, the Beautiful and the Just. St. Bonaventure, who also articulates the whole system of thought in sets of three's, has likewise different sets of names for them. One set of the names he gives them is Brilliance, Radiance and Splendor. Actually, most of the original thinkers tend to come up with their own names in light of the insights they gain. But, if you recall, we have decided at the outset that we would not introduce into the context of the absolute whole anything until we have first understood it. Since this knowledge did not surface for us yet, I suggest that we limit ourselves to the general names of the first class such as Designer(s), Orderer(s), Knower(s), Intelligent Living Being(s), and so forth, names that we have discovered thus far on our own by means of reason alone.

Thomas: Being faithful to our intent has served us well so far. So let's keep it that way.

WHAT-IS:
THE TRUE REALITY

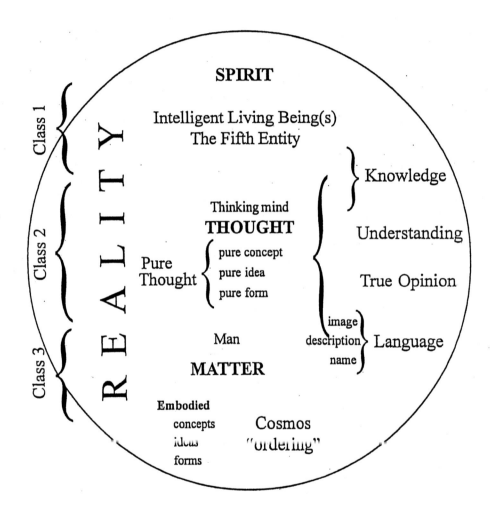

Components of the Major Categories

Diagram 3.5

Diotima: You're a very congenial group and it's a joy to do philosophy with you. Before we move on, please take a careful look at Diagram 3.5 with an updated view of what-is to see if you have any questions about any of the five categories?

Jason: I don't have any questions, but I do have an observation I'd like to share. As I look at the "map" we have sketched, I can see how one can justify pluralism, dualism and monism, without contradicting oneself.

Thomas: With my scientific bent, as I look at it I see a huge atom!

Sophie: I, again, see pure thought as a hub of a huge wheel upon which everything revolves.

Diotima: How interesting! Imagination is a fantastic power with which we humans have been endowed. I'm glad it's at work in you. Suppose we take some time to let each of you describe the image you have in your mind.

Jason: Every category on this page when looked at individually conforms to the definition of pluralism, for each thing has a being and identity of its own that is unlike everything else. At the same time, since the two lower categories are empirical and the upper three are purely metaphysical, therein lies a justification for dualism, the realm of matter and the realm of mind. And since all the categories are connected and form a chain of wholes, reality is ultimately one, hence monistic.

Diotima: Very good observation, Jason. It looks as if we're well on the way to bridging those great epistemic divides. What about your image of reality, Sophie?

Sophie: Let me show you what I mean by drawing an arrow from pure thought to each of the five categories to show its relatedness to it.

WHAT-IS:
THE REALITY

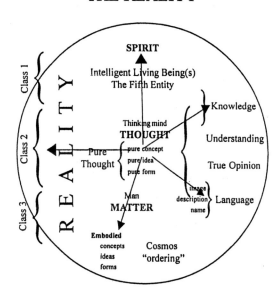

Pure Thought: a Bond of Unity
Diagram 3.6

First of all, pure thought is in the Mind of the Thinker, the Fifth Entity. Thought constitutes the substance of knowledge. Thought is communicated in language. Thought is embodied in matter. Therefore, thought is at the heart of reality as a whole, class two.

Diotima: By pointing out the centrality of thought and its bond with all-that-is, you have shown us that thought is pervasive; it pervades all-that-is. It is that "silver thread" that binds all things into a single whole. For this reason, some thinkers maintain that reality is thought, because all reality is reducible to thought: concepts, ideas and forms. Or, as Parmenides put it: "thought" and "being" are one; "to think" and "to be" are one. This is tantamount to saying, thought and being belong together; they are inseparable. Good thinking, Sophie. And you, Thomas, our scientist, what image are you entertaining in your mind?

Thomas: My view resembles Sophie's, except that I am envisioning reality as being encircled in a three-fold manner with all three circles crisscrossing each other at the center. Here it is. We can enter this image as diagram 3.7, if you will.

WHAT-IS
THE TRUE REALITY

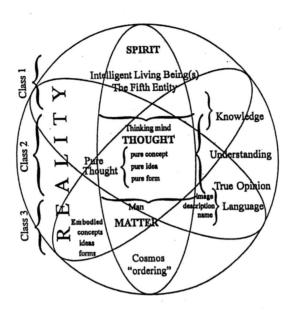

Reality: A Vast Atom
Diagram 3.7

Notice, please, my first circle runs vertically, encompassing all three classed of reality. That is, it encompasses reality *per se.* The second circle extends diagonally from the embodied concepts, ideas and forms in class three all the way to knowledge in class one, with pure thought at the center binding them. They're all "birds of a feather." In this image I see man in the cosmic realm, but as one inquires into the things of this realm, the pure concepts, ideas and forms embodied in theories are his stepping stones to knowledge. And the third circle, the opposite diagonal, spans language, pure thought and class one in general. To me this suggests that through the medium of language in discussion such as we are conducting right now, we are led to class one by means of the pure concepts, ideas and forms. Like Sophie's image, mine too shows pure thought to be at the core of all-that-is, binding it all into one.

Diotima: There is nothing you have said that I could dispute. I may only point out that there is further significance to this image, Thomas. It is bound to surface toward the end of our dialectic. Language at that point will be rendered, as you've hinted at it already, as *discourse,* which is one of the other meanings for the Greek word *logos.* In upgrading our image of reality at that stage, we might be able to explain more fully the reality of the first class. Let's not allow ourselves to forget about your images.

Incidentally, did you notice that in offering your images of reality you have confirmed everything we have said earlier about language?

Sophie: Very true. I find all of this very fascinating, but my intuition tells me there is more to reality than just thought. While what I'm learning satisfies my intellect, it does nothing for my heart. It just doesn't "hit the spot," if you know what I mean. There has to be more to reality than this.

Diotima: Oh, yes! Of course, there is, Sophie. We must find just the thing that can "hit that spot" for you. We're on the way to it already.

Our analysis of the absolute whole, of course, could go on and on with the hope of arriving at the understanding of everything to our satisfaction, but reality being so vast and intricate, such an undertaking would be an insurmountable task. The human mind has been attempting to do just that for several millennia already, and by means of many disciplines at that! We might find a shortcut to the knowledge we're seeking at a more opportune time. You may be glad to learn that for our purposes, what we have established thus far will suffice for now. Eventually we will cross-examine our understanding of the absolute whole by means of Plato's divided line and some other disciplines. Plato has a remarkable way of presenting the very thing we are hoping to understand. His thought withstood the ravages of twenty-four centuries and is as alive today as when he first presented it.

As this session is drawing to a close, before we proceed any further there is one thing I'd like you to keep in mind regarding our visual aids. The diagrams we have drawn with the help of the two symbols, the circle and the line, are delineations to help ourselves understand what-is. They are comparable to the road maps that geographers prepare to facilitate our travels. There are no such markings in reality much the same as there are no fixed boundaries between the States within a country, or among the countries themselves, except when people choose to designate them as such. All such markings are of human making; these are contrived to help us see things more clearly. Consequently, when our dialectic reaches its goal and we will have understood the various aspects of reality in relation to each other, we shall dispense with these symbols to reflect the truth more accurately. At that point such helps should be found superfluous. But until the light of truth dawns upon the horizon of our minds, we shall deem nothing beneath us that conduces to our goal. What's of essence currently is that you have a good grasp of what we've established today in preparation for our next gathering. For at that time we want to raise this discourse to a new level of understanding.

Jason: That's only fair.

IV. COMPREHENSIVE VIEW OF WHAT-IS

A. Reality as a Chain of Wholes

Diotima: Let's begin with our Diagram 4. It enables us to situate each entity independently and as a part of the greater whole. It likewise shows the particular entities in the context of their category as members of their own series or species, and also in relation to all other categories with their own species and series—all eventually tracing back to the First Principles of the Ontological Realm.

Look to the extreme right. We see there three concentric circles with the caption reading "Microcosmic Whole." This whole represents a human being, a person, or simply man in a generic sense of the word. The outer circle represents our body of flesh and blood, that is, our psycho-somatic component that consists of the physical organism. This component of our being is composed of the same elements of matter that enter into the composition of other entities in this world. Because we experience our body firsthand through the five senses with which it comes equipped, even though the human body constitutes no small challenge to understand it with all its functions, no one doubts that we are beings endowed with a body.

The middle circle represents the human mind, our intellect, that is, the thinking, reasoning, contemplative faculty of our being. Our mind, which comes equipped with its own powers, enables us to understand what-is. This intellective faculty uses

our brain and acts by means of it. Although we are diversely gifted (and there is currently much controversy within science about the relationship of the mind to the brain), no one doubts that we have a mind capable of highly intellectual activities. The very quest into its nature, functions and identity—indeed, the human quest for knowledge in general—is an irrefutable proof that we have a mind. Unlike all other species on earth completely oblivious of knowledge, we irresistibly seek it. Truth is important to us.

The innermost circle is likewise known by different names. Some thinkers call it a soul; others name it a spirit. Still others refer to it as the "core" or the "ground of our being," or simply as "the self." Sophie called it a "heart," even though she did not mean by it a physical muscle. Am I correct in assuming that, Sophie?

Sophie: Absolutely! I meant that "something" within us that impels us to love and to aspire to all that is good, beautiful and true—all that we value most! In short, all that lifts us beyond ourselves and gives special meaning to our life.

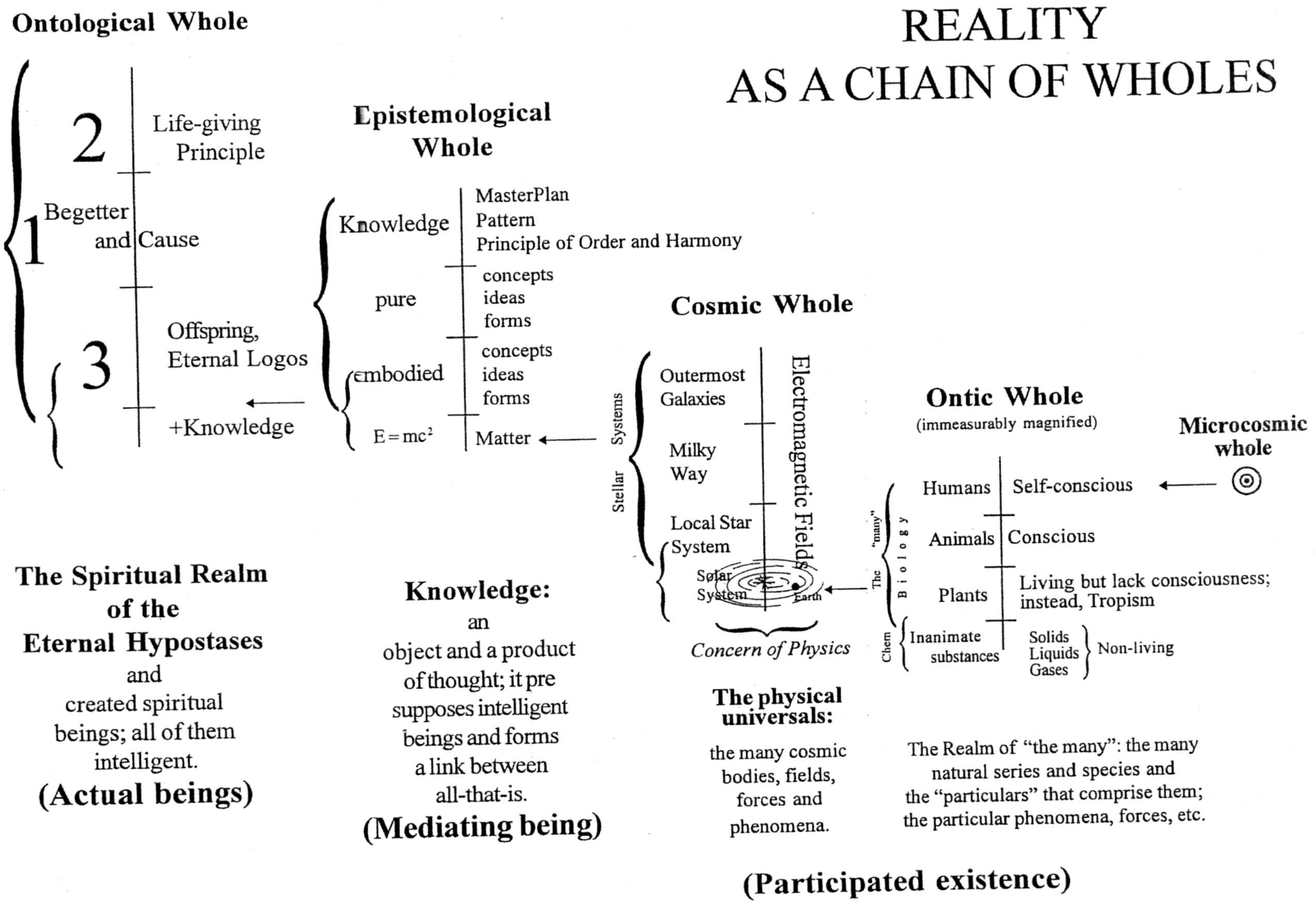

REALITY
AS A CHAIN OF WHOLES

Ontological Whole

2

Life-giving
Principle

Begetter
and Cause

1

3

Offspring,
Eternal Logos

+Knowledge

**The Spiritual Realm
of the
Eternal Hypostases**
and
created spiritual
beings; all of them
intelligent.

(Actual beings)

**Epistemological
Whole**

MasterPlan
Pattern
Principle of Order and Harmony

Knowledge

concepts
ideas
forms

pure

concepts
ideas
forms

embodied

$E = mc^2$

Matter

Knowledge:

an
object and a product
of thought; it pre
supposes intelligent
beings and forms
a link between
all-that-is.

(Mediating being)

Cosmic Whole

Outermost
Galaxies

Milky
Way

Local Star
System

Systems

Stellar

Electromagnetic Fields

Earth

Solar
System

Concern of Physics

**The physical
universals:**

the many cosmic
bodies, fields,
forces and
phenomena.

Ontic Whole
(immeasurably magnified)

Humans

Animals

Plants

Inanimate
substances

Biology

Chem

The "many"

Self-conscious

Conscious

Living but lack consciousness;
instead, Tropism

Solids
Liquids
Gases

Non-living

**Microcosmic
whole**

The Realm of "the many": the many
natural series and species and
the "particulars" that comprise them;
the particular phenomena, forces, etc.

(Participated existence)

Diagram 4.

Diotima: We understand what you mean. Don't we fellows?

Jason: Actually, the name "heart" is not a bad choice at all. Most people know what is meant by it, for that is where we all hold what is dear to us. That's where lie "our heart's deepest longings," as we like to put it.

Diotima: It seems that the physical heart might even be the seat of our spirit, which manifests itself as consciousness, for that is where we experience the warmth of love, where we are conscious of loving and of being loved, both on the human and the divine level. Humanity from time immemorial has been using the heart as the symbol of love and has esteemed love as the highest good. Valentine cards so popular in our culture provide ample proof of it, if anyone needs one. Regardless, understanding that all these names refer to the innermost component of our being, we shall know what is meant by the name whatever appellation happens to be employed. Eventually we may be able to discover which of these names is the most appropriate for it.

At this time there are two points that must be emphasized. First, that each of the three components (body, mind and spirit) comes with its own set of powers as well as its own needs, and each has its own functions to fulfill for the over-all well being of a person. The second point, that these three components or dimensions of our being do not exist in isolation within us as if superimposed upon each other in layers. They permeate each other and function as a single whole. Just as the organs of the human body form an organism that functions as a single whole with each organ performing its own part, so the above named three dimensions, in turn, are completely integrated to constitute a human being and they, too, function in unison with each fulfilling its own part—unless, of course, there occurs some malfunction or deviation from what is normal. Since we are not physicians but metaphysicians, that is, philosophers and not doctors, our focus will be on what is normal and natural. And from this perspective we understand all three dimensions to be fully integrated in the human person.

Thomas: I understand. I wonder, though, why did you call man a microcosmic whole? When I hear this phrase I tend to think of atoms, for I see them as microcosmic wholes.

Diotima: It is true that the word "microcosm" has been used to denote the smallest units of matter. This still holds. However, when you see how man figures in relation to the rest of reality, you will see the appropriateness of this name for a human being. In light of it, you may also agree that the word "infinitesimal" might be a suitable substitute for the smallest elements of matter of which you speak. The answer to your question, Thomas, is upon the horizon. It will soon come to a full view, if you can wait a bit. Are there any other questions or observations you'd like to make?

Jason: Why is the "microcosmic whole" placed by itself? This is not how we exist.

Diotima: I was waiting for this question to surface so that we could come to understand that just as we have taken man out of his context for the sake of study, so every existing entity can be taken out of the context of the absolute whole and made the subject of special inquiry. This is exactly what thinkers do, each one in his or her domain. Such studies create domains that turn out to be different disciplines, or branches of them. Because reality is so vast, it would be too cumbersome to drag along all the knowledge that has been gathered. And because reality is diverse in nature, it makes various delineations into disciplines possible. These divisions facilitate our quest, for they give rise to the many bodies of knowledge along with their divisions and further sub-divisions. It is important to stress, nonetheless, that this is done for the sake of study. When one's goal is reached, it is imperative to return things back into their normal setting. Otherwise we create unbridgeable gaps with each body of knowledge yielding a fragmentary bit of information, which can leave us in the dark as to how the particular information fits into the context of reality and how it contributes to the function of the whole. The consequence of it is regrettable. We thereby lose sight of the unity, coexistence and harmony of what-is.

Putting things back into their context and seeing them subsequently in relation to the other existing things within the context of the absolute whole has an added advantage. Like a newly inserted piece into a jigsaw puzzle, it lends greater intelligibility to each entity and to reality as a whole. Not infrequently it even obliterates doubts or misgivings we had about something. We come to see the incompleteness in what-is in the absence of the component we held suspect. It is the missing component of reality that invites questions and creates "black holes" in knowledge for us. I trust you will come to see this personally in the course of our quest. Now, having established this fact, let us proceed to do what we have just said. Let us place back our "microcosmic whole" where it belongs.

The Ontic Whole. Experience tells us that man does not exist somewhere out in space, all alone, but that he is a part of the *ontic whole* without which his life is unimaginable. The word "ontic" comes from the Greek *ta onta*, the plural form of *to on,* for "being." The ontic whole, then, is the realm of the "many," that is, the many natural series and species we find on this earth and the particulars that comprise them. While speaking about the human race, we have just said that each person is one but consists of three dimensions each with powers of its own, and each further analyzable to its smallest components. To some extent, this applies to all the existing entities within the ontic whole—observing, of course, differences in nature and properties relative to the various series and species.

We notice that the entities within the ontic realm consist of three living categories and one non-living. The latter consists of the inanimate substances studied by Chemistry. These substances, however, on the Periodic Chart of Elements fall into three groups: solids, liquids and gases. Unlike the other three categories, they are an integral part of the ontic whole. For these elements enter into the composition of all that constitutes this realm with respect to the entities themselves, their habitat and the conditions of their survival.

All living things fall into the domain of Biology (from Greek *bios,* life). There are three distinct categories of living things, so divided according to the nature of each. These are: plants, animals and human beings, whence the division of Biology into Botany, Zoology and Anthropology. Plants have life, but lack consciousness and mobility. Their movement is that of tropism, the involuntary turning toward light. Animals are conscious, but they are not conscious that they are conscious. In other words, they lack self-consciousness. Of all the species within the ontic realm only the human beings are self-conscious. This fact places us into the special category by ourselves.

Sophie: Why is it written under the Ontic Whole "immeasurably magnified"?

Diotima: If you follow the arrow pointing to the planet earth, you'll find that our planet in relation to the rest of the cosmos appears only as a dot. Were we to observe the right proportion, our line would have to be the size of that dot. As you can see, we had to magnify it immeasurably to make it legible and intelligible to ourselves.

Jason: If the earth in relation to the cosmic whole is but a dot, this certainly cuts us down in size. I can see now why you have represented us as a microcosmic whole. Here is your answer, Tom.

Diotima: If you consider now the innumerable number of the existing series and species on earth and equally innumerable number of entities within each of them, all coexisting on earth and interacting for the benefit of each other and all of us, it is enough to boggle anyone's mind.

Thomas: Sure does! According to the latest census, there are well over 6 billion human beings on this earth.[7] This is not counting all the land, air and water animals plus the widest variety of plant life. Given the totality, yes, I can honestly see why a person is no more than a microcosmic whole. Unbelievable! Just mind staggering!

Diotima: And yet earth is only a small planet within the cosmic realm.

The Cosmic Whole. Please note further that the *cosmic whole* consists of a solar system and three stellar systems: the Local Star System, the Milky Way and the Outermost Galaxies. The Solar System gravitates within the Gravitational Field of the Sun (GFS) and the Stellar Systems within the Electro-magnetic Field (E-MF). The whole cosmic system gravitates around the *common center* (CC) of the Gravitational Field, which undergirds both. Albert Einstein called the cosmic center the *"cosmological constant."* According to Einstein, the cosmic gravitational field is irreducible to the other two fields. He worked on the unified field theory for thirty-three years. Every attempt to reconcile them had failed. And so the mystery remains.

In spite of that mystery, much has been discovered to thrill one's mind and to pique one's interest. Just listen to what Lincoln Barnett writes in his book *The Universe and Dr. Einstein.* The book comes with a Foreword by Albert Einstein in which he validates what is there. Barnett writes, "For all ordinary purposes of science the earth can be regarded as a stationary system. . . . But to the astrophysicist, the earth, far from being at rest, is whirling through space in a giddy and highly complicated fashion. In addition to its daily rotation about its axis at the rate of 1,000 miles an hour, and its annual revolution about the sun at the rate of 20 miles a second, the earth is also involved in a number of other less familiar gyrations. Contrary to popular belief the moon does not revolve around the earth; they revolve around each other—or more precisely, around a common center of gravity. The entire solar system, moreover, is moving within the local star system at the rate of 13 miles a second; the local star system is moving within the Milky Way at the rate of 200 miles a second; and the whole Milky Way is drifting with respect to the remote external galaxies at the rate of 100 miles a second—and all in different directions!"[8] Imagine: no traffic lights, no speed limits, no guard rails and NO accidents!

Sophie: Wow! Awesome! It's a wonder we're not dizzy.

Diotima: Yes, it's an awesome universe we're a part of. Most people hardly realize this fact. The cosmic whole consists of the physical universals, that is, of the many vast cosmic bodies, fields, forces and phenomena that first and foremost are the concern of Physics.

Jason: Why did you say "first and foremost"? That implies other bodies of knowledge.

Diotima: What we have said earlier about the ontic realm, applies also to the cosmic realm, except on a larger scale. It is true that physics is concerned with the cosmos in general. In its purview are all the non-living things from the universe as a whole down to the tiniest particles of matter that make up an atom. However, because of its immense magnitude and diverse phenomena, many related bodies of knowledge have emerged in conjunction with it. No one discipline can handle it all. Thus physical sciences include astronomy, chemistry, earth sciences and physics. Just as formerly biology, so, too, the earth sciences sub-divide into: geology, geomorphology, geophysics, seismology, geochemistry, meteorology, climatology, hydrology and oceanography.[9] In spite of the great diversity reflected by all the physical sciences, its content is ultimately reducible to matter in motion. And matter, Einstein demonstrated, is nothing other than energy. Energy is convertible to matter and matter into energy. His famous formula reads: $E=mc^2$ (Energy equals mass times velocity of light squared). Yet the source of this energy continues to be a mystery to science.

The Epistemological Whole. Enough knowledge has been retrieved to give rise to the *epistemological whole.* Everything we see reflected on this page is a part of it. Evident here is the master plan at work along with its pattern and the principle of order and harmony. One quick look at Diagram 4 reveals that everything comes in groups of three's plus one. The "plus one" element, although different in nature from the particular set of "three," is always *within* it as a part of it. At the same time, it gives rise the next whole. But the *connecting link* between the given three and the next whole to which the fourth element gives rise is always *third* in each series of three's. To be specific, in the ontological whole there are three Intelligent Beings and knowledge is fourth. Knowledge is within them and a part of them, but it is different from them in nature. This knowledge gives rise to the epistemological whole, but the connecting link to knowledge as a system of thought is the Third, the Eternal Logos, who externalizes it. Is it not the function of any word to communicate thought or to externalize it in some form, be it in language, art, music, poetry, or architecture?

The epistemological whole, in turn, consists of three categories of thought plus energy. Energy is within and a part of knowledge through the *embodied concepts, ideas and forms.* So the connecting link between knowledge and the cosmos to which energy gives rise is thought in the third position again.

The cosmos, in turn, consists of three stellar systems and a solar system. The solar system is within and a part of the stellar systems. Here the planets of the solar system are linked to the stellar system through the sun that is a part of the third group of stars. The ontic whole, again, consists of three living categories and one non-living. The non-living category is within and a part of the living categories, but it is different from them. The non-living category, which consists of the elements of cosmic matter, is connecting the living categories to the cosmic realm through the plants, the simplest form of life that also comes third. And man, a three-dimensional being, is connected to the ontic realm through his body, which is likewise the third component of a human being. Man completes the pattern and closes the circle. Because our bodies are mysteriously knitted together from the same elements that make up the cosmic realm, we are subject to the physical laws like the rest of physical reality. But because our bodies are psychosomatic, we are linked at the same time to the ontic realm by natural life and like all living entities we are subject to the natural laws of nature. Through our mind, we are linked to the epistemological whole, and through our heart, to the ontological whole. Here, too, we need to adhere to the laws that underlie our metaphysical dimension; but we'll say more about this later. Having uncovered the pattern, let us leave all other implications for later. Instead, let us complete our discussion of "reality as a chain of wholes."

The Ontological Whole. The *ontological whole* consists of three Intelligent Beings and knowledge. Because these Beings are intelligent, knowledge *ipso facto* belongs to them. The name "ontological," as we have already seen in conjunction with the ontic realm, comes from the Greek *ta onta* (the plural form of *to on*), which means beings. The ontological whole is the Spiritual Realm of the Eternal Hypostases. The word "hypostases" means Persons. It comes from two Greek words: *hupo,* beneath, and *stasis,* a standing, hence "what stands beneath" all-that-is. And what stands beneath all-that-is, are the First Principles who turn out to be Persons, all Intelligent Beings. These Hypostases are: the Begetter and Cause of all-that-is, the Life-giving Principle and the eternal Logos. The universe and all that came into being came through the eternal Logos, because the eternal Logos is the agent of the Cause.

Thomas: How do we know this?

Diotima: It will take us a while yet, Thomas, for this answer to emerge on its own. Only at that point it will become intelligible. However, since I do not like to dismiss any question without giving at least a provisional reply, let me just state that most of this knowledge comes from the firsthand visions of seers, those mystical "lovers of wisdom" we spoke of earlier. Since this knowledge finds confirmation in the divine revelation and coheres with logic, it is more reliable than any other human knowledge could ever be. You must know, however, that we are speaking here of an awesome mystery. This knowledge startles even the seers who catch a glimpse of it. Understandably, for you, at this point of our quest, this knowledge can be only hypothetical. The understanding we speak of is contingent upon the understanding of the ontological realm in its relation to all-that-is. We, on the other hand, are just building the background for it. In view of the fact that our being and reaching this knowledge presupposes the existence of reality in its totality, it is only logical that we first set the stage upon which the drama of the human life unfolds. Once the context is in place, ascent to the truth we are seeking will be smoother. Here is my advice for now. Hold what we say in this entire section as merely a hypothesis. The challenge of the next round of discussions lies in making these claims explicit. If answers to your questions do not surface in the process of the ascent, be sure to voice them.

Thomas: Fair enough. Let's move on.

Diotima: Picking up where we left off, we can say that in reaching the ontological whole, we have reached the actual beginning, the First Principles in light of which everything becomes intelligible. We have only to reverse the arrows to know how it all took place and we will know even the order in which what-is came to be.

Sophie: Reversing the arrows is simple enough, but things are not quite as obvious to me, at least not yet.

Diotima: They will become clearer for you, too, Sophie, when our dialectic reaches that point. As we have just said, currently we are still gearing up for that ascent. Let me just finish saying what remains to be said about each of the three realms.

Please note that the ontological Beings are the *actual beings*. They are, in fact, the true reality and "the actual object of human knowledge." Until they come to be known in relation to what-is, knowledge of all other entities remains incomplete, hence only a true opinion. The powers and perfections of Actual Beings extend to everything that exists. It is they who render everything intelligible. But the ontological realm also includes two categories of created beings that are immortal that, too, are intelligent.

Knowledge has a *mediating being*, or status. It mediates between the Designers and the designed cosmos. Knowledge has no existence of its own. Knowledge is in the mind of the knower, but it can be communicated. Knowledge can be communicated directly from mind to mind, or by means of language. It can also be communicated by means of some works like art, music, poetry, architecture and the like. It can be communicated by means of matter, as we find it in the universe. Once thought is externalized in some form, it can be retrieved by means of analysis. That is what the scientists have been doing for centuries. Little by little they have been recovering the master plan that has been concealed since the beginning of time. Much has come into light already, but the fundamental questions of science still await the answer. And so the mystery remains.

The cosmic whole, along with the ontic realm that is a part of it, has a *participating existence*. It partakes of their energy, powers and perfections to some extent, and it participates in the existence of the actual, eternal Beings in accordance with their master plan, order and harmony. This realm has a temporal existence. What had a beginning will have an end. That which is composed eventually gets decomposed.

Jason: I find this extremely interesting. It seems to make a great deal of sense, but I still don't know how you got here. You seem to suggest that in the ontological realm, which is eternal, there are some created spiritual beings. Who are those beings and how did they get there?

Diotima: Yes, there are some created spiritual beings there; all of them are intelligent. Some of them were created purely spiritual, and others, with a "spark" of an eternal element within them. Since what is purely metaphysical is indestructible and what is eternal never dies, both categories of those beings live forever.

Sophie: Could it be that one class of these beings consists of angels, and the other of us human beings?

Jason: Are you suggesting, then, that we have an eternal element within us?

Diotima: You are always a few steps ahead of me. The hint to one of your questions surfaces by means of our next diagram, but the answer to both questions will become intelligible only by means of the dialectic, when we make personal ascent to truth. You'll just have to be patient.

Thomas: I know you are eager to move on, but I am still haunted by what you said about those eternal Hypostases. Could you help me understand how, or better, in what sense they are said to "stand beneath" all-that-is?

Diotima: I'll try, Thomas. In fact your question will make it a good finale to our present discussion. I'll ask you to use your imagination. Imagination is a fantastic power we possess. We have only to put it into use a little more. Imagine now that the various wholes on this page, I mean the wholes we have been discussing right along, are like round plastic discs on a board where they can be moved at will.

Thomas: That's easy enough.

Diotima: Slide the little disc of the "microcosmic whole" into the ontic whole where it belongs. Next, slide the bigger disc representing the "ontic whole" on to the Earth. Now, slide the large disc representing the entire "cosmos" on to the epistemological whole. And finally, do the same with the "epistemological whole." Did you slide it on to the ontological whole?

Thomas: Yes.

Diotima: And what happened?

Thomas: We now have the ontological whole underneath all-that-is. It is almost completely covered up. There is just a small uppermost part of it that's visible.

Diotima: What's on top in full view?

Thomas: The cosmic whole containing the smaller wholes within it.

Diotima: And what is "standing beneath" it, as if the ground supporting it?

Thomas: The Hypostases of the ontological whole. I get it. Thanks. That made it clear.

Diotima: Now you can see why some philosophers speak of God as the ground of all-that-is, or refer to Him as a substratum. Please note likewise that by sliding over these wholes, we have placed them into their proper setting, for that is how reality is. In so doing, we have emerged with an absolute whole. Have we not? We had them pulled out of their context and spread out only to help us see things more clearly. Were we to discuss them in the form they really exist, that is, as you see them now, you would have had greater difficulty in understanding what-is. Your difficulty would have been particularly with the two-fold metaphysical component: as concepts, ideas and forms and as components of the true reality in their relationship to the ontological whole. Given the magnitude, multiplicity and complexity of these dynamic wholes continuously in the process of acting and interacting with each other, you can now appreciate better the work of the scientists who must conduct their inquiries looking at reality as it manifests itself.

B. Human's Bond with All-that-is

Diotima: There are a few questions you had posed earlier that I've postponed answering. Let's first pick up the one on how we are related to both the ontic and the ontological realms in terms of our powers. For we already know how we are related to them in terms of their identity. Looking at Diagram 5 helps us to reflect the current aspect under discussion.

Once again for the sake of clarity we are taking the human person out of the normal setting. In keeping with t
he understanding we have acquired earlier, we see ourselves here as three-dimensional beings: spirit, mind and a body that comes with the senses. Since our body is composed of the same elements of matter as the other categories of the ontic realm, we hold certain powers in common with them. We notice at a glance that just as there is a hierarchy in the richness and complexity of their physical make-up, so there is a hierarchy to their powers. With the inanimate substances we hold in common the powers of acting, interacting and becoming. It is by means of their properties and these powers that certain elements combine diversely and in various proportions to form molecules and become natural substances such as water, salt, sugar. Or, through the synthetic processes of man, become such things as medicines, solutions, sprays and other beneficial substances, or some harmful substances such as mind altering drugs, nuclear bombs, chemical or biological weapons of mass destruction, etc.

We know that the elements have their own properties, because when they are placed together, just like people, some of them blend beautifully and produce something new, like hydrogen and oxygen (H_2O) when combined produce water. Others, like oil and water, refuse to combine, and still others readily ignite ($2Mg+O_2=2MgO$), or even explode ($Na+H_2O=NaOH+H$). Plants possess the powers of the inanimate substances, but in addition to these, nutrition, growth and vital generation are their extra powers. Animals possess all of the former powers with sensation, appetition and locomotion coming in as their special prerogatives. These powers enhance animal life and make for a richer and more interesting existence. We know the value of all these powers because we possess them, too. They afford us, among other things, a sense of freedom in mobility. We use these powers in conjunction with our body. The powers we share with the lower forms of life are appropriately judged to be our *lower powers*.

HUMAN'S BOND
WITH ALL THAT IS

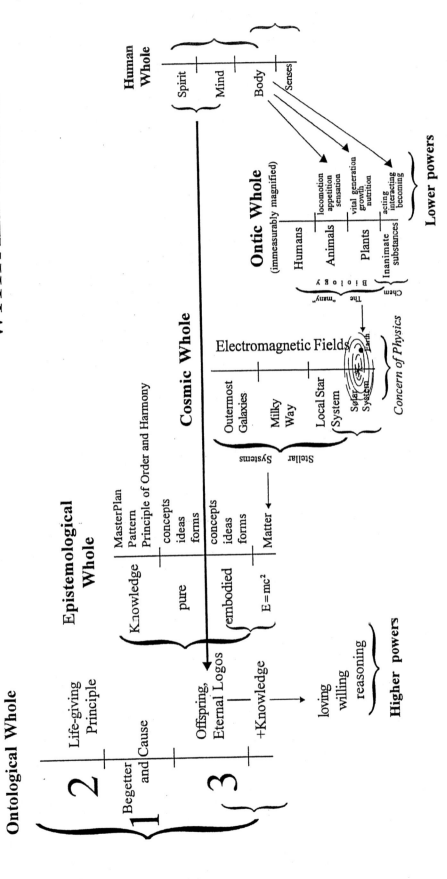

Diagram 5.

Our *higher powers* are those of loving, willing and reasoning. Knowledge, moreover, is of interest only to us. We hold these in common with the Intelligent Beings of the ontological realm to whom we are linked through our metaphysical dimension of mind and spirit—observing, of course, an incomparable difference in degree and in kind. Our bond with them is through the Third, the Eternal Logos. Our spiritual dimension is but a "spark" of the Eternal Living Flame of Love.

Jason: Is this a philosophical name for it?

Diotima: This component of our being is so mysterious that thinkers have been at a loss what to call it. Plato (428-348 B.C.) calls it a "spirited part of the soul," Plotinus (205-270) a "divine emanation," Meister Eckhart, (1260-1327) a "divine spark," Hegel (1770-1831) "spirit in self-estrangement," Scheler (1874-1928) "the ground of being," Heidegger (1898-1975) "*Dasein*" and our contemporary "lovers of wisdom," Thomas Keating (1925-), calls it the "true self" or the "Divine Presence within us," while William Johnston, S.J. (1924-) refers to it by names such as "the inner eye, the eye of the heart, the eye of wisdom, and the eye of love." We shall call it a "spark" of the Eternal Living Flame of Love and provide our justification for it. Each of these names, however, is valid and complements the others, as we shall eventually see. Perhaps it is only a combination of all these names that most closely denotes its true identity. In any event, judging by the time when these thinkers lived, you can see that this knowledge has been with us throughout history and it is not a rare discovery today.

We receive this component in a "virgin" state, as it were, at the moment of our conception. Since this component is by nature metaphysical and what is metaphysical is indestructible, at death it returns to where it came from in the form we give it—provided, of course, we have done justice to our being by living fully in accordance with our nature. At death, the body, which had served the person so well throughout life to realize his or her potential, is laid to rest, while the immortal soul wings its way through the cosmic space to its eternal home there to live forever.

Clearly, we are unlike all other beings in all of reality in that we are a composite of the natural and the supernatural components. For this reason we are subject to two kinds of laws. Moreover, just as our body comes with the senses, so our soul comes with a mind. Senses do not have an independent existence anymore than does the mind. But all work together for the benefit of the person. The senses enhance the life of the body and of the soul. The body enables the person to realize his or her potential. The role of the intellect is to attain knowledge and to help the soul make wise choices for the good of the person; that means for the good of the body as well as of the soul. The human spirit is what gets realized by means of this collaboration. The senses are activated through the prudent guidance of the mind that is sensitive to the needs of the body as well as of the spirit, "the core" of the person's being. Since it is the intelligent spirit within us that distinguishes us from all other created species in the ontic realm, it is this spirit that gives us our unique identity. Because of the spirit, each human being is a person. Actually, it is only when we conduct our life from the core of our being that the whole person is fully engaged and one can be said to be doing justice to oneself.

In light of what has surfaced, we can identify three bonds with the ontological realm in terms of which reality is a tightly knit single whole. These are: knowledge, cosmic energy and humans. It is the human person, however, that is the closest image of the eternal, intelligent Being and is able, therefore, to reveal it best. We come to discover this truth through the actualization of our potential. Our intellect is capable of understanding and explaining what-is, but the ultimate truth of reality comes through the *experience of authentic living* that eventually brings one to the vestibule of the First Principles and reveals them, with absolute certainty, to be the Incarnate Logos, the Holy Spirit and God the Father working as one. Likewise, simultaneously one discovers on the one hand, how these divine Persons relate to us and to reality as a whole, and on the other hand, *who we truly are* and what our life is all about.

Jason: This information is exhilarating and most comforting. I want to believe it is true. My question is: how does one come to know these things *personally* as a fact? I want to know the way that leads to this experience? I like what I am hearing, but I am completely at a loss of how this state can be attained.

Diotima: All that we come to know, Jason, we first learn from others, from those who have already come to know. Subsequently, through education, particularly through certain disciplines, we discover personally how we must live in order to attain to this state of being. Were we to wait until we found out everything personally first, most of our life would have escaped us in just meandering here and there, not knowing what we are looking for. Without knowing the purpose and direction, we would be frustrated by disoriented existence, which would lead us to question the meaning of life itself. The sooner we are set on the right path and directed toward life's ultimate goal, the better it is. This is why in our quest we are following this path. Did you not request at the outset that we follow the path natural to human life? This is it. The next diagram, Jason, will help to disclose the path to the knowledge you are seeking. The specifics of life's journey will be treated at the time when our discourse focuses directly on this topic, that is, as soon as we conclude our inquiry about reality in its entirety.

C.   What-is as a System of Thought

Diotima: Basically, what you see on Diagram 6 you already understand. There are only a few minor, but important additional observations that need to be made.

In our discussion of "reality as a chain of wholes" we have seen that the human species differs from all the animal species in self-consciousness. But we are three-dimensional beings and so we need to see our self-consciousness in terms of all three dimensions. As we approach this discussion we must constantly keep in mind that from the physical standpoint we are insignificant beings on the planet earth, and a mere speck of dust in relationship to the universe, which is boundless. Although the human body is so small, our minds have the power to transcend the whole cosmic sphere, and through knowledge pave the way for our soul to reach its goal, a glimpse of what-is as it is—first, in reason, and subsequently, in vision.

Sophie: What do you mean by "first in reason, and subsequently in vision?"

Diotima: First, we need to understand what-is as it is through our use of reason. That is, first we need to grasp the truth of reason either by means of the philosophical dialectic, or through faith accepting it from those who know, in order to live in accordance with it. To live in accordance with this truth is to live wisely. And to live wisely is to live authentically, which is in accordance with our human nature. When we act wisely, we are gradually led to the knowledge of vision. At the moment when the vision bursts upon the "lover of wisdom," the truth of reason, or of faith, becomes the truth of actual beholding. This is an "Aha!" moment. For it is only at this point that we come to know the truth with absolute certainty, and fully realize what our life was all about.

Jason: Is the truth of reason and the truth of faith the same truth?

Diotima: Not always, Jason. This knowledge will come to light in due time. Were I to give you the answer now, you'd have to accept it from me on faith. I want you to know not only this truth, but also when, how and why the truth of faith is on par with that of reason and, often, even superior to it.

Now, to show how we can come to this truth of actual beholding, we need to portray our ascent all the way to the ontological realm. We shall do so by means of the same line we were using to understand reality. Although the ascent will be made intellectually, because our intellectual dimension is in an embodied form, we have to take our body along. This means that we have to bar all sense of mathematical proportion of the human body to the rest of the cosmos, if we are to help ourselves with a visible image—unless, of course, you'd rather settle for an abstract discourse, which is fine with me.

Sophie: Not I! I find these diagrams very helpful.

Thomas: Yes, these visual maps, as it were, have been of help. They allow, moreover, for an immediate questioning and clarification of concepts.

Jason: I agree. It's difficult to carry on a sustained discourse by means of abstract concepts alone without getting confused, even lost. Especially when that discourse is of the unfamiliar content, as is the case here.

Diotima: Let us take a look at Diagram 6 once again. To our extreme right, we see that on account of our physical dimension, we see ourselves as *sense, body and world conscious.* Because of our mind, we find ourselves *thought, knowledge and truth conscious.* When someone rejects our thoughts, be they ideas or values, don't we feel as if they are rejecting us? We are what we think and believe. That is a part of our identity. Centuries before Anthropology was born as a separate body of knowledge, the Greek thinkers already then defined a human being as a "rational animal." And because of our ontological dimension, we discover ourselves as *self, spirit and God conscious.* Now our principles of conduct and our convictions constitute our identity. At this stage, we do not capitulate to anyone. We live by them and we are ready to die for them, for now we know their true worth. Each dimension, we intuitively apprehend, is sensitive of its own domain and is geared toward its own end. It all happens so naturally. We come to see it only in retrospect.

Our understanding of our "self" as an *embodied spirit* comes last. Initially we understand ourselves as merely *natural beings;* we are totally oblivious of being anything else. With time, as we begin to think more deeply we become conscious of being *rational beings.* Ultimately, we become "self" conscious, that is, self-conscious as *spiritual beings.* Once we reach this awareness of ourselves, we finally come to realize that this dimension was there from the start and acting *incognito.* It was hidden within the depths of our being and patiently awaiting to be

WHAT-IS AS A SYSTEM OF THOUGHT

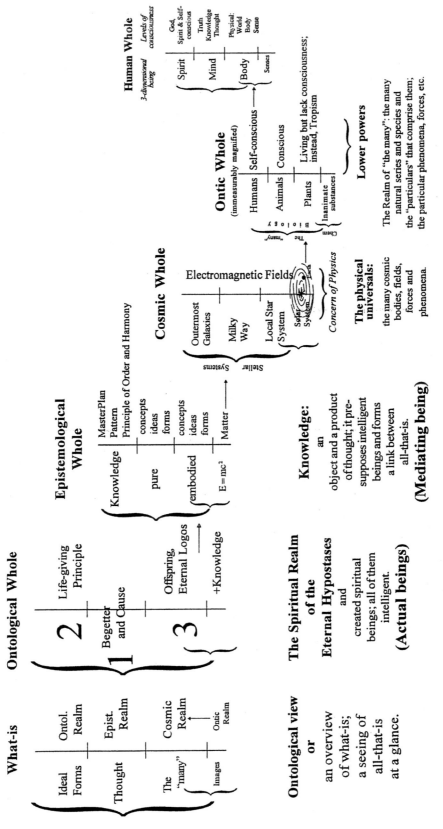

Diagram 6.

recognized. Unbeknown to us, it was this "self" that was our true identity all along. At this point we also recognize personally, our "self" as having been made to the image and likeness of God, a spirit destined one day to be with Him forever.

Thomas: In saying this, are you relying on Revelation or on Philosophy?

Diotima: At this point, I am relying on neither of these, but on the person's firsthand experience, which turns out to be a confirmation of them both, because truth is one regardless of how it is manifested. Each source, in turn, is a confirmation for one's own findings. It is thereby an indisputable proof of the truth, irrespective from where it comes.

In some cases the vision of God bursts upon the lover of wisdom and one already here on earth catches a glimpse of Him and of self in Him. When this occurs, one finally comes to know this truth with absolute certainty. Some souls when wafted on high are granted even a glimpse of the universe from that vantage point. These are the mystical philosophers we spoke of earlier. There are a number of them. Every historical period can point to one. The medieval period had many of them and this knowledge is available to us. We can learn much from those thinkers.

Jason: As I look at the line representing the human person on the extreme right and at the line portraying What-is on the extreme left, I see a correspondence between the two.

Thomas: How? I don't see it.

Jason: What our senses are to the body, so the ontic realm is to the cosmic realm. And what mind is to the spirit, so epistemological realm is to the ontological realm.

Thomas: Yes, I see your point with a big difference though on the lowest level. Senses do not coincide with the ontic realm, do they?

Jason: That's true, but it is through the senses that we perceive things in the ontic realm. Do we not?

Diotima: What you've observed here holds true in other cases as well. In all existing things there is always something that's the same, and something that's different, because things are not identical. For this reason you will be noting a slight change in the sequence of reality as a whole when we get to look at the ordering of what-is. In any event, to see more clearly how the truth of the highest segment becomes accessible to us, let us slide to the left the life-line representing the human person, along with the other wholes, just as we did it before. This time, all the way where we see now *What-is* reflected by means of *a single line.* What we have here is an ontological view, or an overview of the irreducible to each other categories. It is a seeing of all-that-is at a glance.

Let us note further that the human life-line reflecting our three-dimensionality, when moved unto the line representing what-is, shows the human person extending from the ontic realm all the way into the ontological realm. The human body is on par with the cosmic realm from whence it comes, and upon which it depends for its survival. The human mind is eye to eye with the epistemological realm where it first originates, and upon which it draws to reach its goal. And the human spirit extends into the ontological realm from whence it comes, and where it is destined to return. When the person attains to this stage, one catches a glimpse of the eternal Hypostases, and thereby attains the Truth of intellection. This means then that this line reveals us at the heart of reality, and that it leads to three things: the Hypostases, the ultimate Truth, and to the enlightenment of the soul. But this is exactly what Plato's divided line shows. We were planning to use it anyway in order to examine our understanding of the absolute whole. Let us, therefore, take a cursory look at it, first to see what it is and secondly, how the two compare.

1. Plato's Divided Line: What it exhibits

Diotima: By way of a preface let me just mention that Plato's discussion of the divided line takes place in the *Republic,* Plato's major work. Here the various concepts, dealt with individually in other Dialogues, come to bear upon each other presenting an integrated view of human life in the context of society—in those days in a city-state, a republic, whence the name of the Dialogue *Republic.* Some scholars see this book as probably the most influential book of Western civilization; they rank it as second only to the Bible.

Sophie: That's indeed an extraordinary compliment. What makes the *Republic* so highly esteemed?

Diotima: Plato deals here with what is deemed by most to be the deepest concerns of human life. They are also our concerns as well. In this Dialogue, most of these concerns can be seen in conjunction with his divided line.

PLATO'S DIVIDED LINE

Degrees of enlightenment
of SOUL

BEING   **TRUTH**

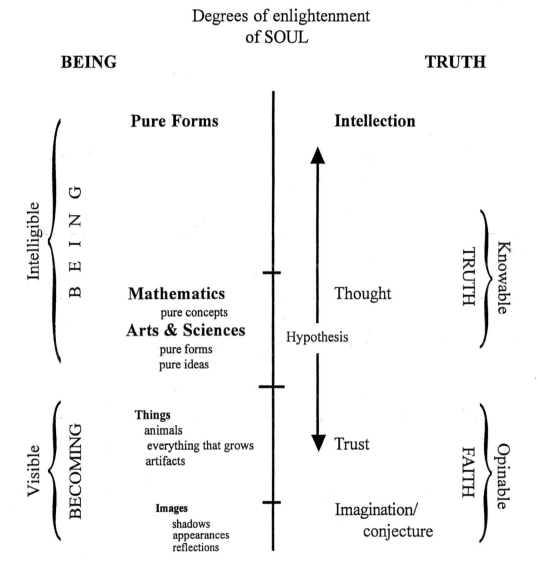

Pure Forms   **Intellection**

Intelligible   B E I N G

Mathematics
pure concepts
Arts & Sciences
pure forms
pure ideas

Thought

Hypothesis

Knowable   TRUTH

Visible   BECOMING

Things
animals
everything that grows
artifacts

Trust

Opinable   FAITH

Images
shadows
appearances
reflections

Imagination/
conjecture

The Actual Object of Knowledge

Diagram 7

The construction of the divided line takes place at the end of the sixth book of the *Republic* (509d-511e). It is preceded by "the sun analogy,"[10] and it is followed by Plato's famous Allegory of the Cave. These three parts constitute the climactic section of the *Republic*. All three parts are relevant to our quest.

As we have already intimated, Plato's divided line (Diagram 7) exhibits simultaneously three different things. These are: Being, the Greek *to on* that translates also as reality; Truth, the Greek *aletheia*, an unconcealment, which turns out to be on par with Being; and Soul in its ascent to the Truth of Being. Below the line is an absolute non-being, and when one reaches the top of the line, one encounters not only the non-hypothetical principle, but also discovers how the Good, the Beautiful and the Just relate to all-that-is. The segments are unequal because what each segment represents is not equal to each other; it is unequal in the form of its existence as well as in its powers.

From the standpoint of reality, the two lower segments represent the *World of Becoming,* the two upper ones, the *World of Being.* The former is *visible,* the latter, *intelligible.*

Jason: If I understand it correctly, what is represented by the two lower segments can be seen with one's eyes; what is represented by the two upper segments, can be seen only with one's intellect, therefore, only understood. Is that what Plato means?

Diotima: That's precisely the meaning. Now from the standpoint of Truth, what is visible is *opinable,* and what is intelligible, is *knowable.* And what opinable is to knowable, so *faith* is to *truth.* Moreover, what segment one (the lowest segment) is to segment two, so segment two is to segment three,[11] and segment three is to segment four.

Sophie: Just to be sure, what does "opinable" mean?

Diotima: The word "opinable" comes from "opinion." In this context it means that when we look at the things which make up our world we form opinions about them based on our perceptions. Since these things are always in the process of becoming, hence changing, and we can see only the external aspect of them, our judgment of them is inadequate. Consequently what we say of them is only an *opinion.* In the discussion on the Good, Socrates said to Glaucon, "no one will ever adequately know the just and fair things themselves, before this [the *idea* of the good] is known" ((506a). The study of the Good, he argued, is "the greatest study" of all (504e-505a). It is worth studying for its own sake and for the sake of understanding everything else.

Jason: What does he mean by faith? Does he mean it in a religious sense?

Diotima: Although Plato's entire philosophy is based on God, more precisely on the Good, the Beautiful and the Just, in this case he does not mean faith in a religious sense. It is rather faith in our own perceptions. As we have stated it earlier, because the forms in the World of Becoming are always in a process of becoming, hence changing, and because we can see only the external aspect of their being, we cannot have accurate knowledge of them. Our understanding here is based on *faith* in our perceptions of them, which is why we can have only an opinion about them. Because the forms in the World of Being are permanent, we can gain *truth* of them.

The four segments of the divided line designate also the *four affections of the soul.* Since one attains knowledge when the soul finally reaches the highest segment, at which time the soul realizes that it has reached the actual beginning and first-rate knowledge, Socrates reverses the order of the segments. He now says, "there are four affections arising in the soul in relation to the four segments: *intellection (noesis)* in relation to the highest one, and *thought (dianoia)* in relation to the second; to the third assign *trust, (pistis),* and to the last *imagination (ekasia).* Arrange them in a proportion, and believe that as the segments to which they correspond participate in truth, so they participate in clarity" (511d). The Greek word *ekasia* also means *conjecture.* You will soon see the appropriateness of both meanings. Do you have any questions about what we have just said?

Jason: Both upper segments seem to yield truth. Is there any difference between them?

Diotima: Yes, there is a difference. The truths of the third segment yield theoretical truths, that is, the truth we come to understand by means of theories produced by the arts and sciences, whereas the truths of the fourth segment are those of intellection or firsthand seeing.

Thomas: That is clear enough. I wonder, however, about the meaning of the word "hypothesis" in Plato and the reason for the two arrows. I am also puzzled on another account. If we cannot know for certain what is visible, what we can see, feel and touch, how can we claim to know what is invisible?

Diotima: Notice, please, that the word *hypothesis* is on the level of thought along with the different forms of human knowledge. Just as reality, we have found, begins with the Hypostases, so the human quest for knowledge begins with the hypotheses. No one inquires into what one knows. That would be superfluous. Since we inquire into what we do not know but want to understand, the quest begins with a hypothesis. Hypothesis is an assumption about something, which then is subjected to a rigorous study proper to each discipline. Because an inquiry can be conducted into anything that is, thought can move downward or upward, whence the reason for the two arrows.

When the inquiry is made into something within the cosmic realm, as is always the case with scientific studies, thought moves down to the object of one's quest. Scientists conduct their experiments and draw data from what they observe about the object of their hypothesis. Since a scientific theory is a description of "the given," scientists never step out of their hypotheses. Their theory in each case is a result of inductive reasoning; hence, the conclusion is most likely so, but it cannot be guaranteed. The reason for it is obvious. Scientific inquiry proceeds by means of studying many samples—never all cases, for that is obviously impossible—hence the conclusion is a generalization based on the studied samples. It always assumes more in its conclusion than the information that was gathered. Given the vast variety and particularity within each species, there is always a possibility that in some cases such may not be the case. Consequently, the conclusion is hypothetical and the end product is a hypothetical theory. Such a theory is subject to subsequent modifications in light of some other pertinent findings.

In the second case, one begins with a hypothesis, but as thought moves upward to mathematics, it steps out of the hypothesis. At that point one leaves the visible objects behind and from then on conducts one's inquiry deductively by means of pure concepts on the basis of logical necessity. This dialectic carries one upward until one reaches the non-hypothetical principle, which is the actual beginning of all things. Because this conclusion is deductively reached on the basis of logical necessity, it is guaranteed or indisputable. Please note: in cases where science raises its inquiry to the mathematical level, it too secures deductive knowledge because mathematics is an exact science. In that case, however, the scientist loses the image of the sense object given in experience. While the mathematical formulae reflect a more accurate knowledge, they are no semblance of the physical phenomena they explain. In light of this understanding, the answer to Tom's question becomes quite explicit. Mathematical concepts are by nature invisible, yet they render more accurate knowledge than do the visible objects given in perception. Does this answer your questions, Thomas?

Thomas: Yes, I see it now.

Sophie: So the hypothesis is an assumption in need of being demonstrated or proven to be true. And the proof can come in different ways. Science provides its proof by means of observation and philosophy by means of dialectic. Both employ reason.

Diotima: Yes. Philosophers sometimes call an *assumption* a *supposition,* but these terms mean the same thing—a belief that something is true. Both terms are used as a starting point of an inquiry and both at first are merely conjectures. As we have stated earlier, no one inquires into what one knows, but into what one wants to know. This means that the starting point of inquiry for everyone is "not-knowing" but surmising, hence, an hypothesis.

Sophie: How does one move from one segment to the next in order to arrive at the knowledge of the fourth segment?

Thomas: You said earlier that what segment one is to segment two, so segment two is to segment three and segment three is to segment four. Can you explain how this is so?

Diotima: Actually, both questions are closely allied. Looking at the divided line and starting from the bottom we see, with respect to Being, that the lowest segment represents the different *forms* of *images;* the second segment, the *visible forms* of the cosmic realm; the third segment represents the *pure forms* of thought, the realm of Arts and Sciences; and the fourth, the *Pure Forms*[12] of the first principles. Please note that each segment is reducible to *forms.* While the forms of the two lower segments are *visible* and the forms of the upper two segments are *intelligible,* they all form a trail of thought that leads to the fourth segment. Each lower segment presupposes the one above it and points beyond itself. Let me explain this by means of an example.

Sophie: Good idea. This should be helpful to all of us.

Diotima: Suppose you've recently moved into the suburbs of a city and are just getting acquainted with the environment of your new setting. One winter morning as you get up and look out the window you see the earth covered with a fresh blanket of pure white snow. While admiring the lovely scene you look down and see footprints in the snow. Immediately your *imagination* goes to work. You wonder whose footprints these might be. You go out and having taken a closer look you *conjecture* that the *image* of the footprints must be that of a deer. You surmise that deer live in the nearby woods and occasionally cross your property as they look for a spring of fresh running water. You have not seen any deer, but the footprints point to a deer, or some such animal. You are not certain. The *image* in your mind reflects *the lowest grade of clarity* and, therefore, of certainty. At the same time, the image of those footprints points beyond itself to the one that made them, hence to something that belongs to the second segment of the divided line.

Thomas: That's clear enough. Let's continue.

Diotima: Later in the day, gusts of strong wind form drifts of snow and cover the footprints. Actually, they are not just covered over but can be retrieved by digging away the snow. No, they do not exist any more. Such images have a quasi-existence. You are, however, on the look out for a real deer, or whatever the animal whose footprints you saw. One day you happen to see it. You were right. Yes, it is a deer. According to Plato's theory, the second segment of the divided line represents *the animals and all the things that can cast shadows and produce images.* All such things have a higher status of existence than do the images below. They have a being and identity of their own which does not rely on anyone's seeing them. Besides, you know when you see something and you know what it is you see, even though without prior exposure to it you may not be able to identify it accurately. Let us assume that as time goes on, you get to discover that deer are seldom seen alone. They usually travel in herds. You learn what habitat they like and where they go as they dart across your grounds. You learn this simply by observing them and form your *opinion* based on your perceptions. You *trust* that your opinion is true. Would you say that you have an understanding of a zoologist?

Thomas: Obviously not.

Diotima: When you pick up a book in zoology with a scientific account of the deer, you will find a wealth of information that was gathered over the centuries by serious scientific investigations. That understanding is a compilation of information secured by means of research that started with an observation, hypotheses and testing to yield the theory you are now reading. There you discover what and how the zoologists have gone about seeking knowledge and how they have come to arrive at their insights. You will also discover what questions are still being asked to make scientific knowledge about deer complete. To that end, additional hypotheses will be set up and experiments carried out to make further inroads into this knowledge.

Scientific theories provide a clearer and a more accurate understanding than we get simply by means of sense perception. Since the world is so large and consists of such diversity of things, there are many branches of science and each provides information relative to its particular area of interest. What is known already, however, reveals certain commonalities about various series and species of existing things. Since there is a consistency in the nature of the species, it is certain that they do not come into being by chance. And since theories reveal an intelligible design in their bodies and a basic pattern in their behavior (something which they lack sufficient intelligence to figure out on their own), it is only logical to conclude that some intelligent being is responsible for their existence such as it is. Scientists do not impose their design upon anything they study. They merely report what they have observed and on that basis draw their conclusions.

From the standpoint of clarity, scientific knowledge, as you yourself see, is superior to what we have encountered on the two lower segments of the divided line. It provides us with *theoretical truths.* This knowledge, however, is not on par yet with the knowledge of the fourth segment of the divided line. As Plato accurately contends, adequate understanding of these entities is possible only in light of the Good (which for Plato is God). Until this knowledge dawns, we cannot know them fully; we cannot know what they really are. This is why, despite all the knowledge that has been attained, there are always outstanding questions in science. Because scientific theories exhibit a highly intricate, intelligible order and harmony in the entities themselves and in their harmonious coexistence in the cosmos as a whole, the knowledge of the third segment of the line points beyond itself to the intelligent Designer(s), hence to the Ideal Forms of the fourth segment of the line. It is, therefore, the retrieved knowledge of what-is below that logically leads us to the original Knowers and Designers. This is how we come to understand the Ideal Forms as the originators of what-is.

Thomas: I must admit, it all does make sense.

Diotima: What we have just said leads Plato to conclude that when we arrive at the knowledge of the Ideal Forms we arrive at the actual beginning and can then explain "everything that is good" in terms of them. *Beginning* then at the beginning, *with the Ideal Forms* [the first principles, the originators of what-is], *we go through the pure forms* [of thought, their ideas], *to the visible forms* [the embodied forms of thought, the visible objects of the cosmic realm], *and end in forms* [the transient images of the lowest segment]. This articulation of reality is known as Plato's Theory of Forms. By means of it he explains all that is good. Since what is good is also beautiful and these are good and beautiful because justice was done to them, you can see now how the good, the beautiful and the just things trace back to the Good, the Beautiful and the Just as their first principles and how these principles render everything intelligible.

2. Comparison of What-is with Plato's Divided Line

Diotima: Placing Diagrams 6 and 7 side by side we see that Plato's divided line consists of four segments, just as ours does, and it too exhibits three different things: *Degrees of unconcealment of Being, Degrees of unconcealment of Truth and Degrees of enlightenment of the Soul.* The highest segment on the side of Being reveals correspondence between his Pure Forms and our Ideal Forms that form the ontological realm. Similar correspondence exists on the third segment, for the third segment being the realm of arts, sciences and mathematics is a realm of thought and, therefore, the epistemological realm. And the two lower segments, which for Plato reflect the World of Becoming, the visible realm, corresponds to our cosmic realm. The difference appears to be on the lowest segment. We have in that place the ontic realm, whereas Plato has images such as shadows, appearances and reflections produced in water and some other bright surfaces (Rep. 509e-510a).

Thomas: Does that mean that one of us is right and one is wrong?

Diotima: Not necessarily. Not if you remember what we have established earlier. We know that the ontic realm is within and a part of the cosmic realm and so we have a little arrow showing where it belongs. Actually, the things Plato names as belonging to the second segment, namely, "the animals around us, everything that grows and the whole class of artifacts" are all from the ontic realm. So there is an agreement between us. The question that could be raised is: Is Plato reducing cosmic reality to the earth? The answer, of course, is *no.* Plato names these objects because everyone is familiar with them. He means to incorporate, however, all that comprises our cosmos, which he calls here the World of Becoming. Whether the forms are large like planets, medium size like animals, or infinitesimally small like atoms, they all are a part of the cosmic realm and all are visible, if not to the naked human eye, then with the help of a telescope or a microscope. We have the ontic realm specifically singled out here for a reason. We want it to keep us mindful of where we are and from where we make our ascent to Being and to Truth. Plato's recognition of the images as an intermediate step between the temporal objects and absolute non-being, which he places below the line, is both perceptive and most appropriate.

Jason: Since the entities of the ontic realm are likewise visible images, in a certain sense, one can justify their being on the level of Plato's images.

Diotima: Yes, they are visible images, but the images on the lowest segment of the divided line do no enjoy the same status of existence as the entities of the ontic realm. Images have only a quasi existence: they are and they are not. They are when light shines upon the objects of the second segment. It is then that they *are* as shadows or reflections in water or in some shiny surfaces. They do not exist in the absence of light, whereas the objects listed on the second segment of the divided line have an independent existence. They exist whether the light shines upon them or not. At night, for instance, when the room is completely dark, you do not see a chair in your path, yet you will discover it is there when you trip over it, or get a bruise. As you can see, objects object to their being overlooked or underestimated. They have a language of their own to manifest their presence.

The only other difference between the two lines, his and ours, is that Plato's divided line does not incorporate Logic. This is only because Logic as a systematic body of knowledge did not exist yet. Plato was mindful of this fact, but apparently ran out of time. He bequeathed this task, and the one of developing an objective moral code in ethics, to the future generations of philosophers. Aristotle, his brightest student, developed the science of Logic and postulated it as a prerequisite for doing philosophy. As to its place in the scheme of other disciplines, Logic belongs at the center of human knowledge. Its place is on the third segment of the divided line, right between Mathematics and the Arts and Sciences.

Thomas: What about ethics? Did any philosopher meet this challenge?

Diotima: By now, there is every imaginable theory of ethics in existence. Not one, however, manages to please humanity; apparently none succeeds in meeting humanity's high expectations. Thinkers always find some reason for rejecting it, or something about it to judge it inadequate. Eventually we, too, will have to address this area because morality is a part of authentic living, and authentic living, we have seen, is the way to assuaging our heart's deepest longings.

And now as we are about to conclude our discussion of Plato's divided line, it may be helpful to add the point made earlier in the *Republic* by means of "the sun analogy" that led to the construction of the divided line. Plato established there the relationship of the two divinities, the good and "the offspring of the good most nearly made in its image," to the two worlds where each is sovereign. The good is sovereign in the World of Being, he tells us, and "what the good is in the intelligible region and to the objects of reason," so "the offspring the good begot in proportion with itself is to the visible world and the objects of vision"(508b-c). The offspring is the cause of everything in the visible realm. Since the subsequent discourse reveals the offspring to be the Just, and we already know from book two of the *Republic* that the Good is God, it becomes clear now how the Good and the Just stand in relationship to the two worlds, the World of Being and the World of Becoming. Are there any questions or reservations you have with respect to the two divinities and their respective realms, before we proceed to insert the divided line into the absolute whole?

Jason: Eager as I am to move on, I have a lingering question that's been weighing on my mind for quite some time. I hope you'll bear with me for asking it now. It might not be even too far afield of our present discourse. I was always under the impression that the Greeks believed in many gods. Does Plato really speak of one God?

Diotima: You are right, Jason. Polytheism was the prevailing view in the Greek culture for centuries. Heavens were populated with all kinds of gods. There was a god responsible for every good and evil in the world. These gods married and were subject to strife. They reflected all human vices and imperfections. Plato sought to rectify this misunderstanding. Immediately after the concept of justice has been given thorough examination in book one of the *Republic*, the next concept that surfaces for scrutiny in book two is that of God.[13]

In founding the city and wanting to make it just, the founders deemed it imperative to admit into the city only what was good, only what would benefit human beings, especially the children who at a tender age are very impressionable and form their basic concepts early in life. "For the young," Socrates says, "are not able to distinguish what is and what is not allegory, but whatever opinions are taken into the mind at that age, are wont to prove indelible and unalterable. For which reason, maybe, we should do our utmost that the first stories that they hear should be so composed as to bring the fairest lessons of virtue to their ears. . . . Adimantus, we are not poets, you and I at present, but founders of a state. And to founders it pertains to know the patterns on which poets must compose their fables and from which their poems must not be allowed to deviate, but the founders are not required themselves to compose" (378d-379a).[14] Consequently, the poetry even of Hesiod and Homer, in spite of their many merits, gets banished, because it attributes to God human imperfections, ill will and all kinds of evil or harmful actions. "The true quality of God we must always surely attribute to him whether we compose in epic, melic, or tragic verse" (378d-379a). Or as Bloom translates it, "The god must surely always be described such as he is, whether one presents him in epics, lyrics and tragedies" (378d-379a).

Having logically established that "God in reality is good," that "no good thing is harmful," that "that which does no harm cannot be the cause of evil," and that "the good cannot be the cause of any evil," nor be "responsible for the bad things," Socrates concludes, "Neither, then, could God . . . since he is good, be, as the multitude say the cause of all things, but for mankind he is the cause of few things, but of many things he is not the cause. For good things are far fewer with us than evil, and for the good we must assume no other cause than God, but the cause of evil we must look for in other things and not God" (Shorey, 379b-c).

Jason: What then is Plato's understanding of God?

Diotima: The rest of book two is devoted to developing proper understanding of God. We are told that God is not a "wizard able treacherously to reveal himself at different times in different forms," wanting to deceive us. He is simple and least likely to depart from his own form; neither is he "wanting in beauty or virtue." It is impossible "for a god to want to alter himself, but since, as it seems each of them is as fair and as good as possible, he remains forever simply in his own shape" (Bloom, 380d-381c). The "god is altogether simple and true in deed and speech, and he doesn't himself change or deceive others by visions, speeches, or the sending of signs either in waking or dreaming" (Bloom, 382e). Consequently, neither mothers, nor teachers or guardians should expose children to anything that would only frighten them, or present God to them in a manner slanderous or unbecoming to Him in any way. So, yes, Jason, as you can see from the cited passages, Plato does speak of one God and him as perfectly good, for which reason he confers upon him the name "Good." You may have noticed, however, that he implies there is more than one entity to this God. In saying "each of them is as fair and as good as possible" he hints at the names the Good (*agathon*) and the Beautiful (*kalon*). The Just (*dikaion*), "the offspring the good begot in proportion with itself" (Bloom, 508b) being the central concept of the *Republic,* is explained by means of the analogy of the sun during the pivotal section of this Dialogue. However, because all three are good, beautiful and just, to distinguish between them, Plato subsequently assigns one of these names to each of them and at one point gives a reason for the hierarchy among them.

Jason: I can see that we are faced here with a profound mystery. Is it possible to gain some insight into it?

Diotima: How it is possible to speak of one God and yet three divine Persons without a contradiction we shall understand better when our dialectic brings us to the discussion of the Ideal Forms. Since our dialectic makes its way to that region by means of the divided line, I suggest that we proceed now to insert it into the context of the absolute whole. Your question, Jason, took us on a little detour. Our initial intent in appealing to Plato's divided line, you may recall, was only to cross-examine our understanding of the absolute whole.

Sophie: The detour was well worth it, Jason. I am glad you've asked the question. The same question was on my mind several times, I just did not want to interrupt the train of thought we were pursuing. I found Plato's reasoning extremely interesting and enlightening. It seems incredible that he, a pagan philosopher, should have had a Christian understanding of what looks to me like the Blessed Trinity. After all, he lived four centuries before Christ was born. And is it not Christ who first gave the world the truth of the Blessed Trinity?

Diotima: My dear Sophie, if only all the Christians were as pagan as this pagan was! This world would be a paradise to live in—just what it was meant to be. As to your question about the explicit knowledge of the Blessed Trinity, it did come through Christ. There are, however, some inklings of the Spirit *(Ruah)* and a promise of the coming of the Messiah in the Old Testament.

Sophie: Amazing! This discourse heightened my desire to know more what Plato had to say. I'm eager to gain a fuller understanding of reality, regardless of how this knowledge comes.

Thomas: What do you mean by "regardless of how this knowledge comes?"

Sophie: I mean, regardless of which body of knowledge makes it accessible, or by whom it is explained.

Diotima: In saying this, Sophie, you reflect the true spirit of philosophy. You are right; it is the truth that matters. Well, then, my friends, let's meet again.

Thomas: You gave us here much to ponder, but, yes, let's set a date.

3. The Divided Line within the Absolute Whole

Diotima: Welcome back. Let's begin by taking a careful look at Diagram 8 to see if there are any further insights, questions or observations you'd like to register.

Jason: What we have understood with respect to the two lower segments of the divided line seems to hold. The visible forms of the cosmic realm appear to be the embodied concepts, ideas and forms. According to this sketch, it also follows that the theories of arts and sciences when viewed independently of the Ideal Forms yield true opinion, that logic and mathematics provide understanding, and that knowledge in the full sense of the word, comes only with intellection.

Thomas: It seems to me that the discourse on the mathematical level should already provide a fairly reliable knowledge. My question is: How is it that the Fifth Entity is said to be "the actual object of knowledge"? Didn't we determine at the outset that the absolute whole is the actual object of knowledge?

Jason: Yes, Tom, that's what we've said. Now we see that the understanding of the absolute whole hinges entirely on the understanding of the Fifth Entity. So, in essence, the Fifth Entity is the actual object of knowledge.

Sophie: I agree, Jason. I wonder, however, if from now on we should not dispense with using that conditional "s" in conjunction with the ontological Hypostases and refer to them in the future as the Intelligent Living Beings. To all evidence, there are three Ideal Forms.

Diotima: Just to be safe, let us wait with this adjustment until we have gained a clearer understanding of this aspect by means of our dialectic. Besides, at least one of the Ideal Forms is the necessary Being, hence the "nonhypothetical principle." Who it is, why, and how it is so, has not yet come to light. What we can grant, though, is that the two symbols, the line and the circle, complement each other, for the circle denotes completeness, a totality, an absolute whole, and the line systematically aligns all that the circle encompasses and gradually leads to the ultimate Truth. Furthermore, because the circle encompasses the metaphysical reality including the ontological realm, once we have inserted the divided line into the circle, we are better able to understand the eternal Hypostases as the "ground" upon which everything rests. As a result of this combination, the two symbols succeed in giving us an ontological view of all-that-is—a vision that far exceeds the ability of the human eye to secure in actuality. Our vision, even when it is 20/20, manages to span, relatively speaking, merely a tiny area of just the ontic whole. Clearly, our forte—and we say this without meaning to underestimate them in the slightest way—are not our senses of perception, but our mind with its powers.

Sophie: Given the full range of what-is with its bewildering diversity, even our mind becomes keenly aware of its limits as it struggles to grasp the sight of the absolute whole. Were it not for the diagrams, I would have been lost long ago.

WHAT-IS:
THE TRUE REALITY

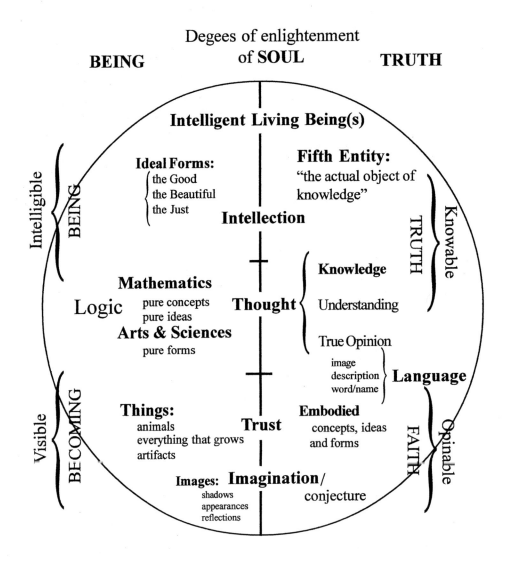

Degees of enlightenment
of **SOUL**

BEING   **TRUTH**

Intelligible · BEING · Visible · BECOMING

Intelligent Living Being(s)

Ideal Forms:
the Good
the Beautiful
the Just

Fifth Entity:
"the actual object of
knowledge"

Intellection

TRUTH · Knowable

Mathematics
pure concepts
pure ideas

Logic

Arts & Sciences
pure forms

Thought

Knowledge

Understanding

True Opinion

image
description
word/name

Language

Things:
animals
everything that grows
artifacts

Trust

Embodied
concepts, ideas
and forms

FAITH · Opinable

Images: **Imagination/**
shadows
appearances
reflections
conjecture

Ontological View of What-Is.

Diagram 8

Thomas: Granting all we have said thus far, I still fail to see how our ascent to the ultimate Truth is to be made in light of Diagram 8.

Diotima: Up to this time we were looking at reality from the ontological point of view. We were trying to understand what-is in terms of the specific wholes, individually and in their relationship to each other. Now that we have a fairly good grasp of what-is, we need to see how this reality translates into human knowledge. Our ascent to Truth, after all, is to be made in knowledge. Because we found reality in all its diversity and multiplicity to be so connected and entwined as to yield ultimately a single absolute whole, we can anticipate the same kind of bonding in knowledge. Knowledge, after all, is of reality. Seeing reality from the epistemological standpoint should help us to see more clearly how our ascent to Truth needs to be made. That means, then, that we need to cast one more glance at the same reality, but this time viewing it from the standpoint of knowledge.

V.   REALITY FROM THE EPISTEMOLOGICAL STANDPOINT

A. Knowledge Accessible to Arts and Sciences

Diotima: Our ultimate goal here is to get a bird's eye view of all the major branches of human knowledge. We want to see how they merge into the sea of knowledge into which the rivers of all the disciplines empty. Such an outcome presupposes an understanding of how they divide, what each of them encompasses and how they network into a vision of an absolute whole. In this way, we will see more precisely what belongs to whom and why; also, the reason for what we shall and shall not be doing. Because we already know that reality consists of three classes (cosmos, the realm of thought and the realm of the first principles), let us find out how each of these classes translates into the existing bodies of knowledge.

We begin with class three, the cosmic realm, because this is where we are. This is the area most familiar to us. Since the ontic realm is within the womb of the universe that embodies the three kinds of entities, there are three basic categories to this knowledge. Diagram 9 helps us to see that these categories are: physical, biological and social. The physical category concerns itself with the inanimate content, the biological with the different forms of life, and the social with matters that relate to human existence.

 Each of these categories, in turn, consists of various divisions and sub-divisions. Although physics is concerned with all the non-living things in the universe as a whole down to the smallest particles of an atom, because there is diversity even among the non-living substances, *the physical sciences* incorporate physics, chemistry, astronomy and a number of earth sciences. Of the latter, for lack of space on our diagram, we have incorporated only the most familiar divisions, namely, oceanography, meteorology and geology. But the list encompasses also geomorphology, geophysics, seismology, climatology, hydrology and geochemistry.[15]

Physics is concerned with the nature and sources of energy, and how energy is changed from one form to another. Into its purview belong the physical fields, forces and phenomena. In conjunction with these, physics concerns itself with electronics, light, magnetism, nuclear energy, mechanics, and engineering, each with its own set of sub-divisions. Chemistry, in turn, which studies the properties, composition and structure of matter, embraces many sub-fields known as: analytical chemistry, organic and inorganic chemistry, physical and nuclear chemistry, and chemical engineering. While the elements of matter forming into various inanimate substances maintain chemistry's link to physics, biochemistry and organic chemistry studying living things constitute a link to biology. Ecology, in turn, links chemistry to environmental and earth sciences. This bonding is an evidence of unity in nature.

Astronomy, commonly known as the study of the heavenly constellations, deals with all kinds of movements of cosmic bodies and matter. It includes astrophysics, astronautics, celestial mechanics and cosmology. Here, archaeoastronomy is a transitional body of knowledge in that it shows astronomy in its relation to archaeology (earth), anthropology (humans), and mythology (early people's concepts, beliefs, deities and heroes expressed in myths).

The biological sciences, whose common bond is life, divide into biology, paleontology and psychology. Biology sub-divides into botany (plant life), zoology (animal life) and anthropology (human life). These sciences incorporate physiology, cytology, microbiology, morphology and anatomy. Biophysics and biochemistry emerge

THE ARTS AND SCIENCES

Knowledge accessible to our natural powers.

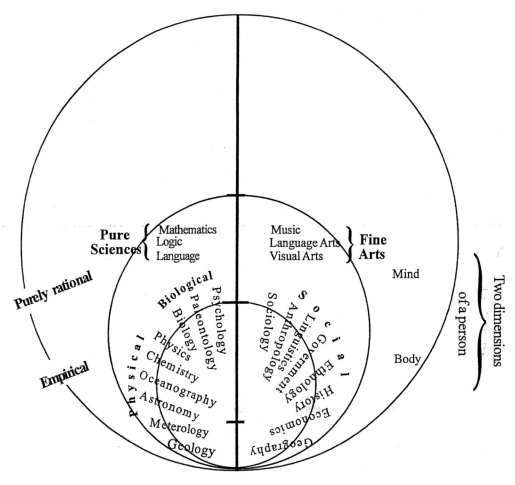

Arts and Sciences

with further sub-divisions

**Many areas of science overlap.
One can study the same object from different points of view, but
each presupposes Ontology.**

Diagram 9

here as connectives between life and the inanimate or inorganic substances. Genetics, embryology, ecology and taxonomy are those other sub-divisions that apply to all three forms of life. In conjunction with these studies arose the field of medicine, which is now considered to be both an art and a science. To the domain of medicine belong dentistry (teeth), podiatry (feet), osteopathy (bones), psychology (behavior), psychiatry (mental disorders) and veterinary (animals). It includes all kinds of specializations of the body such as heart, pulmonary diseases, eyes (with its own sub-divisions), ears, nose and throat, pediatrics, gynecology and so forth. In general, it can be said that these fields are concerned with health, which includes prevention, alleviation, or curing of diseases. Unlike all other branches of biological sciences, this knowledge applies only to animals and human beings.

Paleontology is a science that studies fossils, dealing with the life of past geological periods. Fossils, being remains of plants and animals, provide information about "the phylogeny and relationships of modern plants and animals and about the chronology of the history of the earth."[16] Like the rest of the major branches of knowledge, this one also consists of sub-divisions. These include paleobiology, paleobotany, paleozoology, paleogeography, paleoclimatology and palegeology (a branch that deals with the succession and significance of past life). Clearly, paleontology establishes a link not only between the specific fields of reality, but also between the past and the present.

Thomas: Paleontology is indeed a fascinating field. I wasn't very aware of it. Through the study of fossils we even learn about things that had existed long ago, but don't exist any longer. I mean, for instance, creatures like the dinosaurs. Things like this just baffle my mind.

Sophie: I concur with you, Tom. The more I learn about these things, the more I am seized with wonder.

Diotima: Social sciences, in turn, concern themselves basically with the social and cultural aspects of human existence. Under the umbrella of social sciences we find sociology, cultural anthropology, linguistics, government, ethnology, social psychology, political science, economics and geography; sometimes history is included.[17] While sociology is a study of society, social institutions and their social relationships, social psychology looks into the manner in which one's personality, attitudes, motivations and behavior are influenced by the society in which one lives.

Cultural anthropology deals with human culture. In this context one focuses on social structure, language, law, politics, religion, art and technology. Because language is a critical factor in that it sets us apart from animals, linguistics receives special attention. Whereas physical anthropology compares the human body with those of animals and pays attention to measurement of body parts, archaeology concerns itself primarily with prehistoric cultures and civilizations. The prehistoric cultures give us, among other things, the first inklings of man's life on earth and, through ethnology, an insight into people's relationship with God.

Geography, on the other hand, is the study of the earth's surface, particularly as it impacts on physical and social life of the people. Physical geography incorporates climatology, hydrography and the study of landforms known as geomorphology. These branches of knowledge overlap with the physical sciences, while human geography overlaps with economic, political and social activities. Here are studied dynamics of human populations; demographics include age, gender, births, deaths and migratory movements of people.

Political science, in turn, inquires into the origin, structure, functions, powers and administration of the different forms of government, both on the local and on an international level. Its main concerns are business, labor, natural resources, regional planning and legislative programs. Sometimes history and law fall under its jurisdiction. While the chief concerns of economics are production, distribution and consumption of goods, the chief components of microeconomics are units of activity such as individual farmers, business firms and traders. Output, income and interrelations between different sectors of the economy are the special concerns of microeconomics. All these branches of human knowledge are *empirical* in nature. Studies are conducted by means of observation, testing and experimentation proper to each discipline. Theories begin with a hypothesis and upon securing sufficient evidence yield generalizations that are, notwithstanding, subject to future modifications. In view of the fact that all these sciences constitute a part of human knowledge and as such belong to the second class of reality, we have them start on the level of thought; and because they inquire into things within the cosmic realm, we have them directed downward toward the objects of their inquiry.

Jason: Where does philosophy come in? Isn't philosophy one the disciplines that seeks truth by means of man's natural powers?

Diotima: The content of the empirical sciences is bracketed by Husserl's phenomenological *epoché,* which consists of bypassing objects' external component given in sense perception. As such, it falls outside the ambit of philosophy even though philosophy does inquire into this realm. Unlike the empirical sciences that rely on data secured by means of experimentation and sense perception, philosophy relies upon reason and intuition. Philosophical quest is conducted from the metaphysical standpoint, hence independently of the objects of its inquiry.

Thomas: Mathematics is used in conjunction with all these sciences and yet, I notice, you have it posted squarely in class two.

Diotima: Yes, let's find the reason for it. Class two, being the realm of pure thought, first and foremost, is the realm of pure sciences. The pure sciences are: language, logic and mathematics. We say they are pure, because they are not bound to any specific content. Because they are not bound to anything, they are neutral by nature. Being neutral, they are free to be at the service of every art and science. This is why, Thomas, you have encountered them in studying science. You can expect to find them in conjunction with all the disciplines, both physical and metaphysical, including the arts. Sooner or later, this fact is bound to come to the foreground.

As opposed to the *empirical sciences* that are conducted by means of observation, experimentation, tests and measurements, the *pure sciences,* because they are conducted by reason alone, are said to be *purely rational.* This holds true of them even when they are applied to anything of a physical nature, because the study in pure sciences is carried out independently of the objects of their inquiry.

In addition to the pure sciences, there are also *the fine arts* that belong to class two, for these too originate as works of pure thought. Fine arts, known for their aesthetic value and effects, are creative products of artists. The main divisions of fine arts are: visual arts, language arts and music. Because architecture, sculpture and painting depend on the aesthetic appreciation of eyesight, they are called *visual arts.* Music is *auditory.* And language arts can be both visual (reading literature) and auditory (listening to poetry); sometimes they are a composite of both (drama).

Like the sciences, the fine arts also sub-divide. While the visual arts subdivide into architecture, sculpture and painting with further sub-divisions, so the language arts—which aim at improving communication, both verbal and written—divide into philology (including linguistics), literature (prose and poetry) and drama (a dialogue and action, hence a play). Music, in turn, is the art that combines vocal or instrumental sounds for beauty of form or emotional expression. Usually it is created according to "cultural standards of rhythm, melody, and, in most Western music, harmony."[18] From the world's perspective, music lends itself to various groupings in accordance with the cultural overtones. Apart from the particular style that surfaces at different periods of history, music can be sub-divided into three distinct forms: folk music, classical music and country music. None of them comes as a pure breed, but each is distinct in form. *Folk music,* which comes with many shades of meaning, has its origin with common people of a nation. It is bound to culture and tradition. *Classical music,* also diversely interpreted throughout the centuries, is composed in accordance with established principles and methods. It exhibits excellence, which is recognized as having lasting worth and significance for all times. And *country music* is a style of popular
music, usually based on folk music that has special appeal to particular regions of a nation. Every country has its own form of music.

In the twentieth century in United States there were born other kinds of popular music as, for instance, *rock 'n' roll* and *jazz* that are characterized by a specific style, form and content. This music, having captured the imagination and musical appeal of the contemporary mind and human emotions, is influencing the style of music throughout the world. Because this form of music departs from the characteristics that formerly delineated particular genre and often incorporates elements from a number of them, it obliterates the sharp distinctions between them. *Rock 'n' roll* music, for example, incorporates country, folk, and blues elements, but it gives them its own character through pitch organization, rapidly changing meters, and irregularity in rhythm to generate power, drive and excitement.

Sophie: What is meant by "genre"?

Jason: According to what I have learned, by "genre" is understood "kind" or "style," that is, a particular category of musical, artistic, or literary composition that is distinguished by a specific expression, form and content, such as were mentioned.

Diotima: Music is a vast and fascinating field of knowledge. Interesting as it is, we do not have the time to enter into it, particularly since twentieth-century music through its departure from the hitherto stable patterns abounds in variations of form and styles of expression that resist neat classification. You may want to treat yourself to it at leisure. Our aim here, if you recall, is simply to point out the links between and among the various branches of knowledge in order to show how integrated reality is. Consequently, let the little we've said suffice for now.

Artistic productions as new forms of artistic expressions are often encountered in combination with the other arts. For instance, language arts often appear in combination with music, singing and dance, as we see in drama, opera, symphony, film and other stage productions. Thus, while some works, as those in sculpture, painting, photography, music and literature are single arts, architecture, opera, drama and dance are said to be composite arts.[19]

Lest it be overlooked, there are connections between the fine arts and the cosmic sphere. While we find music and auditory language arts linked to the cosmos through sound, so art is linked to the material world through light with its color spectrum. Artists produce great effects through the interplay of light and darkness, as well as through the various combinations of warm and cool colors. Sculpture, pottery, as also art history and archaeology, through typological classifications, aim to distinguish the varieties of artifacts and place them within broad domains, exposing further the links between the current and earlier civilizations. Objects recovered from archaeological excavations enable scholars to learn something about the early production of art, the material used and the technique employed. All these help them to determine the period from which the artifacts have come. Undeniably, all human endeavors, both in fine arts as well as in science, reveal an overlapping which testifies that all nature is akin.

What remains to be pointed out is that these arts and sciences, at the same time, are closely allied with the two dimensions of the human person, the body and the mind. The empirical sciences account for the physiological, psychosomatic dimension of human existence. This is the dimension we hold in common with the other natural entities within the ontic realm, the difference being only in the degree we possess these powers. Knowledge and language are the initial signs that distinguish us from them all. No animal species has been found to exhibit any interest in theoretical knowledge, nor learn symbolic language. These two powers or abilities, which trace to the intellect, place us beyond the animal species and point to the human intellect as a new phenomenon within the ontic realm. The human mind, in turn, reveals our ontological dimension. For the mind does not exist independently of the spirit. What the eye is to the body, so the mind is to the soul. Primarily, it is the study of the humanities, otherwise known as the liberal arts (although likewise diversely grouped in the course of the centuries), that cultivates the human mind and enables it to plumb the depths and to scale the heights of all-that-is. Since the mind by its nature is directed toward truth, the person will not rest until the light of truth dispels the darkness of one's mind. Because we know when we know, and we know when we do not know, it is certain that we shall know when the coveted moment of truth has dawned upon the horizon of our minds.

In conclusion it can be said that many areas of science overlap. One can study the same object from different points of view, but each point of view presupposes ontology. And this is where philosophy comes in.

Sophie: What do you mean? Can you be more explicit?

Diotima: For example, a botanist, an ecologist, an artist, a poet, and a mystic can look at the same tree but see something else in it. This is because each of them looks at it from a different point of view. All of their views, if they perceive the tree accurately, will have some truth about it. However, like all the bodies of knowledge we have encountered, their views presuppose knowledge of ontology for the full understanding of the tree. By means of ontology, the realm of the first principles, philosophy provides the answer to their unanswered questions and, thereby, completes the human quest for truth.

Sophie: Thanks. I get the idea.

Diotima: In order to see more clearly the path our dialectic needs to take, we must understand philosophy in the context of reality as a whole. This means in relation to all other epistemic disciplines we have just covered. Before merging the two, it seems advisable to see philosophy first as it is in its own right, as a field of knowledge by itself.

B. The Scope and Branches of Philosophy

Diotima: Let us begin by pointing out three basic distinctions between philosophy and the empirical sciences. The first has to do with *the scope of the content*. Diagram 9 made it exceedingly clear that the empirical sciences deal exclusively with the content of Class Three, the universe, whereas philosophy is concerned with all-that-is. The second contrast has to do with *the nature of the inquiry*. Although both disciplines inquire into Class Three, there is no redundancy in their pursuit, for science seeks answers to the questions "how" and "why," and philosophy to "what" and "whence." Science asks: *How* something is or how it behaves, and *why* it behaves as it does? Philosophy asks: *What* something is and *whence* it comes? The third distinction lies in *the nature of the content itself*. Empirical sciences study what is physical, sensible, natural and visible—in other words, that which is given in *sense perception*. Philosophy, by contrast, studies what is by nature metaphysical, supersensible, supernatural and intelligible. This is to say, that which is seen *directly by the mind* but not perceived by the senses. The methodology in each area is governed by the nature of the content. Given these contrasts, it is quite obvious that the two realms of human quest are distinct and are meant to complement each other.

The clue to what philosophy is, what is its function as well as its domain, lies in the very contrasts we've just named. In virtue of the metaphysical inquiry and content into which philosophy inquires, *philosophy is metaphysics*. Its *function* is to arrive at the *ultimate truth* of what-is and, thereby, to supply the answer to the two perpetually out-standing (unanswered) questions in science: What is matter/energy? And, Whence does it come? The "what" and the "whence" are in fact the fundamental questions of philosophy. The first question is the question of *identity*. The second question is that of *origin*, or *source*. These questions, we observe, are raised about *ta onta*, the beings of the cosmic realm, whence philosophy's branch of *cosmology*. Logic, the tool of philosophy, traces *ta onta* to *to on*, the Being of beings, whence *ontology*, another major branch. The product of the philosophical quest is *epistemology* (knowledge), philosophy's third major branch. This branch dovetails with the knowledge of the empirical sciences and complements them. Here the pure sciences constitute the link between the two domains. Epistemology incorporates both the process and the answers, for it is the process that makes the answers intelligible. All the branches of philosophy are metaphysical in nature, much the same as is the nature of its quest.

Furthermore, just as the pure sciences form the link between philosophy and empirical sciences, so ontology is the link between philosophy and theology. Ontology is tantamount to natural theology. Both rely on reason and both find the same first principles to be the origin of the universe, except that they address them by different names. Given this understanding, we can see better why *The Dictionary of Philosophy* states, "Theology, in the widest sense of the term, is a branch of philosophy, i.e., a special field of philosophical inquiry having to do with God" (317).

Once we understand ontology and theology as the realm of the Spirit, we retrieve the source of our third dimension, for the human spirit traces back to the Holy Spirit, the Being of beings.

Jason: What then is the distinction between ontology and theology, if any?

Diotima: Good question! First of all, ontology is the highest branch of philosophy at which metaphysical inquiry arrives. Ontology is the realm of the First Principles or the Hypostases in light of which all of reality becomes intelligible. Theology calls them Persons of the Blessed Trinity. Thus, where philosophy ends, theology begins, and while philosophy's truths are arrived at primarily by means of *reason*, theology receives its truths of "divine wisdom" on *faith*. Upon attaining this knowledge, philosophy reaches its goal, though only to consider next its relevance and application to human life. In this capacity it manifests itself as "love of wisdom." Theology's service lies in helping us to understand what God had revealed and to point out its application to human life. It can be said, then, that philosophy and theology complement each other. Philosophy helps theology to understand the revealed truths, and theology helps philosophy to cross-examine its conclusions. This overlapping makes for a smooth transition from the truths of *reason* to the truths of *faith* and vice versa.

Divine Revelation is theology's privileged domain. The revealed truths are written down in sacred books such as *Bhagavad Gita, Tora, Sacred Scripture, Tao te Ching, Koran,* and so on, each reflecting and promoting the beliefs of its own religion. Because some of this knowledge is passed on orally, as adapted to the changing conditions of the times, another source of this knowledge is Tradition.

Theology enjoys a higher status because its truths have the stamp of divine authority. Indeed, who of us mortals could know better the answers to human life than its Maker? Theology's challenge consists of interpreting these truths accurately and making them intelligible to the human family to facilitate life on earth on its journey back to God. Because the content of ontology is shared by both philosophy and theology, ontology constitutes the link between them. We can say, then, that just as formerly the empirical sciences passed on the torch to the pure sciences, and the pure sciences to philosophy, so now philosophy passes its torch to theology and theology brings it to us—all in a smooth, systematic, orderly manner with each contributing its own share of findings.

Thomas: I'd like to know a little more about the complementary aspect of philosophy and theology and the reason for it.

Diotima: Theology and philosophy, Thomas, as is obvious from what we've just said, make excellent bedfellows. One supplements what the other needs. Both share the same goal and both are in service of life. Unaided human reason emerging from the darkness of the intellect is prone to error. This is amply evident in the conflicting views on any given topic that humans hold and in our trial-and-error approach to discovering what is truly good for us. In such instances, truths revealed by God can be an invaluable help. At the other end of the spectrum

THE SCOPE AND BRANCHES
OF PHILOSOPHY

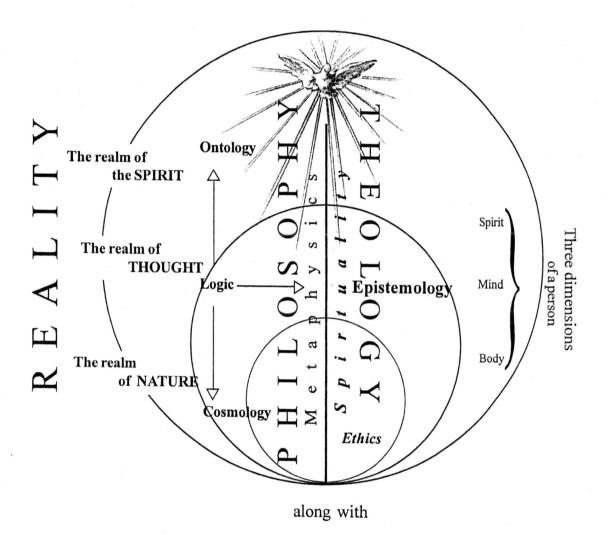

along with

THEOLOGY
Spirituality and Ethics

Diagram 10

the discipline of philosophy can prove to be of assistance. To be sure, the difficulty is always on our side, not on God's; it is due to our inadequate understanding of His Word, because God being Wisdom personified does not contradict Himself. His truth emits pure light and the sound of symphonic beauty but we fail to apprehend it clearly. To help us, God occasionally grants to some individuals glimpses into the ultimate reality. These mystical experiences shed light on those sublime, but perplexing concepts to our mind and help us to discern God's message which always aims at helping us live a good life and be happy.

Thomas: How does this happen? Can you explain it a little more?

Diotima: God grants intellectual glimpses or visions and flights of the spirit to some persons at which time the *intellect* intuits, that is, *apprehends directly* with *utmost clarity* what God wants to communicate. These mystical experiences are for the benefit of all. It is God's way of helping us humans to assuage our unabated thirst for truth, in order to discern more readily the path that leads to Him. Great as reason is, it is beyond its power to attain such knowledge; intellect, the eye of the spirit supersedes it. But this knowledge always comes as God's gift when He wills it, never at our will. We will have much more to say about these things in due time. At this point we need to get our discourse back on track before we lose sight altogether of what we are currently about.

Thomas: I apologize for the detour, but believe me it was not without its merit.

Diotima: Going back to our discussion of theology, we now need to find its place in the scheme of things on Diagram 10. Because theology parallels ontology, it belongs on the fourth segment of the divided line. To preserve its autonomy, we place it on the opposite side f it. However, because theological truths coming from God are meant to help us live our life authentically on earth, we enter theology on the chart starting at the level of ontology and moving downward toward the earth where we are.

Thomas: Isn't there some connection between theology and religion?

Diotima: The term "theology" (Greek *theos,* God, and *logos,* study) is usually a theoretical expression of a particular religion, in which case theology becomes "Jewish," "Catholic," "Muslim," "Hindu," "Presbyterian," and so forth. Theology, however, does not need to have any reference to religion. It can be simply a theoretical discussion about God and God's relation to the world. As such, it can be pursued on a disinterested plane as any other inquiry. Theology, like the rest of the bodies of knowledge, comes with sub-divisions proper to its content. Since we are concerned here with just the major disciplines, we shall not go into them.

Focusing now on philosophy, we need to mention that what we have said thus far belongs to the realm of philosophy as a discipline in its own right. Its function, however, does not end here. Philosophy extends to all the other areas of what-is. There it serves as the system of principles underlying a particular discipline, institution, profession, organization, and the like. Thus we have: Philosophy of Education, Philosophy of Language, Philosophy of Nursing, Philosophy of Science, Philosophy of the Social World, Philosophy of Business, Philosophy of Religion, and so on. One can also speak of the Philosophy of Harvard University, the Philosophy of Alvernia College, or of the Philosophy of the University Professors Association, the Philosophy of Labor Unions, and the list goes on. There is, in other words, a philosophy underlying every human enterprise that is based on a sound foundation and has a clearly defined goal toward which it is systematically oriented. There is even Philosophy of History and a History of Philosophy. Nothing, it seems, nothing rational falls outside its ambit.

Sophie: Which studies in philosophy most directly apply to us as human beings seeking to attain fullness of our being, happiness and our human destiny?

Diotima: Most directly? I believe it would have to be the Philosophy of Human Existence and Ethics, once the truth of metaphysics is established. Without the knowledge of ontology, no body of knowledge is complete or can do justice to anything. It is in the areas of human existence and ethics that philosophy most truly acts in its own name, for as "love of wisdom" philosophy is the bedrock of the science of Spirituality, "the art of wise living," and of Ethics, "the science of human conduct." Both of these areas hold in common the goals you have just named. In this capacity, philosophy is most truly a handmaid of a person. The basic principles of Spirituality provide general direction toward God, leaving plenty of freedom for one's personal relationship; Ethics, through its normative principles guides us in our conduct toward each other and toward nature, in our earthly home. Both Spirituality and Ethics work hand-in-hand. They overlap and enhance each other while guiding us along the path of justice toward self, others and God. Both disciplines are indispensable to one's authentic living and to happiness.

Sophie: So once again there's an overlapping in disciplines.

Thomas: I caught that, too, but I'm somewhat puzzled when you refer to any branch of philosophy or to theology as a science. When I hear the word "science," I immediately conjure activities such as dissecting a cat in a biology class, carrying out experiments in a chemistry lab, or doing medical research in some pharmaceutical laboratories. I don't find that such activities have any place in philosophy. How can I, for instance, understand Ethics as a science?

Diotima: Ethics is a science in a broad sense. It is a science in the sense that it is an *intellectual enterprise,* like all the other bodies of knowledge. Like them, it is a systematic inquiry into its subject matter with the aim of attaining knowledge. The aim of Ethics is knowledge of what is truly good for us *as human beings.* Spirituality as a science must be understood in much the same sense, except for the distinction in its goal. The goal of spirituality is a cultivation of one's inner self; its aim is personal union with God. Both of these disciplines lead to the excellence of our being. We will give them a fuller consideration when we arrive at the conclusive answers with reference to reality as a whole.

Thomas: This explanation is very helpful. It certainly broadens my understanding of the word "science." Where do these two disciplines fit on our chart?

Diotima: Ethics applies to human beings, but it has ramifications for the entire ontic realm. Since we are too insignificant to appear on this chart, we place Ethics horizontally by the dot representing the planet earth, our ontic sphere. Spirituality we place vertically, moving upward from the ontic to the ontological realm, because the goal of spirituality is to guide us to our eternal home within the ontological realm.

By way of summary, we can say, then, that philosophy is metaphysics; that cosmology, ontology and epistemology are its major branches, but that philosophy's domain extends to all that is. Its function, in addition to providing a sound foundation to all the other bodies of knowledge is to attain the ultimate Truth of what-is. Given this understanding, are we ready to merge the two domains, the empirical sciences with philosophy now?

Jason: Wait a minute! Before we do that, let's first see how our ascent to the truth of the ontological realm is to be made.

Diotima: One thing is certain; we are not going to meddle into the affairs of the empirical sciences. Metaphysics points out our route.

Sophie: I am not completely clear yet on what *metaphysics* is. Is there an explanation similar to those you have given us for the other Greek terms?

Diotima: Yes. The Greek word for metaphysics, *meta ta phusika* translates into English as "what comes after physics" for *meta* means "after, beyond," and *phusika,* "the physical reality, the natural world." Because metaphysics inquires into the very *being* or *essence* of beings, it is defined as "the science of being as such." It incorporates all that is not physical and concerns itself, first and foremost, with the "causes," or "the first principles" of existing things. For this reason Aristotle called this study the First Philosophy.

Sophie: Thank you, that's helpful. Once I can connect a new concept with something I already know, I am comfortable with it. The clue for me here is "the first principles." With this clue, I have an idea of what metaphysics is about and how our ascent will proceed. Please pick up now where you left off.

Diotima: In mapping the way, our ascent will take place by means of the pure sciences: language, logic and mathematics. We've been making use of language ever since our discourse began and we will continue to rely upon it. Our quest, like that of the empirical sciences, will begin on the *level of thought* with a hypothesis, hence on the third segment of the divided line and it will be about the cosmic realm, thus the two lower segments of it. This means that first we will have to make a *claim,* our "hypothesis." Since our claim is regarding the cosmic realm, our thought will move *downward,* just as it does in science. Inferences of "inductive logic" will lift us to the level of "deductive reasoning," the third segment. Here our discourse will maintain itself for a while on the horizontal level. Finally, this reasoning on the mathematical level, by means of the *a priori* synthetic judgments will carry us aloft to the fourth segment, *the truth of reason* regarding the first principles. In short, such is our game plan. Don't worry. What exactly all this means will become clearer in the process of making the ascent. As in life, we come to know most things best by doing. We learn to walk by walking and to talk by talking. We learn to read by reading and to swim by swimming. And we learn the art of living by living. So, too, in this case, we shall learn to reason by engaging in the process of reasoning. The new unfamiliar terms that get introduced will be clarified as we encounter them.

C. Reality as Reflected in a System of Major Disciplines

Diotima: Our discussion of philosophy has revealed that philosophy provides a rational foundation to "all that is." We can get this effect by placing Diagram 10 (the contents of philosophy) under Diagram 9 (knowledge of

MAJOR BRANCHES OF KNOWLEDGE

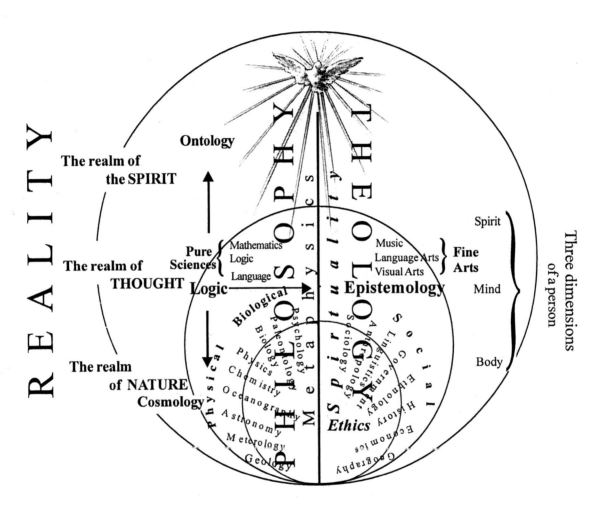

Philosophy, Arts and Sciences, THEOLOGY, Spirituality and Ethics

Diagram 11

the empirical and pure sciences). Looking now at Diagram 11 which combines them, we see a rough composite sketch of the major bodies of knowledge in their relation to each other. What you are looking at here is a product of the human quest over the millennia. This is what the human mind, through the combined effort of all disciplines, achieved throughout the centuries as a result of the mind's relentless search for truth. Each body of knowledge, like a piece of a jigsaw puzzle, is fitted into its place to yield an image of reality in its diversity. All is entwined and interrelated with everything else. Had we inserted all the bodies of knowledge we had named, you can just image how intricate and complex that picture would be. Yet, even then it would be a mere skeleton, although at the same time a more accurate blend of what-is.

Jason: Yes, these would be only the titles of the major disciplines. Each discipline by itself most likely consists of several volumes of knowledge. It's mind-boggling!

Diotima: Take a look again. Is there anything else you observe on Diagram 11 you'd like to share?

Jason: I can spot a pattern even in the way the bodies of knowledge dovetail.

Sophie: And all serve as the steppingstones to the first principles of the ontological realm! To all evidence, what philosophy promises to give us by means of reason, theology can give us on a silver platter as a finished product without sweat and pain. That is, if we are willing to accept it on faith.

Jason: This knowledge, in turn, should shed light on the path of life that comes by means of Spirituality. Does it? Spirituality points us back to the first principles, the origin and source of all things. If what you said is true, then by living in accordance with the light of truth, we should be returning to where we, and the whole cosmic realm, came from—making a full circle! I find this an exciting discovery.

Thomas: So it is a mistake to think that any one discipline can deliver the full truth. It looks to me as if a great deal of collaboration is needed among the scholars of both the physical and the metaphysical disciplines for the picture of reality to emerge in its full splendor and beauty.

Diotima: Well put, Thomas. Let's hope that by carrying out our project to its completion, we can lay a solid foundation for it and thereby help to inaugurate the process of the overall synthesis. Although what we have said about the ontological realm up to this point is still only hypothetical, and as such, in need of being demonstrated, this much is sufficiently clear: Class One, the ontological realm, is the *Realm of the Spirit.*[20] Our spiritual dimension traces to this realm. Class Two, the realm of the mind, is the *Realm of Thought.* All human knowledge merges here. And Class Three, the cosmos, is the *Realm of Nature.* It is true that by "natural things" we commonly understand the immediate entities of the ontic realm, because that is the reality with which we are familiar. Yet, at night, when we look up at the starry heavens and gaze into the rest of the cosmos, we can sense ourselves somehow one with it.

Since our life revolves on earth, all inquiry is conducted from here and most of the bodies of knowledge pertain to this realm, there is a sufficient reason for calling cosmos "the realm of nature." All of reality, however, notwithstanding these classifications, is, you may have noticed, one vast continuum quite fittingly represented by a single line. The concept of the continuum holds true even though along the way at one point one steps out of the realm of time and finds oneself on the shores of eternity. This is another connection that we will note when we come to it later.

V.   DIALECTICAL ASCENT

A. Ascent on the Empirical Level: Inductive Reasoning

Diotima: Do you remember how by tracing things back to the moment of their inception we have thought away the existence of all temporal things and subsequently of absolutely everything?

Thomas: Yes. We were then left with absolute nothingness symbolized by an empty circle.

Jason: Without the human beings, all the branches of knowledge we have just delineated would be nonexistent. So we must eliminate them too. After all, they all are of human origin and had a beginning.

Diotima: That's correct. Assuming nothing else exists, we are faced with absolute nothingness and the question: How did all that is come to be? This absolute nothingness, then, is our starting point. Our first claim is: *The starting principle is necessarily eternal.*

Just in the event, after some exposure to philosophy, you are able to come up with some fresh insights, we ask anew: Can anything come into being out of this absolute nothingness? Ponder this question for a while, as you did before.

Jason: Ever since you've asked this question initially, I have pondered it many times. My answer continues to be the same. No way!

Thomas: I stand by my first answer, too. There are no causeless phenomena.

Sophie: So our first self-evident principle holds: Nothing comes from nothing.

Diotima: Positively. We reason: If there were ever a time when there was absolutely nothing, there would still be absolutely nothing, for nothing comes from nothing. But we, and this whole cosmic realm in all its richness and diversity, exist. We must therefore conclude that there was never a time when there was absolutely nothing.

Now, if there was never a time when there was absolutely nothing, then *ipso facto* two things necessarily follow: (1) that there was *always* "something" or "someone," and (2) that that "something" or "someone" is necessarily *eternal,* meaning, always was, is and will always be.

Sophie: Must it necessarily be eternal?

Diotima: Absolutely. We must grant it is eternal for two reasons: (1) because being itself absolutely first, there was no other prior to it that could have brought it into being; and (2) it could not have brought itself into being, for that would have necessitated acting prior to its existence. This, of course, if you think about it, is logically impossible. Nothing can act prior to its existence. Nothing comes from nothing.

Thomas: That's for sure. Not even God!

Sophie: The concept "eternal" is difficult to understand. I have a hard time envisioning it.

Diotima: Yes, this concept is foreign to our experience because everything in this world is temporal. It had a beginning and it has an end. But what is eternal is uncreated and immortal. If it had no beginning, it will have no end. You may be able to understand it better, and to see more clearly the difference between what is temporal and that which is eternal, by means of the two symbols we have been using, the line and the circle. Notice, a line has a beginning, so it has an end. A circle has no beginning, so it has no end. This is why a line is a good symbol for temporal things, and a circle for what is eternal. Actually, words such as "was" and "will be" do not even apply to what is eternal. These are designations of time, of past and of future, whereas what is eternal simply *is.* As one of the philosophers put it, eternity is an ever present now.

Sophie: I . . . see. . . . I must give it more thought, though, to grasp the full significance of its meaning.

Jason: We must conclude, then, with absolute certainty, that as long as anything exists, that "something" or "someone eternal" necessarily is.

Thomas: Yes, definitely, there has to be something eternal, but what is it? Why couldn't it be matter?

Diotima: To answer this question, Tom, we need to take our first conclusion a step further. Our new claim needs to be: *The "something eternal" is an intelligent being.*

Thomas: How does one go about justifying such a claim?

Sophie: Once we acknowledge that there is something eternal, for me the second self-evident principle, "No one can give what one does not have," provides a conclusive evidence for establishing everything else. I have only to turn my mind's gaze inward on the mystery of my own being. There is nothing in this whole vast universe, least of all matter, that could have given me my intellect with its thirst for truth, a heart whose yearnings nothing in this world manages to satiate, or consciousness that makes me mindful of the grandeur, goodness and beauty of nature. Where did these come from? No one can give what one does not have. Matter does not possess these attributes or components. Just these three examples—and these can be greatly multiplied—are sufficient to convince me that there is Someone, some highly intelligent Being, who possesses these and many other attributes needed to produce the world such as it is. It is because this Being possesses them that it can impart them to me and to what-is. Since I don't see myself as any different from the rest of humanity, I contend that sooner or later others come face to face with the mystery of their own being and, eventually, with the mystery of all that surrounds them in nature. When they begin to relish what eludes their eye, but grips their heart, they will be led to a similar conclusion, even though they may not be able to properly name that source.

Thomas: What about the atheists and all those learned professionals in nearly every field who hold the highest academic degrees but do not concur with your view?

Sophie: They are, I must confess, an enigma to me. If little children can get so excited at the sight of a pretty butterfly or at a little daisy in the grass and in wonder ask all kinds of questions, and if simple people can stand rapt in contemplation gazing at the heavenly constellations or at the majestic mountains towering in the azure sky and experience the presence of some Majestic Presence, it puzzles me that those who should be able to provide intelligible explanation for these phenomena manage only to trace it to the Big Bang of gases and blind, chance-driven evolution. How could those gases give what they do not have? How could they have produced what the most intelligent minds over all these centuries have toiled to understand, and still have not managed to fathom?

Jason: I can understand Sophie's point. It is well based on the second self-evident principle. I, on the other hand, am inclined to base my arguments on the third and fourth principles: "Intelligent activity presupposes an intelligent being," and "The intelligence of the being must be at least on par with its activities." As I ponder the magnitude of reality in its diversity, so intricately designed and harmoniously intertwined, so as to form an organic whole, I can barely form a notion of the intelligence and power required to produce such a stupendous work of art. No wonder Leibniz called it "the best of possible worlds." There is so much wisdom and beauty concealed in the magnificent order and harmony that the universe displays in its co-existence and reciprocity of all that exists in it! We have barely caught a smattering of it in the system of epistemic disciplines (Diagram 11) that reflects it. These, we know, are a product of a host of outstanding intellects over the millennia that are just reporting what they found. None of the thinkers, scientists or humanists ever claimed credit for designing anything in nature, much less the universe. A mere insight into what-is "as it appears to be," was deemed a great accomplishment. What intelligence, what knowledge one must have to even conceive it! What power was involved in converting that design into reality and then to sustain it all in existence! This truly boggles my mind.

Clearly, in light of what I have already discovered in the process of our search, I have no doubt that the first principle responsible for the existence of all that is, is an eternal, intelligent being whose powers exceed my ability to comprehend. As a member of the most intelligent and most gifted species in this world, I cannot make the tiniest bit of paper stay up in space, when I toss it up. Still less, can I sustain it there in an orderly fashion. Yet, look at the solar system. Those incredibly vast cosmic bodies revolve in their orbits like toys. As we have heard from Lincoln Barnett, the universe consists of all kinds of systems that move simultaneously in space with unimaginable speeds. The planet earth itself is involved in different kinds of motions at the same time. What's astounding is that these motions are not just useless gyrations. Each of them has a purpose that has a positive effect upon our life on earth. The knowledge that science has retrieved lends tremendous support to my thesis and renders our third and fourth self-evident principles irrefutable. Intelligible activity, that the universe reveals, presupposes an intelligent being. And if the nature of one's work is any sign of the intelligence that produced it, then the intelligence of the being that designed this universe and sustains it in existence, must be at least on par with it. To my mind, the dynamism at work in the universe, as well as the power that sustains it, can be nothing short of infinite!

Thomas: Although I myself find it more and more difficult to refute your arguments, the classical reply of those who view the universe as a natural spin off from the Big Bang, would be that cosmic functions are all a result of natural laws. Laws such as that of gravitation, complexity, vortex motion in space and the like are sufficient for them to explain all cosmic motions without any appeal to an intelligent being.

Jason: Admittedly, these laws exist and are operative in nature. That's what accounts for its order and harmony. What laws can they point to, though, that have come into being independently of intelligence? Laws are intelligent ordinances that presuppose intelligent beings. They are framed by intelligent beings for a specific purpose, usually for the sake of order and harmonious coexistence among the parties concerned. In case of the universe, they are there for the sake of the order and harmony of cosmic bodies, be they vast or infinitesimal, in their co-existence. We can see the same need reflected in any society and family. Where there are no laws, there is chaos. And where there is chaos, there is neither harmonious co-existence nor peace or happiness. To be effective, of course, laws must be just, that is, they must do justice to all parties concerned. In any event, whether in a family, in a society, or in the universe at large, where there are laws, there is a mind, or minds, behind them.

Sophie: And where there is a consistent, intelligible, purposeful behavior in objects that lack intelligence, as is the case in most of nature, the case is even stronger!

Thomas: Although the latest scientific findings in molecular theory seem to lend validity to order and design in nature,[21] one can point out cases to invalidate your stance.

Diotima: This is true. One can find exceptions to the inductive arguments in philosophy as much as in the empirical theories in science. It is impossible to study every case of any theory. This already always leaves an open window for some possible deviations from the norm. You may recall from our brief study of logic, however, that such exceptions, called *counter examples,* do not invalidate sound arguments. Exceptions to the rule are recognized and acknowledged for what they are, exceptions. Were we to invalidate sound inductive arguments on the basis of counter examples, we would have to invalidate also most of the empirical knowledge. While inductive conclusions cannot be guaranteed in every case, neither can they be dismissed lightly. To be on the safe side, though, it is better to state one's conclusion as "most likely so" or "probably true in most cases." This applies to your arguments as well, Sophie and Jason. Undeniably, evidence is mounting for an intelligent eternal Being as the originator of the cosmic realm; however, a more reliable method of arriving at it is needed to establish it as an irrefutable truth. We just have to raise our discourse to the next level of logic.

B. Ascent on the Rational Level

1. Deductive Reasoning: Logic

Diotima: Deductive arguments, if you recall, unlike the inductive, begin with the whole and move to the parts. Words such as "all" and "no," or their equivalent in the major premise, are usually a clue to an argument being deductive. Conclusions to these arguments never claim more than what was accepted in the premises. For this reason, if the argument is valid and its premises are true, the conclusion is necessarily true. Since an argument usually establishes one thing at a time, sometimes a series of deductive arguments is needed to reach one's conclusion systematically. Pay careful attention to the arguments that follow. If you have any reservation, feel free to interrupt. We shall move slowly and with great care.

Reflecting upon the same reality, our arguments run as follows:

What at some point in time came into being, at one time did not exist.
Man and the objects of the cosmic realm at some point in time came into being.
Therefore, man and the objects of the cosmic realm at one time did not exist.

Now that which came into being, came necessarily through the agency of another.
Man and the objects of the cosmic realm are that which came into being.
Therefore, man and the objects of the cosmic realm came necessarily through the agency
of another.

Since "that which comes into being" is an effect and "that through which" something comes into being is
a cause, given that man and the objects of the cosmic realm are "that which came into being,"
they all are effects of some cause.

Because the being and powers of every effect necessarily trace back to their cause,
given that man and the objects of the cosmic realm are all effects,
it follows that their being and powers trace back to their cause.

Considering that no one can give what one does not have,
the powers found in the effects,
necessarily inhere in the cause.

Since every intelligent being and/or highly complex effect presupposes a highly intelligent cause,
and man is both an intelligent being and a highly complex effect,
it follows that man's being presupposes a highly intelligent cause.

But this is true not only of the human species.

Whatever exhibits an intelligent order and design presupposes an intelligent cause.
Since both man and the whole cosmic realm exhibit a bewilderingly intelligible order and design,
they all point to and reveal a bewilderingly intelligent cause.

Diotima: Well, how do these arguments strike your ear?
Sophie: They are music to my soul.

Jason: I am in agreement with them 100%.

Thomas: Given the internal structure of formal logic, it is difficult to take issue with them.

Diotima: Any questions? Comments? Observations?

Jason: An observation. These arguments merely confirm in a formal way what we have reasoned to on the empirical level. Even though we did not appeal to empirical methods, we did rely on the observation of what is given in our personal experiences. We drew our conclusions on the basis of inductive reasoning by going from our actual or possible experiences to generalizations. I am glad to find out that there is so much truth in those "educated guesses," as the generalizations are sometimes called. No wonder we hold the conclusions of empirical sciences with so much respect. The deductive arguments, however, because of their formal structure are able to yield a much more reliable knowledge on the strength of logical coherence. I am beginning to see the real value of logic.

Diotima: You can understand now why we have said earlier that conclusions of inductive arguments should not be taken lightly. At your leisure, it might be good for you to examine these arguments more closely for the validity and the truth of their premises. Perhaps some questions may surface in your mind at that time. In the meantime, on the basis of what had surfaced can we draw a conclusion?

Jason: By all means!

> *Conclusion:* In view of the fact that a consistent order and harmony in nature are inconceivable without an intelligent orderer or designer, as long as the harmonious ordering in nature exists, the intelligent Orderer or Designer necessarily is.

Thomas: What about the *chaos theory* that some scientists advance?

Diotima: This theory at one time seemed to enjoy some popularity, particularly when Darwin's theory of gradual evolution by natural selection was dominating the scientific scene.[22] Alas, with every advance in science, evidence is mounting for the intelligible design. Michael J. Behe, a biochemist who thoroughly examines philosophical arguments for and against the design, bases his conclusion on the scientific findings saying: "To a person who does not feel obliged to restrict his search to unintelligent causes, the straightforward conclusion is that many biochemical systems were designed. They were designed not by the laws of nature, not by chance and necessity; rather they were *planned.* The designer knew what the systems would look like when they were completed, then took steps to bring the systems about. Life on earth at its most fundamental level, in its most critical components, is the product of intelligent activity.

"The conclusion of intelligent design flows naturally from the data itself—not from sacred books or sectarian beliefs. Inferring that biological systems were designed by an intelligent agent is a humdrum process that requires no new principles of logic or science. It comes simply from the hard work that biochemistry has done over the past forty years, combined with consideration of the way in which we reach conclusions of design every day" (DBB, 193). To the question "When is it reasonable to conclude, in the absence of firsthand knowledge or eyewitness accounts, that something has been designed?" he responds: "For discrete physical systems—if there is no gradual route to their production—design is evident when a number of separate, interacting components are ordered in such a way as to accomplish a function beyond the individual components. The greater the specificity of the interacting components required to produce the function, the greater is our confidence in the conclusion of design" (194). By *design* he means, as we do, the *"purposeful arrangement of parts"* (193).

To us the most familiar example of the case in point is the human person. A person is more than the function of the particular organs like the heart, lungs, kidneys, liver, etc. Yet, if one of these functions were to cease, the person itself would cease (without immediate medical intervention). Thus, the essence of the design is that all parts of a given system work together to produce a certain function beyond that which the individual components can achieve. This would not happen if one of several parts of the system were missing. Behe contends, "This is the essence of the design argument" (DBB, 212). Of course, the design of which we are speaking not only incorporates, but also extends beyond the structure of the particular entities and, in a like manner, encompasses the whole cosmic realm. This is evident in the *harmonious coexistence* of all that is when everything functions in accordance with the design and in *chaos,* when something malfunctions. The malfunction, because of it being an integral part of what-is, has a rippling effect on the rest of the whole. This is true on the individual as well as on the universal level. Behe's scientific proof of design on the molecular level is at once the strongest proof for design on the cosmic level and, as we shall soon see, on the level of the absolute whole.

Thomas: Is this not perchance a view of one scientist?

Diotima: It is interesting, Thomas, that you should make this observation. Ordinarily when science speaks, the general public receives the new information as a pronouncement *ex cathedra*, that is, coming with "authoritative finality." Science spoke, God spoke! Yet in the temple of science there is as much controversy about their matters, as there is in all other fields of knowledge about theirs. Some of it, no doubt, is because not all are at the same level of understanding and acumen. The major reason, however, appears to be due to the fact that each person speaks from the framework of his or her personal life-orientation. We know what we live and we live what we know. This colors our intuitive grasp of things and forms a disposition toward everything else in life. Such being the case, some scientists base their judgments on the presuppositions, rather than on data. Consequently their views do not coincide with those based on the facts. Since the glory of science accrues to it from data, rather than from presuppositions, evidence is on our side. Just listen to what Behe reports: "The knowledge we now have of life at the molecular level has been stitched together from innumerable experiments in which proteins were purified, genes cloned, electron micrographs taken, cells cultured, structures determined, sequences compared, parameters varied, and controls done. Papers were published, results checked, reviews written, blind alleys searched, and new leads fleshed out. The result of these *cumulative efforts* [emphasis ours] to investigate the cell—to investigate life at the molecular level—is a loud, clear, piercing cry of *design!*" (DBB, 232).

The most recent publications in science seem to confirm these findings. Ignatius Press in the year 2000 published *Science and Evidence for Design in the Universe.* The book, co-authored by Michael J. Behe, William A. Dembski, and Stephen C. Meyer includes bibliographical references to papers presented at a conference sponsored by the Wethersfield Institute. This text provides additional glimpses into scientific evidence for design in the universe; it also shows, like the quote above, how painstakingly this knowledge was secured. Even the thinkers who are too enamored of the mystery in the universe to give credence to the mystery of God find it necessary to examine the question again. We see an evidence of it also in the debate between Sir Martin Rees, the British Astronomer Royal, and Canon John Polkinghorne, the former Professor of Mathematical Physics at Cambridge. Rees, despite his atheistic orientation, at a session of the interdisciplinary society "Café Scientifique" in the end emphasized: "The prerequisites for any life—long-lived stable stars, a periodic table of atoms with complex chemistry, and so on—are sensitive to physical laws and could not have emerged from a Big Bang with a recipe that was even slightly different . . . Many recipes would lead to stillborn universes with no atoms, no chemistry and no planets; or to universes too short lived or too empty to allow anything to evolve beyond the sterile uniformity." According to him, this "fundamental mystery should not be brushed aside merely as a brute fact."[23] If so, then the deductive conclusions we have reached merely reinforce scientific inferences, and jointly provide compelling evidence for the eternal intelligent Being as the First Cause of what-is.

Thomas: What we have said thus far, then, establishes only that the originator of the cosmic realm is necessarily eternal and that it is a highly intelligent Being. We still do not know who this Being is. Neither do we know that there are in fact three Hypostases as the first principles, as was intimated earlier. If such is the case, then we need to discover what precisely is their relationship to all existing things, don't we?

Diotima: You are right on target, Thomas. Our next step is to discover what else we can know about this Being, or Beings. When this knowledge comes to light, we hope to gain insight into those other questions as well. To ascertain all this, let's move on to the next level of reasoning. Number concepts are precise. It should be easier for us to understand these abstract concepts by means of them.

2. Deductive Reasoning: Mathematical Level

Diotima: Keep in mind that on the previous two levels our *claim* served as a hypothesis and the arguments proceeded to justify that claim. Here, too, we shall begin with a *hypothetical statement*, hence with a hypothesis. Likewise, it will require a series of arguments to arrive at the conclusive answers we are seeking. There are, however, several movements to this process. Listen carefully: Our reasoning process, as before, is beginning with a hypothesis on the third segment of the divided line. From there, our thought will move *downward* to the realm of "the many," another name for the cosmic realm. Since hypothetical arguments are the "if/then" arguments, we begin in just this manner.

Argument 1. If there are "the many," there is one, because each of the many is one.
Whether "the many" be innumerable in number, or only 9, 5 or 2, there is 1 *per se.*
For unless there is 1 *per se,* there is nothing at all.
This follows from the fact that 4 to be 4 presupposes . . .

Sophie: Hold it, please! You've lost me already. Math is not my forte.

Thomas: Yes, please. Can we go through that slowly again?

Diotima: Certainly. I cannot afford to lose you at this stage. Just relax. This reasoning does not require complicated math. All you need to know is the basic set of ten numbers. You are surely comfortable with these. Are you not?

Sophie: To reduce apprehensions of individuals who, like myself, are not of a mathematical bent of mind, and possibly to minimize misconceptions or expectations of others, it might be helpful at this point to delineate more clearly our goal in this section and how we shall use number concepts to achieve this end.

Diotima: Good idea, Sophie. First of all, please remember that we are metaphysicians, not mathematicians. As such, we are not interested in the whole gamut of mathematical systems, their uses of numerical concepts, and the intricacies inherent in the field of mathematics. As metaphysicians, our goal is to understand reality. Consequently, we are appealing to number concepts to help us refine our understanding of what-is. Secondly, we have seen earlier that mathematics is both a *neutral* science and an *exact* science. Because of these enviable qualities, mathematics makes valuable contributions to all the bodies of knowledge whenever it is appropriately applied.

To legitimize our appeal to it, it is sufficient to point out that mathematical concepts are versatile in their use. They are applied differently in the realm of music than, let's say, in art, physics or economics. In metaphysics, we shall employ number concepts in their simplest form, that is, by appealing to their essential meaning and to the universally accepted sequence of the standard set of ten numbers that subsequently lend themselves to all kinds of applications. And thirdly, it just so happens, that mathematics is our next and the final steppingstone to the understanding of reality. If you recall, we began with our *personal, subjective sense perceptions.* Then, having acknowledged as the next step the *empirical sciences* raising ordinary sense experiences to a higher, *objective* level, we have moved to the *inductive reasoning* and, then, to the *deducting reasoning of logic.* The latter brought us to the doorstep of *mathematics,* which has the power to lead us to reliable conclusions with regard to the first principles and their relationship to the rest of reality. It is the precision of the mathematical number concepts that holds the promise of yielding the indisputable truth we are seeking. Throughout the search, our goal has been the understanding of what-is and this goal remains unaltered to the end. Does this review, my friends, make it clear what we are about in this section? Does it put you at ease?

Sophie: This look in retrospect at what we did and a look forward at where we're going, along with the clear articulation of the goal, is a good preparation for the section upon which we are embarking. Knowing what awaits us not only allays my fears, it makes me eager to take the step that promises to bring us to our goal.

Diotima: Good. To help ourselves envisage what we have just said, suppose we go back to our two symbols, the circle and the line, which served us so well up to this point. These will help us to see more clearly what exactly is happening at this level of our discourse. Let us draw, once again, the absolute whole consisting of three circles to designate the three classes of reality and the divided line running through them to represent all-that-is. In the lowest circle representing Class Three, write the words "the many." In the second circle designating Class Two, write "Math" in its proper place. Parallel to it, on the right side of the divided line, write numbers from 1 to 10 finishing off with the sign for infinity to indicate that numbers could go on indefinitely. Next, draw an arrow from the hypothesis down to the realm of "the many" and from there back to "Math," for this is the path our discourse will follow. Do you have it?

All: Yes.

Diotima: Fine. With our gaze on Diagram 12—where we have the path of our mathematical discourse traced against the background of, and therefore along with, other ways of knowing (sense perceptions, science and logic), let us thoughtfully look once again at the first argument that initially appeared to be unintelligible: "If there are 'the many,' there is one, because each of the many is one." The planet earth is one, a tree is one, you are one, and *each* of "the many" entities comprising our cosmos is one. Are you with me?

Sophie: So far, so good.

WHAT-IS:
THE TRUE REALITY

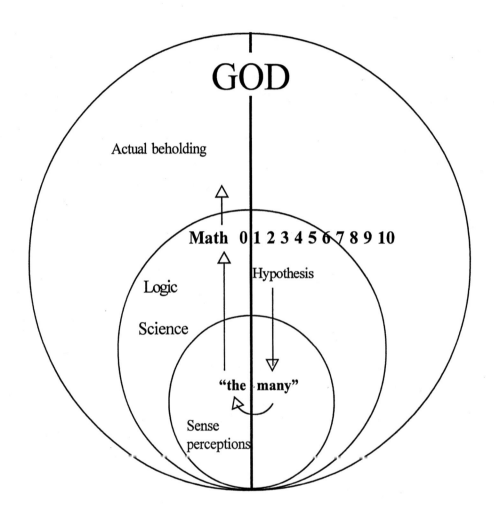

GOD

Actual beholding

Math 0 1 2 3 4 5 6 7 8 9 10

Logic

Hypothesis

Science

"the many"

Sense
perceptions

Stages of Mind's Ascent to Truth

Diagram 12

Diotima: "Whether 'the many' be infinite in number (which they are not), or only 9, 5, or 2, there must be 1 *per se.*"

Jason: Why are you referring to number 1 as "1 *per se*"?

Diotima: Look at your number line. Each of the numbers is one: 9 is one by itself, 6 is one by itself, 3 is one by itself, and so on. We can consider 75, or 1,000,000, or 8,745 each of these three sets, and therefore any other set, as one by itself. The first number could be designating a membership of some association; the second can stand for the sum of money you won in a lottery, and the third number could denote an enrollment in some school. Notice, each of these three combinations of numbers is considered as one, a sum or totality representing one thing. Since any number, whatever be its combination, can be viewed as one by itself, to distinguish number 1 from the rest of them, we refer to it as "1 *per se.*" This number is extremely important, "For unless there is 1 *per se,* there is nothing at all."

Sophie: How is that?

Diotima: This follows from the fact that 4 to be 4 presupposes the being of 3, 2, and 1, even as 2 to be 2 presupposes 1. After all, is 2 not 1+1? If there is no 1, there is no 2. And is 3 not 1+2, 2+1, or 1+1+1? Clearly, without 1, there is no other number possible. Every subsequent number presupposes 1 and builds upon it.

Given this understanding, what is 5 without 1?

Sophie: If there is no 1, number 5 does not exist. And neither does any other number.

Diotima: Excellent, Sophie! I am glad you did not say 4, for you could have reasoned 5 -1 = 4. Your answer assures me you understand the point I am trying to make. And, now, what comes before 1?

Sophie: A zero (0).

Diotima: Since zero is also a number that has a significant role to fulfill, let us place it in front of the number 1. We all know that in this position zero stands for nothing, which means that 1 depends on nothing for its being. We also know that when zero appears in the middle of numbers or at the end, it is a "place holder." This is nothing new.

Now, since numbers are neutral in nature, they can be applied to anything that is, and since they are precise, when they are applied accurately, they lend the same validity to that content. We see them applied practically to everything: objects, money, computations, counting, all kinds of measures such as sizes, weights, ratios, volumes, degrees, distances, as also to all the sciences and arts. How are they applied in music?

Jason: Numbers are applied to measures, to notes, to keeping time, to beats and chords. These are indispensable to producing melody, rhythm, harmony, and so on.

Diotima: What about art?

Sophie: They apply to proportions, measurements and distances. Presumably there are other uses as well, of which I am not aware.

Diotima: Is something comparable true in science?

Thomas: Physics, astronomy, chemistry, in fact all of the physical sciences, are inconceivable without mathematics. Perhaps to a lesser extent, but the biological and social sciences make use of numbers as well.

Diotima: What, then, prevents us from employing number concepts in philosophy? If numbers apply to the particular entities of reality, why should they not apply to reality as a whole? What follows, paves the way to our second argument. Have you an idea of how we should apply the number line to reality?

Jason: I assume vertically, because reality extends through all three classes.

Diotima: And where does number 1 belong, on top or at the bottom of the line?

Jason: Since number 1 starts the number line, and the starting principle is in the ontological realm, I would put it on top.

Sophie: I agree.

Thomas: I suppose it make sense to put it there, unless one insists on the Big Bang as the starting point.

Diotima: Good thinking! The number line extending downward into the World of Becoming can then apply to the ever-new particulars of all the cosmic series and species that can keep on coming indefinitely, just as the numbers sequence can.

Argument 2. Applying now the number line to reality as a whole with number 1 in the ontological realm, we can see that what the mathematical 1 is to the number line and to the science of mathematics as a whole, so the One—we write it with the capital letter to differentiate it from "the many," each of which is one—the eternal, intelligent Being, is to every existing one, each of "the many" and to the reality as a whole. From this it follows that just as every subsequent number relies for its being on the existence of the number 1 and the whole science of mathematics builds up from it, so every subsequent being relies for its existence upon the existence of the One, the eternal intelligent Being, and all-that-is builds up from it. Since the One is just as indispensable to the existence of "the many" as the number 1 is to the number concepts, we are compelled to conclude: *As long as anything is, the One necessarily is.*

Sophie: That's fascinating! Just beautiful! What about the negative numbers? How do they fit into this scheme?

Diotima: Good point, Sophie. The negative numbers have their place here as well. Let's insert them into our diagram by placing on the opposite side of the zero, a corresponding set of numbers with a minus sign in front of them. We do so with the understanding that the negative numbers are possible only because the positive numbers are. A concrete experience from life can exemplify this fact. For instance, you can lose or spend and, therefore, be minus a $5.00 bill only if there is such a thing as a $5.00 bill. I can be short of a penny, only if there are pennies. In other words, you cannot be minus that which does not exist in the first place. So, too, is the case with numbers. We can be minus any number only because there is a corresponding positive number. Since the particulars of reality consist of things that *are,* that is, they are "something" definitive, we have applied positive number concepts to them.

Sophie: Thank you. That was a big help.

Diotima: I'm glad, because this understanding leads to several other conclusions.

Argument 3. Given that number concepts and the science of mathematics are intellectual activities and intellectual activities presuppose an intelligent being, it follows that number concepts and the science of mathematics presuppose an intelligent being.

Argumen 4. Moreover, since the intelligence of a being is always at least on par with its activities and number concepts, the basic components of mathematical activities, terminate in infinity, it follows that the intelligence of the being demanded by the science of mathematics is infinite.

Argument 5. And since an appropriate name names something about the named, and the one being named possesses intelligence that is infinite, it follows that an appropriate name for the Being whose intelligence is infinite, would be *the Infinite.*

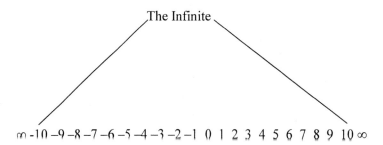

Furthermore:

Argument 6. In view of the fact that the physical sciences are recovering knowledge of the cosmos in mathematical equations, it follows that the cosmos was mathematically designed, which is why it is so "finely tuned." (A comparison: Just as one can fetch peas from the soup only if they were put into it in the first place, so, too, one can recover mathematical proportions in cosmic phenomena only if they were applied to them in the first place.) If so, then mathematics predates the birth of the cosmos and is, therefore both, prior to it and independent of it.

But mathematics consists of intellectual activities.

Argument 7. Since intellectual activities are functions of the mind and the mind has no existence independent of the intelligent being, it follows that mathematics belongs to the being that originated the cosmos.

Argument 8. And since the originator of the cosmos, we have agreed, is the eternal intelligent Being who possesses all powers and perfections, and all that is ultimately traces back to this Being, mathematics being one of those perfections, it follows that mathematics necessarily traces back to the same Being. And if that Being is eternal, so must mathematics be eternal. Were it not eternal and not already always in the mind of the Originator, how would it have come into being, or from whom, when prior to this eternal intelligent Being there was no other to give it birth? Yet, all that came into being gives irrefutable evidence of it.

Clearly, mathematics not only renders the universe and everything within it intelligible and points to, but also demands the existence of the Super-eminent Mathematician as the Maker of the cosmos. Thus, while mathematics is the most precise and reliable body of knowledge, and for this reason the most highly respected science of all, it itself is superseded by its Author who exceeds it both in dignity and in power.

But the service of mathematics does not end here.

Just as philosophy, mathematics applies to the fine arts as well. This is so because the fine arts draw upon the cosmic phenomena of light, heat and sound for their substance. For instance, melody, rhythm, harmony and symphonic beauty of sound in musical compositions are inconceivable without the mathematical precision. And the beauty of form, color and design in artistic productions of art, much the same as in nature, are due to the ratio, proportion, hue in color and symmetry in them. Artists testify to this fact. All this indicates that the mathematical concepts are the basic "buildings blocks" of all that displays beauty, order and harmony, whether in nature or in fine arts.

Considering that human artistry to a great extent is an imitation of Divine artistry in nature as many paintings from scenes in nature indicate, it can be expected that the laws governing the fine arts and nature, would be comparable and that both would trace back to the laws of the original master plan of the cosmos. This confirms our earlier conclusion, namely, that the beauty, harmony and the intelligibility of reality to a great extent depend upon mathematics whether one is aware of it or not. Given these facts, *mathematics undeniably is.* And *if mathematics is, the eternal Super-eminent Mathematician necessarily is.*

Did you notice the sequence? Cosmic phenomena of light, heat and sound that give rise to nature, give rise to empirical sciences and to fine arts. These, in turn, by revealing mathematical underpinnings lead to mathematics. And mathematics necessarily leads to the Super-eminent Mathematician, the eternal intelligent Being. Here surfaces, once again, a chain to what-is, this time with mathematics as "the silver thread" binding all-that-is into one.

Jason: So the universe is a product of the knowledge of the eternal intelligent Being, and human knowledge is a "discovery" or better, a gradual "uncovery" and a "recovery" of the original master plan that displays a fabulous design with an all-over pattern to it.

Diotima: Well stated, Jason. Our intellect aided by the senses enables us to recognize some of the obvious designs in nature. We see the various flowers each with a particular design to it. Dogs, cats and horses, deer, fish and birds, as all else, can be recognized for what each of them is by the respective form that is uniquely designed. With the help of scientific studies we are led to discover an intelligible design not only in the identity, but also in the nature of the particular series and species, individually as well as in their co-existence and reciprocity within nature as a whole. Physics and astronomy have helped us to see the design in the arrangement and motions of the solar system and the stellar systems. The latest triumph in science, right at the end of the twentieth century, although for some reason low keyed, comes with the discovery of a design in biochemistry—an extraordinarily intricate, beautiful design in the development of life at the molecular level. And philosophy has helped us to uncover it in reality as a whole in the pattern and coexistence of the vast wholes. Undeniably, it is the mathematical principles, which undergird the visible world, that allow music to speak of the harmony of sound, science to speak of the harmony of the spheres, and philosophy to speak of the harmony of all-that-is!

Thomas: Interesting, to say the least. Are we ready now to undertake the quest for the three Hypostases? I continue to be haunted by this concept.

Diotima: Before we approach that discussion, let us first take a thoughtful look at the distinctions between the One and "the many." These delineations will serve to forestall some ambiguity when we begin making the more subtle distinctions. On the basis of what you have discovered already, let us see how many contrasts we can list. Will one of you be our secretary as we jointly seek to arrive at these concepts? Thank you, Sophie.

Jason: The most obvious distinction is *eternal* and *temporal.*

Thomas: Intelligent and *non-intelligent?*

Diotima: Since we and animals in general exhibit intelligence in various degrees, it may be more accurate to say *intelligent* and *intelligible*. The term "intelligible" will encompass then the inanimate substances as well, hence, all of "the many."

Thomas: Yes, *intelligible* does make better sense.

Diotima: Anything else? . . . Looking at the number line, you may get a hint at some other sets of appropriate distinctions. . . . Since without the One nothing could be, what does this say about the One?

Jason: That the One is *necessary,* while "the many" are *unnecessary?*

Diotima: True, we are not necessary to the existence of all that is, but we do not want to think of ourselves as being completely unnecessary. Do we? Neither would life be possible without the basic elements of nature, even though they are only inanimate substances. These and everything else in this world are definitely necessary for the human life to survive on earth. How about *necessary* and *contingent?*

Jason: That sounds better.

Sophie: Supernatural and *natural.*

Diotima: Good. Any other? What set of contrasts comes to your mind when you consider that the One does not depend upon anything for its existence?

 Thomas: Independent and *dependent.*

Diotima: And because the One is not conditioned by anything or anyone?

Jason: I guess *unconditioned* and *conditioned.*

Diotima: Very good. And if the One is independent and unconditioned by anything whatsoever, it must be . . . what?

Sophie: Self-sufficient?

Diotima: Good. *Self-sufficient* and . . . ?

Jason: Dependent? But we've used that word. Reliant?

Diotima: Reliant will do; so *self-sufficient* and *reliant.* Now, if someone is self-sufficient, then it must possess all powers and perfections. Otherwise, it will be lacking something and to that extent in need of it. Were it so, it could not be said to be self-sufficient. By means of the number 1 concept, we have seen however that the One relies on absolutely nothing.

Sophie: How about *infinite* and *finite?* I suppose we could also add to our list *the designer* and *the designed, the orderer* and *the ordered*—all those contrasts we have reasoned to earlier.

Jason: That's right! How about *the cause* and *the effects?*

Diotima: Very good. However, because "the many" in generating others like themselves serve as secondary causes, the One, since it had no beginning, is referred to in philosophy as *the uncaused cause.* So let us record it this way. Now, can you think of a term that would encompass all powers and perfections? No one?

Jason: Absolute?

Thomas: Yes! So the set of contrasts would be *absolute* and *relative.* Would it not?

Diotima: Well done, my seekers of truth. These contrasts will suffice to make the point. Sophie, would you please read the list we've assembled?

The One	"the many"
eternal	temporal
intelligent	intelligible
necessary	contingent
independent	dependent
unconditioned	conditioned
self-sufficient	reliant
infinite	finite
designer	designed
orderer	ordered
uncaused cause	effects
absolute	relative

Diotima: An impressive list, don't you think? Please keep these contrasts in mind. They will prevent our faltering in the future.

At this point, let me draw your attention to three other important attributes that belong to the One. They are: *transcendental, transcendent,* and *immanent.* These characteristics do not have corresponding terms for "the many." The word "transcendental" means *fundamental, underlying,* forming *a substratum* for the existence of "the many." By analogy, we can say that the floor of this room is transcendental to everything that rests upon it. If the floor were to fall through, so would everything that rests upon it. In just this sense, the One is said to be transcendental to the existence of everything that is. Without it nothing else would be. You can see now why some philosophers speak of the One as the Ground of all that is. The word "transcendent" means *beyond, above all that is.* From the human standpoint, it would be last reached. Thus, first in actuality, but last approached from where we find ourselves now. And "immanent" means *within, present* or *inherent* in what-is.

Jason: How can something be "beyond" all that is and yet "within" it?

Diotima: These concepts do seem to be contradictory, but they are not. This fact will soon come to light with the help of the number concepts.

Thomas: Is the One, God?

Sophie: What, or who else, could possibly fit the description with all the attributes we've named?

Jason: If I remember correctly, it was Hegel who referred to God as the Absolute. He said that we are barely able to get a notion of all that the name Absolute signifies. And I fully concur with him. For when I try to envisage the Being with all those attributes, I am utterly bewildered. My mind loses itself in thought.

Diotima: Throughout the history of philosophy God was referred to by many of the attributes we have listed. The thinkers simply placed an article "the" in front of it and capitalized the first letter of the word. Thus, God was addressed by names such as the Eternal, the necessary Being, the Infinite, the Transcendent, the Absolute, and so on. Hegel was not the first one to call God by this name. Some philosophers already during the classical period did, and certainly many in the course of the medieval period had reached similar conclusions about God. It was St. Anselm, however, the philosopher of the eleventh century, who gave us a very succinct, but perhaps the best explanation of how God needs to be conceived. He said God is the Highest Thing Thinkable, *aliquid quo nihil majus cogitari potest,* literally, "greater than which nothing can be conceived."[24] That, of course, would be the Absolute, which is why he referred to God by this name, too. For the Absolute could neither be superseded nor exceeded in any way by anyone or anything. Sometimes you may encounter in literature a reference to God as "the Most High." This name probably most closely approximates St. Anselm's understanding of God.

Jason: To me this means that on the continuum of all-that-is, beginning with the Hydrogen atom and moving gradually up the scale through the existing series and species of absolutely all that is, one would eventually come to the highest, the most excellent, the perfect Being to whom everything traces, hence from whom it proceeds, and that would be God.

Diotima: Your articulation, Jason, resembles one of the five ways St. Thomas reasons to the existence of God. It is his argument from the gradation found in nature. He writes: "Among beings there are some more and some less good, true, noble, and the like. But *more* and *less* are predicated of different things according as they resemble in their different ways something which is the maximum, as a thing is said to be hotter according as it more nearly resembles that which is hottest; so that there is something which is truest, something best, something noblest, and, consequently, something which is most being, for those things that are greatest in truth are greatest in being, as it is written in *Metaph.* Ia, I (993b 30). Now the maximum in any genus is the cause of all in that genus, as fire, which is the maximum of heat, is the cause of all hot things, as is said in the same book (993b 25). Therefore there must also be something which is to all beings the cause of their being, goodness, and every other perfection; and this we call God."[25] St. Thomas is handling several examples at the same time, but taken singly, I hope you can see that this argument does resemble your own trend of thought.

St. Anselm likewise has an argument similar to yours. His take-off point is not from the smallest atom in the universe, as yours is, but from the desires of the human heart. He says, "In all our desires there is something that seems to us good in what we desire. It may be a real good; it may be only an appearance of good; we desire it because we think we shall enjoy it, because we think it good for us.

"Now all good things must have their origin in good; therefore since the scale of the finite good things desired by man cannot be infinite and our grading of these good things, however far we carry it, must eventually come to an end, there is one absolute good, one absolute sublime whence all good springs.

"Therefore one absolute sublime, one Highest Being exists; one absolute *Summa Natura.* And this absolute Supreme Being is not a whole, made up of parts, for if it were composite and conditioned by parts it would not be absolute.

"And the Absolute, unconditioned and without parts, created the world we live in *ex nihilo,* out of nothing. What other hypothesis is credible?" (Pegis, 137). No matter from what standpoint you approach it, St. Anselm's succinct definition of God as the being "than which none greater can be conceived" names the Absolute. As you can see, Jason, your own argument resembles and complements the thinking of both, St. Anselm and of St. Thomas Aquinas.

Thomas: I do not deny the legitimacy of these arguments. There is obviously much merit to them, in fact too much for me to assimilate at the moment. I must ruminate on them for a while to get the full benefit of this thought. My nagging question right now is: How can I be sure that this Most High, Sublime Being we've called the Absolute is in fact God and not some other absolute being?

Jason: Tom, why would you want to posit some other absolute being rather than God when God is the name given exclusively to that Highest Being and implies all the powers and perfections that the term absolute denotes? Are you suggesting another absolute being in addition to God?

Thomas: I really don't know. Is that impossible? I am just asking. In spite of where we are in this quest, I'm still uncertain. What logical proof is there that the Absolute is God?

Diotima: The concept of two absolute beings, much the same as of two absolute wholes, is logically untenable, Tom. Let us consider first the possibility of two absolute wholes, for that might be easier to understand. Do you remember what we did when we tried to secure the concept of the absolute whole? We kept on adding things until we have encompassed *absolutely everything.* We've included even that of which currently we may not have any knowledge. Only then were we able to call it *the absolute whole.* Everything we've reasoned about subsequently, we have placed within it. From this it follows that there could be only one absolute. If there were two identical wholes, neither of them would be absolute, for there would be something outside of both—that other whole. On the metaphysical level, as is would be the case with the Absolutes, if there were two, they would collapse into each other, for there would be nothing to set them apart. As you can see, there could be only *one absolute whole,* or the concept *absolute whole* itself becomes meaningless. But this concept is intelligible. We have logically arrived at it and it has been employed meaningfully in the past many a time. It is in fact indispensable to the understanding of what-is. In conjunction with the discussion of the absolute whole two other remarks are apropos. The first has to do with our symbol of the circle, the second, with the concept of the "multiverse."

Having arrived at the concept of the absolute whole, we drew a large circle, a symbol for it to help us envision it, lest we got lost on account of its bewildering magnitude. Subsequently we have incorporated into it two other circles: one to designate the cosmos; the other, knowledge. We did that in order to see them more readily in relation to each other and, although different in nature, both as an integral part of reality as a whole. In doing this, however, we have imposed a boundary upon each of them. In reality, there are no boundaries to what-is. Consequently at the end, when we complete our quest and have the understanding, we will dispense with the circles to gain a vision of the absolute whole just as it is: boundless, spreading indefinitely into oblivion and vanishing even from our inner sight.

Given this image of reality, we can also understand that the concept of the "*multiverse,*" instead of the *uni*verse that some scientists have been recently advocating, is equally untenable. The universe can be conceived as both, *finite* and *infinite.* It is *finite* because it had a beginning and it will have an end. As of late, some scientists place the beginning somewhere around 15 billion years ago.[26] According to the same source, the universe will draw its last breath in approximately about another 15 billion years. The scientists even venture to tell us it will expire in a whimper.[27] Supposedly we are already in the entropy phase, somewhere beyond the half of its life span. But the universe can be viewed also as *infinite* in the sense that it admits of no boundaries. The cosmic galaxies at enormous speeds are dashing outward into the endless expanses of dark space with nothing to contain them or obstruct their flight. The concept of the multiverse implies real boundaries among the particular universes in space. But no boundaries can be found. Since science relies on facts observable in nature, what evidence is there in support of the multiverse? With all the space explorations in progress, no astronaut ever returned from space reporting anything that could even remotely suggest some kind of a boundary. Neither did any of the astronomers with all their finest telescopes, nor an unmanned aircraft circling in space gathering information, find any evidence in support of it. Sir Martin Rees, a contemporary British Astronomer we had mentioned earlier, recently argued for the theory of the multiverse, but eventually conceded that he was merely speculating.[28]

Something comparable holds true of the absolute being that is purely metaphysical. There could be only one absolute being. If there were two, the only way both of them could maintain their own identity would be if one of them differed from the other in some way. One of them would have to have a different form or possess some power or perfection that the other lacked. In that case, the one that lacked something could not be said to be an absolute being. At best, it would be next to it in excellence. Since the concept of the absolute being denotes absolutely all powers and perfections, *the maximum of what could possibly be in itself* and is limited by no particular form, if there were two identical beings they would blend into one for lack of boundaries or any distinctions in them. A crude, imperfect analogy of it might be water in the ocean and that of rain or a river that empties into it. There being no difference in their essential nature, they blend together, forming an indistinguishable single whole.

Thomas: I understand now the impossibility of there being two absolute wholes and two absolute beings, but how can I be sure that the Absolute is God, or that there are three Hypostases?

Diotima: If you understood what we have said thus far, a simple deduction can establish this fact. We reason: Since the name "God" belongs to the Highest, Most Sublime Being "than which none greater can be conceived" and this is precisely what the term "absolute" denotes, the Being who possesses all these attributes is the Absolute. Given that there could be only one Absolute, it follows that the Absolute is necessarily God. Both terms, "God" and "the Absolute," name the Being "than which none greater can be conceived."

Thomas: Diotima, do you *personally* believe that the Absolute is God?

Diotima: No, Thomas, I do not believe that the Absolute is . . .

Sophie: I simply *cannot* believe that!

Thomas: If so, what's the source of your convictions, just logic?

Diotima: No need for consternation, my friends. You did not let me finish my sentence. I was attempting to say: No, I do not *believe* that the Absolute is God. I *know* this for a fact. And I know it with *absolute certainty.*

Thomas: How do you know it?

Diotima: From contact, through my interaction with the Deity. Wouldn't you expect a "priestess of Apollo" to have some firsthand knowledge of the Divine? Read Plato's *Symposium* and you will find out who it was that instructed Socrates in the Great Mysteries; also, how the lover of wisdom "is led and approaches" this Being of awesome beauty and comes to know this truth as a fact from *personal experience.* This knowledge, however, is not meant to be a possession of a select few. It is meant to be a ravishing experience of every human heart, if not already here and now, at least upon death. That's what we were created for, but for it to happen, one must choose to move in that direction and attain the purity of heart *needed* to behold the awesome sight. We were created not only to know the truth *about* God. We were created as partakers of His powers so that we may one day to participate in the fullness of God's life and glory for all eternity. This is our glorious destiny, my friends, and this is what spirituality is all about.

Thomas: Can you explain it a little more?

Diotima: Just as all children who do not disown their parents are heirs to their inheritance, so are we to God's inheritance, also under the same conditions, for we are God's offspring in the real sense of the word. In both instances, moreover, from day one the offspring partakes of its parents' nature and bounty and *with their help* moves toward its own fullness of life. The remarkable part about it is that reaching the coveted state of one's being requires of us only to be true to our nature, but we must develop *fully* what we already always potentially are right from the start. Our life on earth is but a maturing process in all three dimensions of our being; it is a journey in consciousness, a journey that involves growth and transformation through a personal relationship with the Divine. It occurs in the process of our search for the truth of who we *really* are. Eventually, the ultimate truth of our search turns out to be our *bond with God* and a *vision* of Him. Thus, the search for our real "self" is really a search for "God"; and the search for "God" is a search for our "self"; both answers surface at the same time. This is what one discovers in the end and this is what human life on earth is all about!

Thomas: How does one get to that state? Is it through reason?

Diotima: Not by reason alone, Thomas, by love. We have reached the point to which reason alone can take us when we have discovered *that* the eternal intelligent Being or the Absolute, rather than the Big Bang, is the cause of everything that is good and *that* the Absolute *is* God. What He is like is given to each person individually in a *personal experience* through a relationship of love with the Divine. Spirituality is the science that facilitates our development at this our deepest level, the level of the spirit. Here love paves the way and brings one to the ecstatic vision of Him.

Relating now to what we have said earlier about the three dimensions of the human being, we can now see more clearly the process of how one arrives at the ultimate Truth with body, mind and spirit each fulfilling its own task. Just as the human body with its senses has a special work to fulfill through the functions it performs for the good of the whole person and cannot exceed its powers, so our mind and heart or intellect and spirit, each with its powers in its own area has its own work to fulfill through the functions it performs and cannot exceed its powers. The fact that we are alive and well indicates that the body is doing its share. Reason, the faculty of the intellect has been hard at work in us ever since we've undertaken this quest and, as we have already stated, it has reached its goal when we have arrived deductively at the conclusion *that* the Absolute or God *really* exists—more accurately, *is*—and *that* everything good that came into being ultimately traces back to Him.

Notice please, reason does not invalidate or undermine the functions of the body with its senses. It enhances them and, by guiding them properly, raises them to a higher level of excellence on the one hand, and on the other, finds confirmation in them. The confirmation is manifested in the normal growth and harmonious development of personality that exudes joy. It is not within the power of reason, however, to take one to the *vision* of the *living God*, even though reason can draw implications from it once the *intellect* had caught a glimpse of Him.

Sophie: Just when our dialectic was gaining momentum and it looked as if we are but a stone's throw away from the final truth, we are brought to a sudden halt.

Diotima: What we are experiencing subjectively on the personal level in our quest, friends, is not unlike what the empirical and the speculative thinkers experience objectively on the epistemological level in their quest. You're right, Sophie. There is usually much enthusiasm and great anticipation on the part of all truth-seekers, especially when insight by insight light begins to dawn and an intelligible design begins to emerge. The confidence in reaching the full truth intensifies with each step along the way. You've experienced it yourselves. Alas, as so often in life, when the object of one's dreams seems to be within reach, one "hits a brick wall," as it were.

We have only to recall: the whole march of science, on the empirical level, had led to an unprecedented progress. Its triumph occurred when the scientists finally reduced the whole cosmos to matter and matter to energy. But now, instead of the final truth, a dilemma, for they ask: What is energy? Whence does it come? It is this victory *and* these questions that bring the empirical thinkers to an impasse. Science is facing a dilemma beyond the means of its own discipline to resolve. Speculative philosophers, in turn, fully confident in the power of reason, on the strength of logical necessity seek to arrive at the same answers by means of reason. Some of them take different approaches to the study of reality and appeal to different methods, but when unable to reconcile some of their conflicts—and usually to find God—they are brought to the same kind of impasse as scientists. Even those who appeal to logic, as we did, and arrive at the conclusive answers that reason can provide, like yourselves now, they emerge with a sense of disappointment. More is anticipated from reason. Yet, when a mind's search terminates in a system of thought that is free of contradictions and an intelligible vision of reality, reason has honorably fulfilled its role. The fact that all thinkers do not agree, or doubt even when the answer has been reached logically, is a proof that reason falls short of what it takes to satisfy heart's deepest yearnings. What the human heart craves is love and nothing short of the experience of God, but this belongs to the domain of the spirit.

Jason: Didn't we mention at one time that at this point reactions among the thinkers diverge?

Diotima: Good memory, Jason, they do. Some become disillusioned with the power of reason and abandon further search, thinking only their opinion matters. Others are led to conclude that only this world exists and all one's reasoning is futile, nothing more than mere speculating that has no bearing on human life. They turn to the pursuit of wealth, power and prestige instead. Still others relegate all philosophical thinking to merely an edifying discourse. Such thinkers usually abandon the concept of truth altogether. If anything, they deem only the scientific explanations of the world worthy of any credence. The concept of the metaphysical reality is dismissed as nothing more than a phantasm or an illusion. The reactions are almost as varied as the thinkers themselves and the style of life they espouse. The outcome of such thinking is predictable. Once truth is denied and reality reduced to the world of the senses, the absolute gets relativized and the relative absolutized. With this twist, words lose their meaning, confusion ensues and some of the philosophical language gets to resemble more the experience of the Tower of Babel than even an "edifying discourse." Wisdom becomes a lost art. No one even mentions it. Such thinking, as we know from the contemporary situation in the world, is not without deplorable consequences for humanity. Fortunately, there is yet another group of philosophers whose faces upon reaching this stage are radiant with joy and they have heartwarming answers to our questions.

Sophie: How is that? Why is there such a disparity among the philosophers? I am puzzled.

Diotima: There are many possible reasons for it. We will not go into them at this time. Just recall what you have heard me say earlier: We know what we live, and we live what we know. But *we do not know what we do not know,* and we do not know *that we do not know it.* Because no human being knows everything, it is important that we are open to the ideas of others. Otherwise, we can get cheated of what is in our best interest, precisely because we do not know about it. There is a tendency in most of us to live in a comfort zone of our own familiar little world and pay little or no attention to what others have to say. To be sure, there are various reasons for this attitude, too. Primarily, most of us think that we know best what is good for us, so why listen to other people's views? We may also distrust others, particularly if in the past we had some bad experiences acting upon another's advice. Doing so, however, deprives us of the opportunity to examine the ideas that guide us in life.

Jason: You're probably right. But *we* know that we do not know and so I hope this is not the end of our dialectic, is it? We still have unanswered questions. I am eager to learn *how* one gets to the ultimate Truth which we hope to behold one day.

Diotima: Positively, as long as there are unanswered questions, our quest is not over; the human mind will know no rest. Intellect was made for truth; it will not surrender until the light of truth dawns. You can see now, however, that the dilemma on the large scale encountered by the thinkers on the empirical as well as on the speculative level, holds true on the personal level and, precisely, because of it. In experiencing a similar dilemma personally, we are not only discovering, we are also demonstrating the process of how human knowledge of the ultimate Truth is attained.

As to your question, namely, how do we get to the ultimate Truth we hope to behold one day, there is another, a much easier, safer and more direct path that leads to it. We are not just a body and a mind. We also have a spirit, and spirit that has an eye of its own. This deepest dimension of our being, too, has its own function to fulfill. Its basic function is that of faith and love; here faith points the way and love makes the ascent to that Truth. Just as reason with respect to the empirical findings, so now love with respect to reason's conclusions does not invalidate the truths of logic. It simply elevates them to the highest level of clarity. This path turns out to be the simplest, the most direct and, what's of paramount importance, accessible to everyone, not just the intellectually gifted and the educated. We are a product of love, are nurtured by love and are all capable of love. Love is what makes the world go round. Love pursues the track that leads one to both, the Truth of *actual beholding*, putting all questions to rest, and to the *ecstatic experience of God* that satiates every longing of the human heart, filling it with profound peace of mind, incredible freedom of the spirit, and utter contentment of heart—the very things every human heart craves!

Sophie: Can you take us there?

Diotima: I cannot take you there, for that is a work of one's own doing, but I can speak of the path that leads to it. In any event, it looks as if you all are ready for the transition.

Thomas: What do you mean by "transition"?

Diotima: What is involved here is a switch on the *metaphysical level itself* from the track of "reason" to that of the "heart" where our spirit dwells and is awaiting to be discovered. In popular parlance, it is a transition from the "logic of the head" to the "logic of the heart." To reach our final destination in thought, while refining points along the way at some point we will need to pick up our discourse on the number concepts where we left off. That discussion will shed light on how our ascent to the Absolute is made and on the three Hypostases that make it possible—the question, if you recall, Tom asked earlier and we've bypassed at the time. When this understanding dawns, we will be ready to take up the discourse on the journey of human life starting at its actual beginning. From that vantage point the answer to the four perennial questions of philosophy will be much easier to understand.

Thomas: Sounds good. We're with you.

3. Transition to the Logic of the "Heart"

Diotima: For the sake of smooth transition, let us briefly recapture what we have already done and discovered, because there is a pattern to this ascent. Seeing things in context always lends an added measure of intelligibility. Since "repetition with attention is the mother of learning," recasting once more the process that brought us to this point should do us no harm. On the contrary, it should only strengthen our understanding of it.

What we have observed formerly, that is, in the case of the *empirical ascent* and its position to reason, we now find is the case of the *rational ascent* and its position to the *spirit*. Just as the empirical thinkers upon reaching their moment of victory were left with questions beyond their discipline to answer, so now the speculative thinkers upon reaching their moment of triumph in the *enlightenment* about the real First Cause of existing things are left with some questions beyond the power of reason to secure. And just as the *empirical impasse* was transcended and its dilemma resolved by means of another path, the "logic of the head," through *thinking*, the activity of reason, so the *rational impasse*, you will soon see, gets transcended and its dilemma resolved by means of still another path, the "logic of the heart," through *love*, the activity of the spirit. Each succeeding path completes the former until the full truth comes to light. We must emphasize, though, that this result obtains only when each dimension of our being is given the opportunity to fulfill its own function and all three work in unison. Currently we are at the point of the second impasse.

Jason: That's right.

Diotima: As we have hinted earlier, right at the time when some speculative thinkers walk away from the truth of reason in disillusionment, others are in their glory. Having lived a *fully human life*, these genuine "lovers of wisdom" by now are experiencing great intimacy with God and know Him from *personal experience*. They know for certain that the One or the Absolute is God and are reaping abundant blessings of the *divine illumination* that complements and enhances their state of *enlightenment*.

Jason: Does that mean that the level of *divine illumination* on the spiritual level corresponds to the level of *enlightenment* on the rational level but is higher than it?

Diotima: Exactly. The divine illumination advances one's former understanding by means of Divine intervention. An influx of divine light permeates one's intellect and one sees and understands what reason alone was unable to apprehend. Moments of divine illumination for the reason are an "Aha!" experiences. These may come with respect to different things and in different degrees of illumination; eventually the soul is lead to the *actual beholding* of God. It seems that God in His holy impatience, if one can put it this way, cannot wait until their death to reveal His face to the ardent lovers of wisdom. Some of them, additionally, are gifted with some visions and flights of the spirit at which times they are given to see the world from the standpoint of eternity, as God sees it

. Finding oneself in the vestibule of God, even in the sanctuary where He dwells, such a one catches a glimpse not just of God, one gets to see all three Hypostases. One sees them, moreover, in relation to self and in relation to the whole cosmos. Unable to keep this knowledge to oneself, out of overflowing joy as well as of one's love for God and the entire human family, such a person attempts to share this knowledge with others, though seldom revealing it as a personal experience. What one sees is so awesome in its splendor and beauty and so unlike everything in this world, that even when one does try to give an account of these experiences, one falters; one's speaking is but stammering, it comes in halted utterances. When St. Paul was lifted up to the highest heaven, all he was able to tell us is, "Eye has not seen, ear has not heard, nor has it so much as dawned on man what God has prepared for those who love him" (I Cor. 2:9-10). These sublime mystical experiences, on the one hand complete human knowledge of the previous two levels; on the other hand, they provide firsthand confirmation for both, the truths of reason and for the revealed truths of God in sacred writings that the lovers of wisdom initially accepted on faith and lived by. This is why the pre-modern thinkers knew, and all mystical thinkers of all ages know with *absolute certainty* the answers to the outstanding questions of the empirical and the speculative thinkers.

Thomas: Heart-gripping! Is the discussion about the three Hypostases next?

Diotima: There you are, Thomas, proving once again that secondary knowledge is not enough to satisfy one's thirst for Truth. I must agree, though, that only a personal relationship with God and a vision of this Great Mystery alone can quench that thirst.

Jason: Could you give us, then, at least some inkling of the three Hypostases and their relationship to all that is?

Diotima: Actually, it is the understanding of these three Hypostases and their relationship to all that is that clarifies the three attributes of the One: *transcendental, immanent* and *transcendent*—which have no corresponding terms for "the many"—and thereby reveals the truth of reality. Unfortunately, as I have already told you, this knowledge is not attained by means of reason alone. It is given in a mystical experience.

Thomas: But the reason ought to be able to explain it once the intellect apprehended it.

Diotima: Granted, but not always with ease. To be honest, I am very reluctant to undertake this discussion.

Thomas: Why?

Diotima: It is because this discourse calls for an inquiry into the Great Mysteries, and who of us mortals is worthy to gaze at Beauty's very "Self," or to speak of it without reducing it to what it is not? I do not want to mislead you into thinking that one can do justice to what this sacred Mystery really is. Language itself fails one. Language is adapted to the things of this world, whereas here one is attempting to speak of the Infinite, the Absolute, the Triune God—concepts that exceed the ability of a finite mind to fathom, much less to express in human language. Besides, the all holy God deserves our highest reverence. I fear you might end up reducing God to the few insights you gain. Knowing *that* God truly is should be enough to ignite the "spark of love" already within you and to set you on a journey of personal relationship that alone holds the assurance of attaining what you *really* want.

Sophie: Oh, you're not going to back away from speaking of it now, are you? I've been waiting for this moment with great anticipation. Please?

Thomas: Just do what you did with us with respect to the One. We will be satisfied with whatever we are able to distill from it. Otherwise, I might be tempted to revert to the Big Bang theory.

Diotima: I don't think so, Thomas. Not any longer. What you really want, though, is to see God with your own eyes. Not surprising at all! We all do. Although we may not be aware of it, this desire has been implanted in every human heart. That is why, no matter how great are one's achievements, no human heart will ever be fully satisfied, or completely happy until this moment dawns. However, since you insist, let me at least show you that these concepts are not unintelligible.

B. Ascent based on the Promptings of the "Heart"

1. Quest for the First Principles

Diotima: We begin by asking: How many first Principles are there? Since we do not know, let us begin with an empty circle of the absolute whole and once again rely on number concepts to arrive at this understanding. If you recall, that is how far our dialectic brought us. To keep the parallel structure running on track without constantly moving back and forth from the number concept to the Entities they represent here, let us agree that what we state of the number concepts applies equally to the eternal Hypostases. For the most part we shall employ numerals, the symbols of number concepts (1, 2, 3, etc.). Occasionally, when we wish to draw a conclusion or emphasize a point about the Hypostases, we shall convert numbers into words and capitalize them (One, Two, Three, etc.). Keep in mind, however, that the mathematical concepts belong to the third segment of the divided line, while the Entities we will be striving to understand by means of them to the fourth, for they are members of the ontological realm. We will be *applying* number concepts to them but *not equating* the two. Should you have any questions, be sure to voice them.

Thomas: That's rather obvious. Please go on.

Diotima: We already know that to begin with, there had to be at least 1. So insert number 1 into the context of the absolute whole. Now think: if to begin with there were only 1, just this 1, there would still be only 1. For what could you do mathematically with 1? Nothing! To add, subtract, multiply or divide, that is, to carry on the mathematical processes—just as to account for the plurality and multiplicity of the cosmic entities ever coming and passing away—you need more than 1. All you can say of it is that *1 is.* This agrees with what we've established about the eternal intelligent Being, namely, that the *One is.*

Given the above, it is necessary to posit more than 1. Moving cautiously we reason: if not just 1, then 1 more. This means that we now have concepts 1 and 2. But as soon as there is 1 *and* 2, automatically we have 3, for 3, in addition to being the next number on the number line, is nothing other than 1 and 2, or 2 and 1. The 3 is at once the sum of 1 and 2, and an embodiment of them. So, too, is the case with the ontological Hypostases. The Three, that is, the Third Hypostasis is an offspring and an embodiment of the One and the Two, consequently nothing other than They. But 3 is not just any kind of embodiment of 1 and 2. Since 3 is neither less, nor more than what precedes it, it is a perfect embodiment of 1 and 2, hence equal to them. And since 2 is nothing other than 1+1, hence Two but another One in union with the One, and Three is a perfect embodiment of One and Two, it follows that the Three is also One. This means then that if the One is good, all of them are good, if the One is beautiful, all are beautiful, if the One is just, all of them are just, and if the One is God, *each of them is* in virtue of their shared divine nature, as a member of the same original unit.

Please notice that what we have just said of the first three numbers, and thereby of the three Hypostases, does not hold true of any other number. The next number in the number sequence, 4, is not equal to what precedes it. When we add 1+2+3 we get 6, not 4. With each succeeding number in the sequence, the disparity increases. For instance, when we add 1+2+3+4+5, the numbers that precede 6, we get 15 and not 6; and when we add 1+2+3+4+5+6, the numbers that precede 7, we get 21 and not 7. The higher the number the greater is the difference between it and what precedes it.

Thomas: I am amazed! This is quite intriguing. Are you suggesting, though, that there are three Gods?

Diotima: Not quite. There is one God, but there are three Divine Persons. This is why we say, the Three are One and the One, in a certain sense, is Three.

Thomas: How can this be? I don't understand it.

Diotima: This is the most profound Mystery of all. No matter how many insights one gains into it, one can never fully comprehend it. The important thing, Thomas, is to make getting to Heaven our top priority. Once we're there, we will have the rest of eternity to scale the height and to plumb the depth of everything—plenty of time to feast our minds on anything that interests us. The understanding of the Blessed Trinity, most likely, will be reached last even there.

Thomas: I hear you. As for now, let's see how much we can get to understand about it at this point.

a. Three as One and One as Three. Having established earlier that there are three Hypostases, we resume the discussion by focusing on 3.

Thomas: Since each of the Three is one by itself, has a being of its own, and each is divine, could we not represent them as $1 + 1 + 1$?

Sophie: That would certainly show that they have the same nature and value.

Jason: But that would make them a carbon copy of each other. How could they be recognized for who or what each of them is, when eventually one comes to see them? More importantly, if 1 corresponds to the Absolute that would mean there are three Absolute Beings. Didn't we learn that there could be only one Absolute?

Diotima: Good observation, Jason. The fact that the Three are not a product of multiplication of the Absolute can be demonstrated mathematically, for $1 \times 1 \times 1 = 1$, not 3. Here we have a confirmation for the possibility of there being only one Absolute Being. And if the Three are not a product of multiplication, then they are neither a carbon copy of each other, nor are all of them Absolute Beings. The Absolute is God, the First Person of the Blessed Trinity. Notwithstanding, there is some truth to what Thomas said, namely, that each of the Three is itself one, because it has a being of its own, and in being divine that it is 1, hence One. Neither was Sophie wrong in noting that the representation of the Three as three 1's reveals their shared nature and value. We may add to it, that that makes them also a *community* of the same kind of Beings, a family as it were.

Thomas: What other articulation is there?

Diotima: Well, if not $1+1+1$, then as 1, 2 and 3, as we have seen earlier. Here we see that in addition to what they hold in common, each has a being and identity of its own reflected by its form. Each is other than the other two. Neither are they numerically equivalent to each other. Paradoxically, however, since 1 is the Absolute, the other two are subordinate to it and, therefore, lesser to it in status. But this hierarchy is overshadowed by the nature of the relationship among them. Moreover, the inequality would hold if they were ever found to be apart, which is not likely to be the case. If the 3 ever lacked either 1 or 2, it would cease to be itself. The same would be true of 2, if it ever lacked 1. There is among them a giving of themselves to each other to the point of *kenosis,* a total emptying of self. The 1 being 1, gives itself completely to 2; the 2 being a 2 gives itself completely to 1 and to 3; and the 3 being a 3, gives itself completely to 1, to 2 and to the cosmic realm. Because of it, there is a kind of self-transcendence in each case that overshadows the differences among them. It also links them, in an inconspicuous way, with the World of Becoming.

Thomas: A self-transcendence of what?

Diotima: A self-transcendence of eternal life in love, knowledge and perfections! Love captures all of these, just as God does, for God and love are synonymous terms. God's nature is love. And love is not love until one gives it away. The greater the love, the greater is the gift of self. God's love is perfect; consequently, His gift of "Self" is complete, a total emptying. And this is true of all three divine Persons, whence *the circle of an uninterrupted flow of love* in the inner life of the Blessed Trinity making them one. Moreover, where there is perfect love, there is perfect sharing; and where there is perfect sharing, there is perfect communicating, hence also perfect knowing. Consequently, all Three are of one mind and one heart. Because there is only one Absolute, strictly speaking, there is only one God. Because there are three divine Persons sharing the same life and nature, it is also true that there are three Persons in one God. Thus we have the Three in One and One in Three.

Thomas: So God is love?

Diotima: That is how God is experienced ultimately on high; in fact, it is also how He is experienced already here and now when He makes one's soul His permanent abode. And where there is infinite love, it comes with all the attributes of the Absolute, because love is the most creative thing there is. As such, it has an infinite need to express itself and so we have the universe such as it is. And because love is a soul of all God's attributes, it binds everything into one, making God absolute love. As you can see, love has logic of its own. Because the logic of love is the logic of the "heart," love fulfills all the longings of the Divine Heart. It fulfills likewise all the yearnings of the human heart whenever love reigns there. Just keep in mind that by the "heart" we do not mean the physical muscle, but the spirit, the deepest dimension of our being.[29]

Looking at God in terms of the three principles of thought (Non-contradiction, Excluded Middle and Identity), in light of the above it is apparent that the Principle of Identity applies to God alone, for He alone is an undifferentiated whole, a perfect blend of all perfections. Of the Three as One, it is necessary to posit the Principle of Identity-with-a-Difference: identity in nature and powers and difference in being and in form. Because of their identity in nature and powers, all Three are Divine, hence One, and so they share some names in common. Because of their distinctness in being and in form, each is entitled to a particular name as well.

Some names accrue to them in virtue of their attributes, others in virtue of their particular functions. Although all of them are promoting the same master plan, because each has its own specific functions to perform, some names are more appropriate to one than they are to the others. Consequently, since one of them is "that which begets or wills," another, "that which brings forth" and the third, "that through which" the process takes place, there is a good reason for naming the first Principle the Begetter or Father, the primary Cause of what-is; the second Principle, the Life-giving Being or Mother, the Holy Spirit; and the third Principle, in keeping with Heraclitus and Heidegger, the eternal Logos, or as Plato calls the Logos, the offspring that the "father" or "the good begot in a proportion with itself" (*Rep.* VI, 507b, 506e). This offspring turns out to be the agent of the Cause, for through this Deity, as we have seen, cosmos came onto being. All these names are appropriate and do not contradict the fact that each of them is a Cause and each is a Divine Person. They merely more closely identify the role of each, showing what kind of a cause each of them is and how they work *together, as one,* for the good of all. In them we find a perfect community of Persons and an ideal model for the human family and any society.

Something comparable can be said of other names. For instance, from the standpoint of being members of the same Original unit, hence as 1+1+1, it is apparent that being identical in nature each of them is good, beautiful and just. But viewed from the standpoint of their individuality, as 1, 2 and 3, in order to distinguish them from each other, it would be proper to name one the Good, the other the Beautiful, and the third, the Just. And precisely in this order, for what exists, came into being through the Just, and through the Just it returns. It is because the Just did justice to what-is, that he deserves the name "Just" and since everything is beautiful and good when justice is done to it, it becomes apparent that justice is the way to goodness and beauty—a clue to our becoming. When we do justice to the Just and to what-is, we become just and thereby approach the Good and the Beautiful. But to become just is automatically to become not only beautiful and good, but also to become *one with* the Good, the Beautiful and the Just. We can expect the eternal Logos to play a major role in our reaching this goal.

Jason: This is remarkable. I'm looking forward to discovering how this transformation takes place within us.

Sophie: I have a question. Since the "eternal Logos" is an offspring, I assume you mean the Son of God who came into this world some two thousand years ago and is known as Jesus Christ. Why is he called the Word or Logos if He is and always has been a Person?

Diotima: This name is very appropriate for him in terms of one of his major functions. The function of a word, as you already know, is to communicate thought or to externalize it in some form whether in art, music, drama, or the like. Word reveals what is in someone's mind. Jesus initially externalized the Father's master plan for the universe by executing it; the cosmos came into being through the eternal Logos. And when he came into this world, Jesus communicated to us the Father's plan for us human beings. In so doing, he performed the function of the word, and so the name Logos or Word is a fitting name for him.

Jason: Is Jesus not the second Person of the Blessed Trinity? You speak of Him as third.

Diotima: Where there is love, there is no first, second, and so forth. Love is deliberately blind to such distinctions because its focus is not on self but on the good of another. To be sure, love does not obliterate these distinctions; it overlooks them. That's the nature of genuine love. Its properties are humility, generosity and self-forgetfulness. Love makes one totally other-centered. And God is love. This is why each of the Three gives itself completely to the others in love and together they form *the circle of divine love* that constitutes the inner life of the Blessed Trinity. This makes them one.

Furthermore, when we are speaking of *the circle of divine love,* we are speaking of the *co-eternal Deities.* The Blessed Trinity is the *eternal co-existence of divine life of the three Persons.* As in any circle, there is no first, second or third to it. It might be more accurate to say that the ordering we attribute to the Persons of the Blessed Trinity reflects more the order in which we come to know them, than the ordering among them. From this viewpoint, what we are taught is correct. God the Father as the Creator is always automatically first. Jesus is most specifically our Lord. He came into this world for our sake, took our nature and told us about the Father. He also told us how we need to live to come into God's Kingdom that we may be where He is. So to us, Jesus is second. And the Holy Spirit, although the soul of our souls and very much at work in us, is always mentioned third, for we will behold this most mysterious, elusive Person only when we come into the eternal Kingdom, unless someone is gifted with the Beatific Vision while still on earth. If we are to speak of the ordering among them, to which obviously there is some legitimacy, then the ordering we are proposing holds but it needs to be understood from the standpoint of eternity, rather than of time. The view, to be sure, is not without support. Do we not maintain that the Holy Spirit is the "bond of love"? If the Holy Spirit is *the bond of love* between the Father and the Son, then "that which unites the two" is necessarily in the middle position, hence second. We can also gain some insight into this mystery by means of the analogy to the human family, which is based on the Eternal Model. Is not the human offspring always a result of the union in love of the two from whom it springs? But about this we shall say more later. It is only when the awesome moment of that blessed vision dawns and one apprehends the Truth that one gains better insight into the Mystery of their Being. At that point one comes to see all three divine Persons in their respective positions and finds out also how they relate to us personally and to the rest of reality.

Thomas: That was my other question. How do they relate to the rest of reality?

Diotima: Briefly, the Third is Sovereign in the World of Becoming, the Second is Sovereign in the World of Being, and the One, God, being the Absolute who embraces the both worlds, is the King of all-that-is. Initially, we have called the Blessed Trinity the Fifth Entity and placed it in the fourth segment of the divided line because they would be reached last. Now that our discourse approached this segment and we see things more clearly, we find that the ontological realm is co-extensive with all three classes of reality and that the Three form the *ontological transcendentals* that underlie all that is. We have only to subsume the ontological whole under both, the epistemological and the cosmic whole to get a complete image of reality and to see more clearly that they are the Hypostases in the full sense of the word.

Thomas: If the "eternal Logos" is an offspring of the original unit and follows the same principle of *kenosis* and, as you've put it, being a Three it gives itself to the One, the Two and to the cosmos, does that mean that the universe is also divine?

Diotima: Well, let's see if we can generate the rest of the numbers by multiplying 1, 2 and 3. If we can, then we will be generating a universe of gods, if not, then no. Let's see, 1x2x3=6. Try as one may, no matter what the ordering of these numbers, the product always equals 6 and nothing else. Since all subsequent products of these four numbers presuppose the actual being of the complete basic set of 10, and the 10 numbers cannot be generated by *multiplying* 1, 2, and 3, it follows that the universe does not consist of divine beings, although there is something of the divine in it.

This conclusion is a fortunate one for philosophy. While it would be difficult enough to equate sticks and stones with the intelligent Beings, to reconcile the transient, ever-changing natures of "the many" with the permanent, immutable nature of the eternal Three, or to defend the pantheistic view of the world, it would be even more difficult to account for the evil in the world vis-à-vis the perfect nature of the Originals. The conclusion is fortunate also for science, for it gives a hint to the mystery encountered in the universe to which the scientists testify.

Now, if the rest of the numbers cannot be generated by multiplication of 1, 2 and 3, that means that *right from the start* there had to be more than just the Original unit of Three. If so, it is necessary to grant that there was also a 4 and that 4, too, is eternal.

Jason: What would 4 represent in the total scheme of things?

Diotima: The 4 has to be something next in importance to the Three. Observe that 4 is *in* what precedes it, but it is neither equal to them, nor possible without them. This something we postulate to be knowledge, for knowledge is in the mind of the intelligent Beings, yet it is lesser than they and it is inconceivable without them. This means that knowledge, too, is eternal, which agrees with what we have concluded earlier by means of the deductive arguments. Likewise, given that knowledge is one of the perfections of intelligent beings, the Absolute had to possess it right from the start, or it would not have been the Absolute.

Sophie: That is absolutely fascinating! What else can we know about 4?

Diotima: Did you notice that 4 is not contained within any *one* of the preceding numbers, but is in them as a whole? This seems to confirm the fact that the Three hold things in common, just another evidence of their unity.

Furthermore, please note: when we add 1+2+3+4, we get 10, the complete set of numbers basic to all mathematical functions. Since mathematics is a part of knowledge, once we grant that knowledge is fourth and eternal, our difficulty with the rest of the numbers, and thereby with the plurality and multiplicity of the cosmic processes, is resolved. For once there is knowledge, there are pure concepts, ideas and forms, the *epistemological transcendentals*, and the number to multiply them as well as to give them measure, proportion and symmetry. Thus, there is everything that is needed to produce the "finely tuned" beautiful cosmos that it is or, for that matter, any "ordering" that the Absolute could have chosen to bring forth. It is no wonder the ancient Greeks held 10 to be a perfect number.

The artistry of the "ordering" (the Greek word for "cosmos") reveals sequence, creativity and diversity and these depend upon the intelligence, imagination and playfulness of the mind that conceived them. Since the mind that conceived them is that of the Infinite and the Infinite is capable of infinite possibilities, numbers go on to infinity and there is an innumerable variety of series and species with nothing in the way to prevent them from further multiplying under new forms.

Thomas: I can see why concepts, ideas and forms are said to be the *epistemological transcendentals*. I am not quite as clear as to how the three Hypostases are the *ontological transcendentals*.

Diotima: Let us make them, then, the focus of our next discussion.

b. The Ontological Transcendentals. We already know that knowledge is eternal and, since mathematics is an essential part of it, that mathematics too is eternal. Consequently all number concepts are there from the start and do not need to be generated. What we humans have done is only supplied numerals, that is, symbols for these concepts. Notwithstanding, it still remains true that the standard set of 10 number concepts—basic to all the other multi-digit numbers, fractions and mathematical processes, here representing cosmic series—though they can be employed diversely in math, cannot be generated by multiplication of the first three numbers. At the same time, it is equally true that this set of 10 numbers could be reduced to the first three, but not beyond these. For the plurality of number concepts—much the same as the corresponding plurality of the existing things—can be generated by *addition*. For example, once we have 1, 2 and 3, we get 4 by adding 1+3, and 5 by adding 2+3 or 1+4, and so on. Given fractions in addition to whole numbers, the possibilities are endless. Numbers 1, 2 and 3, therefore, can be said to be the *mathematical transcendentals* and since number concepts apply to all that is, we can expect to find this pattern throughout the three classes of reality. This is to say, we can encounter a comparable set of *transcendentals* in the cosmic, the epistemological and the ontological realm.

Jason: This reflection on the relationship of number concepts to each other brings us to the *ontological transcendentals*, doesn't it?

Diotima: Yes, Jason. It leads us also to the discussion of the three concepts spoken of earlier with respect to the One, namely, *transcendental, immanent* and *transcendent*.

Sophie: If I remember correctly, we've defined the word *transcendental* as fundamental, underlying all that is.

Diotima: That's correct. Let us now reflect this meaning in terms of the number concepts understanding that the sequence of 10 numbers represents here all that is, albeit only in a general sense. Once we understand the meaning of the three terms in question, we shall try to identify the categories of reality to which the number sequence corresponds. Below we have the number sequence in conjunction with the *mathematical transcendentals*.

```
1   2   3   4   5   6   7   8   9   10
    1   2   3   4   5   6   7   8   9
        1   2   3   4   5   6   7   8
            1   2   3   4   5   6   7
                1   2   3   4   5   6
                    1   2   3   4   5
                        1   2   3   4
                            1   2   3
                                1   2
                                    1
```

Diotima: What do you observe?

Jason: The most obvious fact is that the One, as the number 1 shows, is basic or fundamental to all that is, that it underlies everything; everything rests upon it, as it were. I can see now why some philosophers speak of God as the Ground of all that is. The term "transcendental" does seem to suggest this meaning.

Sophie: I can also see the appropriateness of the name Absolute for God. For while I understand the 1 *per se* at the very beginning of the number sequence, where it stands alone, to represent God as the only Absolute (absolute in His powers and perfections), through His powers that extend to everything, He is present to all that is and so is in fact the indispensable condition of the possibility of its being. In other words, if the set of 10 numbers does represent all that is, then the Absolute through its powers is co-extensive with the absolute whole.

Thomas: But if the One is present to all that is and forms the Ground of everything, then in addition to being the Ground of possibility of the universe as a whole, it must also be the Ground of each existing entity individually. To me this means that the One is present to both, the cosmos as a whole and to each entity within it. Perhaps it is even inherent in it.

Diotima: You are hinting here at the meaning of God's *immanence.* The move is in the right direction, but understanding God's immanence calls for further refinement of thought on our part. Don't forget that there are three Hypostases, hence *three ontological transcendentals.* There are also three classes of reality. Each of the Hypostases is transcendental to a particular class. The One is *transcendental to the first class*, the ontological realm, namely, the Original unit or the Blessed Trinity itself. The second One, the Being of beings, is *transcendental to class two*, the World of Being that encompasses the created "spiritual beings" all of whom are intelligent. And the third One is *transcendental to the third class*, the World of Becoming or the cosmos. From this it follows that God is present *directly* only to the Original unit, and *indirectly*, that is *through the Second* to the second class, and *through the Third*, to the created entities of third class. This makes the first two Persons of the Blessed Trinity *transcendent* or, *beyond* the cosmic realm. From our place in the ontic realm, the *transcendent Persons* would be reached last. It is the Third that is *immanent,* meaning *within* class three, who is somehow *inherent in it.* For it is through the eternal Logos, that the cosmos and everything in it came into being. This is consistent with everything else we have said earlier.

Early on, if you recall, while looking at all the wholes and their relationship to each other, we have seen that the link among the various wholes, starting with the human beings all the way to the ontological whole, always came through the third component in each case (Diagrams 4-6). The same bears out in number concepts. In discussing the Original unit, we have seen the same pattern of self-transcendence in love. We have said that the 1 being 1 gives itself to 2; the 2 being 2 gives itself to 1 and to 3. And the 3, being a 3 gives itself to 1, to 2 and to the many of the cosmic realm. Since God is not only the Father and Love of utter tenderness, but also a Brilliance of ineffable beauty, and all three Persons share the same nature, all Three are Beings of Light. This means then that we can expect the light emanating from the Third to give birth to the cosmos and inaugurate the processes of its becoming. Since light is energy, we can expect *the energy of light* to be the basic constituent of matter making the universe such a dynamic reality. So, yes, Thomas, there is "something of the divine" in nature. The whole universe traces to the eternal Logos. Itself an eternal offspring of God, it gives rise to its own offspring, the cosmos, where it becomes *its soul* and "the mind" behind its processes.

There is one further point worth mentioning. Did you notice that we have just done away with the need of infinite regress?

Sophie: What do you mean by *infinite regress?*

Diotima: Ordinarily, to account for the cosmic reality, there is an attempt on the part of the thinkers to trace things back through time to the very beginning. Science does it by tracing the cosmic series and species back to the Big Bang, or some such cause. Philosophers do it by tracing everything to the First Principles. But if the First Principle of the cosmic realm is the same in all the particulars, "the many" comprising it even now, which we see is the case, there is no need for the infinite regress. By looking *into* the nature, the *core* of the existing things now, one ought to be able to arrive at "that something" that gives them their being, for it surely must be there. That's what phenomenology attempts to do; by bracketing the external aspect it attempts to get at the very being, *the soul* of the existing entities.

Thomas: That is exactly what I was hinting at, except that I had the wrong Hypostasis. Yes, if it is "something of the Third" that is *inherent* in the things of nature, then to identify the *be-ing* of entities, that is, the life or, whatever the dynamic element in them is in virtue of which they *are* or *exist*, is to identify their link to the Third.

Sophie: You're right about there being no need of the infinite regress. These are eternal Beings. It is not that they *were* but no longer are. They *were, are* and *will always be!* That's, after all, what "eternal" means.

Jason: And since the Originals are intelligent Beings, a study of man ought to reveal this link the best. Given what has come to light, I would not be surprised to discover the presence of the Third *within* us.

Diotima: And through the Third, we might find our relationship to the other members of the Original Unit. That's going to be the major goal of our discourse sometime in the future.

Thomas: You were right in saying that it is the relationship of the three Hypostases to all that is, understood by means of the three terms you've just clarified, that will be our breakthrough to the understanding of reality as a whole. This is heartwarming and certainly much more than I expected to discover. A fantastic transition to science!

Sophie: And to theology!

Diotima: These terms, directly or indirectly, do make for a smooth transition to all the bodies of knowledge, for knowledge is of reality and reality is an integrated whole. We can see now why the scientists find the universe so pregnant with mystery, why they are tantalized by it and enamored of it. They sense its mysterious presence, but are at their wit's ends to identify it. It is this Presence that irresistibly challenges them onward, holds them spellbound, but because of its nature eludes their grasp. As we have seen it earlier, they know the cosmos is reducible to *energy*, $E=mc^2$ and that energy is mass times velocity of *light* squared, but they do not know *what it is* and *whence it comes*. Hopefully our findings will provide a clue for them. Actually, if the questions of science and those of philosophy complement each other and fit together like the hinges in the door, so should their answers. Apparently the door between these bodies of knowledge can swing in both directions and yield new insights on both sides. If what we discover jointly in science and philosophy finds confirmation in theology, that is, in the truths revealed by God Himself, we shall know that we have an indubitable Truth[30] with some understanding of it. This, in turn, should help all of us make better sense of our life.

To be sure, what we are saying about cosmology applies to all the branches of science, not just to physics, chemistry and astronomy; although here the magnitude of power and the intricacy of design is experienced more vividly. Here also are recovered the basic building blocks of cosmic reality and the laws guiding them. Recognition of these things on the basic level is extremely important, for what is determined here impacts upon the interpretation in the remaining branches of science.

Thomas: So how did the cosmic series come into being?

Diotima: The "how" question of existing things, Thomas, belongs to science. As you well know, scientists are hard at work to discover it. We can, however, try to state how things look from our perspective. Eventually, when we have completed our homework, we may want to compare our answers with theirs, but not yet. We have not reached that point, have we?

Jason: Not yet, for I still have some questions. I would like to see next the ordering of what-is in terms of the number sequence. Could we do that now?

Diotima: With your ingenuity, I am sure we can. This may not be easy, because there is a kind of playfulness going on. The 1 hides in 2, both hide in 3 and 3 hides in them *and* in matter, and all this happens behind the veil of divine knowledge. Yet, it is the knowledge we are recovering that betrays them through the intelligible design it exhibits.

c. Quest for the Identity of "the Many." At which end of the spectrum do you wish to begin?

Thomas: Any objection, Sophie and Jason, if we begin with the cosmic realm?

Diotima: Since you are such a compatible group, let's begin there. Once again we begin with what is familiar to us. There is an advantage to this approach for it will confirm something we have encountered earlier. Since you want to see "what-is" in terms of the number sequence, let us first write the numbers from 1 to 10 and then we'll try to place them where they belong.

$$1 \quad 2 \quad 3 \quad 4 \quad 5 \quad 6 \quad 7 \quad 8 \quad 9 \quad 10$$

Keeping in mind that the last thing that came into being has to be something that presupposes the existence of all that preceded it, and consequently what cannot exist independently of it, what do you suppose it could be?

Thomas: According to evolution and certainly from the standpoint of intelligence, man came into being last.

Sophie: This agrees with the Bible, too. Man was created last.

Jason: And it does agree with plain logic. For the existence of the human race presupposes the existence of all that preceded it, and what preceded it existed prior to humans' appearance on the scene.

Diotima: So under the 10 let's write humans or man, however you wish to state it. Given similar requirements for the other species, what do you think had to be next to the last? It has to be something that can get along without human beings but relies on everything that preceded it, which, in turn, could exist independently of it.

Sophie: I assume animals, because the existence of animals presupposes the environment, which can exist independently of them, whereas animals cannot survive without it.

Jason: That sounds right, so under the 9 we write animals.

Thomas: And under the 8, plants?

Diotima: Very good, for animals presuppose plant life and their origin traces back to them. And what do the plants need, without which plant life could not survive? Anyone?

Jason: Soil with its minerals, air, water, light—the elements of nature.

Diotima: In short, these would be the *inanimate substances* of the cosmic realm to which, again, the origin of plant life traces, and without which it could not exist.

Jason: So under 7, we write inanimate substances. And what's 6th?

Diotima: Well, to what did science reduce the cosmic phenomena?

Thomas: First it reduced it to matter and, ultimately, to the energy of light.

Diotima: So 6 is energy. Einstein's equation $E=mc^2$ expresses it best. And now, to what does this energy trace?

Jason: I see. Starting from this end, we are faced here with the dilemma of the empirical thinkers. However, having done our homework in philosophy, we trace cosmic energy to the third Hypostasis, the eternal Logos. But we are still missing something. What does 5 represent?

Diotima: We already know what the first four numbers represent. Do we not?

Jason: Yes. The first three numbers represent the three Persons of the Blessed Trinity. Since they have so many appropriate names, if you don't mind, let's call them the Good, the Beautiful and the Just, the names that Plato conferred upon them. The 4th is knowledge. But 5 has me baffled. To what could 5 correspond?

Diotima: If the universe starts with 6, then 5 must stand for something that is not physical, prior to it, and therefore independent of it.

Sophie: Angels! Angels are metaphysical, prior to the cosmos and independent of it.

Thomas: Angels? Who or what are they? How do you know that they exist?

Sophie: They are the created intelligent spiritual beings who serve as God's messengers. I know of them from the historical accounts, past and current. The Old Testament, which is a record of historical events of the Hebrew people, records instances where angels appeared to humans to carry out God's messages or injunctions. The New Testament also has numerous references to angels. Jesus himself spoke of a "legion of angels." If God exists, why would you doubt the existence of angels? Is it just because they are purely metaphysical beings?

Jason: Did we not say at some point that the mystical thinkers provide a confirmation for the revealed truths? If we can point to someone in this world who saw an angel personally and told us of it, that should be evidence enough. Do you agree?

Thomas: Can you name anyone?

Jason: The most familiar person, I suppose, would be St. Francis of Assisi, the world renowned saint. A six-winged seraph is reported to have appeared to him when he came to imprint upon his hands and feet the stigmata, that is, the wounds of our Lord.

Diotima: St. Thomas Aquinas is called the Angelic Doctor because of his superior knowledge. St. Bonaventure, who is called the Seraphic Doctor because of his great holiness, also had a vision of the seraph. Seraphim comprise but one of the nine choirs of angels, the highest choir. Our initial knowledge about the different choirs of angels comes from sacred writings through prophets, mystics and sages. But the phenomenon of angels is more common than you may suppose. Books on angels are multiplying and have become very popular in recent decades. One has only to read, for instance, *A Book of Angels* (1990) by Sophie Burnham, *Angels: Ministers of Grace* (1988) by Geddes MacGregor, or *The Angels and their Mission* (1957) by Jean Danielou to find abundant knowledge on angels of the past and the present. Sophie Burnham is detailing true stories of how angels served in the past and how they touch *our lives* on daily basis. Programs on TV about the angels enjoy much popularity, too. So yes, there is abundant evidence of the existence of angels. Much of it is based on people's personal experiences of them.

Alongside these accounts, there appears to be just the right spot for such beings in the overall scheme of things. For when we look closely at the entire sequence of what we've identified, from the standpoint of powers and perfections in what-is, the hierarchical scale extending from God down to the inanimate substances reflects a gradual, half-step descent in the kinds of beings and their form of existence. Angels are lower than the triune God, but higher than human beings. Angels are intelligent beings that are purely metaphysical who were created, yet are immortal. As such, they are neither eternal nor temporal. They are not eternal, because they had a beginning, whereas what is eternal has neither beginning nor end. They are not temporal, because what is temporal has a beginning and an end. Angels had a beginning, but will have no end. Since they are neither eternal nor temporal, St. Thomas put them into a separate category, which he called *aeviternal.*

We humans, on the other hand, partake of both, the eternal and the temporal. We have an immortal intelligent soul, which we hold in common with the angels, but we also have a mortal body, which we hold in common with animals. Animals are mortal, they have practical intelligence and, like we do, a natural life; but, unlike us who have a destiny, they are intra-worldly beings. The world has all their little hearts desire and their desires are geared only to what the world has to offer. Since we hold the natural dimension in common with them, like them, we rely on the goods of this world to satisfy our natural needs. Unlike them, however, human hearts crave something else, which none of the things of this world manage to satisfy. The immortal human soul craves its own good, the Highest Good, nothing short of God Himself.

Moving down the scale from animals, plants have life but lack intelligence, appetition and locomotion, while the inanimate substances lack life altogether but have dynamism and properties of their own. According to science, there is a gradual diminution in consciousness throughout the whole spectrum.

Thomas: How do we know that angels are immortal, or that our souls are immortal?

Diotima: We know that they are immortal because what is purely metaphysical is indestructible.

Thomas: I don't get it.

Diotima: Draw a triangle on your paper, Thomas. Can you now erase it, tear it up, or destroy it in some way?

Thomas: Yes. I can do all these things and burn the paper on which I drew it.

Diotima: Please erase it now.

Thomas: I did.

Diotima: Now erase it or remove in some way from your mind. . . . Did you succeed?

Thomas: No. I can't. I still see it in my mind.

Diotima: You have an idea of it, a mental form or a symbol of it in your mind. Because concepts, ideas and forms, like the mind itself, are by nature metaphysical, they are indestructible. We can forget them or store them in our memory, but we cannot destroy them. This holds true in principle. What is metaphysical is indestructible. Things we call physical are composites of the elements of matter. What is composed can be decomposed. What is metaphysical is not composed of parts and so it does not yield to decomposition. Since angels are metaphysical beings, they are immortal, and the same is true of our intelligent souls.

Thomas: I never noticed this distinction in the past. I do see it now.

Diotima: Good. Now that we have clarified our position with respect to the existence of angels and have aligned reality with the number concepts, we can next take a thoughtful look at the categories of what-is to see if anything else comes to light.

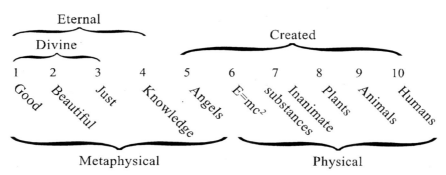

Notice, the first three numbers represent the eternal Deities; the first four reflect what is eternal, and the first five, what is purely metaphysical. Because these are not visible to the human eye, initially we have difficulty believing that they exist. Hopefully our reflections, particularly on the number concepts, which themselves are metaphysical, have helped to dispel this doubt. Beginning with angels everything down the line was created. Starting with number six, it is physical with an admixture of metaphysical.

   (1). Origin of the Cosmos. Cosmic reality, which begins at 6, is the creation of the intelligent *Ontological Transcendentals*. It comes through the Third, the eternal Logos, that Bearer of light who, to all evidence, intended to make the universe a copy of the Eternal Model. For according to the latest findings in science, there are three kinds of energy in the cosmos. Not only can the scientists distinguish and identify them, they supposedly have an exact percentage of each. In his article "The End" of *Time,* June 2001, Michael D. Lemonick reports the "astrophysicists can be pretty sure they have assembled the full parts list for the cosmos at last: 5% ordinary matter, 35% exotic dark matter and about 60% dark energy" (55). By "dark energy" they mean the "unseen" energy. Apparently, when the Logos spoke the word of command, divine energy burst forth from within Him with an immense power giving birth to the cosmos and to time.
   Thomas: Was that the Big Bang?
   Diotima: Science will have to determine that. There is, however, another, a more recent theory in science that is little known to the general public, but perhaps more probable than the famous Big Bang theory. In the above-cited article of the *Time,* the article that speaks of recent reinstatement of Einstein's "cosmological constant" and his "flat view of the universe," we find support for the *inflation theory* of the universe. Alan Guth of M.I.T., we are told, pioneered the inflation theory around 1980.According to this theory (not of astronomical insight, but a study of elementary-particle) "the entire visible universe grew from a speck far smaller than a proton to a nugget the   size   of   a   grapefruit,   almost   instantaneously,   when   the   whole   thing   was .0000000000000000000000000000000001 sec. old. This turbo-expansion was driven by something like dark energy but a whole lot stronger. What we call the universe, in short, came from almost nowhere in next to no time" (55). By the "cosmological constant" Einstein meant *antigravity* or the "dark energy," which "amounted to a force that opposed gravity and propped up the universe" (52). According to this theory, "The unique properties of a cosmological constant would make the universe slow down early on, then accelerate," just what the astronomers are witnessing currently (53). Clearly, Einstein's view of the flat universe and the cosmological constant, as well as the predicted effects of the antigravity, all lend support to the "inflation theory" rather than to the "big bang" theory. Science may want to re-visit this question once again.
   Jason: I am intrigued by these facts.
   Thomas: Why do you think that the inflation theory is more probable?
   Diotima: God's actions are always humbly unobtrusive; they are quiet, delicate and inconspicuous, even if mightily powerful. He reveals Himself in things such as a whisper of a wind, the silent beauty of nature, the delicate prodding of conscience, the gentle inspirations of the Holy Spirit, the sweetness of His love in our hearts, and the hidden designs of nature, all of which nonetheless reveal His incredible wisdom, power and beauty. He is not known to act in violent ways. Besides, the Big Bang theory does not begin at the very beginning. It begins with gases that are already there. Because the universe presupposes an eternal first principle as its starting point, matter has been claimed to be eternal by the proponents of this theory. But if the universe, which is composed of matter, will have an end, as the latest scientific predictions indicate, then matter cannot be eternal. What is eternal has no end. There is, on the other hand, some scientific evidence in support of the inflation theory—provided, of course, that the speculations of how the universe will end are correct. If what starts with a "big bang" ends with a "big crunch" (scientific knowledge born of stars' existence), then if the universe is to expire in a "whimper," the *inflation theory* offers a more likely explanation for the birth of the universe. Does it not?
   Thomas: You have a point there.
   Diotima: Speculations aside, there is something else we can point to in science that has been more confidently affirmed for years and is equally intriguing. It is likewise no less revelatory. We have only to take a thoughtful look at the Periodic Table of Elements to find another evidence for the cosmic realm being *a copy* of the Eternal Model which, in turn, can help us to determine the true beginning. There is an amazing resemblance between God and the hydrogen atom. God, we saw, is the *first* Entity in the structure of reality as a whole; hydrogen is the *first* element in the structure of the cosmos. Both are *one,* yet *three.* God is one, yet there are three divine Persons: Father, Holy Spirit and Son; hydrogen is one, yet there are three isotopes: Protium, Deuterium and Tritium (Latin names for First, Second and Third). And not only that! Hydrogen, like God, is also the *only element* that has three isotopes with two names for it. The *first* name, "God," is common to all three divine Persons; the name "hydrogen" is common to all three isotopes. The *second* name in both instances reflects their particular identity, each as

an entity in its own right. The "common name," both in God and in hydrogen, refers to their *essential nature* which they hold in common, the "special name" reflects the particular identity of each. The difference in their *individual identity* is due to the *inner composition* or *form* and the particular *function* proper to each.

Sophie: How do the three isotopes differ from each other to express their individuality?

Diotima: Here is their visible representation according to science.

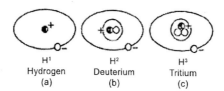

Fig. 1. Three isotopes of hydrogen.

Reproduced with permission.

As you can see, Protium—as of late called simply "hydrogen"—consists of just one proton and one electron. Deuterium consists of a proton, neutron and an electron. And Tritium has a proton, two neutrons and an electron. Hence, just as each of the three Persons in the Blessed Trinity, each isotope has its own identity. And in the Blessed Trinity, too, the first Person is ordinarily referred to as "God," but all three are understood to be Divine, much the same as all three isotopes are understood to be hydrogen, but only the first one is called by this name. What needs to be noted is that nothing comes into being without them. Both are *first* in what follows each, both inaugurate the *starting process* of their respective whole, and both, albeit in a different way, *enter into the composition* of everything that follows them. That is, all other elements are formed by various combinations of the *components of hydrogen*, much the same as all created entities are formed by various combinations of the *powers of God.*

Sophie: By what are they followed?

Diotima: Hydrogen is followed by helium, the element of light—the *physical light of the sun* (the celestial bodies), and God is followed by the metaphysical light—the *metaphysical light of knowledge*. Both are a form of light and since there are two kinds of light, there are two isotopes of helium apparently symbolically to reflect this fact. Since both entities that come "second" in their respective ordering incorporate something of the first, both are contingent upon the existence of their *first,* both are inconceivable without it, and both reveal something about the nature of it.

Jason: How do they reveal the nature of the *first?*

Diotima: Remember the second self-evident principle?

Jason: Yes, I do. No one can give what one does not have.

Diotima: Looked at in reverse, we can say: If what issues is light, that which emits it must also be light, precisely because no one can give what one does not have and God, if you recall, is a homogenous Being. This means that God is the Being of Light. It must be so, because this understanding coincides with the reporting of mystics who with the help of the sun analogy describe God as "Brilliance of ineffable beauty." And if all three divine Persons share the same nature—just as the three hydrogen atoms and the two isotopes of helium, each share theirs—all three divine Persons must be Beings of Light. We can understand now why the Seraphic Doctor, St. Bonaventure, quoting St. James (1:17) speaks of God as the "Father of Lights" (*New Jerusalem Bible*, "Father of all light") and describes the three Persons of the Blessed Trinity as "Brilliance, Radiance and Splendor."[31]

Thomas: I can see the reason for the names "Brilliance, Radiance and Splendor." I am not just as clear on what he means by "lights" or "all light." This saying conceals more than it reveals, at least for me.

Sophie: I assume he is referring to *wisdom*, the light of eternal life, to *knowledge*, the light of the mind, and to the light of day, the *physical light* of the sun and other stars, because being absolutely first, God is the "ultimate from which" these lights come. Besides, you probably remember that the entities in all three classes of reality are ultimately reducible each to its own kind of light. These lights, in turn, trace back to God as the Source of all lights, whence the name "Father of all light."

Thomas: Yes, I do remember that. I suppose you're right, Sophie, because electrons are components of light, and this is what goes forth from the hydrogen. We can see it by analogy as well as by means of the all-over pattern, that what went forth from God is light and energy or better, energy in the form of light. This analogy helps me to see also the Son as the "Bearer of light" and God as the "Father of lights"— the light of wisdom, light of knowledge, and light of radiant energy.

Sophie: This is indeed revelatory. I am not sure, though, how exactly helium differs from hydrogen and how it incorporates the components of *hydrogen.*

Diotima: Here is a scientific portrayal of it.[32]

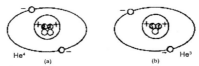

Fig. 2. Two isotopes of helium.

Reproduced with permission.

The most common isotope of helium, we are told, consists of two protons, two neutrons and two electrons, the second isotope of two protons, one neutron and two electrons. In either case, as you can see, helium contains the same components as hydrogen. Although the components are the same, their identity is different, which is why it is given a different name. If you notice, its identity is different due to its *internal composition* that gives it its particular form—the exact thing we have seen to be true of the Eternal Model by means of number concepts and the glimpses of mystics. This leads us to conclude in principle that it is the *internal composition* of each existing thing that determines its identity. Thus, while all other elements also contain components of the hydrogen atom, each succeeding element has a different combination of what it embodies and that alters its *particular composition.* The latter gives it its own identity, which then calls for a different name. Given the all-over pattern and the principle at work in what-is, it is safe to grant that it is also the *internal composition* in us humans that constitutes our being and determines our identity. We need to keep this insight firmly in mind when we come to reflect upon our nature, identity and name.

Sophie: Could it be that the distant position of helium from hydrogen on the Period Table of Elements is symbolic of the great difference that exists between the triune God and the rest of created reality? After all, otherwise, being the second element in line, helium is the closest to it and in its nature most closely resembles hydrogen. It should, therefore, like the rest of the elements on the chart following each other, be right next to hydrogen. Wouldn't you agree?

Diotima: Your guess is as good as mine, Sophie. Only the Artificer who fashioned the cosmic realm with such artistry and beauty knows exactly why He did things as He did. If by then we don't figure out the answer to this question by means of some additional data, we may have to ask Him when we get to see Him face to face. In the meantime, there are several other things we need to consider.

Thomas: Did we overlook something?

Diotima: When we were speaking of the components of the hydrogen atom being in all other elements, we have failed to establish the correspondence with reference to God. To complete the exposé of the parallel structure between the Eternal Model and its copies we need to mention that just as the components of hydrogen are present in all other elements of nature, so the Divine powers are present in all created entities as a whole, and while their identity is different due to their inner composition, the *bond* between them on both the physical and the metaphysical level is never severed, precisely because the former *inheres* in the latter. Thus, not only is it true that God and hydrogen are both *first* and the *starting point* of their respective whole, it is also true that they constitute the "core" of the beings' being. As such, they are *inconceivable without them, indispensable to them* and are *inseparable from them* as long as they exist.

Jason: Amazing! That makes hydrogen *immanent* and *transcendental* to the cosmic realm, just as God is *immanent* and *transcendental* to reality as a whole. Doesn't this follow?

Diotima: Not quite. Immanent, yes; transcendental, no. Here we note a difference. Hydrogen is the smallest known entity there is; it is always *within* things and, therefore, it is in some degree *always lesser* than they. Because it enters into the composition of all material substances and bodies, it is present *within* all of the cosmos, so it is *immanent.* But hydrogen does not underlie the universe as a whole, consequently it is not transcendental. Because God's powers enter into the composition of all that is, He is *immanent,* but God is infinitely more than that in Himself. As such, He is also *transcendental* and *transcendent.* Thus far we were concentrating on similarities, but there are contrasts between them too. This is one of them. There are others as well.

Sophie: Before we go any further, I have a question about the process. How does hydrogen, and for that matter God, become the "core" of the entities' being?

Diotima: Observe that while the components of hydrogen, as indeed the powers of God, enter into the composition of what follows each, neither of them thereby loses its own being and identity. It must, therefore, be concluded that although *essentially* different by nature, both are *dynamic entities* and that each of them gives being to beings by means of *projecting itself,* or *emanating something of itself,* into otherness. Thus, each of the "firsts" in addition to being "something in itself," by thus projecting outward gives being to other beings and continues to exist also in them "in a new way." Because "what gives being" is *dynamic* by nature, "that which comes into being" bears the same nature. Once inaugurated, the process continues to move onward passing from one generation to another as time moves on. Since what followed hydrogen were elements of matter, the elements became the "dynamic building blocks" of the endless series of the ever-new others that eventually built up into the gigantic superstructure we call cosmos, and now continue to give being to its ever-new particulars. And since what followed and continues to follow God is absolutely everything, including the cosmos, His powers subsisting in all that is constitute the "being of beings" making all of reality a *dynamic whole.* Because the "created physical entities" embody something of both "firsts," they are a *mixture of the physical and the metaphysical,* and God is their ultimate *Source,* the *Giver of being and life,* and the *Sustainer* of reality at large. Consequently, "God is all in all," and reality is ultimately one—just as Teilhard de Chardin, a famous paleontologist of the twentieth century about whom we will be speaking soon at greater length, and some other mystical thinkers have been telling us right along. Given this fact, it also follows that if God were ever to go out of existence, everything simultaneously would cease to exist. Of course, this is impossible! What is eternal never ceases to be.

Thomas: What other differences can you name?

Diotima: Contrasts between them are many, for God and hydrogen find themselves at the opposite ends of the spectrum of reality. God is the *absolute actual Being* with *infinite* powers and perfections, hydrogen is the *smallest infinitesimal entity* with *limited* powers and a *potential* for becoming more than it is. Hydrogen *enters into* the composition of the *physical* entities only, whereas God's powers enter into *absolutely everything* and He *encompasses absolutely all that is.* At the same time, did you notice that while the components of hydrogen, just as the powers of God, enter into the composition of all that follows each, "that which follows" although it comes to be by addition of something, yet upon receiving an increase is *not equal to* what precedes it? We can see this clearly exemplified in helium. Helium is *not equal* to the three isotopes of hydrogen even though it is formed by adding the 4th hydrogen nucleus to the existing three. Helium is born, we are told, when "four hydrogen nuclei fuse" through a series of reactions on the sub-atomic level. Yet helium, as we have already seen, consists not of four but of just two protons, two neutrons and two electrons, or two protons, one neutron and two electrons. What we see to be the case with helium holds true in principle, if for no other reason than "that which follows," being a composite of all that precedes it, is contingent upon it for its very being.

Sophie: How does this happen in the case of hydrogen?

Diotima: Put simply, some of the radiant energy is transformed into matter as Einstein's equation $E=mc^2$ reflects. What it means is that with the creation of helium *matter was born,* and that matter is nothing other than radiant energy *in a new state.* The equation reads: Energy *equals* mass times velocity of light squared. This makes *matter the first miracle* in the creation of the universe.

Thomas: I like what I am hearing, but I am wondering why you are describing matter as a miracle? Besides, I always heard it said that God created the world out of nothing, *ex nihilo* as the early thinkers put it.

Diotima: The two statements are not contradictory, Thomas; they complement each other. To say that something was made "out of nothing" means that it was made without any *pre-existing material.* To bring something into being "out of nothing" is *to create,* and to create is to work a *miracle.* None of us humans can ever do anything like that on our own. While we are highly gifted and creative beings, to give expression to *any idea* we must have some kind of material that *already exists* out of which it could be made, or in which it could be embodied to become an entity in its own right and be visible to others. Otherwise nothing will happen. No matter how wonderful an idea it might be, it will remain just an idea in the mind of the thinker and never see the light of day. Can you agree with this?

Thomas: By all means!

Diotima: Suppose one day you were able to make something out of nothing, even as small as a grain of sand or a blade of grass, would you not consider it a miracle?

Thomas: That would be a MEGA miracle for me!

Diotima: It is in this sense that I am using the word "miracle" with reference to the creation of matter. All of God's creation is a miracle because it was made out of no pre-existing substance. Prior to creating matter there was nothing there out of which the universe could have been made. It was just an idea in God's mind. To give concrete *being* to this idea, God chose to create *matter.* Then out of this *substance* He fashioned everything that makes up the cosmos. Since matter was created first, *matter is the first miracle* in creating the cosmos. You may find it interesting to learn that the Greek word *cosmos* has two meanings. The one with which most of us are familiar is "an ordering." It is an ordering because everything in the universe from the tiniest elements of matter to the largest bodies in space is harmoniously ordered. The earlier meaning of this word was an "ornament" or an "enhancement." We can see matter as an enhancement of reality—an enhancement that makes reality, which is by nature metaphysical and imperceptible, visible to our sight. Ideas embodied in matter became the *phenomena* of this world. They are "that which manifests reality" by making it seen. This is what the Greek word *phainomenon* means. This is also why this world is said to be the "World of Phenomena."

Jason: This is all very interesting. My question is: How does science explain creation of matter?

Diotima: Even though scientists carry out their research strictly by means of "the given," that is, by studying the phenomena, every scientific theory (if accurate) is really an "un-covery" or a "discovery" of *what already is* and an explanation of something *how* it is. On the basis of how things behave now, they infer how things *must have happened when they first came to be,* for everything in this world had a beginning. In this case—although the scientists do not say so, for this knowledge falls beyond the ambit of their discipline—theirs is an explanation of *how* God must have carried out His plan in creating matter in the first place. Because the process of producing matter, once it was started at the beginning of time, continues to go on in the sun and other stars, the scientists had ample time to study it sufficiently well to be able to give us a plausible explanation of it. For the sake of accuracy let us go to the experts in the field for this information.

Ronan, whom we have already cited, speaks of the sun as the "nuclear powerhouse." He writes, "Our sun is a ferocious ferment of energy that owes its power to reactions between miniscule particles deep in its interior" (106). To justify this statement he explains, "In the center of the Sun, huge temperatures and pressures push protons – the nuclei of hydrogen atoms – so close together that some of them fuse. Through a series of reactions, four hydrogen nuclei are joined to produce one nucleus of helium. But one helium nucleus is only 3.97 times the mass of four protons, so during this reaction 0.0075 grams per gram of fused hydrogen are lost altogether, or annihilated. Matter that is annihilated turns to energy, and the amount of energy released is given by Einstein's equation $E=mc^2$ – in which energy equals mass annihilated times the speed of light squared. So for each gram of helium made, the 0.0075 grams of matter lost produce 6.75×10^{11} joules – or enough energy to run a 1KW electric heater for about 20 years" (106). Can you imagine that?

Jason: It's awesome!

Diotima: Yes, it is. To help us appreciate the magnitude of what is taking place in the sun constantly, of which we are completely oblivious, Ronan provides an analogy. He states, "The energy produced by the Sun is equivalent to millions of hydrogen (or fusion) bombs going off each second." Can you fathom that! We know what devastation and havoc one hydrogen bomb can wreathe, yet million of them going off per second, surprisingly work to our benefit giving us warmth and light and allowing nature to go on with its processes as ordained. Life on earth without the sun is inconceivable already at the lowest strata of reality and without it nothing else could exist. Can you envision your life on earth without the sun?

Sophie: No. Just a few days with an overcast sky makes life dreary and depressing. I can't imagine existence without it.

Diotima: Rightly so, Sophie, because there is no existence without the sun and stars. We all know that it is the flow of photons that gives us light. What we may not know is that photons are formed in the core of the sun and to give us light they must make their way to the surface. Getting to the surface, however, is not so simple because the matter at the core is very dense to begin with and a photon "cannot travel for more than ½ in (1cm) before it interacts with matter. Each interaction scatters the photon in a random direction, and it takes about a million years for the energy of one of the photons given off in the core to reach the sun's surface" (107). Despite the random motion of photons, there are several predictable effects. We have a steady stream of light, there is a normal pattern to days and nights, to seasons and years and, unless we upset nature's balance in some way, the cosmos for the most part exhibits harmonious co-existence and reciprocity in all its parts.

Jason: Given these facts, it is evident that cosmic energy did not come in a haphazard manner.

Diotima: Scientists tell us that although the energy of light came with great force—whether by means of "inflation" or in some other way—it came gradually and thoughtfully creating first the elements of matter, each with carefully endowed properties, and in their wake, the conditions necessary for the emergence and survival of the various forms of life (178-79). With this explanation, Ronan goes on to adduce startling evidence of how it all happened. He even provides an illustration of it in color (198). He writes, "None of the chemical elements existed when the universe began – they have been built up one by one. [This statement alone is sufficient to discredit the "big bang" theory of gases. The rest of the quotation reveals how *they* came to be.] Most of the elements we know were made by nuclear fusion in stars, starting from just hydrogen and helium" (168-69).

Yes, to begin the process there had to be a strong blast but, given our findings, of *radiant energy,* not of gases. According to Planck, it was a "unified force" (199). His theory appears to coincide with that of Guth's *inflation* theory. Slowly and gradually the sub-atomic particles formed first into hydrogen, and subsequently to helium and other elements that took the form of solids, liquids and gases. If there were no elements when the universe began, and they were built up one by one starting from hydrogen and helium, there could not have been any gases to condense and to cause the "big bang." There is an incongruity between the "big bang theory" and this explanation. The theory suffers from lack of internal coherence. Surprisingly, this disparity seems to escape notice among most of the scientists.

Jason: Doesn't Ronan subscribe to it?

Diotima: Yes, he does (198), apparently because the scientific community has accepted it as a fact. When one works so closely with the subject matter from day to day concentrating on the minutest details of it, it is easy to overlook the big picture, especially when that something was established "authoritatively." The "Big Bang theory" was endorsed by science decades ago and currently it is taken almost for granted. A stranger to the field not encumbered by the details and free of the prevailing attitude has a better chance of spotting a discrepancy. This is why for the sake of truth, which we all seek, it is advantageous for scholars from different fields at least occasionally to get together and cross-examine their findings. Hopefully one day at the roundtable most of the incongruities will be worked out to allow the light of truth to appear in its full splendor and beauty. I venture to claim that by now enough knowledge has been garnered by the different disciplines to make the assembling of the jigsaw puzzle of reality possible.

Sophie: There appears to be a curious link between the One, the *Alpha and the Omega* of this world, and the *alpha* particles of Helium emitted by the sun in the *alpha rays.* The very name *alpha* suggests to me this link, since *Alpha* is the first letter of the Greek alphabet and *Omega* the last letter. When I checked *Webster's New World College Dictionary* (1999), I found out, it is also a name for "the beginning of anything" (40).

Diotima: Since God is the *beginning* and the *end* of "all that is," these names have been applied to God from who knows when. However, since this world came into being through Christ, the eternal Logos, this is His Kingdom, and all will first return to Him, Christ is invoked as the *Alpha and the Omega* of this world.

Thomas: Since something of the Logos is *inherent* in the cosmos, couldn't the *alpha particles* and *alpha rays* be the link we are seeking? Couldn't they be our direct contact with the divine from which the cosmos is built up?

Diotima: The phenomena of the cosmic realm do point beyond themselves to the divine Logos as the source of radiant energy, so this Being is said to be the "cosmic soul and mind" behind the cosmic processes. In Himself this Person is much more than this. Don't forget that the members of the Original Unit are "purely spiritual intelligent Beings," whereas all cosmic phenomena are "composites of matter." It is *through their powers* that we are led to Him. The astronomer Guy Consolmagno, S.J. says, "*alpha rays* are really the nuclei of helium atoms traveling at a high speed; *beta rays* are high-speed electrons; and *gamma rays* are very energetic protons."[33] All three kinds of rays trace back to helium, hence to matter, whereas the names *Alpha* and *Omega* refer to the divine Persons. Consequently, these rays must correspond to something on the metaphysical level, most likely to the ontological transcendentals permeating the cosmos, but not to the Persons themselves. Insofar, however, that everything within the cosmic realm is permeated with the divine power, so are these rays. Once we put together the concepts we have retrieved into a system of thought it will be easier to see how these things fit together. And when we finish our homework, we shall invite the scientists and the theologians to cross-examine our system of thought from the standpoint of their disciplines. If the concepts fit in and complement each other, we shall know we have found the answer to our quest. Do you think that we are at this point now?

Thomas: I am beginning to see how things are falling into place, but I'm not at the point of seeing it all as integrated whole.

Diotima: If we persevere in our search, the answer is bound to surface. Superficial as this explanation is, I hope it is sufficient to answer your questions, Sophie and Jason, about matter. I am hoping that as a result of this conversation all of us have come to appreciate *matter* as a marvel of the almighty God, His own power "in a new form," or better, *His power made visible.* The consistency in the behavior of the cosmic phenomena makes knowledge of the universe possible. There is, therefore, hope that the longed-for human dream of understanding of what-is will soon become a reality.

Jason: What I have called earlier *earth, air, water* and *fire*, Ronan explains in terms of the elements of matter. Each of the elements, he tells us, came with individual properties to serve a specific purpose. These elements in their diversity are the building blocks of the vast variety of existing things that make up the universe as a whole. Understandably, the foundations of the cosmos had to be set first and the basic elements of nature carefully endowed before any form of life would be possible. Foreseeing all the needs billions of years in advance presupposes infinite intelligence and an unimaginable wisdom!

Sophie: I find it interesting that the elements also fall into three categories: solids, liquids and gases. And that it is the various combinations of these elements that produce different molecules and eventually different substances that come in turn with their predetermined properties, reflecting already at their earliest stage diverse patterns and designs.

Diotima: It is tempting, I must agree, to step into the field of science to see those findings complement our own, but we must return to our quest, lest we get accused of having lost our way. In our way to the "light of truth," we are like those photons on their way to the surface of the sun to give us "their light." At every step we take, it seems, we too meet up with other concepts that call for an interaction scattering out attention in different directions. Since we do not have million years, like they do, to reach our destination, we must forge ahead. I wonder if you even remember where we were deflected from the main thrust of thought in our discourse and what caused this detour.

Thomas: We were discussing the big categories of "what-is" on the number line, and it was the transition from the metaphysical to physical realm that caused the delay. More accurately, it was our attempt to understand *energy* and *matter* or energy *as* matter, as well as its role in the scheme of things, that consumed the time. I'm sure though the discussion was not without benefit, but we're ready to move on now.

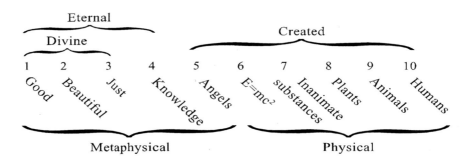

(2). Origin of Substances, Series and Species. Resuming our search, then, we recall that numbers 6 through 10 are naming just the major categories of what-is. We also know that each of these categories consists of innumerable numbers of series and species that sub-divide into classes, genera, phyla, sub-phyla, and so on.

Thomas: Yes, so how can we account for them all by means of just these five numbers?

Diotima: Mathematically, between any two numbers, it is possible to envision an infinite number of points. Each of these points, for us here, represents a progressively higher, more complex and more endowed form of a composite, substance, organism and/or entity. To be specific, what begins at number 7 with definite properties of an inanimate substance, beyond the mid-point into 8, begins to exhibit properties common to the simplest forms of plant life. An example of it could be coral. Corals come in the vast variety of forms and colors. If you consult your dictionary, you will find different definitions for corals. Some speak of it as a "living organism" of marine life, others as a "hard stony skeleton," and still others as a "stone" used in jewelry. Corals have properties of each of these. Such an entity makes it difficult for the biologist to determine what it is, an inanimate substance or a form of life? The further one moves up toward number 8, the entities take on more and more properties of plants and at number 8 they reflect fully and distinctly all the characteristics attributed to plant life. Yet, even at this stage, we are already speaking of an organism that has a highly complex form of existence. It is only recently that even the scientific community came to appreciate more fully the wealth of information that a single cell contains. John B. Fenn, one of the three recipients of the Nobel Prize in Chemistry in 2002,[34] who received his award "for the development of methods for identification and structure analysis of biological macromolecules," tells us there is more information in one cell than in all the volumes of the *Encyclopedia Britannica.* Can you imagine that?

Jason: This is mind-boggling!

Diotima: Comparable patterns exist on the next level, that is, between plants and animals, as the variety, richness and complexity of life progressively increases. At 8 unequivocally starts a plant life, but by the time development of species reaches the mid-point into 9, one encounters something called *euglena,* an entity that has the characteristics of both a plant and an animal. Here, too, the scientists have difficulty determining where it belongs. *Webster's New World College Dictionary* (1999) defines it as "any of a genus (*Euglena*) of green protests with a single flagellum, a reddish eyespot, and a flexible body shape" (490). Were we to encounter it, we too would be completely at a loss to determine what it is. But euglena, too, is already "miles" beyond amoeba, the one cell animal that reveals considerable complexity.

In light of this, we can expect the case to be no different on the next level, within the whole spectrum of life that falls between numbers 9 and 10. It seems incredible that what starts off as bacteria, develops into the bewilderingly enormous variety of life forms that, in turn, branch out into innumerable classes, genera and species of the animal kingdom. It is at the transitional stages between the classes and between the species that we encounter animals such as emus and penguins that possess properties of the two neighboring divisions and make their placement difficult. The closer the species approaches 10, the more characteristics it will share with the human beings on the biological level. Before the birth of the science called Anthropology (Greek *anthropos* for "man" in a generic sense), a human being was defined as a "rational animal" and was studied in Zoology. Apparently an in-depth study of human nature revealed a significant difference between animals and humans that necessitated the birth of a new branch in Biology, now known as Anthropology.

What is amazing is that despite the tremendously increased *complexity* along the way, everything from the hydrogen atom on becomes so intricately entwined and integrated so as to form a single cosmic whole. It is a whole, moreover, of incredible balance, co-existence and reciprocity throughout. Were it not for the unhappy effects on human life, when the original order and harmony in nature was upset, this balance is so natural and inconspicuous that it might have escaped our attention. Alas, some of the disturbances in nature can hardly be overlooked, so threatening are their consequences to the survival of all the inhabitants of the earth. The new science of Ecology was born precisely out this concern. It is no wonder the British physicist Freeman Dyson, who gave us a vision of a "finely tuned universe" says: "The more I examine the universe and study the details of its architecture, the more evidence I find that the universe must have known that we were coming" (Cornwell, 4). Dyson's evidence for the "fine tuning" or the "anthropic principle," reports Cornwell, "involves the citation of many numerical accidents in the laws of physics that make our universe hospitable to life and to human higher-order consciousness." He adds, "Some of these 'accidents' are to do with force fields. For example, the strength of the attractive nuclear forces is so peculiarly precise that were it even slightly different hydrogen would be a rare element, stars like the sun could not exist, and the emergence of life would have been impossible. Had the nuclear forces been weaker, on the other hand, hydrogen would not burn, and there would be no heavy elements, and hence, again, we would not have a universe hospitable to creatures like us. The universe, moreover, is constructed on such a scale that stars in a typical galaxy are twenty million million miles apart; were the distances between stars just two million million miles, life could not have survived on our planet.

"These numerical accidents—on the macro and micro levels—accumulate to build an orchestration of diverse and finely poised balances."[35]

Sophie: I find this mind-boggling! No wonder there are so many branches of knowledge. One can barely scratch the surface of all there is to know in one's lifetime, even if one were to live to a hundred.

Jason: I am still trying to discover what made it possible for this vast procession of new forms of life to come into existence. Didn't we learn that all the entities within the cosmic realm are composites of the same elements?

Diotima: If such precise conditions and properties in the elements of nature had to exist for the universe to develop as it did, it is inconceivable that those conditions could have developed independently of the intelligence capable to construct the universe of this magnitude and complexity. If the finest minds among us for centuries found it so difficult to fathom what *already is,* then to design it, to convert the design into reality and to make it work as it does, demands nothing short of the infinite mind of God. It is in accordance with His wisdom that there had to occur gradual changes in the conditions of nature, that allowed the new forms of life to emerge. It is these environmental changes impacting on the already existing forms of life that eventually yielded new forms of existence, while some other species ceased to exist. The transitional phases, at which time genetic mutations in the organism ensued, were no doubt chaotic stages along the way. But these made it possible for the new forms of life to emerge.

The good had to come along with the bad, John Polkinghorne writes. "The more science reveals about the world, the more it looks like a package deal. We tend to think if we were in charge of creation we'd keep all the good and throw away the bad. But the world cannot be divided that way. Consider genetic mutation, which has driven the amazingly fruitful history of life on Earth, eventually turning bacteria into human beings. Genetic mutation is a geared good, but that same process allows some cells to become malignant. So you can't have the fruitfulness of evolution without cancer, which is a terrible anguish."[36]

Polkinghorne backs up his views with Dyson's conclusions in *Origins of Life* (Cambridge University Press, 1999) where he speaks about "the necessary sloppiness of life" and explains how life "must be able to tolerate error" in order to achieve its highest form. "Novelty comes from the very edge of chaos. If something is too reliable, it's just rigid and nothing new happens. If it's too chaotic, it falls apart. It's in that region of openness and preservation that things really happen.

"And that's a dangerous place—but necessarily dangerous. And it's not because God is careless or incompetent, it's just the necessary cost of great fruitfulness" (Polkinghorne, 23). Reading this passage, one is reminded of Hegel's historical dialectic that paves the way of progress. It is by means of strife or tension between the given historical situation (thesis) and an opposite emerging order (antithesis) that a new understanding (synthesis) is reached, which results in a *higher* form of *existence*. The progress comes as a result of *confrontation* in some form, a *struggle* of two opposite forces that is chaotic and difficult to endure. But it lifts one's life to a higher state of consciousness. The pattern, apparently, holds true on a personal and the social level, much the same as on the natural and cosmic level. The contemporary situation in the world is an indubitable proof of it.

Jason: I can see this principle at work in human life. It is consoling to know that the struggles and adversities we experience have a positive side to them, that they are the necessary challenges to our growth and development in the attainment of excellence of our being.

Diotima: Excellent insight, Jason. What Polkinghorne says here is true in principle. Remember to bring this point to our attention when our discussion will be focusing on human existence. And now kindly take one more look at the sequence of what-is. For at this point I have a question for you.

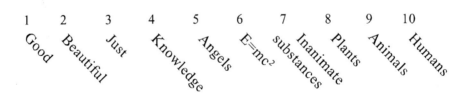

(3). Origin of Evil. Tell me, please, where do you see evil in this scheme of things? No answer? Do you think there is evil in the world?

Thomas: Plenty of it!

Diotma: Whence does it come?

Thomas: It must be man, human beings. I don't see it anywhere else.

Diotima: Do you see yourself as an evil person?

Thomas: No, I don't.

Diotima: Look at the display of what-is. Did God create anything evil?

Sophie: Impossible! Nothing here is evil. Besides, we have seen that God is the Highest Good and the source of all good things. This is why we have called Him *the Good*. There is certainly nothing in this sequence that's evil.

Jason: You're right, Sophie. Since God is the Absolute who possesses all perfections, it is inconceivable that God would have created anything evil.

Diotima: So where did evil come from?

Jason: Some of it definitely traces to our human actions because of our free will and, often, ignorance.

Diotima: It would be difficult to disagree with that. Is there any other source of it? Is it possible that evil came into being prior to human existence? After all, we've come into being last and evil already existed.

Sophie: I get it! Prior to humans, God created angels with an intellect and free will. According to the Bible, some of the angels disobeyed God and were driven out of Heaven. They became evil spirits. So it looks like evil came into being before we did. Consequently, some evil traces to the angels who disobeyed God, and some to us, whenever we disobey God's commandments.

Thomas: What do you mean? What commandments are you speaking of?

Diotima: Your question, Thomas, leads into the discipline of Theology, which is beyond our purview at the moment. We shall, however, touch upon laws, principles of conduct, and the like, from the philosophical viewpoint later when we seek to determine what is truly good for us. Then you will have the opportunity to address this type of question. Currently, however, we need to complete our quest of reality. We are almost there. I believe that we have reached the point when we can insert the ontological whole into the context of the absolute whole, unless you have a question or comment to make on the material we've just covered.

Jason: I didn't want to interrupt at the time the word was introduced, but I am not clear on the meaning of the word "pantheistic." What does it mean?

(4). Pantheism versus Panentheism. The word "pantheism" comes from two Greek words: *pan,* which means "all things" and *theos,* which you already know means "God." Therefore the word pantheism means, "all things are God," and conversely, "God is all things." Given this interpretation of reality, it is easy to draw the next conclusion, as some do, that *this world is God* and there is no God apart from this world.

Jason: How do they reach this conclusion? Is it because they misunderstand God's immanence?

Diotima: You're right on target, Jason. To forestall our falling into this fallacy, I had you draw a list of contrasts between the One and "the many." We did it in advance so that when you become exposed to those three new terms, particularly the concepts *transcendental* and *immanent,* you would not overlook the difference between the two kinds of reality. Do you remember those contrasts?

Sophie: I'm sure we all do, for you made us think and emerge with those answers on our own. Once an idea enlightens one's mind, even if the word escapes one's memory, the understanding is there. I've heard, however, another strange claim made by some people. Surprisingly, the people from whom I heard it are staunched believers. They say that the universe is God's body, because they experience God's presence in nature. I knew intuitively they were wrong, but I didn't know at the time how to refute that claim.

Diotima: I am so glad you can see it now that this erroneous view traces to the misunderstanding of God's immanence. Some people even go on to say that if God is *within* me, then I am God. This fallacy, in turn, leads to a host of other disastrous conclusions and, eventually, to negative consequences.

Thomas: What do you mean?

Diotima: Well, if I understand myself as God and believe there is no such being as God, then I can follow my fancies without fearing any consequences. As Dostoyevsky noted, "If there is no God, everything is permissible." With that mentality, morality is nullified. Once this occurs, selfishness in all its forms takes over and concepts such as good and evil, right and wrong, virtue and vice, law and order, justice and equity become obsolete. Unfortunately, as a result of lawless living one's mind gets darkened, confusion ensues and wrong decisions become a way of life, a sure way down the path of destruction. With these effects, evils multiply and there is nothing to restore peace, order and harmony, neither within a society, nor in the lives of individuals, who as a result of it, are hurting. All of these unfortunate consequences can come because of misunderstanding God and our relationship to Him.

Thomas: Then how is God's immanence to be understood?

Diotima: The word that correctly conveys God's immanence is *panentheism.* Please notice the insert *en,* which means "in" in the word "pan-*en*-theism." Given the meaning of the insert *en,* what do you make of the word panentheism?

Thomas: All things are *in* God. And, apparently because of God's immanence, God is *in* all things? This must be right. For if God is the Absolute who encompasses all that is, then all things are in God. And if He is immanent, then He must be in all things. No, that's wrong! How can the Absolute be in finite things? Something here is still unclear to me. For if God is in all things, then what's wrong with seeing the universe as God's body?

Jason: We have also learned that God is *transcendent.* You're overlooking this aspect of God, Tom. I can think of several reasons why it would be incorrect to think of the universe as God's body. First of all, because of what I've just said, namely, that God is transcendent and as such beyond the cosmic realm. If God is beyond the cosmos, the cosmos cannot be God's body. Secondly, God is eternal whereas the universe is temporal. That would mean that prior to the creation of the universe, God was minus His body, now He has it, and when the world comes to an end, God again will lose His body. On the one hand, that would make God incomplete from the start, which is incompatible with the concept of Absolute. On the other hand, having a body would make God partially mortal, which is inconsistent with God's eternal, purely metaphysical nature. Third, the universe consists of parts, particles of matter, and of a vast variety of cosmic bodies, and a still greater variety of forms in "the particular many." These forms set limits on the entities and give them thereby their specific identity. God, on the other hand, to be Absolute cannot be limited by any form. It is for all these reasons, Tom, that the universe cannot be God's body.

Diotima: Good thinking, Jason. The statement "God is in all things" means that some of God's *powers and perfections are in all things,* like "life" or "being" of some sort with powers to act in a certain way. But in Himself God is infinitely more than this. As we look at the numbers sequence we see that God is *first* and *last.* He is *first* as the Originator of all things, and He is *last* reached whether as the Ground of beings or in a sequence from our standpoint. God is, moreover, *utterly simple* and *boundless*: simple because there are no parts to His being, He is homogeneous throughout. God is boundless, because He is not limited by any definitive form. And because God is not limited by any form, He encompasses all that is. He is *present everywhere*, yet *contained nowhere*. He is *supremely One*, always fully Himself, yet *all-inclusive,* containing all things in Himself. Nothing falls outside His Presence or eludes His all-seeing, omniscient mind. He is *transcendental* and *transcendent*. As Xenophanes, a Greek thinker, six centuries before Christ accurately put it and Jaeger, a scholar of the ancient Greek philosophy, quoting him writes, the "One God 'sees as a whole, thinks as a whole, hears as a whole.' Thus God's consciousness is not dependent upon sense organs or anything comparable."[37] Xenopahanes' God, moreover, is a personal God who is absolutely calm as "effortlessly he sets all things astir by the power of mind alone" (Jaeger, 45). In another passage he states,

"One god is the highest among gods and men;
In neither his form nor his thought is he like unto mortals" (Jaeger, 42).

Sophie: These descriptions clearly explain that neither is God an oversized human being, as some suppose.

Thomas: Your remark, Sophie, triggered another question in my mind. If God is a Person but does not possess the human form, and I assume you hold the same of all Three Persons of the Trinity, then why is it said that we are made into the image of God? Where is the resemblance?

Diotima: It certainly is not in terms of our physical body, because God is purely metaphysical. The word "person" denotes a being that has an immortal soul, intelligence and free will; likewise, someone who has an ability to know, to love, to communicate, and to act rationally. A person, moreover, is someone who cares. In short, a person is a being with rights and duties who is capable of choosing wisely and acting responsibly. Our likeness to God resides in these things. We are made in His likeness according to the powers with which we are endowed, even though we possess them only in a limited way.

Thomas: The word "person" somehow does connote to me someone with a human form. I cannot imagine myself speaking to a Deity who is not like a human being.

Sophie: Not surprising, Tom, because that is the only kind of an intelligent being we know of in this world. Even Jesus, the Son of God, took the human form when He came into this world, and Jesus always called God his Father. All this leads us to imagine the divine Persons in the human form, but I don't think this is bad if it helps us to enter into a loving relationship with Him.

Diotima: Admittedly, this analogical language does help us to communicate with the Divine Persons more easily. Only when we get to Heaven shall we know what each Person looks like. Numbers 1, 2 and 3 hint at a difference in the form of the Three; each seems to possess a particular identity by which it can be recognized. And since Jesus has a human form, it is easy for us to attribute the same kind of form to each Person of the Blessed Trinity. That, however, is the least of our problems.

You may find it interesting to learn that Xenophanes, the thinker we mentioned earlier, sought to rectify humanity's anthropomorphic view of the Deity. He also explained why we confer on Deity the human form. Since his writings are in verse form, I'll quote him in this form. He stated,

But if cattle and horses had hands, and were able
To paint with their hands, and to fashion such pictures as men do,
Then horses would pattern the forms of the gods after horses,
And cows after cattle, giving them just such a shape
As those which they find in themselves.

. . . The gods of the Ethiopians are black with snub noses,
While those of the Thracians are blond, with blue eyes and red hair (Jaeger, 47).

The reason for it is that each creature is capable of thinking only on the level of its nature and its limited intelligence. Unable to know in any other way, it sees itself as the highest form of existence. For this reason, by conferring on the Deity its own form, it means to bestow upon it the highest honor it can. Thus, cows would see their gods as cattle, horses as horses, and we imagine them as human beings. We humans go even further. This fact is vividly exemplified in the manner that different races represent Jesus or our Blessed Lady. In the December 1994 issue of *Life* magazine, there were depicted sixteen images of Jesus.[38] Just by looking at the facial features of each, it was evident what race and culture the particular image reflected. People even clad their images of Deity in the attire that is culturally acceptable to them. The artists do this to help us identify with our Deities more closely in order to facilitate our communication and bond with them more easily. As we grow in our relationship with God, our image of Him continues to be upgraded. But when eventually we come to see Him face to face, we still will be utterly surprised. For God is wholly Other, far beyond our imaginings. Rather than focusing on God's form, we do better when we concentrate on the personal love He bears for each of us, and strive to reciprocate that love as best we can.

2. Quest for Unity of What-is

A look in retrospect at this point can prove to be a profitable delay. It can help us capture the big picture of life's journey and that of our quest. The two are really the same journey, for as we live, so we learn. Up to this point, we have been taking baby steps asking questions about everything we've encountered on the way. As a result of it, the big picture escaped us. You may have not even noticed that our discourse made almost a full circle, and that currently we find ourselves at the doorstep of the answers to the questions we had when we launched our quest. We have only to close the circle. In the light of what surfaces, the answers to our questions will be within reach. Do you remember what those questions were?

Jason: They were the four perennial questions of philosophy: Who really am I? Whence do I come? Where am I going? What am I doing in this world? These were my questions, so I remember them well.

Diotima: We have learned, however, that sooner or later these questions surge up from *within* in everyone's life and become extremely important. Embarking upon the path of our search, we've soon realized that the answers to these questions are contingent on the understanding of reality, because we are a part of it and our life is inconceivable independently of it. Now, hopefully, we understand more clearly why it is so.

True to the human experiences of life, we began our search on the level of the *senses*, in the context of the physical world where we live. Reflections on this level led us to note that reality consists of two realms: the physical, which is the subject matter of science, and the metaphysical, the subject of philosophy. Aligning our questions with the latter, we adopted the method of inquiry proper to philosophy. Taking up the dialectic on the *inductive level of logic*, we've moved next to the *deductive level*. Finally, by raising our discourse to the *level of mathematics*, by means of the number concepts, we grasped the vision of the absolute whole, both in *its diversity* and in *its relationship to all that is*.

With the help of the number *sequence*, we have understood the *ordering* of what-is and the logical necessity for it. In identifying the categories of what-is, we started here with what is familiar to us, hence, with ourselves at number 10. Applying the same rationale of logical necessity to the existence in the series and the species of what-is, we have recovered not only the order in which things came to be, but also the hierarchical scale of what-is. Our discourse, if you recall, started with the search for the *first principles* and brought us to *them*, yielding a higher level of understanding of what-is.

This enhanced vision of reality allows us now to begin at the real beginning, with number 1, hence with the ONE. As soon as we understand the ONE to be a Trinity, we will be in a position to recast the story of creation as it must have evolved

along the way to be what it is. When we reach number 10, the human family, by exposing our bonding with the Triune ONE and the cosmos as a whole, we shall close the circle. Along the way the meaning of the three enigmatic terms, namely, *transcendental, transcendent* and *immanent*, will become explicit, enabling us to understand reality in terms of its major "bonds" that make it an integrated whole—one, moreover, of incredible order, beauty and harmony, despite its magnitude, diversity and the hierarchy in what-is.

Thomas: Grand plan! I like it, but are we up to it?

Diotima: To help our finite minds to envisage what we are setting out to accomplish, we shall revert to the use of the two symbols that served us so well in the past. The circle, just as at the outset of our quest, will depict reality as the absolute whole. And the divided line, likewise as formerly, will enable us to understand the absolute whole in terms of its classes. Just remember that these symbols are merely a device; eventually they will have to be dispensed with, to approximate more closely what-is *as it really is.*

Sophie: I am glad we can continue the use of symbols. Without them, I confess, I would have been lost long ago.

a. Reality as the Absolute Whole. As before, we begin with just a large circle, our symbol for the absolute whole. The space within it looks empty but, as in science, we know that there is no such thing as an empty space. So our space within the circle, too, is teeming with an incredible variety of life forms, all engaged in all kinds of activities proper to them, making what-is a dynamic whole. Given this fact, we shall be merely inserting the names of what we know is there already. We shall proceed in the order of the priorities we have recovered. Since the first image encompasses all that is, we begin as at the outset with the big circle, our symbol for absolutely all that is, hence

<h2 style="text-align:center">THE ONE REALITY:
THE ABSOLUTE WHOLE</h2>

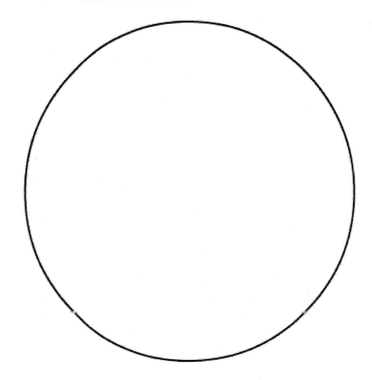

The Actual Object of Knowledge
Diagram 13.1

Jason: Obviously, we begin by inserting the ONE first.

Diotima: You're right, Jason. Since this focuses on the specific realm of reality, let us begin with it.

b. Reality at the Ontological Level. Because nothing could exist without the ONE, we enter the ONE first. In light of this addition, the new Diagram 13.2 calls for an updating in wording. Consequently, we add to *THE ONE REALITY,* the words, *THE ABSOLUTE* and *THE ABSOLUTE WHOLE,* for that is what this whole now

THE ONE REALITY:
THE ABSOLUTE
and
THE ABSOLUTE WHOLE

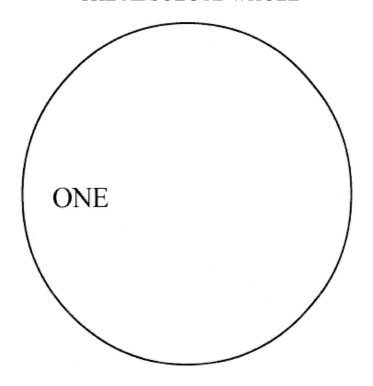

ONE

The Actual Object of Knowledge
Diagram 13.2

exhibits. We understand the ONE to be GOD and His powers to be co-extensive with the absolute whole.

Sophie: Since the same symbol covers both, the Absolute and reality as an absolute whole we must be careful to keep this distinction in mind because the two, I assume, are not convertible, are they?

Diotima: Good observation, Sophie. Can you explain why not?

Sophie: The first difference that immediately comes to my mind is that God is eternal, whereas the absolute whole incorporates also all of creation, the things that had a beginning.

Jason: We can say, then, the two are commensurate or coextensive, but not identical.

Thomas: Good, Jason, easy distinction to remember.

Diotima: Moving on we recall that our search for the first principles revealed that the eternal ONE is not just one, but that there are three Divine Persons to the Original Unit (1+1+1). These Persons are co-eternal and divine in virtue of their shared nature and perfections. Since this image purports to reflect their *ontological co-existence* prior to the creation of anything, they should be entered hierarchically, as 1, 2 and 3 vertically, with the ONE on top, the Two in the middle, and the Three in the lower part of the circle. However, since our aim here is to show each of them not only how it relates to reality as a whole and forms the "bond of unity" in the scheme of things, but also to illustrate the meaning of the terms *transcendental, transcendent* and *immanent,* the position of the Three as reflected in Diagram 13.3 is more apropos.

THE ONE REALITY:
THE ABSOLUTE
and
THE ABSOLUTE WHOLE

The actual object of knowledge

Eternal Life of the Triune ONE

Diagram 13.3

Considering that knowledge is one of the perfections of intelligent Beings, it *ipso facto* belongs to the eternal Three. And since having knowledge is tantamount to knowing the master plan along with the pattern and the underlying principles of order and harmony of all-that-is, we include *knowledge* as *4ᵗʰ* along with what it exhibits: *a master plan embodying pattern or design, and the principles or laws of order and harmony.* We observe that this realm is purely *metaphysical.* In light of what Diagram 13.3 represents, underneath the representation we add the words: *The Eternal Life of the Triune ONE.*

Needless to say, at this point, knowledge is internal to the Three, that is, it is only in the mind of each divine Person. When it becomes externalized in creation and we appear on the scene, it will be gradually retrieved by us and one day, having been embodied in the symbols of language it will be given an independent status in books.

And now a question: From the standpoint of "bonding," which of the Three do you judge to be the bond of their unity?

Jason: Number concepts make it clear that on the *ontological level*, Two (2) or the Second Person is the bond of their unity, for it comes between One and Three.

Thomas: In another sense, though, Three (3) can be said to be the bond of their unity in that it embodies both One and Two.

Sophie: Viewed this way, so is the One, for One is within both Two and Three.

Diotima: Whether you meant it or not, in noting this fact about the Three you have testified to their shared co-existence and reciprocity.

Jason: I always viewed math as irrelevant to matters of deepest import. Little did I know that it would be this discipline that would lead me to the insights that matter most to me!

Diotima: I'm glad to hear this, Jason. If next we enter into the circle the divided line that symbolically aligns "all that is" without going into anything in detail, it becomes instantly apparent that the ontological realm constitutes the Ground for all that now rests upon it. Notice, please, that what rests upon it includes everything that came and is still coming into being. Given this understanding we can say that Diagram 13.4 portrays *THE ONE REALITY: THE ABSOLUTE WHOLE* as the *Ground* and *All-that-is.*

Considering that all this is the actual object of knowledge, we can see that to understand it all is to possess at once *Absolute Knowledge* and *Absolute Truth.* Of course, only the Absolute can have absolute knowledge. With so much to learn, we shall be busy acquiring this knowledge all our life, both here in this life and throughout eternity.

Thomas: Indeed, there appears to be plenty to keep our minds on edge even in eternity!

Diotima: By Two (2) in this diagram we understand the Holy Spirit.[39] It is readily evident that this Person of the Blessed Trinity is Sovereign in the *World of Being*, which includes the created spirits or angels all of whom are intelligent beings. It is equally obvious that Three (3) represents the eternal Logos or God's Son who is Sovereign in the *World of Becoming* with its cosmic series and species and us human beings as its crowning glory. And the ONE is the King of all that is. All of this is taking place in accordance with the Mind of God: His Master Plan reflecting a harmonious pattern that's based on the principles or laws in accordance with which all is erected. Actually, we can say that Diagram 13.4 depicts the whole world of *noumena*—the Greek *noumena* being "spirit"—the world of all spiritual beings, human beings included. We understand this image to be *The World of Noumena,* because we see everything here in terms of its metaphysical dimension, as concepts, ideas and forms endowed with "dynamism" or "life" or/and "spirit", as the case may be, that give being to beings—just as it first was, and is, in the mind of God. It is also what will remain when the created cosmos ceases to exist as a physical phenomenon. In saying this, of course, we are billions of years either prior to our appearance on the scene, or after its physical decomposition.

Jason: What do you mean?

Diotima: We came into being last. Our existence presupposes the existence of the created universe in its entirety. According to science the universe was several billion years old by the time we made our appearance in it. And, if scientific speculation is close, it will take several more billions of years before the universe expires. At that point, the created cosmos having realized its potential, the two worlds, the uncreated and created, will become a single, undifferentiated whole.

Because we are speaking here of it as it is in the mind of God who already always sees it in its complete metaphysical state, we provide merely the "gravitational field of the Third" where the cosmos is in time realized.

Thomas: I am glad to know, and want to believe that the universe will continue to exist even after the dissolution of its elements, but how is it that you are skipping the phase of time, the time of its coming into being?

Diotima: We are at the threshold of this phase right now, Thomas.

THE ONE REALITY:
THE ABSOLUTE WHOLE
GROUND AND ALL-THAT-IS

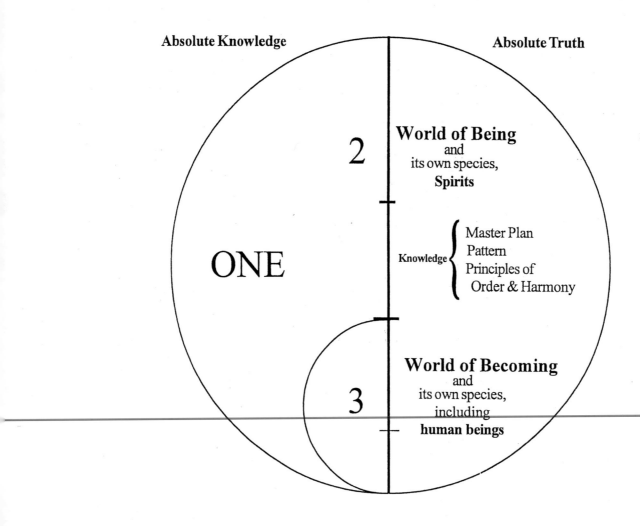

The World of Noumena

Diagram 13.4

Thomas: Before we undertake this discussion, there is one other question prying on my mind. Why did God create the world?

Diotima: Who of us can claim to know the mind of God? From the looks of what is surfacing, however, it looks as if the universe, the World of Becoming, is the Father's gift to His Son meant to be *His Kingdom.* This is no different from what the parents like to do for their children on the natural level. Perhaps we can illustrate this by analogy. For instance, when Prince Charles of the United Kingdom got married to Diana, Queen Elizabeth, his mother the Queen (rather than her husband who does not hold the title of the King) gave him the Windsor Estate, a part of "her kingdom" as a place of his own. Apparently God the Father, being able to give more, wanted His Son to have nothing less the universe as His Kingdom, which He co-created with Him and the Holy Spirit. Notice, though, the Son did not receive His Kingdom as a finished product, anymore than we get our life in a finished form. In both cases there is room left for the person's freedom and creativity, as well as for gaining satisfaction and credit for one's own accomplishments.

Thomas: I can accept this rationale, perhaps because I find an echo of it in human life on a smaller scale.

c. Reality at the Cosmic Level. According to the latest estimates of science the universe sprang into being about 15 billions of years ago, with much forethought, ingenuity, and apparently already then with us humans in mind. As you can see, the focus of Diagram 13.5 is the *Cosmic Superstructure.* We see here *The World of Phenomena* against the background of *The World of Noumena.* It looks as if right from its foundation the created world is a copy of the ontological realm. We notice that what the *gravitational field of the cosmic realm* (G.F.) is to the ontological realm, so the *gravitational field of the solar system* (G.F.S.) is to the electro-magnetic field (E-M.F.) of the stellar systems. And just as the *light of the Third* is the link between the ontological and the cosmic realm, so *the sun,* the *star of the local star system, which is third,* is the link between the stellar systems and the solar system. When God's plan of creation was to be realized, it was sufficient for the eternal Logos to utter the word such as "GO!" or "NOW!" or some such word, for the divine power, in the form of light, to burst forth with great might. At that moment, of the Son, the Sun-like Deity, eventually our sun, a star along with other stars, was born, giving thereby birth to the cosmos and to time. You may recall what we have said earlier, that according to the *inflation theory,* "the entire visible universe grew from a speck far smaller than a proton to a nugget the size of a grapefruit, almost instantaneously, when the whole thing was .0000000000000000000000000000000000001 sec. old [10^{-43} of a second]. The turbo-expansion was driven by something like *dark energy* [emphasis added] but a whole lot stronger. What we call the universe, in short, came from almost nowhere in next to no time" (Lemonick, 55). Agreeing with Guth, Ronan writes, "within 3 minutes the universe was many light-years across" the cosmic space (178-79). Apparently, ever since then it has been in the process of evolving as it moves towards the Pleroma point of its existence. This account of its birth does not require any prior material, such as the gases of the Big Bang, to be already there out of which the universe could come into being. We have seen earlier with the help of science, that all the elements were created out of *hydrogen and helium.* This means that as soon as the radiant energy burst forth from the Third, it created *matter,* the basic stuff of the universe, out of which everything else evolved and is now composed.

Now the "dark energy" is Einstein's *antigravity,* the force that in opposing gravity "propped up the universe," and this *antigravity* is his *cosmological constant.*[40] Directing our gaze to Diagram 13.5 it looks as if the CC, the *cosmic center* of the universe around which the cosmic bodies revolve and Einstein's *cosmological constant* coincide with both, Pierre Teilhard de Chardin's *Cosmic Christ* and our third Person of the Blessed Trinity, *the eternal Logos,* through whom the cosmos came into being. To all evidence, it is His Mind and "unseen" powers that are behind the cosmic processes. If so, it must be He who is holding the reins on the speed of the outermost galaxies preventing them from flying apart. Furthermore, if it is the intelligent Being, rather than the static natural laws, that guides the cosmic order, there is no saying how the behavior of the cosmic forces might be altered in the future. The rate of speed early on and subsequent modification of it indicates that a change can happen again in unpredicted ways. Will God ever allow us to catch up with His doings?

Thomas: Are you not assuming that the cosmic center, cosmological constant, Cosmic Christ and the eternal Logos are the same center?

Diotima: In any circumference there is only one center. Think about it, Thomas. If you reach a different conclusion, we can talk about it.

Jason: Were it not that the scientists are setting a time on when the various occurrences took place, I would be tempted to say that God continues to add new things to what-is just to keep our search going, as if He were playing a game with us.

THE ONE REALITY:
THE ABSOLUTE WHOLE
GROUND AND ALL-THAT-IS

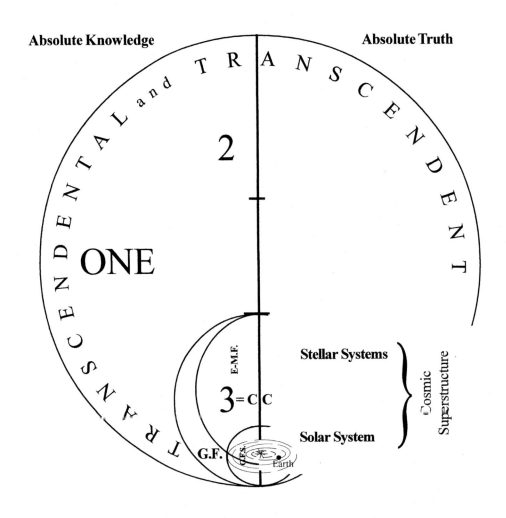

The Actual Object of Knowledge

The World of Phenomena

Diagram 13.5

Diotima: One thing seems certain, with light being the first cosmic phenomenon, the stellar fires had to be ignited first, the elements of matter formed and planets adequately prepared; in short, the whole cosmic superstructure had to be carefully set in place, before the forms of life could appear. Pierre Teilhard de Chardin, the paleontologist calls this phase of creation *cosmogenesis,* the birth of cosmos. This phase corresponds to our interval between numbers 6 to 7. Advancing "the fundamental currents of the universe with 'cosmic' tenacity and intensity to make continuous progress," through the process of 'complexification' *cosmogenesis* gave birth to *biogenesis* (life forms corresponding to our number 8). The latter gave birth to *psychogenesis* (forms of animal life, number 9), which, in turn, gave birth to *noogenesis* (number 10) bringing humanity on the stage only to lead on to *Christogenesis.* We, being an embodiment of His spirit, are in a process of putting on the mind of Christ and becoming one with Him. Our bonding with Christ closes the circle. In keeping with our findings, de Chardin wrote, "Christ is the instrument, the center, the end of all animate and material Creation; by Him all things are created, sanctified, made alive."[41]

Sophie: Was de Chardin the first to point out the link between creation and eventually our link to the cosmic Christ, and Him as the completion of the cosmos?

Diotima: Actually, there is a whole history of development to it. George Maloney, S.J. in his book *The Cosmic Christ* traces the history of this understanding. St. Paul, scarcely a generation after Christ had ascended to heaven, was the first to capture the understanding and to articulate this vision. Many others over the centuries have elaborated on it. Teilhard de Chardin's explanation, however, is the most thorough in the twentieth century.[42] "De Chardin recaptured the vision of the cosmic Christ so dear to earlier Christians," writes Maloney, and having assimilated it into his whole being, "succeeded in expressing it in terms that men, groping in the new complexities of the twentieth century, could understand and make a part of their living experience." By Christ "assuming a material body," he goes on to explain, "God inserted himself into the heart of his created cosmos. By his death and resurrection, Christ, in his gloriously spiritualized humanity, became present, and is even now present, to the cosmos in a new manner. Not only is he the exemplar, the divine Logos according to whom, as St. John tells us in his Prologue, God created all things and in whom all things have their being, but also he is this Body-Person who has become the working agent to effect the fulfillment of God's plan of creation" (15).

Sophie: Then why don't we hear about it?

Diotima: Thinkers who advance this tradition have been primarily mystical theologians and philosophers and they, for some reason, are shunned even though they have the richest insights and the most profound understanding of reality. Most of humanity cannot appreciate this knowledge because spiritually it is not advanced far enough. In Maloney's book there are references made also to Karl Rahner, the outstanding theologian of the twentieth century, who affirms the same view. Maloney writes, "Christ is, as Karl Rahner expresses it, even more than the peak of cosmic realities. He becomes the goal toward which the whole cosmos is moving and in whom the cosmos will find its completion. In Christ we have God's gift of himself to us, irreversibly given" (10-11). Finally, Christ himself tells us that he came from the Father (*Jn.* 16:28) and the Father who lives in him is accomplishing his works through him (*Jn.* 14:10). Christ also counsels, "Live on in me as I do in you" (*Jn.* 15:4), which confirms our own reasoning. Just how Christ is in us will become more explicit in the next discourse when the spotlight will be on us. At this crucial juncture, there appears to be much correspondence between physics, astronomy, paleontology, metaphysics and theology, with confirmation coming from mystical spirituality. It looks as if insights from all these disciplines are converging to lend validity to our findings. Needless to say, separate studies will be required to verify what looks to us like the answer to the nagging questions we all are asking in our respective disciplines. This understanding, nonetheless, is a good preparation for elucidating further the three concepts that pertain to the Divine Persons but lack a corresponding set in the realm of "the many."

d. Transcendental, Transcendent and Immanent. With the help of Diagram 13.5, it is apparent that while all three divine Persons are *transcendental* and *transcendent* to all that is, only the Third is *immanent.* He is *within* the cosmic realm as the source of beings' *being—* their power "to be." God and the Holy Spirit are *transcendent,* although they are present to us from their own stance and through Christ.

Thomas: Your last clause creates a problem for me. How can they be *transcendent,* yet present to us from their own realm?

Diotima: We can understand it by means of the analogy of the sun. The sun is above us, hence transcendent to us, yet the light emanating from the sun is present to us, touches the whole earth and makes life on earth possible. We all know that without the sunlight, plants would be unable to carry on the process of photosynthesis and without plant life no other life would be possible. What follows plants in time relies upon them for survival and they themselves rely on what preceded them in time, namely, *the Transcendent God* and the cosmic superstructure of the inanimate substances. Given the process, we can say that just as without the sunlight plants could not survive, so neither could anything else survive without God. What is interesting and marvelous about God is that as the Absolute, He is present to everything and everyone always and everywhere. No one ever has to make appointments to speak with Him, or wait one's turn until He is free to give one His attention. He is present to us always and everywhere. However, because He is transcendent and spiritual, that is, purely metaphysical by nature, we cannot see God face to face until we come into His Kingdom and see things in a manner comparable to His. The Holy Spirit will escort us to Him when at last we are ready to be caught up in the warm embrace of His eternal Love, for God the Father dwells in an inaccessible light. No one can approach Him directly.

Diagram 15.6 combines the World of Noumena and the World of Phenomena, giving us a thumbnail sketch of the absolute whole as we have come to understand it. We need to emphasize, though, that Divine knowledge at work in creating what-is is not written down anywhere. God has no need of it, as He has no problem with His memory. Some of this knowledge, nonetheless, has been preserved for us in fossils, while most of the other, having been embodied in nature, is now being recovered by means of various disciplines. In addition to it, some of God's knowledge has been communicated to us by means of His messengers such as angels, seers and prophets. But the most important knowledge, namely, knowledge relative to the meaning and purpose of our human existence, was unambiguously revealed to us by the Son of God in person, when He took on our flesh and came to dwell among us some two thousand years ago. Besides, He is the *Dasein*, the "there-being" in the depths of our own being, ever ready to communicate with us. He is the eternal Logos whose voice unceasingly calls us to authenticity through our conscience. Thus, the knowledge needed to live authentically in order to come into His Kingdom is available, and those who make use of it find much joy in living.

In conclusion, let me draw your attention to one more point to which we have alluded earlier, but which is more explicit now. Notice that the One, like the number 1, is both *first* and *last*. It is *first* as the first Cause of all that is, and it is *last* as the Final Cause toward which everything returns. This fact is abundantly clear from the human standpoint. It holds true from both, the viewpoint of the ground of our being as well as from our place in the sequence of all that is. To touch the "ground of one's being" is to touch the "immensity of God" *and* the "shores of eternity." Because we humans have come into being last and embody something of everything that preceded us, on this account we are most richly endowed and are the most complex beings of all. For this reason also we must descend *deep into the ground of our being* in order to meet Him at our core. But to approach one's core, is to approach Christ within. Since Christ is "the ground" of the cosmic realm and "the core" of our being, He is *the Alpha and the Omega* of the cosmos in general, and of our being in particular. However, because Christ is always in communion with the other two Persons of the Blessed Trinity, to find Christ is automatically to be in proximity of the Father and the Holy Spirit. Christ is, literally, *the way* to *eternal life* and *the gate* to Heaven. There is no other access to it.

Now, just as Christ is the "ground" of the cosmic realm and of our being—the first in the order of creation—so God the Father is the "absolute ground," for He is first to absolutely all that is, and so everything, ultimately, redounds to Him. This makes God the Father *the Alpha and the Omega* of absolutely everything. Thus, to reach the ground of one's being is also to come, through Christ, into contact with God. Upon coming into contact with God, one experiences the love of His Presence burning in one's heart with inexpressible delight. At that point one comes to realize what that *eternal component* within one is, and has been from the moment of one's conception. It is the "spark" of Divine Love now aflame with God's own love. What is more, it is also to discover *personally* who God is, (Love), who one is (spirit incarnate formed into the image and likeness of the Triune God), whence one came (from God), where one is going (back to God), and therefore, what one's life has been all about (becoming God-like and one with God to live together for all eternity). But all this becomes possible only through Christ because "all that the Father has he gave to the Son" (*Jn.* 16:15). The Father gave Him all authority over humankind subjecting all things to him (*Jn.* 17:2). As St. Paul so accurately concludes, "When, finally, all has been subjected to the Son, he will then subject himself to the One who made all things subject to him, so that God may be all in all."[43] Currently, however, as Heidegger put it in agreement with Heraclitus about the *sophon*—"One (is) all"—this *sophon*, the Being in whom all beings have being, is making an "appeal" and seeking our correspondence. The "correspondence listens to the voice of the appeal" and in "heeding the appeal" man establishes the "relationship" that makes "the unfolding" of Being possible (WIP, 75-77). "Being is gathering together—*Logos*" (WIP, 49). It is because the access to God is through this Being, "the forgetfulness of Being" makes God inaccessible, which is why today God is known in the world only "through absence," Heidegger contends.

THE ONE REALITY:
THE ABSOLUTE WHOLE
GROUND AND ALL-THAT-IS

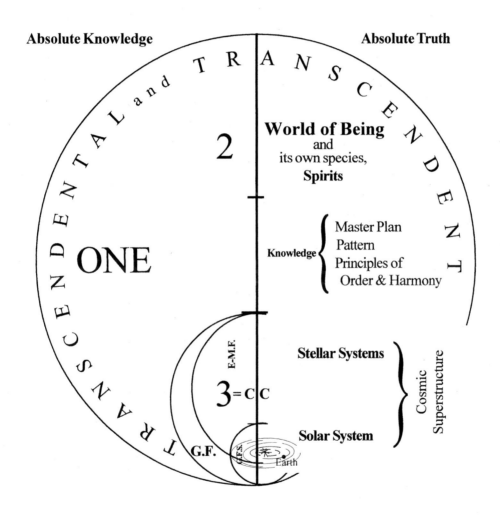

The World of Noumena and of Phenomena

Diagram 13.6

Jason: At last I can understand the underlying reason of the contemporary crisis in the world. This leaves me wondering what we must do to overcome it.

Diotima: The diagrams, as you can see, make it exceedingly clear that all things are *in God*, while the *experience of love* in one's heart testifies that God is *in* one who loves. In the last analysis, my friends, everything is reducible to God, which is why Karl Jaspers said, "That the Deity is suffices."[44] The mystical thinkers like Meister Eckhart, St. John of the Cross, Julian of Norwich, Teilhard de Chardin and others put it simply, "God is all in all," the Latin *"Erit in omnibus omnia Deus"* (FM, 306).

Diagram 13.6 merely combines the World of Noumena and the World of Phenomena to reflect *THE ONE REALITY* as an integrated whole, showing God's own Son to be the link between the two worlds.

Sophie: So *Christ* is the bond of unity not only of the human family. He is the bond of cosmic unity as a whole, and a bond of the cosmic realm with the ontological realm, making reality an integrated whole.

Jason: Knowledge, too, must be viewed as one of the bonds of unity in that it leads a thinking being to this understanding.

Diotima: Knowledge is an *epistemological bond* of unity, whereas Christ is an *ontological bond* of reality and the direct "mediator" between God and the world at large.

Given this understanding, are you ready now to dispense with the symbols?

Jason: We can try. After all we can always return to them, if we need to. What's next on our agenda?

Diotima: Just as at the outset of this section we have captured the big picture of our journey's quest, so now it may prove to be an equally rewarding experience to catch a bird's eye view of reality as *an organic whole*. Our purpose here is to uncover the pattern behind the concepts we have retrieved and by means of it to get a stronger sense of unity of what-is.

Jason: Sounds great! But, with the territory we have covered, it's beyond me how this is possible.

3. Bird's Eye View of the Organic Whole

The magnitude, multiplicity and complexity of reality extending over the inexhaustible spectrum of all-that-is, which otherwise eludes the mind's grasp, can still be understood at least in terms of its basic units, *the transcendentals*. We will do so with the help of Diagrams 14.1 and 14.2. Next, starting with the retrieved building blocks of reality we shall attempt, in light of what we've learned to reconstruct reality from the ground up (Diagrams 15.1-15.5). Once we have a firm grasp of it, by pursuing the sub-divisions on the cosmic level far enough, we shall arrive at an understanding of human nature as it had surfaced in the course of our quest. Finally, to ascertain veracity of the conclusions we have reached, we shall cross-examine our finding by entering into a dialogue with a representative from each of the disciplines that's relevant to our quest.

Thomas: I think cross-examination is an excellent idea, especially if we are to draw upon this knowledge for the understanding of life's journey.

a. Transcendentals of Reality. As we have already seen time and again reality extends from the *infinite ONE, GOD*, at one end of the spectrum, to the *infinitesimal one*, the *hydrogen atom* that itself is a composite of tiny subatomic particles, at the other end. The two ends are mediated by *pure thought*, which unites them (Diagram 14.1). Thus, the basic units of reality are: *the infinite God* in the ontological realm, *pure thought* within the epistemological realm, and the *hydrogen atom* in the cosmic realm.

Sophie: I'm not sure I understand just how *pure thought* is a "link" between the infinite ONE and the infinitesimal hydrogen atom. Can you explain?

Diotima: The same thought that originally is in the mind of the Thinker in its *pure form*, once it is send forth or externalized in some way, becomes *embodied* in that something. In the present case, the *thought* of a hydrogen atom at the moment of creation was embodied *in matter* and became a *hydrogen atom*. Whenever thought is embodied in something, be it in matter, language, art, music, nature and the like, it is then in the mind of the thinker *and* in that which embodies it. In thus binding the two, it becomes a *link* between what it unites making them one. This is how thought becomes a *link*, or as we have called it earlier metaphorically "the silver thread," that binds reality into one. At the transcendental level, *pure thought* becomes *the medium* linking the *eternal infinite God* with the *created infinitesimal hydrogen atom*, and eventually with everything else that falls in between.

Sophie: Now I see it, thanks. I do recall our early discussion of this concept. I believe I compared thought at that time to a hub of a wheel.

Thomas: Yes, you did, Sophie. I remember that discussion very well.

Diotima: Taking the next step, we note that each of the three basic units gives rise to its own set of transcendentals, namely, *ontological, epistemological* and *physical* respectively. Each of these units consists of three particulars. The *ontological unit,* God, incorporates the three divine Persons: the *Good,* the *Beautiful* and the *Just* or the *Brilliance* of ineffable beauty, *Love* personified, and the *eternal Logos.* The *epistemological unit,* pure thought, consists of *concepts, ideas,*

and *forms.* And the smallest *physical unit,* the hydrogen atom, like the members of the ontological unit, consists of three isotopes: *Protium or simply Hydrogen , Deuterium* and *Tritium.* The Greeks saw in this three-fold classification of reality: the *archetype* (the eternal model), the *prototype* (original form, type or pattern that serves as a basic model), and the *ectypes* (perceptible copies of the above).

The hydrogen atom, the basic building block of the cosmic realm, is but the first and one of the many infinitesimal units of the cosmic *physical phenomena* of *light, heat,* and *sound,* and the three *physical universals*: *electricity, magnetism* and *gravitation,* the physical forces that form into electro-magnetic and gravitational fields within which all physical bodies revolve. These fields, forces and phenomena jointly constitute the physical transcendentals.

Thomas: What we've said thus far is common knowledge. My question is: How does one arrive at the same pattern on the other two levels?

Diotima: All our knowledge has its basis in human experience. Consequently, before we can move on to the other two sets of transcendentals we need to incorporate ourselves into the diagram. Without us even this knowledge could not be had; indeed, it would be irrelevant to the rest of the creatures in this world.

b. Transcendentals on the Human Level. We insert ourselves with *the three dimensions* of our being: *body, mind* and *spirit* through which knowledge becomes accessible to us. In doing so, we can see better how each dimension of our being traces back to its own set of transcendentals at the general level and how one relies upon it for the realization of one's potential in attaining fullness of one's being. Although each of our dimensions stems from and draws upon a different set, we place ourselves within the cosmic realm because that's where the planet Earth is and so that's where we are.

We already know that our bodies are composed of the same elements of matter as the rest of the natural beings and that we, like they, rely upon everything in this world for our survival on Earth. It is through the *physical senses* of our body that we, the intelligent beings that we are, *perceive, observe* and *experience* the *physical phenomena* (light, heat and sound along with everything that evolves from these), and the *physical universals* (electricity, magnetism and gravitation), the physical forces that form into fields within which everything revolves. But it is our intellect that interprets this information. Since intellect is metaphysical in nature and as such belongs to another category, transition to that level is both natural and inevitable.

(1). Ontological Transcendentals in Humans. Unlike the physical, the ontological phenomena are foreign to the consciousness of our co-habitants on Earth. Of all created physical beings, only we are conscious of knowledge and are concerned about truth. Only we humans seem to have a problem with our identity and only we seem to be unable to find complete fulfillment and happiness by means of what we find on Earth. This is because we are beings of time *and* of eternity. We begin on the natural level, but have to develop from the "ground up" on both the natural and the spiritual level to attain fullness of our being. Although we begin here, Earth is not meant to be our final abode, which is why in time we die and leave it. Because of our spiritual dimension, our heart is restless. The light of truth beckons us on to ever-new heights and to ever-new depths. Until the truth of our inmost being appears upon the horizon of our mind, it is certain that we shall know no peace. The *ontological dimension,* which constitutes the inmost component of our being, is waiting to be discovered. Initially, it is in a dormant, passive state. Lying concealed in its depths, it is waiting for the body, its natural home that is being prepared for it, to develop—only to be aroused one day and prepared to assume the leading role.

We are speaking here of our *spirit,* which we already know to be the "core" or the "ground" of our being. This dimension having come from the ontological realm relies upon the *ontological phenomena* for the fulfillment of its being. These phenomena *experienced* by us, are *communicated* to each person *individually* in the depths of one's being and calls for listening. The *logos* speaking in *love,* communicates the *light of wisdom.* Its purpose is to direct one's actions to love and to God. One's positive response of love, to that love, eventually manifests itself in the *experience of love*, that delectable fire we all have experienced at one time or another, which burns in one's heart. It is these *experiences* that enable us to identify the ontological phenomena within us.

The *ontological phenomena*, then, are: *light of wisdom, love,* and *logos* (the speaking of the *Dasein* within us). These phenomena trace back to the Divine and are given exclusively to us human beings. They nurture our spiritual dimension and guide us to our eternal inheritance. The spiritual phenomena are *intuited* by one's spirit and *experienced* by the heart as the warmth of love. We can see now that just as the physical phenomena oblige the physical dimension of our being and the epistemological our intellect, so the ontological phenomena oblige our spiritual dimension. Because there is a special personal bond between the Triune God and the human person through the indwelling of the *spirit*, the human heart, consciously or subconsciously, craves its own goods, the *ontological elements* of *goodness, beauty,* and *justice* that emanate from *the Good, the Beautiful,* and *the Just.*

Tracing their presence to the *Universal of universals*, the ONE or GOD, the same *elements* manifest themselves in nature as the *ontological universals,* whence nature's goodness, beauty and splendor. Because these *ontological transcendentals* permeate nature, we *experience* them first in nature and, eventually, within ourselves if we live authentically. Order, harmony and reciprocity in nature, *the epistemological transcendentals* indicate that the Just was at work, for justice has been done to everything in it. And since we are a part of nature, whether we realize it or not, we possess them likewise. This is why we seek them in our life.

(2). Epistemological Transcendentals in Humans. On the basis of the aforementioned *human experiences* within us and *scientific findings* in nature, the human mind postulates the corresponding set of the epistemological transcendentals. The *epistemological phenomena* are: *intellectual light* (of knowledge), *consciousness* and *truth,* and the *epistemological universals: master plan, pattern* or design, and *the principles* or *laws of order and harmony.*

Jason: Are you saying that the epistemological universals are of a human positing? Does that mean that we impose them upon reality?

Diotima: They are a human articulation, but they are not arbitrarily imposed upon reality. Rather, they are "un-covered" or "re-covered" by means of the objective findings of research in the realm of metaphysics and in empirical studies. One thing is certain, we shall never find God's architectonic blueprint of the cosmos. God had no need of one. He has no problem with memory. To the extent that the physicists "discover" the laws operative in nature, to that extent they approximate the Master Plan that God must have had in mind while creating the cosmos. Here, as in mathematics, on the basis of the two known facts, one can arrive at the unknown. The *basic elements* of His plan are, as we have noted earlier, the basic units of *pure thought: concepts, ideas and forms,* the "prototypes" of the "ectypes" that fill this world. And so this is what the scientists ultimately give us by way of *theories.* A scientific theory is an *explanation* of what the scientists have "discovered" to be operative in nature.

Jason: What evidence is there to prove that the laws science is postulating are accurate? Doesn't much of science consist of speculating?

Thomas: Scientific theories are based on facts that have been discovered, analyzed, tested and cross-examined. Technology, for one, is a proof of the validity of those findings, Jason. Technology is built on the laws of nature.

Diotima: There are other proofs as well. Michael Behe, the biochemist we have cited earlier, writes: "The laws of physics are now so well understood that space probes fly unerringly to photograph worlds billions of miles from earth. Computers, telephones, electric lights, and untold other examples testify to the mastery of science and technology over the forces of nature. Vaccines and high-yield crops have stayed the ancient enemies of mankind, disease and hunger—at least in parts of the world. Almost weekly, announcements of discoveries in molecular biology encourage the hopes of cures for genetic diseases and more" (Preface, ix). So yes, there is sufficient evidence to prove that human knowledge, though greatly limited, is a fairly accurate approximation of Divine knowledge at least in some things. It is these findings that reveal God's Master Plan at work. As to what you term "speculations," those are the "educated guesses" of inductive reasoning based on the available data. For instance, questions about the universe at large or about its beginning fall into this category because there is no way that any scientist could have a direct access to these areas. This is why there are in existence conflicting theories about these things and their conclusions are subject to change. However, that is how scientific knowledge progresses until it arrives at its objectively valid conclusions, like those Behe named above.

THE TRANSCENDENTALS

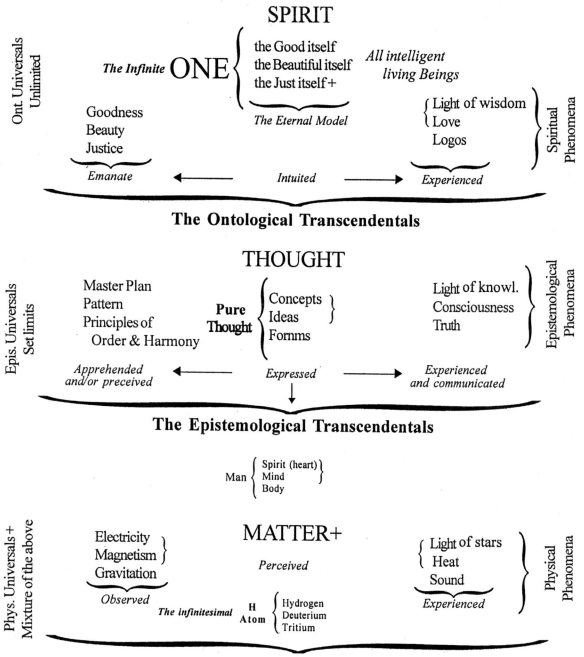

SPIRIT

Ont Universals Unlimited

The Infinite ONE { the Good itself / the Beautiful itself / the Just itself +

All intelligent living Beings

Goodness
Beauty
Justice

{ Light of wisdom / Love / Logos } Spiritual Phenomena

The Eternal Model

Emanate ← *Intuited* → *Experienced*

The Ontological Transcendentals

THOUGHT

Epis. Universals Set limits

Master Plan
Pattern
Principles of
  Order & Harmony

Pure Thought { Concepts / Ideas / Fornms }

Light of knowl.
Consciousness
Truth } Epistemological Phenomena

Apprehended and/or preceived ← *Expressed* → *Experienced and communicated*

The Epistemological Transcendentals

Man { Spirit (heart) / Mind / Body }

MATTER+

Phys. Universals + Mixture of the above

Electricity
Magnetism
Gravitation }

Perceived

Light of stars
Heat
Sound } Physical Phenomena

Observed

The infinitesimal **H Atom** { Hydrogen / Deuterium / Tritium }

Experienced

The Physical Transcendentals

Basic Units of Reality

Diagram 14.1

Notice please that just as epistemology itself, so is our mind in the intermediate position. While each dimension of our being receives its own goods through *its own medium,* it is the intellect that renders everything intelligible. Initially, one's mind upon being awakened is developing by receiving input from others in the form of concepts, ideas, and forms communicated to it. Later, it assumes an independent role as it integrates the input, makes valuable observations, and draws sound conclusions. Through both of these activities the mind develops its own potential and powers that prepare it for a leading role. It is in the latter capacity that our mind postulates *the master plan, pattern,* and *principles (laws) of order and harmony* as the *epistemological principles or forces* behind the workings of created things, which they exhibit.

While our *senses* play a primary role, at least initially, in perceiving most of the physical transcendentals, it is *consciousness itself,* one of the essential powers of the intelligent spirit that *intuits* the ontological transcendentals. The function of the *mind* is to interpret and arrive at truth of all that is. What is given in a personal experience to *consciousness* is *apprehended* and *interpreted* by the mind personally. What is *expressed* in and *communicated* by nature is initially *sensed,* or otherwise *perceived, observed, tested* and interpreted scientifically. Consciousness turns out to be at the heart of reality and at the heart of human existence. The quest for the understanding of what we become conscious, gradually leads to the light of knowledge and eventually to the truth of all that *truly is.* But this moment dawns in its full splendor and beauty only when one realizes fulfillment of one's own being. Everything prior to that moment conduces to it.

Like all concepts, all universals are abstract. The ontological universals are by nature abstract; being devoid of form, they are *unlimited.* The epistemological universals *set limits* on created things by the form they impose and by the principles in accordance with which they are made to function in view of the Master Plan. And the physical universals are a *mixture of the above* embodied in matter. The latter is what reveals the existence of the former two, for by their nature they are invisible to the human eye.

Recapping what Diagram 14.1 in essence depicts, it can be said that the ontological realm is the realm of the SPIRIT (from whence comes our intelligent spirit and the realm for which it craves), the epistemological realm is that of THOUHT (the goal of which is truth that tantalizes the human mind), and the cosmic realm is the realm of MATTER +, the plus being what it evinces from the other two realms. (From the elements of this realm our body is fabulously knitted together.) While the body houses our two-fold metaphysical dimension, it is the latter that permeates it through and through and is meant eventually to play a *leading role* in one's life.

Sophie: Are you suggesting that Diagram 14.1 depicts things as they exist in reality?

Diotima: No, Sophie. Diagram 14.1 reflects the transcendentals as *three sets,* each according to its nature; it exhibits them in isolation to help us see more clearly what each of them is. This is not how they exist in reality. In reality they co-exist as one, just as they do in a human person. To see them as they are given in human experience, with the help of our imagination, we must do what we did once before, reassemble them. Just as formerly in the case of Diagram 6 we had to keep sliding each of the smaller wholes into the next bigger one of which it was a part to see it in its rightful place until we finally found it in the context of reality as a whole, so now we must *slide up* the physical transcendentals upon the epistemological transcendentals in order to see first how these two belong together. Having mentally done so, we see now the physical transcendentals as the "embodied concepts, ideas and forms," the underpinnings of their existence that give them form and render them intelligible in addition to being visible. While we perceive the *phenomena* that manifest them, it is their underpinnings—the *concepts ideas* and *forms* retrieved from them—that make their way to books, charts and images of all kinds where they are explained through theories in the various branches of the *empirical* bodies of knowledge. Such being the case, when we read books and study theories about them, we envision the objects themselves in our mind and find them intelligible. We see them, moreover, according to their specific *pattern* and in terms of *laws* by means of which scientific theories explain them—all as a part of the *Master Plan* that the cosmos at large displays in its harmonious coexistence and reciprocity.

Next, when we *slide up* this combined set over the ontological transcendentals, we see the same phenomena with the *dynamic element* in them, exhibiting their full splendor, beauty and goodness. We see them now as "emanations" of the Triune ONE: the Good, the Beautiful and the Just, embodying and reflecting their perfections in some degree. This makes it possible for us to understand why and how the ontological transcendentals are said to be *convertible with Being.* This dimension of nature is experienced by all of us in various degrees, but it is the artists, poets and thinkers of the *metaphysical* bodies of knowledge that address it, each in a manner proper to its own discipline.

Thomas: Don't the metaphysicians, be they theologians, philosophers, artists, poets, musicians and the like, emerge with concepts, ideas and forms? That's what we find in their books too.

Jason: You're right, but what they say does differ. They do not speak of the same thing, even when they address the same phenomena of nature.

Diotima: The fact that their theories do not coincide, even when they speak of the same object in nature, indicates that they are focusing on a different, though complementary, aspect of it. And the fact that they all emerge with concepts, ideas and forms, is a proof that *thought* plays a mediating role in all of reality. Consequently, all bodies of knowledge need to be viewed as complementing each other. The need for seeing them in their convergence is currently being acknowledged and it is assiduously pursued.

Sophie: I'm so glad to hear this is happening.

Diotima: The understanding springing from the convergence of insights from physics, metaphysics, mysticism and theology, is a relatively new phenomenon. Teilhard de Chardin was the first to articulate it, but he was a man ahead of his time. Not that the thinkers of the past did not arrive at the same conclusions. There is a wealth of comparable knowledge in philosophy, mysticism and theology, but up to now it was attained by means of *faith,* or by *reason,* and in a few instances by faith *and* reason. As of late, *empirical data* is surfacing to lend concrete evidence in support of it. It is only because science in the twentieth century has made unprecedented strides in understanding cosmic phenomena, and philosophy is venturing "to bridge" the great epistemic divides by establishing links with, and among, the existing bodies of knowledge, that there is a possibility of putting the whole "jigsaw puzzle" together. We now know that theology, which relies on Divine Revelation, is on firm ground, that philosophy based on faith and reason is not such a bad combination after all, that human reason, provided one lives a fully human life, is capable of rising to the truths of objective knowledge, and that the mystical utterances are in fact reports of glimpses into the heart of reality Itself. What is even more exciting and consoling is that through the *spiritual phenomena,* all, even those who lack formal education, can come *to experience* and *to know* personally not just their emanations and the three-fold phenomena in nature, but also the Divine Presence *within themselves*: here and now *in their own heart,* and at death *face to face.*

Thomas: Are you implying that all three sets of phenomena are given in experience to every human being?

Diotima: They are open to everyone and eventually *can* be experienced by every human being. Whether or not they are, depends on how one lives one's life. One is free to turn away, even to reject what one does not want. Consequently, only those who live authentically, a three-dimensional life in accordance with the promptings of the Holy Spirit and are realizing their three-fold potential that come to experience them.

Jason: I think it is incredibly good news that all of us have a chance to attain the highest good.

Sophie: I concur with you, Jason. Now that we have the good news and the understanding of reality in terms of its transcendentals, I'd like to see *how* we arrive at this knowledge objectively, in terms of the respective disciplines.

Diotima: A valid and an important question, Sophie. To be effective, the answer to your question needs to emerge in the process of our deliberations. We can expect it to surface when we will be endeavoring to build the reality from the ground up. Before we get to it, however, I'd like to ask you to cast one final look at the transcendentals to note the subtle pattern that reality even at this level exhibits.

(3). Pattern in Transcendentals. Please observe the special *bonding* between the first two concepts in each set of three. There is a kind of *inseparability* to them, as also *interiority* and *concealment,* as it were, which is revealed by the "third" in each set. The third in each case has a special role to fulfill. It "goes out," draws attention, interacts, communicates something, and *points beyond itself* to the other two, be they entities, elements, components, dimensions, phenomena, whatever the case happens to be. Look at the specific "trio's" and see if you can find what I am suggesting.

Sophie: Remarkable! Looking at the ontological set of transcendentals we've seen that while all three divine Persons are transcendental, the Good and the Beautiful are *transcendent,* purely metaphysical and inseparable. Only the Just, the eternal Logos, is *immanent* in the cosmic realm and being the Third, points beyond itself to them.

Thomas: I am not sure I understand how this happens.

Sophie: If the word *Logos* means "Word" and "speaking," these concepts presuppose a speaker or speakers. There is no speaking without intelligent beings. Consequently, when we hear a word or speaking, even if we do not see the person(s), we know that intelligent beings are somewhere near. In the case of the ontological transcendentals, the eternal Logos "goes out" and by revealing itself, points beyond itself to the other two Persons. This occurred also historically.

As to the inseparability of the first two Persons, that came through clearly to me when we sought to understand the Eternal Model by means of the number concepts. At that time we saw that 2 in being 2 presupposes 1 and is nothing other than 1+1, that is, 1 in union with the 1. This means that 2 is not only most like the 1, but also to maintain its identity, it necessarily incorporates the 1. (Without the 1, 2 ceases to be 2). This kind of "inseparability" manifests the closest "bonding" possible in the relationship. Their presence "within" the Third denotes their "interiority" and "hidden-ness" or "concealment" of their Being, both in Him and subsequently in nature. Moreover, if we can come to see them in Person only "in Heaven," there is likewise "interiority" and "hidden-ness" to them in this sense, too.

Justice, in turn, whenever it is at work effects goodness and beauty, whether in us, in nature, in the particular entities, in societies or in the world at large. Through our acts of justice, with the help of the Just, we too become just, and thereby, beautiful and good. And it is by means of the *spiritual phenomena* that the *divine Logos* (speaking within us) communicates to us *love* and *light of wisdom* that enable us to become those faithful copies of the Eternal Model. Consequently, the pattern holds in the *ontological universals* as well as in the *ontological phenomena*.

Diotima: Your explanation, Sophie, reflects good understanding of that realm. Upon further reflection you may note that just as the Just is an "offspring" and an "embodiment" of the Good and Beautiful, which automatically makes Him beautiful and good, so He, by doing justice to the things of the created realm, made them in turn so beautiful and good. Justice itself in being an offspring and an embodiment of goodness and beauty confers the same attributes upon what it produces. Similarly, the communicated divine Logos being an offspring and an embodiment of divine love and wisdom, by communicating with us imparts them to us. In this way it produces the same kinds of effects within us. The more you ponder the relationship within and among the transcendentals, the more insights you will gain. And, incidentally, the more faithfully you live in accordance with this wisdom, the more intensely you will experience its effects in yourself. Thus, with each step along the way you will come to appreciate more and more God's beautiful Master Plan. Eventually, you will come to *know* this truth not just theoretically, but firsthand, *from personal experience.*

Now, what about the other two realms on Diagram 14.1? Can you see anything comparable there?

Jason: Since Sophie addressed the ontological transcendentals and I think Tom will feel more comfortable interpreting the cosmic realm, I am willing to focus on the epistemological set. Tom, would you like to be next?

Thomas: Thanks, Jason, it's thoughtful of you to let me zero in on the area with which I'm more familiar. I promise not to get too technical. Actually, there's not much to this set, as portrayed here. Most of it, I think, is common knowledge. To all evidence, though, the pattern holds true of this realm as well.

Since the birth of the universe traces to hydrogen, which gives birth to helium and from these the whole universe spins off, it seems only proper to see the infinitesimal atom as the foundational block of the cosmic realm. Like the divine Persons, each hydrogen isotope has an identity of its own, yet what goes out of each is the same thing—the electron. A proton, carrying a positive charge (+), and a neutron which has no charge, are "within" the nucleus, while the electron carrying a negative charge (-) "goes out" encircling the nucleus.

Something comparable is true of the *cosmic phenomena* of light, heat, and sound. For here, too, light is always accompanied by heat; it is one with it and inseparable from it. What goes out from them is sound. We see this fact clearly manifested in an electric storm. The sound of thunder is often the first to "go out." It draws our attention to the approaching electric storm, which brings with it lightning. Because lightning is always accompanied by intense heat, it has the power to ignite a combustible object when it strikes it.

The same holds true in case of the *physical universals.* The cosmic universal *forces,* namely, electricity, magnetism and gravitation that create *cosmic fields* (within which large cosmic bodies gravitate) exhibit the same design. Each of the three forces is distinct and produces effects peculiar to it. Yet here, too, electricity and magnetism are found to be inseparable from each other. Wherever there is electricity, there is a magnetic force, and magnetism is always surrounded by an electric field. The planet Earth, for instance, behaves as if a short, thick bar magnet were buried within it and the electric currents surround the Earth. Physicists think that Earth's magnetism is largely due to the electric currents *in* the Earth. Since these two forces are never encountered apart, physicists prefer to speak of them simply as the *electro-magnetic force,* as if the two were one. As we have seen formerly, stellar systems gravitate within the electromagnetic field (E-MF). The solar system, connected to them by our sun, revolves within the gravitational field of the sun (GFS), but the universal gravitational field (GF) undergirds both of them giving unity to the cosmic realm.

Sophie: I thought that there were also nuclear forces. Where do these come in?

Thomas: What we have represented here are the *vast cosmic forces* and *fields* within which large cosmic bodies like stars and planets gravitate. Nuclear forces are "within" *atoms*. Scientists observe two kinds of nuclear forces, strong and weak. These two forces bind atomic nuclei and break them apart under certain conditions. The *strong nuclear force*, first of all binds protons and neutrons against strong electric repulsions that exist between positively charged protons. But nuclear particles, physicists recently discovered, consist of still smaller particles called *quarks,* and it is the strong nuclear force that binds the quarks permanently together. Because of their cohesion, individual quarks are never seen apart, but it is believed they form into "triplets" and in this form they are called *hadrons.* As opposed to the strong, the *weak nuclear force* does not exert any pull or push, but it allows for a change. Ronan explains, "For instance, when a neutron decays into a proton, an electron, and a neutrino, the weak force changes one of the neutrino's three quarks. . . . The weak force," interestingly enough he adds, "has three types of bosons [the force involved in nuclear reactions]: the W+, the W-, and the Z, each controlling a different force field. The W+ and the W- are charged like protons and electrons; the Z is neutral like a neutron" (171). From this it follows that the sub-atomic particles themselves, just as the vast cosmic bodies, have their own electromagnetic forces and fields of activity. Their activity is primarily due to the fact that protons and electrons have a charge, while neutrons being neutral assist both and these three are the main architects of the cosmic realm. The weak force in atoms allows for a change in the arrangements of protons and neutrons. This, in turn, accounts for the diverse combinations of the particles of matter, which gives rise to the formation of different elements, molecules, compounds, and eventually substances out of which gradually the whole cosmos evolves.

Sophie: There appears to be a special kind of link between the electrons and electricity. Doesn't their very name suggest it? And since electricity produces light, there must be also a link between it and the cosmic phenomenon of light.

Diotima: Interesting observation, Sophie. If this link exists, it should come to the foreground in our next discourse. Currently we need to allow Jason opportunity to give us his views on the epistemological realm. After his presentation we will be able to conclude our discourse on the transcendentals and proceed to the phase where the answer you're seeking is likely to surface. Are you ready, Jason?

Jason: Yes I am. I just hope that I can do as well as Sophie and Tom did.

As I look at the realm of thought, I am inclined to begin with *consciousness*, because it is our consciousness of the goodness and beauty of everything in this world that first arouses wonder and provokes all kinds of questions.

Diotima: Excellent start, Jason!

Jason: In *pure thought*, there is undeniably a close similarity, almost an identity between concepts and ideas. Both in themselves lack form and for this reason, both are abstract. And since knowledge is *intellectual light*, concepts and ideas being components of it are *bits of intellectual light*, which is why they yield understanding. Concepts are more illusive than ideas, for even in their embodied form as, for instance, in light, heat and sound, or electricity, magnetism and gravitation they lack concreteness of form. The metaphysical concepts like goodness, beauty and justice, or truth, virtue and consciousness are even more difficult to envision. One may grasp their general meaning but one cannot conceive them as an image. For this reason they are more difficult to understand for the neophyte. Ideas take a *form*, the third element in that trio, which makes them perceptible. Once they are embodied in some form they become objects of perception. Because we have an experience of objects such as a tree, a star, a dog, and so on, through these visible forms we get at the understanding of ideas. And through ideas we are led to the comprehension of concepts. As we have noted above, it is the "third" element, here the *form* (of a particular entity) that first reveals the idea and yields conceptual seeing of what-is, only to make eventually the universal concepts intelligible.

When the human mind comes to understand ideas and concepts, these, being bits of light of knowledge, produce insight into something. Thus, one by one they enable one's mind to approximate the truth of what-is. However, since the *light of knowledge* is really the *light of truth*, when truth is communicated, the light of knowledge dawns upon our consciousness. At this level, it seems, that either one can come first, the truth about something, or some knowledge about it; both are *light* that enlightens the person. In either case, the *intellectual light* comes by means of concepts, ideas and forms, unless it comes first through experience.

With respect to the epistemological universals, it is one's observation of order and harmony in nature that points beyond itself, gradually revealing the design and the Master Plan at work behind the phenomena. There is, therefore, a close relationship between the pattern and the intelligible Master Plan.

THE TRANSCENDENTALS

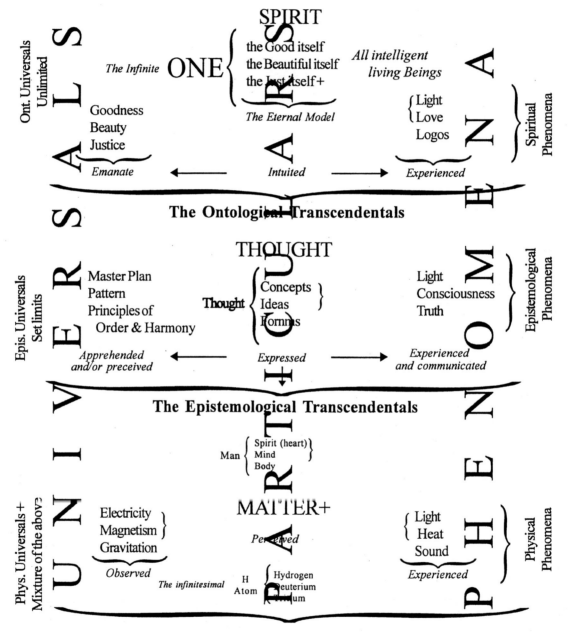

SPIRIT

The Infinite ONE {
the Good itself
the Beautiful itself
the Just itself+
}
The Eternal Model

*All intelligent
living Beings*

{ Light
Love
Logos

Goodness
Beauty
Justice }

Emanate ← *Intuited* → *Experienced*

U N I V E R S A L S

Ont. Universals
Unlimited

P H E N O M E N A

Spiritual
Phenomena

The Ontological Transcendentals

THOUGHT

Master Plan
Pattern
Principles of
Order & Harmony

Thought {
Concepts
Ideas
Forms
}

Light
Consciousness
Truth

Epis. Universals
Set limits

*Apprehended
and/or preceived* ← *Expressed* → *Experienced
and communicated*

Epistemological
Phenomena

The Epistemological Transcendentals

Man {
Spirit (heart)
Mind
Body
}

MATTER+

Electricity
Magnetism
Gravitation }

Perceived

{ Light
Heat
Sound

Observed   *The infinitesimal*   H
Atom {
Hydrogen
Deuterium
Tritium
}   *Experienced*

Phys. Universals +
Mixture of the above

P A R T I C U L A R S

Physical
Phenomena

The Physical Transcendentals

Universals, Particulars and Phenomena

Diagram 14.2

Did you notice any discrepancy in what I said? There is a breakdown in the pattern, if I can call it a breakdown, in the area of the epistemological phenomena. Consciousness was equally a consciousness of knowledge and of truth. I sense something different about consciousness, but I don't know what it is.

Diotima: You are very perceptive, Jason. First of all, you are right in stating that consciousness is a consciousness of knowledge and of truth (and other things besides). Although both yield intellectual light, consciousness, like the mind, lacks independent existence. Both consciousness and mind are attributes of the "self"; they are powers of the spirit. Because the "self" or spirit is the real *you*, by means of these powers *you* are conscious of what-is. And because the human "self" is an *intelligent self*, we can come to comprehend the truth given in our consciousness. When we perceive the truth about the *consciousness* of our "conscious self," we become *self-conscious*. At this point we *know* ourselves as *rational, thinking beings,* and we know *that we know* it. But this is not yet the highest form of self-consciousness possible.

Thomas: How did we see ourselves prior to this awareness?

Diotima: Initially, we were conscious of the phenomena around us and of ourselves as one of the *natural beings,* hence, in terms of our physical dimension; we were not conscious of the fact *that* we are conscious. This fact simply eluded us; it had not entered yet our consciousness and so we were unmindful of it. Lacking maturity, our seeing and therefore understanding, was superficial. We tended to judge things by appearances. Consequently, even though we saw ourselves superior to natural beings, we may have seen ourselves as different from animals only in degree, but not in kind. We were not conscious that such a difference even existed. It is our *self-consciousness* as *rational beings*, which places us above the animal species, even though the highest species among them exhibit a high degree of practical intelligence. Eventually, our *self-consciousness* is that of being *spiritual beings*. The "self" emerges as "spirit incarnate" tracing its origin to the divine.

Thomas: Is there any concrete evidence in support of this view?

Diotima: In pursuit of this answer, all kinds of studies have been carried out over the years by the related bodies of knowledge. As soon as we complete our dialectic we shall inquire into them. Hopefully at that time, a satisfactory answer will come to light.

Thomas: How will we know into which bodies of knowledge we need to inquire? There are so many sciences that pertain to humans. You're not suggesting that we have to look at all of them, are you?

Diotima: There is something, no doubt, in all of them that would enhance our understanding of ourselves, were we to inquire into them. That's not our plan, though. By building reality from the ground up and seeing it in terms of the respective bodies of knowledge, the answer to your question should become readily apparent. We are almost at the doorstep of that undertaking. Are there any other concerns, or questions any one of you has? . . . If not, by way of summary on transcendentals we can say that each set of the three categories of *phenomena: physical, epistemological* and *spiritual* (running vertically the length of the page on the right side) is similar and related to the other two, yet each itself is distinct, both as a set and individually (Diagram 14.2).

Through the experience and study of these three-fold phenomena we are led to the understanding of *the particulars* (running vertically through the center of the page from the infinitesimal hydrogen atom up to the Infinite God). Each of these particulars is itself one *and* a part of the universal to which it belongs. For example, a leaf on a tree is itself one *and* a part of the tree to which it belongs. And the particular tree, though itself one, is a part of other trees in the forest, and so on. In other words, each particular is both, individual *and* a member of a large unit, just like a human being is a person in its own right and a part of humanity.

Through the study of the particulars, in turn, we arrive at the knowledge of the *universals* (again vertically, but on the left side of the page). And all the universals eventually lead to the *Universal of the universals*, the Tri-une God, the source and bond of all that is where everything finds its origin, has its being, and returns to as its final end.

The *ontological universals*, along with the *epistemological universals*, in accordance with the Master Plan permeate all the particulars and the universals of the cosmos. That is, both upper sets of the universals are present throughout the cosmic realm—uniquely present in the human person—and are retrieved by the various bodies of knowledge. It is these bodies of knowledge that help us to understand reality as well as ourselves and enable us thereby to assume responsibility for our life.

In any event, these transcendentals, my friends are the building blocks of all reality and the Infinite ONE, its Master Builder.

Jason: If these are the building blocks of what-is and we've understood how they fit together, we should be able to re-construct reality from the ground up, isn't that right?

Sophie: That would be a good test of our understanding. Should we try?

Diotima: Why not?
Thomas: Let me try.

c. Reality from the Ground up. Given that the infinitesimal hydrogen atom is the first element and the one that gives birth to helium, whose light creates *matter* from which subsequently everything else comes into being, hydrogen must be seen as "the ground" from which the whole cosmos is built up.

Sophie: It is true, Tom, that hydrogen is the first element and as it were the main "architect" of the cosmos, but hydrogen itself is built up of the elementary particles of matter.

Thomas: Yes, currently six quarks and six leptons (total of twelve particles) are considered by science to be the elementary or fundamental subatomic particles of matter. All others are derived from these.

Sophie: If you were to start with the first cosmic phenomenon, according to Alan Guth's Inflation Theory you would have to start with a "speck far smaller than a proton." But even if you began with it, we still wouldn't be starting with the "real" ground. Whatever that first "speck" was, it had to have come from something eternal. Remember? Nothing comes from nothing. There had to be something eternal to give it a start, sustain it and be able to carry out the process to its completion. This fact became clear to us during our mathematical reflections. We have seen at that time that 1, hence the ONE, being absolutely first, had to be eternal for anything else to come into being. Because that "speck" *came into being*, it cannot be eternal. And if it is temporal, then it is also perishable. It is therefore impossible that it would be the "real ground" of what-is. Since only God is eternal, God must be the *ultimate* Ground of everything that is. However, since that "speck" of *cosmic energy* traces directly to the eternal Logos, who thereby became *immanent* in the cosmos, it is He who must be affirmed as the *immediate* ground of the universe. He is its starting point and its transcendental ground. *Transcendental*, after all, means fundamental, basic, like the natural ground underlying all that "stems from it" and "draws upon its riches for survival," or simply "rests upon it."

Jason: I think Sophie is right, Tom.

Thomas: Since we were to move from the ground "up" I was under the impression that it meant moving from *the infinitesimal atom* to *the Infinite One* as depicted on Diagram 14.1. But I agree with you, the "speck" or "particle" of *dynamic energy* whose origin continues to baffle science, had to come from something eternal and transcendental to it. I must concede that to start with anything other than with the ontological transcendentals is ultimately to reduce the universe to a big fat question mark.

Jason: Perhaps a detour, but this conclusion brings to my mind an important question. At the outset of our dialectic we have agreed that something had to be eternal. We concluded at that time that it had to be either *God*, or *matter*. Now we see that matter was created. If so, matter cannot be eternal. This leaves only God as the conclusive answer to our query. Doesn't it?

Sophie: Fortunately, this conclusion is consistent with everything else we have discovered *en route*. While we're on this detour, though, let me pose my question. We are using two concepts almost interchangeably, which I used to hear spoken of as incompatible, certainly exclusive of each other, if not outright contradictory. They are *creation* and *evolution*. Our reflections on the ordering of reality by means of number concepts from 1 to 10 showed that what-is had gradually evolved. That supports *the evolutionary view*. Yet, here we are seeing that matter was "created" and all else came from it. This means that the universe *was created*. I have a sense that the two views are not contradictory, but I have always heard that they are. How do you see it?

Jason: These views are not contradictory, Sophie. I see them as complementary. *To create*, as we have already seen, means to make something out of nothing, that is, to bring something into being by not making use of anything external to oneself. An example from the ordinary human experience can make that clear. When we want to "create," more accurately "make" something, let's say a collage as an artistic production we need materials out of which to make it. If we want to write something, we need *something* to write with: a pen, a pencil or some technological device like a computer, and *something* to write on. If we want to build a house, we need appropriate materials out of which to construct it. Strictly speaking, we never *create*; we just make a creative use of the materials that are already in existence. But God in creating the universe did not need anything external to Himself. Besides, prior to creation, there was nothing there He could have used. He created the universe through *His own power,* that is, through *the energy* that went forth from Him. In other words, God created first the material, *matter,* and out of it, in accordance with His Master Plan, He fashioned this awesome universe of exquisite beauty. So the universe is truly God's *creation*. But God did not create each thing individually. Instead, He chose to achieve His end by the process of *evolution*. While our reflection on the mathematical sequence of numbers led us to understand the process of evolution, it is our acquaintance with the knowledge of how the basic elements of matter were formed that helps us to see how the concept of *evolution* needs to be understood—yet not in a Darwinian way! It is plain, though, that the two concepts *creation* and *evolution* are not contradictory but complementary.

Sophie: I am glad to get your explanation, Jason. You've made explicit for me something I implicitly knew but had difficulty articulating it. It seems to me that the concept of evolution we have come to understand by means of the elements coincides with that of Teilhard de Chardin.

Diotima: You're right, Sophie. Are there any other questions we need to address before we return to the main thrust of thought?

Thomas: This detour presents an excellent opportunity for me to ask now my question. I don't think it's entirely out place here, for it has to do with the ontological ground of the cosmic realm. My query is about the "cosmic Christ." I understand why the Son of God is called the eternal Logos and why He was understood as such prior to His incarnation. I also understand that at incarnation He assumed a human body and having become like us, was given the name Jesus. The name Christ, "the anointed one," accrues to Him in terms of His mission on Earth. But I have a problem understanding Him as the "cosmic Christ." I know we've talked about it before and what was said did make sense. Yet, there is some ambiguity still lingering in my mind regarding it. What does this concept connote? How does the "cosmic Christ" differ from the historical Christ? I find it difficult to envision Him under this name.

Diotima: As you yourself have just pointed out, the eternal Logos, Jesus, Christ, and the cosmic Christ are merely different, historically relevant, designations for the same divine Person. When we are focusing on Him as "the co-creator of the universe" we address Him as the "cosmic Christ." We have seen that the universe is *Christo-centric*, that it came into being through Christ, His dynamic power permeates it and His wisdom guides it to the moment of the Pleroma, the completion and the consummation of all things. As a "starting principle," Christ is its life-giver or its *soul*, as its "ruler," He is its *center*, and as its "ultimate goal," He is its *end*. The universe is His Kingdom and He is its King. This, in essence, is the meaning of His title as "cosmic Christ."

Thomas: What do you mean by "Pleroma" or the "consummation of all things?"

Diotima: In agreement with Christ's disciples St. Paul and St. John, Teilhard de Chardin explains to us "the consummation of all things" as "the mysterious Pleroma, in which the substantial *One* and the created *many* fuse without confusion in a *whole* which, without adding anything essential to God, will nevertheless be a sort of triumph and generalization of being."[45] And what is "the active center, the living link, the organizing soul of the Pleroma? . . . It is He in whom everything is reunited, and in whom all things are consummated—through whom the whole created edifice receives its consistency—Christ dead and risen *qui replete omnia, in quo omnia constant* [who fills up all things, in whom everything holds together]"(DM, 101).

Thomas: How does this happen?

Diotima: De Chardin says, "Christ who saves and suranimates the world . . . does not act as a dead or passive point of convergence, but as a center of radiation for the energies which lead the universe back to God through His humanity, the layers of divine action finally come to us impregnated with His organic energies. . . . As a consequence of the Incarnation, the divine immensity has transformed itself for us into the *omnipresence of christification*" (DM, 101).

Christ's presence on Earth in the physical form was but a fleeting moment of His existence. This sun-like Deity—sometimes invoked as the "Sun of Justice" (DM, 100-101)[46]—prior to Incarnation was as abstract, elusive and incomprehensible to humanity as the Godhead Himself still is. Christ assumed our human flesh and became one of us for our sake. He did so that we may know who we really are and how we need to become partakers of His life in order to live this life to the full and one day be where He now is, with the Father. In other words, He came to bring the *good news* about the Father's plan for us regarding our glorious destiny. He came not just to tell us who we are and what's good for us. He became one of us to be able to exemplify this truth for us and so to help us to better understand what our life is all about. Redeeming us became a part of His total mission. Having redeemed us, He now wants to make *with us* and *through us* this truth accessible to everyone and to redeem the whole world from its corruption.

Shortly before His death, three of the apostles (Peter, James and John), who accompanied Jesus to Mount Tabor saw Him transfigured. They had a sneak preview of the resurrected Lord. They saw Him in His full splendor, majesty and glory of resurrection. After the resurrection, Christ was no longer subject to the limitations of fleshly existence. He was able to be where He willed without having to conform to the laws of nature. He walked into the room through the closed door and found Himself in any place He wanted without physically going there.

He appeared and disappeared from others' sight at will without their understanding how this was possible. Already then He was exercising His Divine powers as the Lord of glory and Master of the universe.

A few decades later He appeared in His brilliance to St. Paul on his way to Damascus. Apostle Paul then, on the basis of his personal experience, testified that Christ who died and was buried had risen and is now alive. Through this encounter, Saul, as he was then called, that zealous persecutor of the Christians became an ambassador for Christ and spent the rest of his life sharing the truth of Christ's mission. Eventually he gave up his life for it. Here you have a faint image of the cosmic Christ, the resurrected Lord and the Radiant Light of this world who, like the sun, is something in Himself, the divine Person. But through the powers emanating from within, He irradiates the whole cosmos and so is present everywhere. Thus, in Him we live, and move and have our being. His Presence within us draws us to "our center," where He dwells, in order to help us attain the fullness of our being.

When the blessed warmth of His Presence within us becomes one's personal experience, already in this world we come to know with absolute certainty that He dwells in our hearts and that we have our life in Him. Once we become one with Him, He acts *in us* and *through us* in moving His cosmic plan onward toward *Parousia*, that is, the apex and consummation of world's being. At that point in time we shall behold Him in Person *as He is*, the triumphant Lord of Glory, our Judge and our Gateway to eternal life. Teilhard de Chardin says, "The Messiah who appeared for a moment in our midst only allowed Himself to be seen and touched for a moment before vanishing again, more luminous and ineffable than ever, into the depths of the future. He came. Yet now we must expect Him—no longer a small chosen group among us, but all men—once again and more than ever. The Lord Jesus will only come soon if we ardently expect Him. It is an accumulation of desires that should cause the Pleroma to burst forth upon us" (DM, 134-35). To get a more satisfactory understanding, I recommend you read Teilhard's *The Divine Milieu* in its entirety and to familiarize yourself with some other sources that give evidence of this knowledge.

Thomas: Are you suggesting there are some other sources of this knowledge? What are they?

Diotima: A similar view of this Deity is found in Hinduism. Hindu religion, unlike most others, has its origin not with a particular person but in the experiences and teachings of the ancient mystics. Those seers and sages lived thousands of years ago, that is, prior to the dawn of organized religions, but what they bequeathed to posterity is wisdom of the highest sort. This wisdom constitutes the basic beliefs of Hinduism. Of all world religions, this religion most closely approaches Christianity and the insights we have gleaned. *Brahman* and *Atman* correspond to our numerically derived concepts of 1 and 2. *Brahman* is *Atman* (God is Spirit), and *Atman* is *Brahman* (the Holy Spirit is God). The *Purusha*, in turn, corresponds to the cosmic Christ. For *Purusha* in the Hindu Sacred Books (*Vedas, Upanishads* and the *Bhagavad Gita*) is spoken of as "the cosmic Person" and "the Lord of the universe." Svetasvatara Upanishad tells us "we need to pass through him to achieve or activate our immortality."[47] He is "the immense one hidden in all beings, in each according to his kind, and who alone encompasses the whole universe—when people know him as the Lord, they become immortal. I know that immense Person, having the colour of the sun and beyond darkness. Only when a man knows him does he pass beyond death; there is no other path for getting there."[48] As you can see from this brief statement, here, too, this Deity is the Lord of the universe, the Being of all beings and the Gateway to eternal life.

Another source, although less obvious than the former, is found in Buddhism, the religion of total *immanence*. Like all religions, Buddhism acknowledges existence of the Ultimate Reality and its goal is sainthood (*arahat* is saint). That reality in their experience, however, is non-theistic; consequently, more like the concept of the "cosmic Christ" than the historical Christ. But the concept of a personal God, hence even of the "cosmic Christ" is foreign to Buddhism.

The aim of Buddhist religious practice is Enlightenment, which brings with it the experience of being one with the whole cosmos and the state of *nirvana*, bliss. Meditation, renunciation, and one's deeds (*karma*) are the way to this state. The main objective of the practice of renunciation that eventually leads to this state consists of freeing oneself of all cravings, desires and attachments to things of this world, for these are obstacles to the true vision of reality, to inner freedom and to happiness. A person begins to see things correctly only when not distracted and encumbered by things of this world. In hearing these words one is reminded of St. John of the Cross, the highly revered Spanish mystic and Master of Christian Spirituality, from the sixteenth century. He likewise counsels those striving for union with God to seek nothing, "*nota, nota*" apart from God. The desires we need to renounce, he tells us, are "the external things of the world, the delights of the flesh, and the gratification of the will,"[49] the very things Buddhism also counsels. Why? On the one hand, because satisfying them does not quiet them, it only intensifies them. On the other hand, they rob the soul of inner peace and of freedom, thereby preventing union with God: of peace, because like buzzing flies they are a constant annoyance; of freedom, because they hold one captive by constant clamoring for new things. Saint Teresa of Avila and most of the Masters of Christian Spirituality are of the same mind. They include even the desires for spiritual favors and consolations. St. John of the Cross gives us the reason for it by means of an analogy, a bird's flight is held back equally by a "thin thread," as by a "cord" (143). But not all desires are negative, both sides agree. The wise man perfected by his practice of virtue can discern them.

Both religions, Buddhism and Christianity, admit the progress is slow and painstaking. By freeing oneself of the natural cravings, one begins to see things more clearly. It is only when one succeeds in liberating oneself from all disordered attachments, that one feels completely free, happy and in union with all of existence. Both religions also call for "dying to self" as the path that brings one to the much coveted moment. Buddha's emphasis on *karma* [self-denial] finds an echo in Christian spirituality in the words of Jesus, "The seed must fall to the ground and die . . . ." Confirmation for this stance comes in the words of St. Paul who having "died to self" said, "It is I, no longer I, but Christ who lives in me" (Eph. 2:20).

The climatic mystical experience symbolically representative of this state that is found in both Buddhism and Christianity, is a "drop of water" falling into the ocean and becoming one with it. There is, however, a marked difference in what souls in the two religions seem to experience and, therefore, report. In Buddhism at the point of *nirvana*, the soul becomes conscious of the Ultimate Reality as "the unity of all things" and, having become an indistinguishable part of the ocean it loses its own "self." By losing itself in it, an understanding of this Ultimate Reality eludes the soul. In Christianity, though the soul also becomes totally absorbed into the ocean and to all external appearances of the human eye becomes an indistinguishable part of it, the soul never loses consciousness of being its own "self"; it remains its own "self" and knows it is *in God* and *one with Him* for ever more. There is, therefore, a difference in what is meant by "dying" or "losing" one's "self."

As we have heard from St. Paul, in Christianity this experience is preceded by the experience of being transformed into Christ, and Christ not only tells us, but sometimes lets a soul to see and to experience what lies beyond, hence what awaits us there. Buddha refrains from making judgment on what happens to the soul after death, as it is irrelevant, he says, to the practice of religion.[50]

Although the Buddhists do not recognize this union with ultimate reality as union with the cosmic Christ, that's what it is. What cosmic element, or what different *ultimate reality* other than the cosmic Soul, is there that could possibly hold the whole universe in unity? Upon death, when the Buddhists will see the full Truth, they will have no difficulty accepting Christ. Right now He is drawing them unto Himself *incognito.* Hopefully, awareness of this truth will dawn upon them already here and now. The possibility of it happening lies in the inter-religious dialogue, but on the level of the *heart*, rather than *reason.* (Age-old doctrines dutifully, often furiously, defended get in the way.) It must spring from the heart and be born of genuine love for the Truth and for each other. It may need to begin with a sharing of what each religion had found to be the richest and most effective aspect in its spirituality and is eager to share it with others. Later on, the sharing can move on to looking at our common mystical experiences in mutual trust and sincere effort to understand accurately God's manifestations of Himself, because mystical experiences are just that, God's revelations of Himself for the good of humanity. They carry profound messages, which at the most profound level are difficult to discern. The sharing of insights thus received can enhance the understanding of those engaging in dialogue and through them of all others. If we, humanity as a whole, see ourselves as members of the same human family and offspring of the same Ultimate Reality, through such a sharing we all can refine the concepts of our own Faith, profit from the wisdom of one another's religion and draw closer to each other in reverence and love. Such a movement is bound to make this world a better place for all and lead it faster to *Parousia.*

Thomas: If there is such similarity between Christianity and Buddhism, why is it that the two religions seem to be a world apart?

Diotima: Actually, these two religions, as of now, are diametrically opposed to each other. Buddhism is a non-theistic religion and Christianity is not only theistic, but also Trinitarian. All other religions fall somewhere in between. Thus, if the differences between these two religions could be reconciled, all others could be resolved as well. Fortunately, that reconciliation is in sight. By the end of this discussion it should become apparent to everyone theoretically, why we differ, how the reconciliation is possible, and where the crux to this harmony lies. Knowing it, however, is one thing, making it a lived experience is something else. We humans are a proud breed of creatures. It may, therefore, take some time but the longed for moment cannot be too far away.

To be sure, there is a justifiable reason for the disparity in views between Christianity and Buddhism. Siddhartha Guatama Sakyamuni, who became Buddha, that is, the Enlightened One, lived six centuries before

Christ was born (c. 563 B.C.). At that time no one had, or could have had, the *Christo-centric* understanding of the world. The Greeks of that century who alluded to Him, referred to Him by a different name: Heraclitus as "the eternal Logos" and "the Being of all being," and Plato as *demiourgos* and the "world soul." Christianity did not exist yet. Hebrew people were just awaiting the promised Messiah.

Sophie: Isn't it true that even when Christ came, Hebrew people didn't acknowledge Him as the promised Messiah?

Diotima: You're right, Sophie. This is why they are still waiting for Him. Yet Hinduism, one of the oldest religions of the world, which predates Christ's incarnation by more than a thousand years, coincides with the vision of the cosmic Christ. Those ancient mystics had come to acquire their knowledge neither by historical tradition, nor by reason, but by firsthand experience of God, as we have learned. Their utterances indicate that the Lord of the universe pre-existed the cosmos, is immanent in it from the moment of its inception and, therefore is who He said He is. Given their description of *Purusha*, He could be no other than the subsequently incarnate Christ of history and, now, the Risen Lord of Glory. Buddhists, believing their Master had found the secret to Truth and to happiness, intent on attaining the same effects cling to his teaching and method. Whether for lack of communication or limited means of transportations in those days, and for whatever other reason thereafter, they never accepted the historical Christ for who He really is. Yet, it is only when Christ became incarnate, when that long-awaited Messiah finally came, that humanity received the full truth. But His truth is still waiting to be convincingly heard and lovingly embraced by all, for it to be able to change the face of our troubled world.

Sophie: What is a Buddhist understanding of Christ?

Diotima: It is difficult to speak for all of them, but let me quote what one of them has to say, presumably expressing the view of many others. Kevin R. O'Neal, a Buddhist monk and President of the American Buddhist movement, states: "The value, for a Buddhist, comes not from proving whether he [Christ] did exist. His significance lies in the lessons of the Jesus story. The scholar in me keeps going back to wondering if he existed, but as a Buddhist I say: Values are more important than flesh-and-blood facts. If people say he existed, then he existed, because the lessons of the life that we are told about are important indeed" (Josh Simon, 68). This statement, if nothing more, reveals a tacit readiness for a dialogue and openness to Truth.

Until recently, people of various religious persuasions were convinced that their Faith was the true one and were satisfied with it. They knew little or nothing about the other religions and so, more often than not, they looked at other believers as strange, if not as enemies of their own beliefs and values. It is only in recent decades that there arose interest in other Faiths, including Eastern religions. A dialogue that sprang up among them is revealing some very interesting commonalities. A humble dialogue focused on truth, can bring about undreamed of effects in the lives of individuals personally and in the world at large. This world of ours, which having become a global village, is now in dire need of a harmonious co-existence.

Although the Christian and Buddhist mystical experience of oneness with all of reality coincides, for Buddhism it is the experience of an impersonal Higher Reality, because what is experienced is a pure and total unity of all things, signified by the ocean, without the vision of a personal Deity. The cosmic Christ as the cosmic Soul is not seen at that point. But then is a human soul ever seen by anyone? It is only at the end of time that Christ will reveal Himself as the Risen Lord of Glory. Independently of knowing Christ and the transcendent Godhead, the Buddhists' description of that mystical experience, and their interpretation of it is most likely the closest articulation that can be had. Even for a Christian, the meaning of the same experience is at first rather elusive. What one experiences is consciousness of being one with the cosmic reality and of being carried onward somewhere by the current of time. The Christian, however, who formerly had the firsthand experience of God and a foretaste of eternal life in Him, has a strong sense at that point of being *one with God and with all that is,* but while still on Earth—like the waters of the ocean moving on—of being carried onward somewhere, apparently toward the *Parousia,* at which time Christ will turn over His Kingdom to the Father and *ALL* will be one in the *ONE*. It is, therefore, a high time for inaugurating the interfaith dialogue on the one hand, and with science on the other, that the full truth of reality may come to light. For religion to be a formidable strength against the destructive forces of evil and ignorance that threaten to annihilate the world and rob us of peace, we must first be united in mind and heart on both fronts. Only then, in partnership, can we reverse these trends in our society and prevail. Since this reversal presupposes reconciliation and reconciliation a clear understanding of reality, let us pick up our discourse where we left off and carefully prepare a suitable platform for the round-table discussions where the existing incongruities could be ironed out. Who remembers where we left off?

Thomas: We were attempting to build what-is from the ground up. With Sophie's observation we've all agreed that to do so it is necessary to start with the eternal Logos because this Deity is the world's transcendental ground, its first principle, and its organizing center. I began with the hydrogen atom bypassing this fact. I also overlooked the evolutionary process that started as *energy* with a "speck" smaller than a proton and only after having gone through its formative stages from the sub-atomic particles eventually surfaced as a hydrogen atom—the first building block that gave birth to helium, matter and the rest of the elements from which the cosmos was built.

Diotima: Now that we have this understanding of how the universe came to be, we have only to recall the major bodies of knowledge portrayed on Diagram 9 that seek further understanding of this realm. Diagram 10 depicts the main branches of philosophy, and Diagram 11, a combination of all the basic bodies of knowledge. The latter gave us an overview of the organic whole, for there we see the various aspects of reality in relation to each other and as a part of the absolute whole. What we need to do now is first to recap some what we already know and from there, while exposing our access to it follow the track into those subdivisions of major branches that lead to the in-depth understanding of our nature. Do we have a volunteer?

Thomas: This is quite a challenge, but counting on your collaboration I'm willing to give it a try. Feel free to chime in any time. I'll begin with what we already know.

(1). Delineations of Knowledge into Disciplines. From Diagram 14.1 we know that the physical phenomena (light, heat and sound), the subject matter of *Physics*, starting with the hydrogen atom trace back to the sun and the luminous cosmic bodies in the firmament which belong to the science of *Astronomy*. We call this realm "Heavens: The Realm of Astronomy." Since the physical bodies exhibit *physical forces* and gravitate in the *fields* into which they form, electricity, magnetism and gravitation fall into the purview of these disciplines. In essence, then, the two vast bodies of knowledge, *Physics* and *Astronomy*, encompass the entire cosmic realm (Diagram 15.1).

The scope and the amount of information amassed in both of these areas as well as the diversity in existing things that sprang from the primary components of matter necessitated appropriate subdivisions. These in due time became independent bodies of knowledge. For instance, analysis of matter into its *basic elements*—initially known simply as earth, water, fire and air—now listed on the Periodic Chart of Elements, gave birth to *Chemistry*. These elements are found basically in three states: *solid, liquid* and *gas*. We may add that here, as is true of all other delineations in knowledge, elements too come with other and further classifications. Some sub-groups comprise the transitional phases among the solids, liquids and gases.

Because the elements of matter form into animate and inanimate substances, there arose the need for another major division. As a result of it Biology became a distinct discipline. As its name indicates (*bios,* life), *Biology* focuses on life. Initially Biology encompassed all living things. The multiplicity and diversity found in the forms of *life* soon made it imperative to subdivide Biology into *Botany* (plant life), *Zoology* (animal life), and, eventually, into *Anthropology* (human life). I am not quite sure, though, what criterion was used for making the last breakdown.

Diotima: This subdivision seems to have been made on the basis of different *kinds* of *consciousness.* Max Scheler, a philosopher of the twentieth century who did an in-depth study in this area, argues that plants lack internal structure for conscious activities. And indeed, if by consciousness is understood an awareness of one's thoughts, feelings and all that is happening in one's surroundings, plants' functions do not exhibit consciousness, at least not overtly. That's not their primary mode of surviving. Their movement is rather that of *tropism,* an involuntary movement toward light that enables them to carry on the process of photosynthesis. Animals are *conscious,* whereas we humans alone in this world become *self-conscious.* We need to emphasize here the word *become,* for as we shall later see this is not the state with which we begin but where we end.

Thomas: In any event, these are the major branches of science. To be sure, they all come with a number of further subdivisions and interconnections, but for our current purposes this much, I believe, will be enough to consider. The lower part of Diagram 15.1 reflects what I've just said.

The information provided here appears against the background of the epistemological and the ontological transcendentals that constitute the metaphysical realm, "Heaven: Realm of Eternal Light and Life."

Diotima: Since this realm is purely metaphysical and initially a mystery to us, our challenge here lies in showing access to this knowledge. Any idea of what it might be?

Sophie: The human person. Didn't we say that *human experience* is the inroad to human knowledge?

Diotima: Absolutely! How do you propose we proceed?

Sophie: First we need to update our image of ourselves, that is, we need to indicate that we are a composite of *body, mind* and *spirit.* Through the body we are linked to the natural realm. And through the two-fold

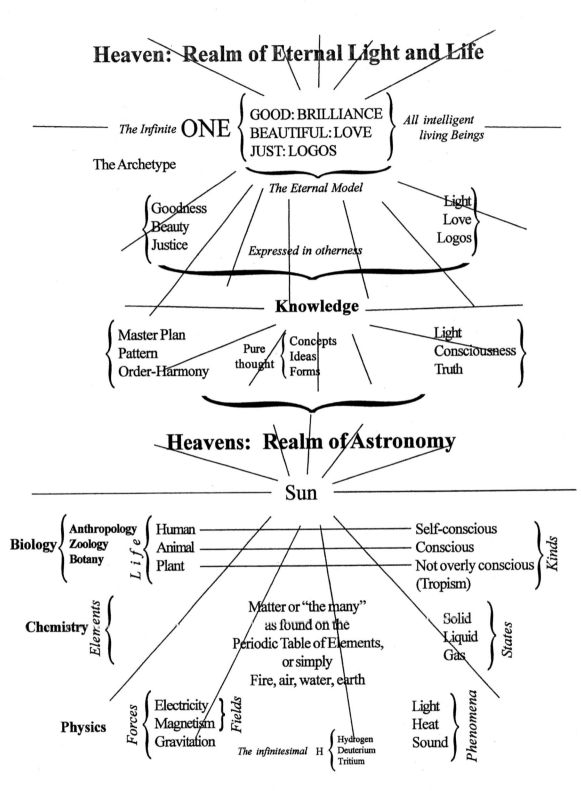

Heaven: Realm of Eternal Light and Life

The Infinite ONE {
GOOD: BRILLIANCE
BEAUTIFUL: LOVE
JUST: LOGOS
} *All intelligent living Beings*

The Archetype

The Eternal Model

{ Goodness
Beauty
Justice

Light
Love
Logos }

Expressed in otherness

Knowledge

{ Master Plan
Pattern
Order-Harmony

Pure thought { Concepts
Ideas
Forms

Light
Consciousness
Truth } }

Heavens: Realm of Astronomy

Sun

Biology { **Anthropology**
Zoology
Botany } *Life* { Human
Animal
Plant

Self-conscious
Conscious
Not overly conscious
(Tropism) } *Kinds*

Chemistry *Elements* {

Matter or "the many"
as found on the
Periodic Table of Elements,
or simply
Fire, air, water, earth

Solid
Liquid
Gas } *States*

Physics *Forces* { Electricity
Magnetism
Gravitation } *Fields*

The infinitesimal H { Hydrogen
Deuterium
Tritium }

Light
Heat
Sound } *Phenomena*

Disciplines with Focus on Life

Diagram 15.1

metaphysical dimension of spirit and mind *concealed* "within" the body, we gain access to the two metaphysical classes.

Jason: So the pattern holds. Just as Class Three *conceals* "within itself" something of the two metaphysical classes and its phenomena point beyond themselves to them, so our body *conceals* "within itself" the two-fold metaphysical dimension of *mind and spirit* and its activities point beyond itself to them.

Thomas: And "through the activities of these two dimensions" we gain access to the two metaphysical classes of reality. It all falls neatly into place. Through the spirit, by way of the *spiritual phenomena* we gain access to the spiritual realm and eventually to God Himself, while the mind looking in both directions paves its way to knowledge of both realms.

Diotima: Given this understanding, it is apparent that knowledge, more accurately the whole middle class is in the minds of the eternal intelligent Beings, its Originators, and some of it is embodied in matter. What is thus embodied, because of *our* intelligence it is gradually "recovered" from its state of *concealment* (Diagram 15.2). Were it not for the human mind, knowledge reflected in this diagram, or any diagram for that matter, would be non-existent in this world. No other creatures need it and therefore none show interest in it. It may be worth our noting that human studies, whether in science or in humanities, consist of "peering into" what already always *is*, and is therefore simply a reporting of what the researchers find. The flip side of this coin is that, unlike in the area of fine arts, we can never take any credit either for the existence of the natural phenomena or for the creative design within the cosmic realm that gets recovered. Of course, this is obvious also from the fact that we came into existence last. Everything was already in place by the time we showed up on the scene, leaving to us the challenge of figuring out how it all came to be.

Sophie: As far as our system of thought is concerned, I can see that what we have reasoned at the beginning about an idea being a link between the Thinkers of Class One and the entities of Class Three, now applies to the whole realm of pure thought.

Diotima: Notice further that as soon as we incorporate into the diagram the three components of our being—*body, mind,* and *spirit*—it becomes evident that our human body is but a small step up from the animal kingdom. True, the human body is more richly endowed, greatly refined and fine-tuned, but given the step-wise progression in what-is, it can be expected that there would be many similarities between our body and the bodies of the highest phyla of the animals.

Jason: If a more refined, fine-tuned body were all there is to us, it would make us different from animals only in degree. It is evident that it is our two-fold metaphysical dimension that distinguishes us from them, placing us into a category of our own. No animals reveal any signs of interest in the other two classes, the very classes that are of such great importance to us.

Diotima: Did you notice that although we humans are an integrated whole, unbeknown to us we are a product of all three kinds of light and our life is sustained and shaped by them?

Thomas: How is that? I'm not sure I get it.

Diotima: Well, did you not notice that each dimension of our being can be said to spring from its own light and that *that very light* is responsible not only for nurturing it, but is also instrumental in the process of the person's total development? Each form of light obliges its own dimension but all work hand-in-hand throughout our life leading us to the excellence of our being and the attainment of our destiny.

Sophie: Could you be more specific?

Diotima: We already know that our physical dimension, like the rest of the universe, traces to the "fourth" hydrogen, making it helium, the "spark of natural light" that gives birth to matter from which the human body is knitted together. Intellectually, each of us is God's unique idea, and ideas are but "tiny sparks of the light of knowledge," the light of the mind, which is also "fourth" in the total structure of what-is. These sparks of light, little by little, enlighten our mind and lead us to the light of truth. And our spirit is the "spark of the divine Light itself," the Light of the eternal Logos (the sun-like Person of Upanishads) from whom it proceeds. He is the Light of eternal life in this world, the One into whose image and likeness we were created. The light of this Logos, namely, "the light of wisdom" nurtures our spirit, promotes our spiritual growth as it effects transformation within us, and leads us to spiritual maturity, the end product of which is our union with God who Himself is Brilliance of ineffable beauty. Since there are three Beings of eternal Light, the "spark" that goes out to give us being is likewise "fourth." Thus, the pattern holds also here and what the ontological light is to our spirit and the epistemological light is to the mind, so the physical light is to the body.

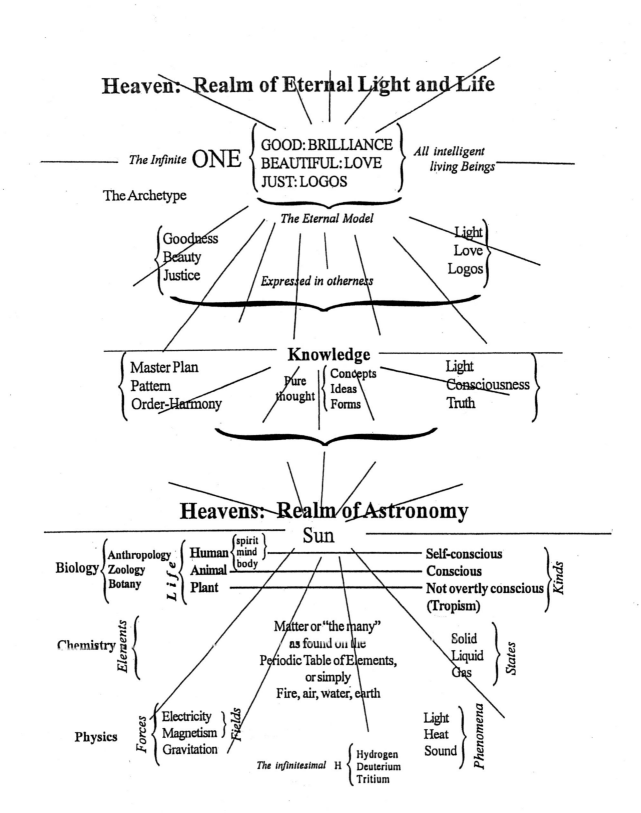

Heaven: Realm of Eternal Light and Life

The Infinite ONE
GOOD: BRILLIANCE
BEAUTIFUL: LOVE
JUST: LOGOS
All intelligent living Beings

The Archetype

The Eternal Model

Goodness
Beauty
Justice

Light
Love
Logos

Expressed in otherness

Knowledge

Master Plan
Pattern
Order-Harmony

Pure thought

Concepts
Ideas
Forms

Light
Consciousness
Truth

Heavens: Realm of Astronomy

Sun

Biology { Anthropology Zoology Botany } Life { Human { spirit mind body } Animal Plant } — Self-conscious — Conscious — Not overtly conscious (Tropism) } Kinds

Chemistry { Elements

Matter or "the many"
as found on the
Periodic Table of Elements,
or simply
Fire, air, water, earth

Solid
Liquid
Gas } States

Physics Forces { Electricity Magnetism Gravitation } Fields

Light
Heat
Sound } Phenomena

The infinitesimal H { Hydrogen Deuterium Tritium }

Life in Terms of Consciousness

Diagram 15.2

Our natural life is sustained by the natural light through plant life, for physical light is indispensable to plants' survival and we rely on them for our sustenance. And not only to plants and us, light is indispensable likewise to animals, for many of them too are nourished by plants. Admittedly, without the lower forms of life neither could we survive. It is not just that there would be no life on Earth without the natural light. If you think about it, there would be no cosmos at all. This realm begins with the natural light, builds on it and is sustained by it. Without the physical light, even if anything could exist in this world, which is inconceivable, there would be a perpetual night of pitch darkness. Can you envision such a reality? Actually, if you remember our mental exercise when in an effort to arrive at the first principles we thought away the existence of absolutely everything, that is, of everything in space, knowledge, angels and God, you told me that your mind found itself in complete darkness. This is another proof that reality is light. Now we see that light comes in three forms and manifests itself as we have discovered it to be. The higher forms give birth to the lower, which it then underlies, permeates and generating it perpetuates the process. Thus it is that in His light we see light and come to understand it.

Despite the presence of the physical light and the physical world in its full splendor and beauty, our life begins with the three-fold darkness: the physical darkness of the mother's womb, the intellectual darkness of ignorance, and the spiritual darkness of separation from God. This being so, human life turns out to be time and process of dispelling darkness and of coming to the light on each of these levels. As is already evident to us, like the rest of natural creatures, we partake of and rely on everything that emerges from the *natural light*. Endowed with an intelligent soul and responsible for our existence, our intellect seeks the *light of truth*, the truth of what-is as well as the truth of our own identity, purpose and meaning of life. In the process of this search, the darkness of our ignorance is dispelled by the light of truth.

By enlightening our mind, the light of truth eventually reveals to us our link with the Divine. Once it becomes our way of life, the *light of wisdom* received through our relationship with the Divine, in turn, liberates us from the darkness of sin and

gradually transforms us into God-like beings who upon having realized our potential are ready for eternal life with Him. All this occurs in accordance with our nature and God's Master Plan that guides us along the way. At death separation occurs with each dimension returning to *what* and *whence* it came. Our body returns to the Earth, turning back to the elements of matter from which it was composed, while the intelligent spiritual soul returns to God, Heaven, the realm of eternal light and eternal life from whence it came. In saying this, I am reminded of the ancient fable Heidegger cites in *Being and Time* to help explain *Dasein's* pre-ontological understanding of itself as "care."

Thomas: What is that fable? I haven't heard of it.

Diotima: Here it is. "Once when 'Care' was crossing a river, she saw some clay; she thoughtfully took up a piece and began to shape it. While she was meditating on what she had made, Jupiter came by. 'Care' asked him to give it spirit, and this he gladly granted. But when she wanted her name to be bestowed upon it, he forbade this, and demanded that it be given his name instead. While 'Care' and Jupiter were disputing, Earth arose and desired that her own name be conferred on the creature, since she furnished it with part of her body. They asked Saturn to be their arbiter, and he made the following decision, which seemed a just one: 'Since you, Jupiter, have given its spirit, you shall receive that spirit at its death; and since you, Earth, have given its body, you shall receive its body. But since 'Care' first shaped this creature, she shall possess it as long as it lives. And because there is now a dispute among you as to its name, let it be called '*homo*', for it is made out of *humus* (earth)" (B&T, 242). Since Jupiter and Saturn are mythical names of Greek deities, the implication is that the complex problem of human identity presupposes knowledge of our roots and is fairly resolved with the help of the Divine.

Thomas: It looks as if the conclusions we have reached coincide with this fable. Of course, fables and myths are not necessarily true, are they?

Diotima: Myths and fables teach profound lessons of life, Thomas. Because the lessons they teach are of the most profound mysteries of reality that elude straightforward articulation, they are better understood by means of myths and fables. Like poetic expressions, everyone knows they are not meant to be taken literally, yet the truth comes through with utmost poignancy. Consequently we need to understand them as *scientific truths expressed in a poetic way*. What is remarkable about them is that one does not need any education to understand them. Even the unlettered can capture their meaning. This fable is an evidence of it. Don't you agree?

Thomas: By all means! I marvel at the wisdom of the ancients. Ironically, we tend to think that those people were "know-nothings." I have been surprised many times when you cited passages from ancient sources. Jaspers is apparently right when he says that we have transcended them in our knowledge of science, but have not as much as approximated them in wisdom. I believe he was speaking of the Greeks when he made that comment.

Heaven: Realm of Eternal Light and Life

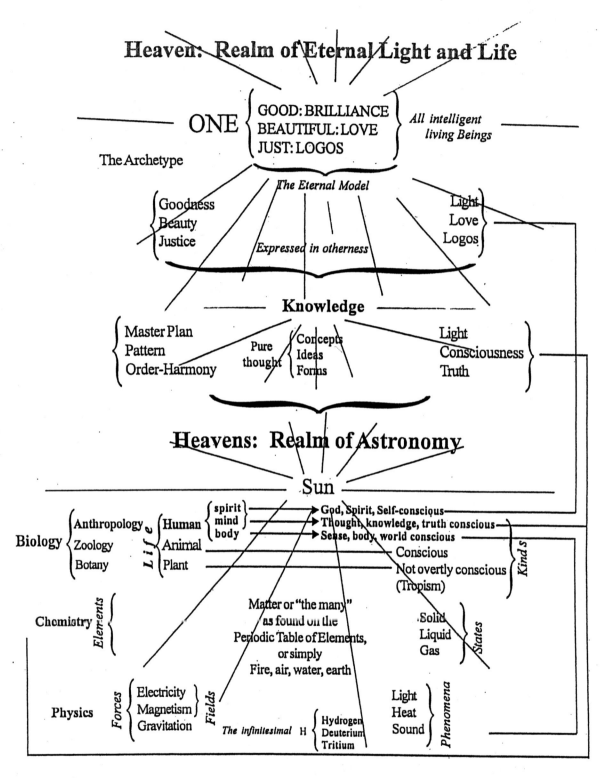

ONE
{ GOOD: BRILLIANCE
BEAUTIFUL: LOVE
JUST: LOGOS }

All intelligent living Beings

The Archetype

The Eternal Model

{ Goodness
Beauty
Justice }

{ Light
Love
Logos }

Expressed in otherness

Knowledge

{ Master Plan
Pattern
Order-Harmony }

Pure thought

{ Concepts
Ideas
Forms }

{ Light
Consciousness
Truth }

Heavens: Realm of Astronomy

Sun

Biology { Anthropology
Zoology
Botany }

Life { Human
Animal
Plant }

{ spirit
mind
body }

→ God, Spirit, Self-conscious
→ Thought, knowledge, truth conscious
→ Sense, body, world conscious
Conscious
Not overtly conscious (Tropism)

Kinds

Chemistry { *Elements*

Matter or "the many"
as found on the
Periodic Table of Elements,
or simply
Fire, air, water, earth

Solid
Liquid
Gas

States

Physics

Forces { Electricity
Magnetism
Gravitation }

Fields

The infinitesimal H { Hydrogen
Deuterium
Tritium }

Light
Heat
Sound

Phenomena

Human Life and Forms of Consciousness

Diagram 15.3

Diotima: You're right, Thomas. And now, before we move to the last sub-topic on our agenda before submitting our findings to cross-examination, let us update our diagram with respect to our nature. While we await the verdict of the related bodies of knowledge on all other conclusions, it is safe to state that because of our physical dimension we are *sense, body,* and *world conscious.* On account of our mind, we are *thought, knowledge* and *truth conscious.* And because of the *spirit* within us, we are *God, Spirit* and *Self-conscious* (Diagram 15.3). Each dimension is conscious of the realm from which it comes and toward which it is impelled by its nature. As we shall eventually see it more clearly, these are but progressive *stages* in our *consciousness* on the journey of total development and realization of our potential.

Because the human person is three-dimensional, there are three major branches to Anthropology: *physical, cultural* and *philosophical* (Diagram 15.4). *Physical Anthropology,* as its name indicates, focuses of the physical component of our being.

It seeks to establish the origin and development of the human species as it looks at similarities and gradual differences among the primates and between them and the human body. You can already see that the insights gleaned in this area can be hardly overestimated.

Cultural Anthropology, in turn, inquires into what is specifically human about humans, hence into the other two-fold metaphysical dimension of our being. Cultural anthropology is a vast field with a long history to it. It takes into account, like the physical anthropology archaeological findings of the recovered materials such as tools, graves, buildings and pottery excavated from prehistoric period, ethnological evidence of cultural origins, beliefs and sociological systems—factors that influenced cultural growth and development of peoples. It looks also at linguistics, social and psychological data that reach back to the earliest times. It is from these sources that scholars extract data of man's earliest manifestations of intellectual development and spiritual awareness.[51] We shall inquire into Ethnology, for it is this branch of cultural anthropology that is relevant to our study at this point.

Philosophical Anthropology, in turn, takes into account the whole person. It looks at a person from the standpoint of behavior that encompasses human activities at all levels of human existence. The study in this area should expose our identity and difference vis-à-vis all other entities on earth.

While the three named branches of anthropology constitute the first set of disciplines into which we need to inquire, there are three further delineations that are equally relevant. Earlier, the content of these delineations once upon a time was the subject matter of philosophy. Because of the diversity in human dimensions and a different orientation of each dimension, in time, analysis of human nature led to sub-divisions. Today these sub-divisions are disciplines in their own right. They include psychology, psychiatry and spirituality.

Psychology, the latest offshoot of philosophy, is a behavioral science that delves into the realm of human *psyche* with the focus on "natural behavior." Through *depth psychology* it reaches down to the ground of our being. *Psychiatry,* a medical field, concerns itself with the *mind* and *Spirituality* with our *spirit.* Since according to our study, spirituality leads directly to the third Person of the Original Unit, the eternal Logos, or "that through which" the cosmos came into being and whose "spark" of life constitutes the very ground of our being, we incorporate 3, meaning the Third Person of the Blessed Trinity, to reflect this fact (Diagram 15.5). Because these three disciplines (Psychology, Psychiatry and Spirituality) have made great inroads in the understanding of human nature, their insights will necessarily play a crucial role in assessing our findings.

Yet, human knowledge does not end here. One cannot step into the realm of spirituality without getting drenched in *theology, religion* and *ethics.* For spirituality overlaps and is deeply immersed in *God's own teachings* from where one receives guidance, in *religion* through which one relates to God, and in *morality,* one's relationship to other human beings, where one implements God's teachings and encounters God in others as well as in nature. By now, each of these areas, as was the case with all other disciplines, constitutes its own field of knowledge. *Theology* is concerned with God's revealed teachings and His relationship to us. *Religion* is but a distilled and highly refined area of Ethnology that has to do with the ways we relate to and worship God. And *Ethics* is the study of morality that seeks to provide objectively valid normative principles for judging goodness or rightness of human conduct with respect to self, others and nature. As you will later see, so entwined are these branches of knowledge that there is no way one can set foot into spirituality without treading upon the content of these disciplines. In fact, the transition from one to the other is so natural and fluid that one is already there before one realizes it had happened. These areas will inevitably become a subject of our further discussion without a deliberate effort to address them directly. With this inclusion we hope to do justice to all the major bodies of knowledge we've named here. Do you find this choice of disciplines, my friends, objectively valid?

Thomas: I don't think anyone could accuse us of manipulating anything. I am eager to see, though, what these bodies of knowledge have to say.

Heaven: Realm of Eternal Light and Life

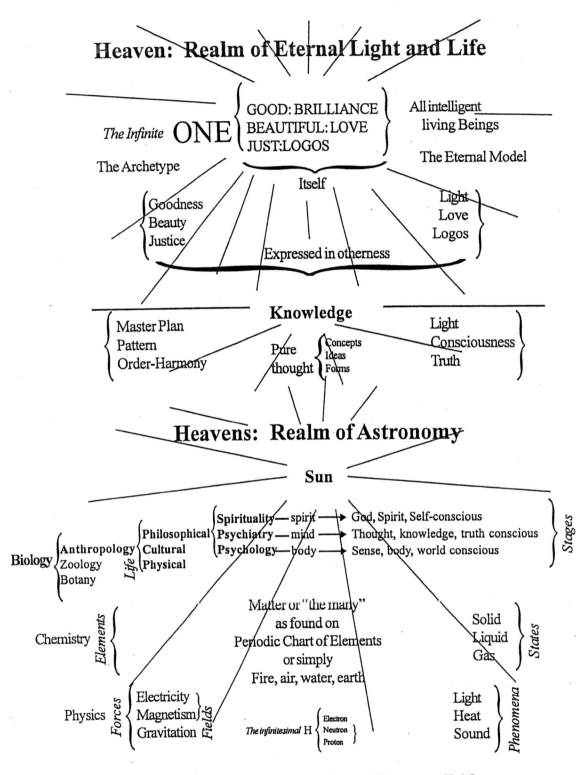

The Infinite ONE
{ GOOD: BRILLIANCE
BEAUTIFUL: LOVE
JUST: LOGOS }

All intelligent living Beings

The Archetype

The Eternal Model

Itself

Goodness
Beauty
Justice

Light
Love
Logos

Expressed in otherness

Knowledge

Master Plan
Pattern
Order-Harmony

Pure thought

{ Concepts
Ideas
Forms }

Light
Consciousness
Truth

Heavens: Realm of Astronomy

Sun

Biology {
Anthropology
Zoology
Botany
}
Life {
Philosophical
Cultural
Physical
}
{
Spirituality — spirit ——▶ God, Spirit, Self-conscious
Psychiatry — mind ——▶ Thought, knowledge, truth conscious
Psychology — body ——▶ Sense, body, world conscious
} Stages

Matter or "the many"
as found on
Periodic Chart of Elements
or simply
Fire, air, water, earth

Chemistry { Elements

Solid
Liquid
Gas
} States

Physics { Forces
Electricity
Magnetism
Gravitation
} Fields

The infinitesimal H {
Electron
Neutron
Proton
}

Light
Heat
Sound
} Phenomena

Disciplines Relevant to Human Life

Diagram 15.4

Diotima: Let's proceed, then, to complete the diagram by matching the rest of the content with the respective disciplines on Diagram 15.5.

Looking at this diagram, one glance is sufficient to see that the *empirical sciences* (physical, natural and social) aim at knowledge of everything in Class III, the *pure sciences* (Language, Logic and Mathematics) and *the fine arts* (Art, Language Arts and Music) of Class II serve as media and as stepping-stones of ever-greater accuracy in leading us to the light of ultimate Truth—the First Principles of Class I (the Good, the Beautiful and the Just) that render everything intelligible. Please note: the goal of *Spirituality* is holiness of our life, and of *Theology* God, the Highest Good and goodness of everything that comes from God (creation and His words of wisdom to guide us). *Fine Arts* of Class II aim at beauty and *Philosophy* at justice, therefore, rightness and truth of everything. As you can see, all bodies of knowledge have a specific purpose and all have an appropriate place in the scheme of things.

Sophie: Could we take a thoughtful look at what you've just said?

Diotima: Diagram 15.5 gives us a bird's-eye-view of all the major branches of knowledge. Now that we see how the respective disciplines of all three classes complement each other, we can discuss each of them individually, if you wish. Before we do so, however, let me draw your attention in Class Three to the Third, the "Offspring" (of One and Two) or the eternal Logos. Notice that this Being is "that through which" everything came into being and, at the same time, the One "through whom" we have access to the other two divine Persons.

Thomas: How do we come to them *through* Him?

Diotima: We do so through spirituality. *Spirituality* is the science of the spirit that helps us to make the journey in *consciousness* and reach our destiny. Growth on this level takes place by means of the spiritual phenomena of His *logos, love and the light of wisdom* which we intuit in the depths of our being and find in Sacred Scripture. These lead us to right actions that effect *holiness* and bring us to the encounter with Him. Because this Person conceals "within" itself something of the first two Persons, we encounter them first in Him. Eventually we come to behold them directly, because the Third, like every "third" in each set, points us beyond itself. Ordinarily, it is only at death that one is brought to the direct encounter with the first two Deities in Person. What makes this ultimate conquest in life attainable is one's response of love to love. In genuinely loving God, others, oneself and one's earthly home or environment, one does justice to all that is. Through acts of *justice* one partakes of goodness and beauty. The *just acts* transform one into a *just person* and one thereby becomes beautiful and good in one's being, making union with the Good, the Beautiful and the Just realizable.

Although the various paths of spirituality are articulated by human beings, the Masters of Spirituality base their helpful guidelines on the *revealed truths of God* and on the *reliable paths of the saints* (genuinely good human beings) who relied heavily on the promptings of the Holy Spirit as they prudently carried them out in *loving service of others*. These avenues are open to every one of us. They are simply a matter of choice.

Jason: The phrases you've emphasized seem to denote that spirituality does encompass the three branches of knowledge that we have enumerated last, namely, Theology, Religion, and Ethics.

Diotima: Please note that here converges a whole series of links: between Spirituality and Theology, between Spirituality and Religion, and between Spirituality and Morality; likewise, between faith and reason, between knowledge and wisdom and between mind and heart—all working hand-in-hand for the good of the person!

By way of synthesis we can say then that *Theology*, as its name indicates (*Theos*, God and *logos*, study) is a study about *God, the Highest Good,* and about *goodness* of everything God created. Theology helps us to interpret the revealed Word and enables us to understand ways of applying it to our life that we may comply with God's wisdom and reciprocate His love.

Thomas: So Faith is really a shortcut to Truth.

Jason: Look at how long it took us to get the understanding we now have and we can hardly claim to know even the basics. Most people lack either the means or the time to pursue this knowledge. Some even lack the ability to do so personally. Besides, unaided human reason, as our period unabashedly attests, is unable to arrive at the ultimate Truth on its own, especially if one is not living a three-dimensional life. We have seen that everyone is preordained for Heaven. Consequently, God does us a big favor by giving us answers essential to a good life, since that is the prerequisite for life with Him in Heaven. People do not have to understand everything. They just have to accept that knowledge on faith and abide by it to the best of their ability. Because the basic ingredient of spirituality is love expressed in good deeds, and everyone is capable of such love, it's a choice one makes. Thus, everyone has an equal opportunity to attain life's goal and be happy.

Diotima: Good explanation, Jason. As you can see, Class Two turns out to be the *Realm of Aesthetics and of Symbolism.* God's Master Plan, pattern and principles of order and harmony operative in nature, whether in the

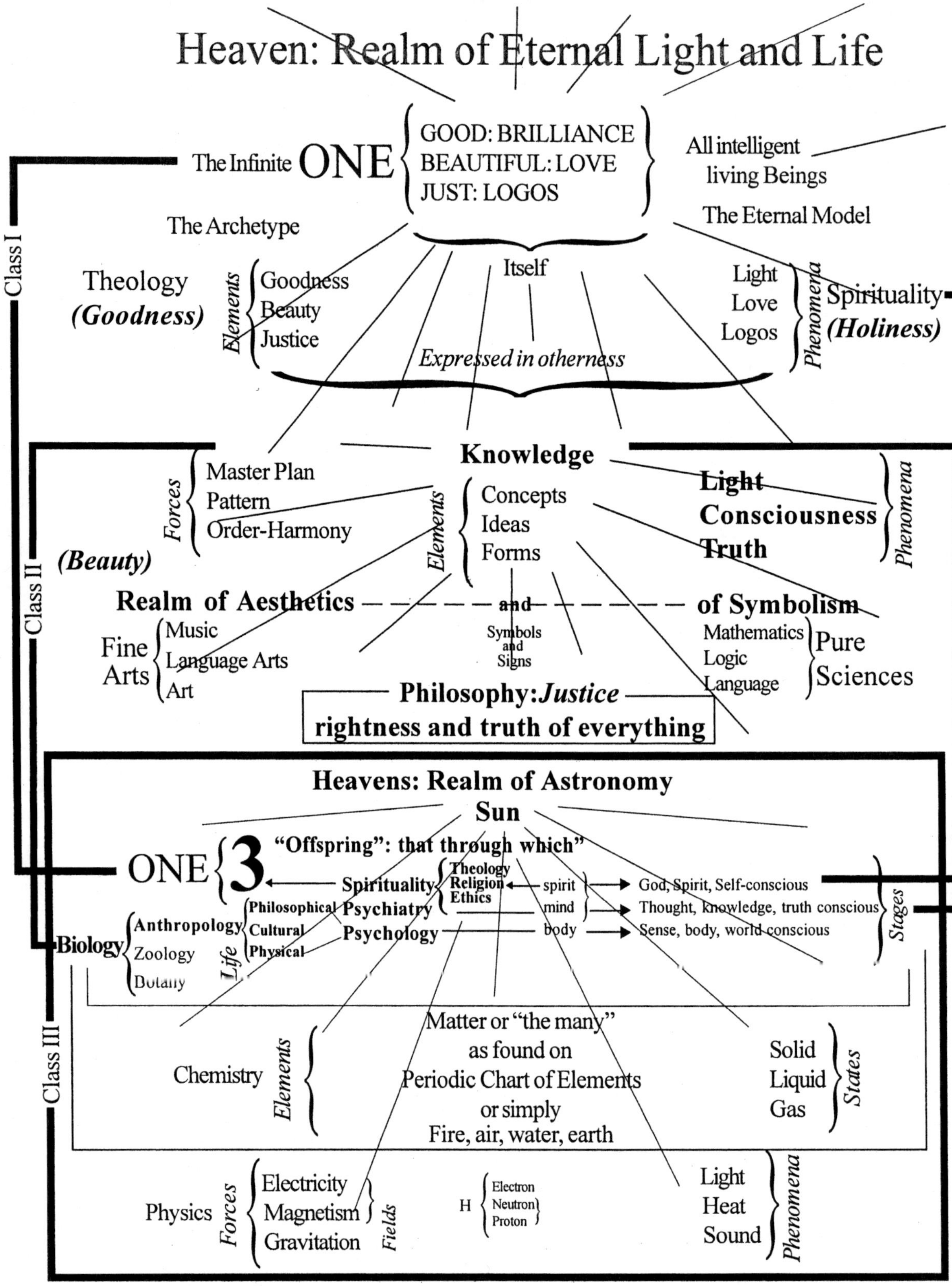

Heaven: Realm of Eternal Light and Life

The Infinite ONE
$$\left\{ \begin{array}{l} \text{GOOD: BRILLIANCE} \\ \text{BEAUTIFUL: LOVE} \\ \text{JUST: LOGOS} \end{array} \right\}$$
All intelligent living Beings

The Archetype

The Eternal Model

Theology **(Goodness)**

Elements $\left\{ \begin{array}{l} \text{Goodness} \\ \text{Beauty} \\ \text{Justice} \end{array} \right.$

Itself

$\left. \begin{array}{l} \text{Light} \\ \text{Love} \\ \text{Logos} \end{array} \right\}$ Phenomena

Spirituality **(Holiness)**

Expressed in otherness

Knowledge

Forces $\left\{ \begin{array}{l} \text{Master Plan} \\ \text{Pattern} \\ \text{Order-Harmony} \end{array} \right.$

Elements $\left\{ \begin{array}{l} \text{Concepts} \\ \text{Ideas} \\ \text{Forms} \end{array} \right.$

$\left. \begin{array}{l} \textbf{Light} \\ \textbf{Consciousness} \\ \textbf{Truth} \end{array} \right\}$ Phenomena

(Beauty)

Realm of Aesthetics — — — — — **and** — — — — — **of Symbolism**

Fine Arts $\left\{ \begin{array}{l} \text{Music} \\ \text{Language Arts} \\ \text{Art} \end{array} \right.$

Symbols and Signs

$\left. \begin{array}{l} \text{Mathematics} \\ \text{Logic} \\ \text{Language} \end{array} \right\}$ Pure Sciences

Philosophy: *Justice*
rightness and truth of everything

Heavens: Realm of Astronomy
Sun

ONE $\left\{ 3 \right.$ "Offspring": that through which"

Biology $\left\{ \begin{array}{l} \textbf{Anthropology} \\ \text{Zoology} \\ \text{Botany} \end{array} \right.$ | Anthropology $\left\{ \begin{array}{l} \text{Philosophical} \\ \text{Cultural} \\ \text{Physical} \end{array} \right.$ Life

Spirituality

Psychiatry

Psychology

$\left. \begin{array}{l} \text{Theology} \\ \text{Religion} \\ \text{Ethics} \end{array} \right\}$

spirit → God, Spirit, Self-conscious
mind → Thought, knowledge, truth conscious
body → Sense, body, world conscious

Stages

Chemistry Elements $\left\{ \begin{array}{l} \end{array} \right.$

Matter or "the many"
as found on
Periodic Chart of Elements
or simply
Fire, air, water, earth

$\left. \begin{array}{l} \text{Solid} \\ \text{Liquid} \\ \text{Gas} \end{array} \right\}$ States

Physics Forces $\left\{ \begin{array}{l} \text{Electricity} \\ \text{Magnetism} \\ \text{Gravitation} \end{array} \right\}$ Fields

H $\left\{ \begin{array}{l} \text{Electron} \\ \text{Neutron} \\ \text{Proton} \end{array} \right\}$

$\left. \begin{array}{l} \text{Light} \\ \text{Heat} \\ \text{Sound} \end{array} \right\}$ Phenomena

Class I
Class II
Class III

Disciplines that Guide Human Conduct

Diagram 15.5

form of a collage, a plot, a theme or a composition, consciously or unconsciously form the underpinnings of Fine Arts. For *Fine Arts* (Visual Arts, Language Arts and Music), the human creativity in a given media (if intelligible and aesthetic), is to some extent an imitation of Divine creativity in nature. Whether they instruct, entertain or inspire, these artistic productions all convey a message that has an *aesthetic appeal and value*. Insofar as artists embody the concepts of thinkers or those embodied in nature, they likewise depict truth even if only in an oblique way. Artists express it through *beauty*.

While Fine Arts aim at *beauty*, the *Pure Sciences* (Language, Logic and Mathematics) aim at *truth*. They communicate through *signs and symbols* making the realm of thought also one of *symbolism*. Although all three disciplines make use of symbols; to be intelligible they too share the same underpinnings, each in its own way. And while all three make use of language, the ascendancy among them leads to a more rigorous thinking and a more precise articulation of knowledge that terminates in truth.[52]

As to *Philosophy*, since this body of knowledge is in essence Metaphysics and as such belongs to the realm of pure thought, we locate it in Class Two. However through its branches (Cosmology, Epistemology and Ontology), philosophy concerns itself with reality in its totality and therefore stretches from one end of the spectrum to the other, just as Diagram 10 accurately reflects. When philosophical discourse is guided by the principles of logic and the three basic laws of thought, philosophy arrives at reliable conclusions and does *justice* to all that is. In this capacity philosophy leads to the First Principles or the Hypostases of the world of phenomena, provides a foundation to all other bodies of knowledge, and guides the "lover of wisdom" on a personal journey to the *truth of actual beholding*. In its attempt to do *justice* to all that is, philosophy aims at "rightness and truth of everything." And since its achievement is that of *reason*, philosophy can be said to be *a path and a guardian of reason*.

In philosophy, as indeed in all other disciplines, *consciousness* plays the central role. One knows when one knows, and one knows when one does not know. When truth dawns upon the horizon of one's mind, one knows that he or she knows for the light of truth floods one's mind and renders what one sought to understand fully intelligible. Doubt, lack of clarity, misgivings and outstanding questions are a proof that one has not reached this goal yet.

Jason: It seems to me that we have manifested this knowledge not only in word but also in deed. I mean, we did not just say how this knowledge is attainable. We have taken the steps, carried out the process, and arrived at it. Thereby, we have demonstrated the *path* and emerged with *the truth of reason*, better known as "the truth of logical coherence."

Diotima: So philosophy has discharged its duty to humanity, has it not? The second step, if you recall, consists of living one's life in accordance with this truth and that is always the work of one's own doing. This is where *wisdom* comes in. Truth is theoretical, whereas wisdom is practical. Wisdom consists of applying truth to life. It is the second step that brings one to *the truth of intellection in vision:* that is, "the truth of actual beholding" which makes all the struggles of life worthwhile.

Jason: These conclusions certainly surpass the expectations that brought me to this dialogue.

Thomas: I, too, am pleasantly surprised.

Diotima: Having understood all this, it remains to be acknowledged that since knowledge is an *intellectual light*, the place of knowledge is the mind of the knower (s), uncreated and created. Knowledge does not exist independently of the mind, unless it is embodied in some form. Metaphysical by nature, it does not occupy any space like the physical phenomena do. And when it is transmitted into some perceptible form like books, videos, films, maps, graphs, artifacts and the like, it is then within the ontic realm, that is, on Earth with us. But if knowledge is only in the mind and in the natural and manmade objects that embody it, then Class Two in reality does not exist by itself, as we have been representing it right along. Consequently, we can dispense with the middle circle, can't we?

Jason: Hold it, please! That throws off our whole system of thought.

Thomas: It certainly creates a hole in it.

Sophie: I thought we saw concepts, ideas and forms at the core of reality. We've compared thought to a hub of a wheel on which everything revolves, haven't we? At this point, given the way the various bodies of knowledge pair off with reality, I would even venture to say that thought constitutes the framework of what-is. How can we dispense with it?

Diotima: Everything we've said about concepts, ideas and forms as the components of knowledge is still true. inaccessible, which is why today God is known in the world only "through absence," Heidegger contends.

They are very real bits of intellectual light. It is just that they do not have any existence apart from the mind in their pure form, *and* in that where they inhere. So, yes, Sophie, they do constitute a "backbone" of things and do form the "framework" of the entire edifice of reality, but only because they are embodied therein.

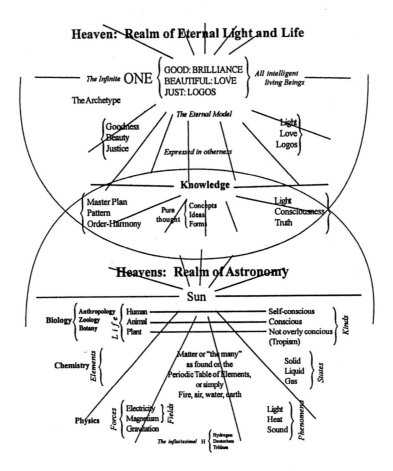

Knowledge as Bond of All-that-is

Diagram 15.6

   Look at Diagram 15.6. This fact is well reflected here. They are in the mind of the Triune God who conceived them and some of them are in His creation that embodies them.

   Furthermore, neither do goodness, beauty and justice have any existence of their own, that is, independently of the Good, the Beautiful and the Just from where they emanate and permeate creation.

   Sophie: I can't believe it. Are we on to some kind of reductionism?

   Diotima: If the Just—so called because He did justice to all that came into being—is *immanent in the cosmic phenomena* and is, at the same time, a member of the original community of Persons, then the Good and the Beautiful cannot be far off. From them, like the light and warmth from the sun, emanate goodness and beauty that permeate all of nature doing justice to what-is and making it delightful to the eye of the beholder. And if goodness, beauty and justice are properties inherent in the Good, the Beautiful and the Just *and* in creation, then like concepts, ideas and forms, they have no special existence independent of them. At the same time, because these attributes as well as concepts, ideas and forms are embodied in nature, the universe is intelligible and reflects the grandeur of God. This is what scientists recover from matter, philosophers declare in thought, mystics glimpse, musicians render in sound, artists depict on canvas, and what poets capture in verse when they look at nature. Listen to how one of the poets expresses it.

God's Grandeur

The world is charged with the grandeur of God.
    It will flame out, like shining from shook foil;
    It gathers to a greatness, like the ooze of oil
Crushed. Why do men then now not reck his rod?
Generations have trod, have trod, have trod;
    And all is seared with trade, bleared, smeared with
        toil;
    And wears man's smudge and shares man's smell:
        the soil
Is bare now, nor can foot feel, being shod.

And for all this, nature is never spent;
    There lives the dearest freshness deep down things;
And though the last lights off the black West went
    Oh, morning, at the brown brink eastward, springs—
Because the Holy Ghost over the bent
    World broods with warm breast and with ah!
        bright wings.

Gerard Manley Hopkins

*Thoma*s: I don't know if I should rejoice or be dismayed.

Jason: I don't really seem to be able even to formulate a question at this point.

Diotima: Should we then move on?

Sophie: Not today. I think we all need some time to absorb the enormity of it all. There is too much to process and to reconcile.

(2). Facing Dilemma. Diotima: Welcome back. I am glad to see you all. Are you ready today to pick up where we left off?

Jason: Yes, we're all back but I'm afraid with some more questions.

Diotima: Is there a problem?

Thomas: Let me begin by asking if you reduced the three classes of reality to just the universe?

Diotima: Not really, but I did reduce them to an integrated whole. We are not reneging on anything that we have established along the way. We are simply trying now to get it all to conform more accurately to reality as it is experienced by us. The Good and the Beautiful are still transcendent spiritual Beings and Heaven is as sure as they are. It is what emanates from them, the ontological universals that permeate the whole cosmos. But since what emanates from the Divine is present to and envelops the whole cosmos, it unites God with it, much the same as the light of the sun is present to and envelopes all things upon the planet Earth, making them ultimately one, yet without reducing them to each other.

Sophie: Does that mean that the eternal commingles with the temporal? How can this be? Didn't we say earlier that eternity is the ever-present now?

Diotima: Yes. But with creation time was born. When eternity broke into time, it made time a moving image of eternity. From that point on we have the past, the present and the future, and with the passing of time history came into being. For history is a record of those events. Plato figured that out four centuries before Christ came into this world. When we see this state of affairs portrayed in greater detail in another discourse, this will become amply clear. Diagram 16 gives us a hint of it.

Jason: I get it! The eternal does commingle with the temporal through the Eternal Logos. Didn't we see that this Hypostasis is *immanent* in creation? My question is: Did eternity's breaking into time make spiritual reality just another dimension of the universe, or is it something beyond it?

ETERNAL RECURRENCE
OF THE SAME

"Time is a moving image of eternity"
(Plato, *Tim.* 37 c-e)

Everything is entwined, interrelated and constitutes
a part of the absolute whole.

Diagram 16

Diotima: At this point it is both, but eventually it will be all one. Currently, because of divine immanence in the universe, the spiritual reality is but another *dimension of time*, while Heaven, the realm of the Transcendent Deity, is the *realm of eternity.* Thus, those who die pass on from temporal to eternal existence. At the point of Pleroma, when the cosmic Christ having consummated all things in Himself subjects Himself to the One who made all things subject to Him, all will be one, so that God may be all in all, and all in Him.

Thomas: If the spiritual is entwined with the cosmic phenomena, how did the thinkers get to aim at their turf, if I can put it that way?

Diotima: Delineations of disciplines is a product of several thousands of years, though it has been accelerated in the nineteenth and twentieth centuries. It is an effect of tedious work and much dedication to the cause of truth. It came gradually and it started simply with the look of wonder at the world of phenomena given in human experience. What the phenomena kept on revealing to the mind of the thinkers as time went on, led to the various divisions, sub-divisions, branches, and so forth. This breakdown into smaller units became a necessity because the accumulated knowledge became unmanageable for a given discipline to handle, and there was enough distinction in the content to justify the separation. With constant progress in knowledge still being made, there may be a need for further branches and delineations. We are far from having exhausted everything there is to know. Fortunately, what is currently coming to light on a number of fronts is pointing to the unity of all things.

Jason: Isn't it the way we began our quest? We, too, have started with a simple look at what is given in human experience when we were building up to the concept of the absolute whole.

Diotima: Yes, indeed. What the human eye gazing at the cosmos beheld in its splendor and beauty and what the human heart captured intuitively to its own delight, the mind wanted to understand. This is how it was then, and how it is now. It is those experiences that led to the analysis of the phenomena. As the phenomena kept revealing their secrets, there arose a need to create new categories and eventually new disciplines. It is the richness, depth and intricacy of reality itself that led to the multiple disciplines. Historically, just as in our own case, analysis was undertaken for the sake of understanding reality. To see the particular things more clearly, we even drew them out of their natural setting, as Diagrams 4, 5 and 6 illustrate. Now that we have acquired basic understanding of what-is, it is time to restore things to their original state of complexity and unity.

Thomas: That's what we had determined to do when we introduced the two symbols, the line and the circle, I recall.

Diotima: I believe we have reached the point at which we can let go of the crutches and emerge with "the vision of the organic whole." By placing things back into their proper setting and eliminating the barriers we've created (circles) to help us understand all that is, we've secure vision of reality, which though complex, is now more intelligible. Otherwise we will have missed the purpose of our venture.

Jason: I'm not sure what you mean.

Diotima: Our look at the past with which our discourse began, historically brought us to the understanding of the current situation in the world. We saw that each thinker in the course of the centuries intended to improve humanity's plight by what he proposed. Progress was made but instead of the hoped for utopia, we were brought to the present-day crisis of fragmentation, alienation and meaninglessness of life, with an impending threat of total annihilation. Sensing something was askew, we've set out to see what went wrong and why. Not knowing what it was, we started from scratch, with the analysis of the absolute whole.

Sophie: We found one reason for the contemporary crisis, humanity's oversight or willful elimination of God and spirituality in people's life. If I remember correctly, this occurred first in sophistry, then in science and in ideologies. These movements in thought left a mark initially on the lives of some individuals, then on societies, only now to afflict most of the world.

Diotima: You are right, Sophie, but there is also another reason working hand in hand with what you've observed. Strange as it may sound, knowledge itself, which was sought to improve humanity's plight, turned out to be a contributing factor to the current crises.

Jason: Knowledge? I thought knowledge was the key to resolving human problems.

Diotima: History shows that knowledge, at least what we humans consider to be "knowledge," has the power to either resolve or create problems. The effects depend upon the prevailing factors at the time and on how human beings choose to employ knowledge. We are seeking knowledge to understand what went wrong and to find ways to rectify the problem in order to restore peace, order and harmony for which humanity longs. Given the contemporary state of affairs it is obvious that knowledge is not enough. We certainly have more knowledge today than humankind ever had in the past. Yet, we seem to be in a worse crisis than any period in history. Some of the knowledge is being misused and is affecting humanity in a negative way. What is needed to resolve the problems of today has not yet surfaced in our quest.

Jason: In what sense is "knowledge" contributing to the world's demise?

Diotima: An avalanche of facts and focus on the minutest components of reality on the one hand obscured humanity's image of reality as a whole, and on the other hand, boundaries between the major disciplines "froze" fast, thereby preventing progress toward the vision of the whole. With so many specializations in place and on the rise, experts know more and more about less and less. It is difficult even for some of them to see how the details of their expertise are meant to serve the whole. That question does not even surface in their mind. At the other end, professionals in their respective fields tend to see their own area of knowledge as a kingdom by itself, with the exclusive access to truth. So, the twain cannot meet. Perhaps an analogy can make that clear.

Thomas: That usually helps.

Diotima: Imagine yourselves coming upon a scene where, on the ground, you see a pile of small pieces of something sparkling in the sun. These pieces come in all forms, shapes and sizes, each nonetheless exhibiting rare beauty. Those at the scene are holding some of the bigger pieces in their hand admiring them and venturing their opinion about what it might be that they are examining. Finally, someone having firsthand knowledge of it appears in the midst and tells the assembled group that these are small fragments of a smashed diamond. None of the bystanders, or you, ever saw that diamond in its original form. If you were asked to assemble these pieces as best you can to restore it to its original state, would you have any idea of how to approach the task?

Jason: That would be a Herculean task even for the one who saw the original diamond! Without having seen it, I would have no way of knowing if I am approximating its original form.

Sophie: I suppose, first of all, you would need to get much help from others. Secondly, your clue to it would be the accuracy in fitting those pieces back together. I believe I get the point you're driving home. Assuming the large diamond is reality, to understand it, it is necessary to put the various components of it together. The tiny pieces, I think, are really the embodied ideas and forms that belong to it. By slowly putting them together, one would be approximating the vision of what reality truly is.

Diotima: Very good, Sophie. Your interpretation brings us to the second difficulty with knowledge. Carrying the analogy a step further, we can say that the various groups of scholars working in their specific fields have assembled an impressive amount of those fragments. They are pleased with their accomplishment, even though there appear to be some pieces still missing. They have, instead, some extra pieces that do not belong to the composite they've assembled and they do not know what to make of them. Despite this awareness, they are reluctant to approach the other groups to see if these might not be the missing pieces to their project, or if perchance they might not have what they themselves still need.

Jason: Why the reluctance? Are they possibly afraid of losing hold on their little kingdom?

Thomas: How do you see this happening, Jason?

Jason: Once the loose pieces are properly inserted, the particular wholes might merge. Should that occur, who knows who, if anyone would have greater claim to the new composite? I suspect some pride, prestige, and power is at stake here.

Sophie: Or it could be fear and insecurity. Fear, that what I have rejected is true after all. If so, where does that leave me?

Diotima: Without imputing anything to anyone, it is sufficient to point out some things that are common knowledge. It is no secret that the scientists take great pride in the work of their field, which they zealously pursue, teach or practice, without paying much attention to the insights in the realm of the humanities. Yet scientists are missing answers to some of the questions beyond the limits of their discipline to attain. Artists, passionate by nature, are so absorbed in the world of their own art, that they have neither interest nor time to question the veracity of anything. Attuned to the spirit, values and incongruities of the time, their creative productions reflect the prevailing trends of the period. What philosophers propose, they depict in their field. They are abreast of the spirit of the time. The question of truth falls beyond the ambit of their concerns. Theologians of the various religious persuasions, again, suspicious of the findings in science, scrupulously guard their own privileged domain. They are wary of new insights even in their own religion, forgetting that God chose to reveal Himself through creation, hence in history. And history, being a gradual unfolding of God's Master Plan, advances by means of slight changes along the way. These provide room for new insights that call for adjustments in our understanding of what-is. Philosophers, in turn, are not budging out of their ivory tower. They are used to basking in the title "lovers of wisdom," even though nowadays there is hardly a shadow of true wisdom left. One is hard pressed to hear a word about wisdom even at the philosophical conferences that are regularly held each year. Wisdom has become a forgotten art. Everyone's focus today is on knowledge, unfortunately on knowledge in its fragmented form. And that's part of humanity's problem today. Consequently, had we failed to emerge with a system of thought that reflects a well-integrated organic whole, we would have missed the purpose of our undertaking.

Thomas: How is that? I don't get it.

Diotima: Fragmentation in knowledge has far-reaching ramifications. There is a domino effect to it. For one thing, fragmentation in knowledge undermines objectivity of knowledge itself, the aim of which is ultimate Truth. Some argue that if the conclusions of the various epistemological areas do not coincide, there is no such a thing as truth. And if there is no truth, there is no objective knowledge. All we can have then is an opinion. Since opinions differ, everything is relative. Once this position is assumed, "man becomes the measure of all things." Doesn't this statement have a familiar ring for you?

Jason: Sophistry once again!

Diotima: With it, individualism is enthroned, subjective goals override objective good, a sense of values is lost, vice and virtue claim equal rights, moral decadence ensues, evil gains an upper hand, and society suffers violence. Ironically, what is sought in the name of freedom and under the banner of "I know best what's good for me" enslaves the person and in time brings humanity to the brink of destruction!

Jason: What you've just said seems to describe perfectly the state of affairs in our world today.

Diotima: Such are the consequences, however, only when, and because, one had overlooked the fact that the various groups of scholars are inquiring into different aspects of reality. All their findings are only partial results. They are meant to complement, rather than undermine each other. It is only when all the existing bodies of knowledge, like the pieces of a jigsaw puzzle, are fitted into their proper place that truth can emerge.

Combining bodies of knowledge into an organic whole is a work of synthesis that has its basis in logical coherence. The synthesis of knowledge currently needed is one on a higher level. We say "on a higher level," for the new synthesis has to incorporate the knowledge of the "large pieces" of knowledge, those that already were analyzed and synthesized by various disciplines. These well-understood aspects of reality now need to be fitted together in order to restore reality into its actual form of existence as one big whole. The state with which humanity historically began the study of reality, was one of the harmoniously integrated whole. That was true of us, too, first when we came into this world, and then when we began this quest. Initially, we saw everything as a whole. In all those instances, historically and now, we humans are the ones who created those boundaries. This was done to help ourselves understand what-is. It is, therefore, our obligation to restore things back to their original state. We may not have all the pieces of the "huge diamond" in place yet, but if we put together what we've already retrieved, it will be easier to find and to insert the rest. True. At that point, we may lose claim to "our own turf," but we all will have gained a much greater victory—a joint conquest of truth! Such a triumph is bound to come with a bonus, the spirit of genuine solidarity with all, mutual respect, and sincere appreciation of each other's accomplishments!

Jason: The very prospect of it sends chills down my spine.

Thomas: A worthy dream, indeed!

Sophie: Let's keep it alive.

Diotima: To all evidence we've reached our goal. A concise summary of it is all we need to grasp the image of it in its broadest terms.

(3). Summary Glance at What-is. If you recall, in the course of converting reality into corresponding bodies of knowledge we have pointed out the links among the various disciplines (Diagrams 9, 10 and 11). Diagram 15.5 helped us to understand what constitutes the content of the major categories of what-is. Casting one final look at it, we can only marvel at how beautifully it all fits together and complements each other: Theology is concerned with *goodness,* primarily of the Revealed Word of God, Fine Arts with *beauty* in its many forms, Spirituality with *holiness,* Sciences with *truth*: the Empirical Sciences with the *truth of correspondence* in the created world; the Pure Sciences with *truth of logical coherence* in general. And Philosophy is concerned with *justice:* through "reason" it seeks rightness and truth of everything; through "love of wisdom" it paves the way to *the truth of actual beholding* and establishes *unity* of all-that-is. It is worth noting also that these very things: goodness, beauty, justice, truth and holiness along with consciousness and knowledge are all absolute attributes of God. Thus, by retrieving knowledge in any of these areas, we are retrieving knowledge of God's attributes embodied therein. Consequently, whether we realize it or not, we all are approaching God through our respective disciplines.

Thomas: This is the most exciting thing I have heard yet! Hurrah! Science, too, is on its way to God.

Jason: Yes, provided scientists are pursuing knowledge objectively, with openness to truth and willingness to accept it when it surfaces anywhere, I assume. If they are, this insight should be a moment of great rejoicing for them, too.

Diotima: The very overlapping and entwining in all of these areas has all kinds of ramifications, in addition to proving that reality is ultimately one and traces to one God.

Jason: What further implications can there be?

Diotima: While it is true that various disciplines concern themselves with the particular categories as just stated, every one of the epistemic disciplines, just by partaking of and participating in the same reality, exhibits something of the attributes proper to all other bodies of knowledge. There is some goodness, beauty and truth in all of them, if justice is done to them. Knowing this, it should make the collaborative venture of synthesis easier and more enthusiastically espoused. The challenge of the universal synthesis belongs to future generations. On our part, anticipating the triumphant moment of that accomplishment one day, we open up the floodgates of all the disciplines and let their waters rush into the ocean where they all merge beautifully, just as reality itself does.

Having already deleted the middle circle with all boundaries to knowledge and bequeathed the challenge of final synthesis to future generations, we have one final step to take. In order to provide an adequate platform for the scholars with ample room for everyone at the roundtable where those details need to be worked out, we need to dispense with the rest of symbols, the line and the remaining two circles. I believe that we are now able to envisage reality independently of them.

Sophie: We can try. Let's see what happens.

Diotima: Recalling that there are no boundaries in space fencing in the cosmos, let us delete the smaller circle to reflect this fact.

Jason: Without it, we see the universe "within" and as an indistinguishable part of the absolute whole.

Sophie: And we understand the absolute whole, although not identical with it, to be co-extensive with the Absolute Itself.

Diotima: Wonderful, Sophie! I am glad you've become comfortable with our "reductionism." And now, since the philosophical understanding of the concept "absolute" is one reality that is uncreated, timeless, limitless, unmodified, unified and complete in every sense, hence perfect and *unrestricted* in any way, we dispense with the large circle for it is placing limits on the Absolute who is Infinite. One of the ancient thinkers facetiously denotes this fact by saying: "God is an infinite sphere whose center is everywhere and whose circumference is nowhere."[53] This is his way of saying that God is beyond limits and beyond human comprehension; no image can do justice to Him.

Thomas Cleverly expressed, I like it. This implies one other thing. Since the Absolute, although indispensable to it, is *purely metaphysical* and as such *invisible*, only the universe is perceptible to the human eye.

Diotima: Yes, and only a minute part of it, at that! You can see now why those who rely only on what is given in sense perceptions and empirical studies reduce all of reality to just the cosmos.

Jason: Indeed, we can. Notwithstanding, we have arrived at the organic view of reality that is a single, well-integrated whole!

Sophie: Ironically, this whole conceals more than it reveals.

Diotima: Well put, Sophie, however because of the extraordinary powers with which we humans have been endowed by our Maker, we are able to experience gradually all that is, and some day, not only to understand it well, but also to relish it all to our heart's content!

Thomas: That is, if our findings hold up to the test.

Diotima: That's true, so without further ado let us subject them to that test. Whatever be the cloud that still hovers over any of concept we have discussed, it should be dispelled in our next discourse.

NOTES

1. *Dictionary of Philosophy* Ed. Dagobert D. Runes, Ph.D. (New York: Philosophical Library, Inc. 1942), p. 250. Henceforth: page only, unless another source is cited in between. In that case DP with a given page.

2. The flightless birds like penguins and emus belong to the transitional categories. They are like the coral that possesses characteristics of non-living and living things, or like the euglena that shares the characteristics of plant and animal life. We will deal with the transitional entities later.

3. George J. Wallace, *An Introduction to Ornithology,* Second Edition (New York: The Macmillan Company, 1963), pp. 35-37.

4. Carl J. Wilson *Botany* (New York: The Dryden Press, 1952), p. 274.

5. Carl J. Wilson *Botany* (New York: The Dryden Press, 1952), p. 281. Speaking of nature's creativity, Wilson tells us that the tree species are so numerous that botanists hardly venture to submit the complete number (pp. 272-281).

6. We are indebted to Plato for the understanding of what-is, although we arrive at it in an original way. Plato discusses these concepts in *The Seventh Epistle*. Plato. *Epistle VII,* 342a-b, Post translation in *The Collected Dialogues* (New York: Pantheon Books, 1961). R. L. Bury in the Loeb Series, *Plato. With an English Translation* (Cambridge, Massachusetts: Harvard University Press, 1966), *Epistle VII,* 342a-b.

7. U.S. *Census Bureau, Population Division:* Maintained by Laura K. Yax (Population Division). Last Revised: October 30, 2001. There is a slight discrepancy. According to the U.N. World Population Estimate, there are 6,237,624,600 people on earth. According to the USA Census Bureau, there are 6,250,417,451 people. Dynamic versions of U.S. and World POP Clocks. (Netscape only).

8. Lincoln Barnett, *The Universe and Dr. Einstein* Revised Edition. Foreword by Albert Einstein (New York: Bantam Books, Inc., 1974), pp. 39-40.

9. This classification of the sciences, though highly condensed, comes from *Encyclopedia Britannica*, the section on sciences, *http://search.eb.com/ebi/article?eu=299058* [Accessed September 30, 2002].

10. The sun analogy attempts to explain the relationship of the good and its offspring, the two divinities, to the two worlds where they are sovereign. The good is sovereign in the World of Being, and "the offspring of the good most nearly made in its image" is sovereign in the World of Becoming (506e). The latter divinity is the cause of everything in the visible realm. Eventually this divinity turns out to be the Just. The analogy establishes: what "the good is in the intelligible region and to the objects of reason," so "the offspring of the good which the good begot to stand in proportion with itself" is to "the visible world, to vision and the objects of vision" (508b-c). The Allegory of the Cave, in turn, depicts the soul's journey from the realm of shadows into the realm of light. The journey requires a knowledgeable guide who points the way and enlightens, encourages and prods the soul to move on when the going gets rough. The soul makes this journey by means of education and actual ascent, hence in word and in deed. Book seven is devoted to educating us as it enacts the journey of the soul's ascent to the realm of light (514a-ff).

11. Mathematically, segments two and three are equal. Not so, content-wise. Content-wise each lower segment presupposes the one above it, which enjoys a higher status of existence. This does not hold in reverse even in the case of segments two and three where the length of the line is the same.

12. In preparing Plato's divided line we shall keep to his terminology, hence Pure Forms. At the time of comparing the divided line with the absolute whole, we shall upgrade the terminology in this case and other instances as well.

13. Some translators, as does for instance Paul Shorey, render the concept of God with a capital letter; others, like Allan Bloom, to be faithful to the syntax of the Greek language, leave it in a small letter. We shall provide evidence for both. On our part, since we have agreed earlier to capitalize all words that pertain to the Fifth Entity, we shall capitalize all such words, except when they are a part of a quotation.

14. .*Republic,* Trans. Paul Shorey, *The Collected Dialogues of Plato,* op. cit., (379a). Allan Bloom's translation of the same passage reads as follows: "A young thing cannot judge what is hidden sense and what is not; but what he takes into his opinions at that age has a tendency to become hard to eradicate and unchangeable. Perhaps it's for this reason that we must do everything to insure that what they hear first, with respect to virtue, be the finest told tales for them to hear. . . . It's appropriate for founders to know the models according to which the poets must tell their tales. If what they poets produce goes counter to these models, founders must not give way; however, they must not themselves make up tales" (378d-379a). Henceforth we shall provide the translator's name along with the numbering of the section.

15. For the classification of the bodies of knowledge and their subfields we have consulted sciences: the *Britannica Student Encyclopedia http://search.eb.com/ebi/article?eu=299058. 2002 Encyclopedia Britannica, Inc.*

16. *Webster's Third New International Dictionary,* Editor in Chief Philip Babcock Gove, Ph.D. and The Merriam-Webster Editorial Staff (Springfield, Massachusetts: G. & C. Merriam Company, Publishers, 1961), p. 1624.

17. The reason for including history with the sciences is due to the fact that there is a whole history of development to all of these bodies of knowledge. There is, however, more to history than this, and for this reason history is rightfully placed with the humanities.

18. Definition from the *Encyclopedia Britannica Online,* http://www.elmhurst.edu: 8081/search?ct =&query=Art% 2Fmusic&submit.x=6&submit.y=18.

19. The following paragraph from the *Encyclopedia Britannica Online,* op. cit., gives an excellent portrayal of how many artistic skills are sometimes required to produce the works of great beauty. "The great religious structures of medieval and Renaissance Europe were the results of collaboration among architects, stonemasons, glassmakers, sculptors, painters, and mosaicists, to name a few. An opera brings together a dramatic plot, music that is both played and sung, well-designed scenery and costumes, acting, and perhaps dance. A modern motion picture brings together writers, actors, directors, musicians, costume and set designers, camera operators, and a great variety of other technicians. Ballet combines dance, music, plot, costume, and scenery."

20. The ontological realm at this stage of our inquiry is being understood as *the ultimate realm of metaphysics*, the realm of the first principles. When the dialectic reaches its final stage and we come to understand how the three Hypostases relate to the rest of reality, this view will be further upgraded to reflect the full Truth. At this point, we are seeing only "a tip of the iceberg," as it were. By now, we all should know from personal experience that the light of Truth surfaces in stages and degrees. The full truth is expected to dawn only at the moment when one catches a glimpse of God. Everything prior to it is an approximation of it.

21. In his book *Darwin's Black Box, The Biochemical Challenge of Evolution* (New York: The Free Press, 1996), pp. 232-233, Michael J. Behe writes: "Over the past four decades modern biochemistry has uncovered the secrets of the cell. The

progress had been hard won. It has required tens of thousands of people to dedicate the better parts of their lives to the tedious work of the laboratory. . . . The result of these cumulative efforts to investigate the cell—to investigate life at the molecular level—is a loud, clear, piercing cry of '*design!*' The result is so unambiguous and so significant that it must be ranked as one of the greatest achievements in the history of science. The discovery rivals those of Newton and Einstein, Lavoisier and Schrödinger, Pasteur, and Darwin. The observation of the intelligent design of life is as momentous as the observation that the earth goes around the sun or that disease is caused by bacteria, or that radiation is emitted in quanta. The magnitude of the victory, gained at such great cost through sustained effort over the course of decades, would be expected to send champagne corks flying in labs around the world. This triumph of science should evoke cries of 'Eureka!' from ten thousand throats, should occasion much hand-slapping and high-fiving, and perhaps even be an excuse to take a day off." But no such things have happened. "Instead, a curious, embarrassed silence surrounds the stark complexity of the cell. ... Why does the scientific community not greedily embrace its startling discovery? Why is the observation of design handled with intellectual gloves? The dilemma is that while one side of the elephant is labeled intelligent design, the other side might be labeled God." Could it be that the scientific community is selective in what it discloses to the general public? This is a rather awkward stance for the discipline that adheres to the principle of honesty and objectivity. Yet, neither science nor God, is, nor needs to be, a threat to the other. The march of science can move forward as before. Now, however, it would be inquiring into how God must have ordained the progressive change in conditions, which always had to be "just so," for the various forms of series and species to evolve and eventually to produce a fitting environment for His masterpiece, the human person. Future references to this book DBB and page(s) within the body of a paragraph.

22. Michael J. Behe in his book *Darwin's Black Box, The Biological Challenge to Evolution,* op. cit., in the section entitled "Irreducible Complexity and the Nature of Mutation" writes, "Darwin knew that his theory of gradual evolution by natural selection carried a heavy burden" for he wrote—here Behe quotes Darwin: "If it could be demonstrated that any complex organ existed which could not possibly have been formed by numerous, successive, slight modifications, my theory would absolutely break down." Darwin, C. (1872) *Origin of Species,* 6th ed. (1988), New York University Press, New York, p. 154. Quote on page 39. According to Behe, by now science has found many such organs in the living cosmos, so Behe's view, to all evidence, is not without sufficient scientific proofs.

23. John Cornwell. "The universe – a divine recipe?" in *The Tablet* (March 9, 2002), pp. 4-6.

24. St. Anselm contends we can conceive of the Absolute after the manner of the rational human soul, consequently God as the rational soul in its perfection: "Fullness of being, of life, of reason, of health, of justice, of wisdom, of truth, of goodness, of greatness, of beauty, of immortality; fullness incorruptible, fullest blessedness, fullness eternal, fullness of power, fullness of unity." Joseph Clayton, F.R. Hist. S. *Saint Anselm* (Milwaukee: The Bruce Publishing Company, 1933), pp. 137-139.

25. *Basic Writings of Saint Thomas Aquinas ,* Vol. I. Edited and annotated, with an Introduction, by Anton C. Pegis (New York: Random House, Inc., 1945), p. 23. Henceforth: Pegis and the page. References to *Metaphysics* are those of Aristotle. Aquinas refers to him in his writings as "the Philosopher."

26. The age of the universe is still a highly controversial matter in science. According to the *Time* (March 6, 1995), pp. 77-84, Michael D. Lemonick and J. Madeleine Nash, report that Allan Sundage continues to insist that the cosmos is 15 billion to 20 billion years old. In contrast to this theory, Wendy Freedman, "who happens to work just down the hall from Sandage at the Carnegie's center in Pasedina, California," and her collaborators, "peg the age at somewhat between 8 billion and 12 billion years" (p. 77). Apparently they settled for a compromise, because the *Time,* June 25, 2001 issue, puts it at about 15 billion years.

27. In the June issue of the same magazine Frederic Golden writes: "Now about halfway through its estimated 10 billion-year lifetime, our sun is slowly brightening. In about 1 billion years, its energy output will have increased at least 10%, turning Earth into a Venusian hothouse where plants wither, carbon dioxide levels plummet and the oceans boil off. . . . If we're still around, we will have to seek out homes on other planets orbiting other warming stars. . . . And in the end, not even such a sanctuary would save our descendants, or any other life-forms still inhabiting the universe, from its last, dying gasp" (55).

28. According to John Cornwell's article "The universe – a divine recipe?" in *The Tablet,* op. cit., the concept of the multiverse was first introduced in 1990 by Sir Denys Wilkinson at a meeting in Jesus College, Cambridge, England. Since then, interest of the scientific community in this theory steadily mounted. In 2002 it became the subject matter of the discussion between the Astronomer Royal, Sir Martin Rees, and the former Professor of Mathematical Physics in Cambridge, Canon John Polkinghorne. The debate between the two diametrically opposite views about the universe, agnostic and theistic respectively, was held under the auspices of the Science and Human Dimension Project likewise at Jesus College in England. Participants of "the inter-disciplinary society" that sponsored the session had ample opportunity to pose questions and to offer their reactions. Judging by the synopsis offered by Cornwell, the debate was stimulating and challenging, to say the least. Rees sought to defend his position of the multiverse. "But in the end," Cornwell writes, "Rees had to admit that his multiverse was purely speculative, happily coinciding with Polkinghorne's caveat from the very outset" (5).

29.You may want to reread the part of our earlier discussion that explains this concept in section entitled "IV. A COMPREHENSIVE VIEW OF WHAT-IS." Under the sub-topic: "A. Reality as a Chain of Wholes" we have devoted two pages to elucidating the meaning of this dimension of our being, which is known by many other equally appropriate names. Sophie called it a "heart" and we found some good reasons for adopting this name.

30. Indubitable Truth is one that is too obvious to be doubted; unquestionable.

31. *The Works of St. Bonaventure,* Vol. 5, *Collations on the Six Days.* Trans. Jose de Vinck (Paterson, N.J.: St. Anthony Guild, 1970), pp. 195-6.

32. Figure 1, the three isotopes of hydrogen, and Figure 2, the two isotopes of helium are reproduced, with permission from Brooks/Cole, a part of Cengage Learning, Inc, which currently hold the rights to this material. Henry Smart, *Fundamentals of Physics*, Fourth Edition (New York: Holt, Rinehart and Winston, Inc., 1966), p. 623. www.cengage.com/permissions.

33. Guy Consolmagno, S.J. *". . . the way to the Dwelling of Light": How Physics Illuminates Creation* (Vatican Observatory Foundation, 1998), footnote, p. 108.

34. The other two chemists who received the Nobel Prize are Koichi Tanaka of Japan and Kurt Wüthrich of Switzerland. http://www.nobel.se/chemistry/laureates/2002/index.html.

35. The author states that there are other scientists who have much to add about "the prodigality of fine balances" in the universe. He cites John Barrow and Frank Tipler, who in their famous book *The Anthropic Principle* in 1988 provide even more detailed evidence leaning in favor of "the existence of creator."

36. Sir John Polkinghorne, "The universe is a mystery," *Science & Spirit* 12: 6. (November-December, 2001), p. 23. Henceforth: Polkinghorne and page.

37. Xenophanes, B 24. Werner Jaeger in *The Theology of the Early Greek Philosophers* (New York: Oxford University Press, 1947; rpt., 1968), p. 44. Henceforth: Jaeger and page.

38. The sixteen images of Jesus, page 66, were: Korean, Russian, Haitian, Native American, Hungarian, Mexican, Filipino, Female, Croatian, Swedish, African American, Chinese, Mexican Indian, Japanese, West African and European American. Josh Simon, "Solving the Mystery of JESUS and Why it Matters Today?" *Life*, December 1994, pp. 66-82.

39. There is a considerable difficulty in speaking of the Holy Spirit, primarily in the use of pronouns. Words have their meanings and their use is prescribed by grammatical syntax of each language, but those words were coined for the things of this world, especially when they come with gender. This creates a problem when we apply them to Divinity that transcends such distinctions. It is particularly true when we speak of the Holy Spirit. There is a difficulty in finding an appropriate pronoun for this Person of the Blessed Trinity. "Spirit" by its nature, is neither male nor female. In fact, like life, it must be neutral to be present in both male and female on the human level. But that leaves "it" as the only alternative. The pronoun it, even if we were to capitalize that IT, reduces the SPRIT OF WISDOM to an object, which is totally unacceptable. Because the Hebrew word *Ruah* for the "spirit" and "breath" is feminine, and "Wisdom," another name rightfully associated with the Holy Spirit, is also feminine, and there is a feminine element to the Triune God, there is a sufficient reason to employ the feminine pronoun for the Holy Spirit. Moreover, traditionally, the Holy Spirit is understood to be "the Giver of life" or "the one that brings forth life." Since "the one that brings forth life" in the natural order is mother, there appears to be another justification for employing the feminine pronoun for the Holy Spirit.

To be sure, the Holy Spirit *does not* have a female human form—she has her own beautiful form, which, one day, we shall come to behold face to face. The female titles for the Holy Spirit accrue in virtue of the functions. Part of one's identity comes from what one does. The Holy Spirit is very motherly in giving and nurturing our spiritual life. Above all, just as a natural mother is a "heart" of a family and a bond of love among all the members in the family, so the Holy Spirit is the "heart" and the bond of love between the Father and the Son, and of Their bond of love in us and with us. (We shall elaborate on these concepts in due time.)

It may be helpful to add that God the Father is also Spirit and does not have a male form, but He is "the Begetter of life" and we rightfully attribute to Him the name Father and the masculine pronouns, both in terms of His functions. Not only does this title make Him very close and dear to our hearts, God Himself delights in being our Father, for that is how He loves us. Those who come to know Him as a Father experience incredible tenderness of His love and fondness that is lavished by fathers on their little ones. Certainly Jesus never addressed God in any other way than Father. No doubt, this is at least one of the reasons why Jesus encouraged us to be like little children.

What we are saying here, *in essence*, is not entirely new. John O'Donnell, S.J., a theology professor, while teaching at the Gregorian University in Rome, in 1988 published a book *The Mystery of the Triune God* in which he devotes a section to "The Femininity of the Spirit" (97-99). To justify his thinking, in the Preface of this book he assures us "This book is written by one who thinks, lives and prays within the Roman Catholic tradition. This tradition" he adds, "has given me the theological air which I breathe." He is able to draw his insights from it, because "the living tradition of the faith of the church is a constant invitation to reflection." (London: Sheed & Ward, Second Edition, 1992), Preface vii-viii. What we say in this text is done in the same spirit and with the same commitment to the teachings of the Catholic Church.

40. It is true that when Edwin Hubble in 1927 provided some evidence that the universe was expanding, a theory that contradicted Einstein's general theory of relativity the basic tenet of which was the concept of the "cosmological constant," Einstein abandoned the cosmological constant as "the greatest blunder of his career." Despite this fact, the idea of the cosmological constant was not abandoned entirely, even after Einstein's death. And at the turn of the century, it became reinstated. In 1998-2001 Adam Riess helped to prove that "Einstein was right in the first place; a mysterious antigravity force

that acts like Einstein's cosmological constant is evidently quite true," concludes Lemonick along with a group of physicists and astrophysicist who are reaching complementary conclusions from different approaches to the study of the cosmos. *Time*, "The End," pp. 50-56.

41. Pierre Teilhard de Chardin, *The Future of Man*, Translated from French by Norman Denny (New York: Harper & Row, Publishers, 1964), p. 304. Henceforth: FM and page.

42. Maloney writes, "This book treats, as architects of this tradition, Paul, John, Irenaeus, Clement of Alexandria, Origen, Athanasius, Basil, Gregory Nazianzen, Gregory of Nyssa, Cyril of Alexandria, and Maximus the Confessor. The concluding chapters treat Teilhard de Chardin's christological contribution . . ." *The Cosmic Christ* (New York: Sheed and Ward, Inc. 1968), p. 14. Henceforth: Maloney and page, or simply page, if the author is understood from the text.

43. St. Paul, in I Corinthians 15:28, *The New American Bible* (Catholic Publishers, Inc., 1971), p. 1272.

44. Karl Jaspers, "On My Philosophy" in *Existentialism from Dostoevsky to Sartre* Edited by Walter Kaufmann (Cleveland and New York: The World Publishing Company, 1956 and 1968), p. 142.

45. Pierre Teilhard de Chardin, *The Divine Milieu*. Trans. Wm. Collins Sons & Co. (New York: Harper & Brothers, 1960), p. 100. Henceforth: DM.

46. The name "Sun of Justice" for the "Son of God" is found in numerous other places. For instance, *Christian Prayer: The Liturgy of the Hours*. Revised by decree of the second Vatican Ecumenical Council (New York: Catholic Publishing Co., 1985), p. 1373 "Sun of Justice, the immaculate Virgin was the white dawn announcing your coming ..."; p. 1246 "Your birth, O Virgin Mother of God, proclaims joy to the whole world, for from you arose the glorious Sun of Justice, Christ our God . . . "; and p. 796, "To enlighten the world, Father, you sent to us your word as the sun of truth and justice shining upon mankind." Such references can be multiplied, pp. 130,764,773, 792, 785, 792, 811, 1091, 1335, 1385, 2018—all in just this one book. Light, sun, truth, and justice are all metaphorical names for Christ, the Son of God; all appropriate in virtue of His identity and functions.

47. Wayne Teasdale, *The Mystic Heart* (Novato, California: New World Library, 1999), p. 54. Henceforth: Teasdale.

48.*Upanisads* Svetasvatara Upanishad 3:8. Trans. Patrick Olivelle (New York: Oxford University Press, 1966). Cited by Teasdale in *The Mystic Heart*, p. 54.

49. St. John of the Cross, *The Ascent of Mount Carmel* in *The Collected Works of St. John of the Cross*. Trans. Kieran Kavanaugh, O.C.D. and Otilio Rodriguez, O.C.D. (Washington, DC: ICS Publications, 1991), p. 119.

50. Buddha is quoted as having said, "Bear always in mind what it is that I have not elucidated, and what it is that I have elucidated. And what have I not elucidated? I have not elucidated that the world is eternal; I have not elucidated that the world is not eternal; I have not elucidated that the world is finite; I have not elucidated that the world is infinite; I have not elucidated that the soul and the body are identical; I have not elucidated that the monk who has attained (the arahat) exists after death; I have not elucidated that the arahat [saint] does not exist after death; I have not elucidated that the arahat neither exists nor does not exist after death. And why have I not elucidated this? Because this profits not, nor has to do with the fundamentals of religion; therefore I have not elucidated this.

And what have I elucidated? Misery have I elucidated; the origin of misery have I elucidated; the cessation of misery have I elucidated; and the path leading to the cessation of misery have I elucidated. And why have I elucidated this? Because this does profit, has to do with the fundamentals of religions and tends to absence of passion, to knowledge, supreme wisdom, and Nirvana." Henry Clarke Warren, *Buddhism in Translation* (Harvard University Press, 1922), p.122 (Majjhima Nikaya 63). Cited by John B. Noss/David S. Noss *Man's Religions*, 7th Edition (New York: Macmillan Publishing Company, 1984), p. 114.

51. Given the scope, as it can be expected, there are further sub-divisions to cultural anthropology such as origin and development of human society or Sociology, religion or Ethnology and, morality or Ethics. At the moment, we shall concern ourselves with Ethnology. Because the latter branches of cultural anthropology overlap with Spirituality that incorporates Morality, Religion and Revelation, we shall address these later.

52. There are, of course, other kinds of signs and symbols. For instance, there are road signs, traffic signs, billboards, different body language signs and the like. Among the most common symbols are heart, a symbol of love, anchor a symbol of faith, rose a symbol of life, nation's flag a symbol of the country, lion a symbol of courage and strength, etc. But we do not need to go into those, as they are irrelevant to our undertaking.

53. This saying is quoted by Meister Eckhart and Pascal. It is taken from *The Book of the Twenty-Four Philosophers*, Edited by C. Baeumker, *Festgabe Georg Freiherrrn von Hertling*, Freiburg im Breisgau, 1913, p. 31. Quoted also by Armand A. Maurer, CSB in *Medieval Philosophy*, Revised Edition (Toronto, Ontario, Canada: Pontifical Institute of Medieval Studies, 1982), p. 292.

54. The Poem *God's Grandeur* by Gerard Manley Hopkins, S.J., edited by Robert Bridges in 1918 belongs now to Public Domain. Project Gutenberg's Poems of Gerard Manley Hopkins, by Gerard Manley Hopkins: http://www.gutenberg.org/files/22403/22403-8.txt.

CITED SOURCES

Avey, Albert E. *Handbook in the History of Philosophy.* New York: Barnes and Noble, Inc., 1961.

Audi, Robert, ed. *The Cambridge Dictionary of Philosophy.* UK and New York: Cambridge University Press, 1999.

Barnett, Lincoln. *The Universe and Dr. Einstein.* Albert Einstein, Foreword. New York: Bantam Books, Inc., 1974.

Becker, Lawrence C. and Charlotte B. Becker, eds. *Encyclopedia of Ethics.* Second Edition. Volume One. New York: Routledge Publishers, 2001.

Behe, Michael J. *Darwin's Black Box: The Biochemical Challenge of Evolution.* New York: The Free Press, 1996.

Black, Max. *Models and Metaphors: Studies in Language and Philosophy.* Ithaca, New York: Cornell University Press, 1962.

Christian Prayer: The Liturgy of the Hours. Revised by Decree of the Second Vatican Ecumenical Council and published by authority of Pope Paul VI. New York: Catholic Book Publishing Co., 1985.

Clayton, Joseph, F.R. Hist. S. *Saint Anselm.* Milwaukee: The Bruce Publishing Company, 1933.

Coward, Harold. "Hindu Christian Dialogue" in *World Religions: Hinduism.* Maryknoll, NY: Orbis, 1990.

Cross, Neal M., and Leslie Dae Lindau. *The Search for Personal Freedom.* Volume One. Second Edition. Dubuque, Iowa: Wm. C. Brown Company Publishers, 1961.

Cross, Neal M., Robert C. Lamm and Rudy H. Turk. *The Search for Personal Freedom.* Volume One. Dubuque, Iowa: Wm. C. Brown Publishers, 1972.

____. *The Search for Personal Freedom.* Volume Two. Dubuque, Iowa: Wm. C. Brown Company Publishers, 1974.

De Beauvoir, Simone. *Force of Circumstance.* Richard Howard, trans. New York: G. Putnam's Sons, 1965.

De Chardin, Pierre Teilhard. *The Divine Milieu.* Wm. Collins Sons & Co., trans. New York: Harper & Brothers, 1960.

____. *The Future of Man.* Norman Denny, trans. New York: Harper & Row, Publishers, 1964.

Durant, Will. *The Story of Philosophy.* New York: Washington Square Press, Inc., 1962.

Eliot, Charles W., ed. "The Golden Sayings of Epictetus" and "Fragments" in *The Harvard Classics.* Hastings Crossley, trans. New York: P.F. Collier and Son Corporation, 1968.

Foy, Whitfield, ed. "Zoroaster" in *The Religious Quest.* New York: Routledge, Chapman and Hall, Inc., 1988.

Goff, Richard D., George H. Cassar, Anthony Esler, James P. Holoka, and James C. Walts. *A Survey of Western Civilization.* Volume One. St. Paul, MN: West Publishing Company, 1987.

Gove, Philip Babcock, ed-in-chief and the Merriam-Webster, ed. staff. *Webster's Third New International Dictionary.* Springfield, Massachusetts: G. & C. Merriam Company, Publishers, 1961.

Hamilton, Edith and Huntington Cairns, eds. *The Collected Dialogues of Plato.* New York: Pantheon Books, 1961.

Heidegger, Martin. *What Is Philosophy?* William Klubach and Jean T. Wilde, trans. New Haven, Conn.: College and University Press, 1956.

____. "The Way Back into the Ground of Metaphysics" in *Existentialism from Dostoevsky to Sartre.* Walter Kaufmann, ed. New York: The World Publishing Company, Meridian Books, 1956.

____. *Being and Time.* John Macquarrie & Edward Robinson, trans. New York: Harper & Row, Publishers, 1962.

____. *Kant and the Problem of Metaphysics.* James S. Churchill, trans. Bloomington: Indiana University Press, 1968.

Jaeger, Werner. *The Theology of the Early Greek Philosophers.* New York: Oxford University Press, 1968.

Jaspers, Karl. "On My Philosophy" in *Existentialism from Dostoevsky to Sartre.* Walter Kaufmann, trans. & ed. Cleveland and New York: The World Publishing Company, Meridian Books, 1956.

John of the Cross. *The Ascent of Mount Carmel* in *The Collected Works of St. John of the Cross.* Kieran Kavanaugh, O.C.D. and Otilio Rodriguez, O.C.D., trans. Washington, DC: ICS Publications, 1991.

John Paul II. *On Catholic Universities: Ex Corde Ecclesiae.* Vatican City. Washington, D.C.: Office for Publishing and Promotion Services, Publication No. 399, 1990.

Just the Facts Learning Series. *The Middle Ages.* Thousand Oaks, California: Full Circle Entertainments, Inc., 2001.

Kiley, John Kantwell. *Why It's Okay to Get Your Hopes Up.* Unpublished Document.

Konstantinov, F.V. et al. *The Fundamentals of Marxist-Leninist Philosophy.* Moscow: Progress Publishers, 1974.

Lawler, Peter Augustine. *Postmodernism Rightly Understood: Return to Realism in American Thought.* Lanham, MD: Rowman and Littlefield Publishers, Inc., 1999.

Lescoe, Francis J. *Existentialism: With or Without God.* New York: Alba House, 1974.

Maloney, George. *The Cosmic Christ.* New York: Sheed and Ward, Inc., 2968.

Mill, John Stuart. *Utilitarianism.* George Sher, ed. Indianapolis: Hackett Publishing Company, 1979.

Newberg, Andrew, M.D., Eugene d'Aquili, M.D., Ph.D. and Vince Rause. *Why God Won't Go Away: Brain Science & the Biology of Belief.* New York: Random House, Inc., Ballantine Books, 2001.

Noss, David S. and John B. Noss. *Man's Religions.* Seventh Edition. New York: Macmillan Publishing Company, 1984.

Miceli, Vincent, S.J. *The Gods of Atheism.* New Rochelle: Arlington House, 1971.

O'Donnell, John J. *The Mystery of the Triune God.* Second Impression. London: Sheed & Ward, 1992.

Owens, Joseph, C.Ss.R. *A History of Ancient Western Philosophy.* New York: Appleton, Century, Crofts, Inc., 1959.

Pegis, Anton C., ed. *Basic Writings of Saint Thomas Aquinas.* Volume One. New York: Random House, Inc., 1945.

Plato. *Apology* in *The Collected Dialogues of Plato.* Hugh Tredennick, trans. Edith Hamilton and Huntington Cairns, eds. New York: Pantheon Books, 1966.

_____. *Epistle VII.* Loeb Series. R. L. Bury, trans. Cambridge: Harvard University Press, 1966.

_____. *Letter VII* in *The Collected Dialogues of Plato.* L. A. Post, trans. Edith Hamilton and Huntington Cairns, eds. New York: Pantheon Books, 1966.

_____. *Republic I.* Loeb Classical Library. Volume Five. Paul Shorey, trans. Cambridge: Harvard University Press, 1969.

_____. *Republic II.* Loeb Classical Library. Volume Six. Paul Shorey, trans. Cambridge: Harvard University Press, 1970.

_____. *The Republic of Plato.* Allan Bloom, trans. New York: Basic Books Inc., 1968.

_____. *Symposium* in *The Collected Dialogues of Plato.* Michael Joyce, trans. Edith Hamilton and Huntington Cairns, eds. New York: Pantheon Books, 1966.

_____. *Theaetetus* in *The Collected Dialogues of Plato.* F. M. Cornford, trans. Edith Hamilton and Huntington Cairns, eds. New York: Pantheon Books, 1966.

_____. *Timaeus* in *The Collected Dialogues of Plato.* Benjamin Jowett, trans. Edith Hamilton and Huntington Cairns, eds. New York: Pantheon Books, 1966.

Powell, John. *Fully Human Fully Alive.* Allen, Texas: Tabor Publishing, 1976.

Ramsey, Ian. *Models and Mystery.* London: Oxford University Press, 1964.

Roszak, Theodore. *Where the Wasteland Ends.* New York: Doubleday and Company, Inc., 1972.

Runes, Dagobert D., ed. *Dictionary of Philosophy.* New York: Philosophical Library, Inc., 1942.

Sartre, Jean Paul. *Being and Nothingness: An Essay of Phenomenological Ontology.* Hazel Barnes, trans. New York: Citadel Press, 1943.

_____. *The Words.* Bernard Frechtman, trans. New York: George Braziller, Inc., 1964, First Vintage Books Edition, 1981.

_____. "Existentialism is a Humanism" in *Existentialism from Dostoevsky to Sartre.* Walter Kaufmann, ed. New York: The World Publishing Company, Meridian Books, 1956.

Simpson, D. P., ed. *Cassell's Latin Dictionary*. New York: Macmillan Publishing Company, 1968.

Smart, Henry. *Fundamentals of Physics*. New York: Holt, Rinehart and Winston, Inc., 1966.

Solomon, Robert C., and Kathleen M. Higgins. *A Short History of Philosophy*. New York: Oxford University Press, 1996.

Teasdale, Wayne. *The Mystic Heart*. Novato, California: New World Library, 1999.

The Book of the Twenty-four Philosophers, Festgabe Georg Treiherrn von Hertling, Freiburg im Breisgau, 1913.

The New American Bible. Catholic Publishers, Inc. Camden, NJ: Thomas Nelson, Inc., 1971.

The Middle Ages. Just the Facts Learning Series. Thousand Oaks, California: Full Circle Entertainments, Inc.

The Works of St. Bonvaneture, Vol. 5, *Collations on the Six Days*. Vinck, Jose de, trans. Paterson, NJ: St. Anthony Guild, 1970.

Upanishads. Svetasvatara Upanishad 3:8. Patrick Olivelle, trans. New York: Oxford University Press, 1966.

Ussher, Arland. *Journey Through Dread*. New York: Bilbo, Tannen Booksellers and Publishers, 1955.

Varga, Andre C. *On Being Human: Principles of Ethics*. New York: Paulist Press, 1978.

Wallace, George J. *An Introduction to Ornithology*. Second Edition. New York: The Macmillan Company, 1963.

Wansbrough, Henry, gen. ed. *The New Jerusalem Bible*. Doubleday Standard Edition, 1999.

Warren, Henry Clarke. *Buddhism in Translation,* Majjhima Nikaya 63. Cambridge: Harvard University Press, 1922.

Wetter, Gustav A. *Soviet Ideology Today*. London: Heinemann, 1966.

____. *Dialectical Materialism*. New York: Praeger, 1958.

Wilson, Carl J. *Botany*. New York: The Dryden Press, 1952.

ARTICLES

Cornwell, John. "The universe – a divine recipe?" *The Tablet* (March 9, 2002): 4-6.

Lemonick, Michael D. and J. Madeleine Nash. "Unraveling Universe." *Time*, 145/9 (March 6, 1995): 77-84.

____. "The End" *Time*, 157/25 (June 25, 2001): 48-56.

Mauron, Alex. "Is the Genome the Secular Equivalent of the Soul?" *Science*, 291/5505 (February 2, 2001): 831-832.

Polkinghorne, Sir John. "The universe is a mystery." *Science & Spirit*. 12/6, (November-December, 2001): 23-25.

Simon, Josh. "Who was Jesus?" *Life* 17 (December, 1994): 67-82.

INTERNET SOURCES

Encyclopedia Britannica. Online, http://www.elmhurst.edu: 8081/search?ct=&query=Art% 2Fmusic&submit.x=6&submit.y=18.

Encyclopedia Britannica, the section on sciences. http://search.eb.com/ebi/article?eu=299058.

Encyclopedia Britannica Student Encyclopedia. http://search.eb.com/ebi/article?eu=299058.

Hopkins, Gerard Manley. "God's Grandeur" in Project Gutenberg's *Poems of Gerard Manley Hopkins*: http://www.gutenberg.org/files22403/22403-8.txt. First published in 1918 [EBook #22403], Robert Bridges, ed. Belongs to Poems 1876-1889 [Poem 7], now in Public Domain.

Loy, David R. "The Religion of the Market." http://www.bpf.org/market.html.

Roszak, Theodore. "Awakening The Ecological Unconscious." *In Context: A Quarterly of Humane Sustainable Culture*. http://www.context.org/ICLIB/IC34/Rshak.htm

INDEX

ABOUT THE AUTHOR

Jacinta Respondowska, OSF., holds a Ph.D. in Philosophy from Duquesne University, Pittsburgh, Pennsylvania. She taught philosophy at Alvernia College, serving at the same time in other administrative capacities since 1972. Recently she became Professor Emerita and is devoting her time to writing. Her goal now is to share what she has discovered on life's journey, hoping thereby, to evoke in a reader an unswerving commitment to what really matters in life. A desire for personal excellence and a love for learning will pave the way to Truth that carries one aloft to the fulfillment of one's noblest dreams.